Understanding IFRS Fundamentals

International Financial Reporting Standards

Nandakumar Ankarath   Dr. T.P. Ghosh

Kalpesh J. Mehta   Dr. Yass A. Alkafaji

Technically reviewed by Ian Hague, Principal, Accounting Standards Board (AcSB), Canada

WILEY

JOHN WILEY & SONS, INC.

ISBN: 978-0-470-39914-9

10 9 8 7 6 5 4 3 2 1

CONTENTS

PREFACE

The International Financial Reporting Standards (IFRS) are now adopted in more than 100 countries. The recent decision of the U.S. Securities and Exchange Commission (SEC) to allow foreign private issuers to list their securities on U.S. stock exchanges using IFRS (without reconciling to U.S. GAAP) and the expectation that more than 150 countries will have adopted IFRS by 2011 has made it incumbent upon accounting and finance professionals, bankers, regulators, educators, and trainers to understand and apply IFRS.

We embarked on this project because there was an urgent need for an easy-to-understand IFRS book; most books covering the accounting standards contained explanations and interpretations of complex technical issues from standards.

In this book, we have explained in simple terms the most important parts of these complex standards through easy-to-follow examples and case studies. It also provides a quick source of reference to find answers to issues of interest to financial statement preparers, users, and analysts. We have also included extracts from published financial statements to illustrate practical implications of applying IFRS.

We have received immense support and assistance on this project from several people around the world. We express our sincere appreciation and gratitude to Ian Hague, a Principal with the Accounting Standards Board (AcSB) in Toronto, Canada, for his detailed review of the entire manuscript. The various amendments to the IFRS that came into effect during the time of writing this book required quite a few chapters to be rewritten and amended. We will be failing in our duties if we did not thank John DeRemigis and the editorial and marketing staff of John Wiley & Sons for their tremendous patience in bearing with the delay in meeting the initial deadlines set for publication. We also thank Abbas Ali Mirza, Partner with Deloitte Middle East who has been our inspiration for his valuable guidance and unstinting support.

We are also grateful to all our family, friends, and colleagues who contributed in their own way to ensure the completion of this book.

All the views expressed in this publication are ours and do not represent those of the firms or organizations of which we are part.

Nandakumar Ankarath
Dr. T.P.Ghosh
Kalpesh J. Mehta
Dr. Yass A. Alkafaji

ABOUT THE AUTHORS

Nandakumar Ankarath is a Fellow Member of The Institute of Chartered Accountants of India and a Senior Partner with Moore Stephens, Chartered Accountants, United Arab Emirates. Nandakumar has over 25 years of postqualification experience in auditing, accounting, financial and management consultancy in various business environments in India, Bahrain, and the United Arab Emirates. He has also served as a member of the Committee on Accounting Standards for Local Bodies formed by the governing body of the Institute of Chartered Accountants of India to formulate accounting standards for local bodies, autonomous bodies, and nonprofit organizations in India.

Dr. T.P. Ghosh is a professor of accounting and finance at Management Development Institute, India, and a visiting professor of Wollongong University in Dubai, United Arab Emirates. Dr. Ghosh, who has served as the Director of Studies of the Institute of Chartered Accountants of India, New Delhi, has authored two important reference books for accounting professionals that include *Accounting Standards & Corporate Accounting Practices,* 8th edition, 2008.

Dr. Yass A. Alkafaji is an Associate Professor of Accounting at the American University of Sharjah, United Arab Emirates. Dr. Alkafaji, who was the founder of Alkafaji & Associates, Ltd., a Chicago-based public accounting firm, has been a faculty member at Mississippi State University, Bowling Green State University, and Northeastern Illinois University in the United States. He has also been published in various journals including the *International Journal of Accounting*, *Accounting Research Journal*, *International Journal of Management,* and *Managerial Auditing Journal.*

Kalpesh J. Mehta is a Fellow Member of the Institute of Chartered Accountants of India and is a founding member of the CA Section at M.T. EDUCARE (P) LTD., a premier institution for imparting quality education in India. He is also a faculty member at the Institute of Chartered Accountants of India.

REVIEWER

Ian Hague is a Principal with the Accounting Standards Board (AcSB) in Toronto, Canada, and the Chair of the AcSB IFRS Advisory Committee that is leading the AcSB's implementation of IFRS for Canadian publicly accountable enterprises. Ian is a Chartered Accountant in both Canada and in England and Wales and was with Deloitte in Toronto and in London, England, before joining the AcSB.

INTRODUCTION

International Financial Reporting Standards (IFRS) are presently being followed in more than 100 countries and it is expected that by 2011, more than 150 countries will have adopted them. The recent decision of the U.S. SEC to allow foreign private issuers to list their securities on U.S. stock exchanges using IFRS and without reconciling to U.S. GAAP has also made it incumbent upon accountants, finance professionals, analysts, and bankers, even in the United States, to become proficient in IFRS.

This large-scale global adoption of IFRS has created an urgent need for an easy-to-understand IFRS book.

Most books covering the accounting standards contain explanations and interpretations of complex technical issues from standards. What they do not contain is simple explanations of the most important parts of these complex standards through easy-to-follow examples and case studies. This book contains basic explanations of IFRS to demonstrate their practical application and provides

- A quick source of reference to find answers to issues of interest to financial statement preparers, users and analysts;
- An easy way to understand IFRS through simple explanations of the most important parts of IFRS standards;
- Easy-to-follow illustrations explaining IFRS standards, keeping in mind the layman; and
- Excerpts from published financial statements to illustrate practical implications of applying IFRS.

1 INTRODUCTION TO INTERNATIONAL FINANCIAL REPORTING STANDARDS (IFRS)

THE NEED FOR A COMMON SET OF ACCOUNTING AND FINANCIAL REPORTING STANDARDS

With the rampant rise of globalization, one would find it rather difficult to disagree with Thomas L. Friedman, the author of the world-renowned book, *The World Is Flat*, who said that right around the year 2000 we entered a new stage of globalization (a whole new era that he refers to as Globalization 3.0) which, according to him, is shrinking (figuratively, of course) the size of the world from small to tiny. Some people believe that this magical phenomenon of globalization has led to the emergence of a global village that we all live in.

With such a robust wave of globalization surging through the world, businesses across the globe cannot remain unaffected by it no matter how hard they try. With the advent of the World Wide Web and the knocking down of trade barriers across national boundaries through global initiatives such as the setting up of the World Trade Organization (WTO), international trade between businesses across the globe has become quite simple and attractive.

If we agree with the old adage, "accounting is the language of business," then business enterprises around the world cannot afford to be speaking in different languages to each other while exchanging and sharing financial results of their international business activities and also reporting the results of business and trade to their international stakeholders. As one school of thought believes, since business enterprises around the world are so highly globalized now and need to speak to each other in a common language of business, there is a real need for a single, universal set of accounting standards that would unify the accounting world and, more important, solve the problem of diversity of accounting practices across borders.

Historically, countries around the world have had their own national accounting standards (some countries have treasured these for whatever reason, most likely due to the pride of national sovereignty). However, with such a compulsion to be part of the globalization movement, wherein businesses across national boundaries are realizing that it is an astute business strategy to embrace the world as their workplace and marketplace, having different rules (standards) of accounting for the purposes of reporting financial results would not help them at all; rather, it would serve as an impediment to the smooth flow of information. Businesses, therefore, have realized that they need to talk to each other in a common language.

The adoption of accounting standards that require high-quality, transparent, and comparable information is welcomed by investors, creditors, financial analysts, and other users of financial statements. It is difficult to compare worldwide financial information without a common set of accounting and financial reporting standards. The use of a single set of high-quality accounting standards would facilitate investment and other economic decisions across borders, increase market efficiency, and reduce the cost of raising capital. International

Financial Reporting Standards (IFRS) are increasingly becoming the set of globally accepted accounting standards that meet the needs of the world's increasingly integrated global capital markets.

WHAT ARE IFRS?

IFRS are a set of standards promulgated by the International Accounting Standards Board (IASB), an international standard-setting body based in London. The IASB places emphasis on developing standards based on sound, clearly stated principles, from which interpretation is necessary (sometimes referred to as *principles-based standards*). This contrasts with sets of standards, like U.S. generally accepted accounting principles (GAAP), the national accounting standards of the United States, which contain significantly more application guidance. These standards are sometimes referred to as rules-based standards, but that is really a misnomer as U.S. standards also are based on principles—they just contain more application guidance (or rules). IFRS generally do not provide bright lines when distinguishing among circumstances in which different accounting requirements are specified. This reduces the chances of structuring transactions to achieve particular accounting effects.

According to one school of thought, since IFRS are primarily principles-based standards, the IFRS approach focuses more on the business or the economic purpose of a transaction and the underlying rights and obligations instead of providing prescriptive rules (or guidance). IFRS provides guidance in the form of principles.

This significant difference in approach to standard setting between IFRS and U.S. GAAP is the main reason that the length of the text of the IFRS is less than that of U.S. GAAP. U.S. GAAP extends more than 20,000 pages of accounting literature as opposed to IFRS, which is approximately 2,000 to 3,000 pages in length.

A BRIEF HISTORY OF THE INTERNATIONAL ACCOUNTING STANDARDS COMMITTEE (IASC)

The International Accounting Standards Committee (IASC), the predecessor of the IASB, was established in 1973 and came into being through an agreement by professional accountancy bodies from Australia, Canada, France, Germany, Japan, Mexico, the Netherlands, the United Kingdom and Ireland, and the United States. The objective behind setting up the IASC was to develop, in the public interest, accounting standards that would be acceptable around the world in order to improve financial reporting internationally. Over the years, the IASC saw several changes to its structure and functioning. For example, by the year 2000, IASC's sponsorship grew from the original nine sponsors to 152 accounting bodies from 112 countries, that is, all professional accountancy bodies that were members of the International Federation of Accountants (IFAC). Such fundamental changes to the IASC may have helped it achieve the objective for which it was set up: changing the perception of the global standard setters about the international nature of participation in the standard-setting process. As part of their membership in IASC, professional accountancy bodies worldwide committed themselves to use their best endeavors to persuade governments, standard-setting bodies, securities regulators, and the business community that published financial statements to comply with IAS. This also drew the world's attention to the fact that there exists a truly representative international accounting body that could ultimately qualify as a global standard setter and be able to develop a single set of accounting standards that would be acceptable to most, if not all, countries worldwide.

Over the years, the IASC worked hard to achieve the objective of developing accounting standards for the world. However, due to several factors (the most important one, according to one school of thought, being availability of national accounting standards in certain leading jurisdictions that were quite well developed and recognized by other leading jurisdictions as well) the standards promulgated by the IASC were unable to achieve the status of an international accounting standard setter whose standards were accepted by leading jurisdictions.

A BIRD'S EYE-VIEW OF THE STANDARDS PROMULGATED BY THE IASC AND INTERPRETATIONS COMMITTEE (SIC) THAT ARE STILL IN FORCE

During its existence, the IASC issued 41 standards, known as the International Accounting Standards (IAS), as well as a *Framework for the Preparation and Presentation of Financial Statements*. While some of the standards issued by the IASC have been since withdrawn or superseded (for example, IAS 30, *Disclosures in the Financial Statements of Banks and Similar Financial Institutions,* was withdrawn and IAS 22, *Business Combinations,* was superseded by IFRS 3, *Business Combinations*), many are still in force. In addition, some of the interpretations issued by the IASC's interpretive body, the Standing Interpretations Committee (SIC), are still in force.

IAS Still in Force for 2009 Financial Statements

IAS 1, *Presentation of Financial Statements*
IAS 2, *Inventories*
IAS 7, *Statement of Cash Flows*
IAS 8, *Accounting Policies, Changes in Accounting Estimates and Errors*
IAS 10, *Events After the Reporting Period*
IAS 11, *Construction Contracts*
IAS 12, *Income Taxes*
IAS 16, *Property, Plant, and Equipment*
IAS 17, *Leases*
IAS 18, *Revenue*
IAS 19, *Employee Benefits*
IAS 20, *Accounting for Government Grants and Disclosure of Government Assistance*
IAS 21, *The Effects of Changes in Foreign Exchange Rates*
IAS 23, *Borrowing Costs*
IAS 24, *Related-Party Disclosures*
IAS 26, *Accounting and Reporting by Retirement Benefit Plans*
IAS 27, *Consolidated and Separate Financial Statements*
IAS 28, *Investments in Associates*
IAS 29, *Financial Reporting in Hyperinflationary Economies*
IAS 31, *Interests in Joint Ventures*
IAS 32, *Financial Instruments: Presentation*
IAS 33, *Earnings Per Share*
IAS 34, *Interim Financial Reporting*
IAS 36, *Impairment of Assets*
IAS 37, *Provisions, Contingent Liabilities and Contingent Assets*
IAS 38, *Intangible Assets*
IAS 39, *Financial Instruments: Recognition and Measurement*
IAS 40, *Investment Property*
IAS 41, *Agriculture*

SIC Interpretations Still in Force for 2009 Financial Statements

SIC 7,   *Introduction of the Euro*
SIC 10,   *Government Assistance—No Specific Relation to Operating Activities*
SIC 12,   *Consolidation—Special-Purpose Entities*
SIC 13,   *Jointly Controlled Entities—Nonmonetary Contributions by Ventures*
SIC 15,   *Operating Leases—Incentives*
SIC 21,   *Income Taxes—Recovery of Revalued Nondepreciable Assets*
SIC 25,   *Income Taxes—Changes in the Tax Status of an Entity or Its Shareholders*
SIC 27,   *Evaluating the Substance of Transactions Involving the Legal Form of a Lease*
SIC 29,   *Disclosure—Service Concession Arrangements*
SIC 31,   *Revenue—Barter Transactions Involving Advertising Services*
SIC 32,   *Intangible Assets—Web Site Costs*

THE BIRTH OF THE INTERNATIONAL ACCOUNTING STANDARDS BOARD (IASB)

With tremendous pressure on the IASC to transform itself into a truly global standard-setting body by addressing some of the serious concerns of established standard setters around the world (grievances were time and again quoted in the international media as serious shortcomings of the IASC), in the year 2001, fundamental changes were made to strengthen the independence, legitimacy, and quality of the international accounting standard-setting process. In particular, the IASC Board was replaced by the International Accounting Standards Board (IASB) as the body in control of setting international accounting and financial reporting standards. This significant structural change to the manner in which the IASC functioned for several years since its inception was brought about as a result of the recommendations of the Strategy Working Party, which was specially formed to take a fresh look at the then-existing IASC's structure and strategy. One dramatic change in the structure and functioning of the Board that is worthy of mention was the replacement of part-time volunteer board members who sat on the IASC Board with, for the most part, full-time IASB board members.

Based on the recommendations of the Strategy Working Party a new constitution was adopted effective July 1, 2000. Under these new rules of governance of the international standard-setting body was born the IASC Foundation. The name of the organization that comprises both the IASB and its Trustees is the International Accounting Standards Committee Foundation (IASC Foundation). The objectives of the IASC Foundation, as stated in its Constitution, are

a.   *To develop, in the public interest, a single set of high-quality, understandable, and enforceable global accounting standards that require high-quality, transparent, and comparable information in financial statements and other financial reporting to help participants in the various capital markets of the world and other users of the information to make economic decisions;*
b.   *To promote the use and rigorous application of those standards; and*
c.   *In fulfilling the objectives associated with (a) and (b), to take account of, as appropriate, the special needs of small and medium-sized entities and emerging economies; and*
d.   *To bring about convergence of national accounting standards and International Financial Reporting Standards to high-quality solutions.*

At its first meeting in 2001, the IASB adopted all outstanding IAS and SIC issued by the IASC as its own standards. Those IAS and SIC continue to be in force to the extent they are not amended or withdrawn by the IASB. New standards issued by the IASB are known as IFRS. New interpretations issued by the International Financial Reporting Interpretations

Committee (IFRIC) are known as IFRIC Interpretations. When referring collectively to IFRS, that term includes IAS, SIC, IFRS, and IFRIC Interpretations.

GOVERNANCE AND STRUCTURE OF THE IASC FOUNDATION, IASB, IFRIC, AND THE SAC

IASC Foundation and the Trustees

The governance of IASC Foundation rests on the shoulders of the Trustees of the IASC Foundation (the IASC Foundation Trustees or, simply, the Trustees). The Trustees comprise 22 individuals who are chosen from around the world. In order to ensure a broad international representation, it is required that six Trustees are appointed from North America, six from Europe, six from Asia/Oceanic region, and four from any part of the world, subject to establishing overall geographical balance.

The Trustees are independent of the standard-setting activities (which is the primary responsibility of the Board members of the IASB). The Trustees, on the other hand, are responsible for broad strategic issues, such as

- Appointing the members of IASB, the IFRIC, and the Standards Advisory Council (SAC);
- Approving the budget of the IASC Foundation and determining the basis of funding it;
- Reviewing the strategy of the IASC Foundation and the IASB and its effectiveness including consideration, but not determination, of the IASB's agenda (which if allowed may impair the Trustees' independence of the standard-setting process);
- Establishing and amending operating procedures, consultative arrangements and due process for the IASB, the IFRIC, and the SAC;
- Approving amendments to its constitution after consulting the SAC and following the required due process;
- Fostering and reviewing the development of the educational programs and materials that are consistent with the objectives of the IASC Foundation; and
- Generally, exercising all powers of the IASC Foundation except those expressly reserved for IASB, the IFRIC, and the SAC.

Lastly, in order to enhance public accountability of the IASC Foundation, while maintaining the operational independence of the IASC Foundation and the IASB, the Monitoring Board, a new body, was created in 2009. The Monitoring Board comprises capital market authorities (e.g., representatives of institutions such as the International Organization of Securities Commissions [IOSCO], the U.S. Securities and Exchange Commission [SEC], and the European Commission) and its responsibilities include participating in the appointment of the Trustees of the IASC Foundation, advising the Trustees in the fulfillment of their responsibilities, and holding meetings with the Trustees to discuss matters referred by the Monitoring Board to the IASC Foundation or the IASB.

International Accounting Standards Board (IASB)

The IASB is responsible for standard-setting activities, including the development and adoption of IFRS. The Board usually meets once a month and its meetings are open to the public—in person and via the Internet.

The IASB shall comprise 14 members appointed by the Trustees; 12 full-time members and 2 part-time members. With recent amendments to the constitution of the IASC Foundation, the size of the IASB is to be increased from 14 to 16 members by 2012.

Stringent criteria have been laid out in the IASC Foundation constitution for the appointment of IASB Board members. They are

- Demonstrated technical competency, knowledge of financial accounting and reporting, and ability to analyze,
- Effective communication skills,
- Awareness and understanding of the global economic environment,
- Ability to work in a congenial manner with other members and show respect, tact, and consideration for one another's views and the views of the constituents, and
- Capability to take into consideration varied viewpoints presented, weighing the evidence presented in an impartial manner, and arriving at well-reasoned and supportable decisions in a timely fashion.

The Board members, who are appointed for a term up to five years, renewable once, are chosen from a mix of backgrounds, including auditors, preparers of financial statements, users of financial statements, and academics. The members of the IASB are usually individuals who possess professional competence, high levels of technical skills, and have diversity of international business and market experience; possessing such personal attributes would normally ensure that the Board members are able to contribute to the development of high-quality, global accounting standards.

The IASB has the complete responsibility for all IASB technical matters including preparation and issuing of IFRS and Exposure Drafts that precede issuance of the final standards (i.e., the IFRS).

IFRS Issued by the IASB to December 31, 2009

IFRS 1, *First-Time Adoption of International Financial Reporting Standards*
IFRS 2, *Share-Based Payment*
IFRS 3, *Business Combinations*
IFRS 4, *Insurance Contracts*
IFRS 5, *Noncurrent Assets Held for Sale and Discontinued Operations*
IFRS 6, *Exploration for and Evaluation of Mineral Resources*
IFRS 7, *Financial Instruments: Disclosures*
IFRS 8, *Operating Segments*
IFRS 9, *Financial Instruments*
IFRS for SMEs**

In July 2009, the IASB promulgated the much-awaited **IFRS for Small and Medium Enterprises (SMEs). It provides standards applicable to private entities (those that are not public accountable as defined in this standard).*

Standards Advisory Council (SAC)

The Trustees appoint the members of the Standards Advisory Council (SAC). The primary responsibility of the SAC is to provide advice to the IASB on agenda decisions and priorities in the IASB's work. The SAC provides a forum for organizations and individuals who have an interest in international financial reporting and who have diverse geographical and professional backgrounds.

The SAC shall comprise 30 or more members. Members are appointed for a three-year renewable term. Currently, the membership of the SAC includes chief financial and accounting officers from some of the world's largest corporations and international organizations, leading financial analysts and academics, regulators, accounting standard setters, and partners from leading accounting firms.

International Financial Reporting Interpretations Committee (IFRIC)

The Trustees appoint the members of the International Financial Reporting Interpretation Committee (IFRIC). The IFRIC is the IASB's interpretive body and is in charge of developing interpretive guidance on accounting issues that are not specifically dealt with in IFRS or that are likely to receive divergent or unacceptable interpretations in the absence of authoritative guidance. The Trustees select members of the IFRIC keeping in mind personal attributes such as technical expertise and diversity of international business and market experience in the practical application of IFRS and analysis of financial statements prepared in accordance with IFRS.

The IFRIC shall comprise 14 voting members. The Trustees, if they deem fit, may also appoint nonvoting observers representing regulatory bodies, who shall have the right to attend and speak at the meetings of the IFRIC. A member of the IASB, the Director of Technical Activities or another senior member of the IASB staff, or another appropriately qualified individual, shall be appointed by the Trustees to chair the IFRIC. The IFRIC shall meet as and when required, and 10 voting members present in person or by telecommunication shall constitute a quorum. Meetings of the IFRIC (and the IASB) are open to the public but certain discussions may be held in private at the discretion of the IFRIC. It is important to note that an IFRIC Interpretation requires the IASB's approval before its final issuance.

IFRIC Interpretations Issued to December 31, 2009

IFRIC 1,   *Changes in Existing Decommissioning, Restoration and Similar Liabilities*

IFRIC 2,   *Members' Shares in Cooperative Entities and Similar Instruments*

IFRIC 3,   *Emission Rights* (withdrawn)

IFRIC 4,   *Determining Whether an Arrangement Contains a Lease*

IFRIC 5,   *Rights to Interests Arising from Decommissioning, Restoration and Environmental Rehabilitation Funds*

IFRIC 6,   *Liabilities Arising from Participating in a Specific Market—Waste Electrical and Electronic Equipment*

IFRIC 7,   *Applying the Restatement Approach Under IAS 29 Financial Reporting in Hyperinflationary Economies*

IFRIC 8,   *Scope of IFRS 2* (withdrawn)

IFRIC 9,   *Reassessment of Embedded Derivatives*

IFRIC 10,   *Interim Financial Reporting and Impairment*

IFRIC 11,   *IFRS 2—Group and Treasury Share Transactions* (withdrawn)

IFRIC 12,   *Service Concession Arrangements*

IFRIC 13,   *Customer Loyalty Programs*

IFRIC 14,   *IAS 19—The Limit on a Defined Benefit Asset, Minimum Funding Requirements and Their Interaction*

IFRIC 15,   *Agreements for the Construction of Real Estate*

IFRIC 16,   *Hedges of a Net Investment in a Foreign Operation*

IFRIC 17,   *Distribution of Noncash Assets to Owners*

IFRIC 18,   *Transfer of Assets from Customers*

POPULARITY AND ACCEPTANCE OF IFRS WORLDWIDE

In the last few years, the popularity of IFRS has grown tremendously. The international accounting standard-setting process has been able to claim a number of successes in achieving greater recognition and use of IFRS.

A major breakthrough came in 2002 when the European Union (EU) adopted legislation that required listed companies in Europe to apply IFRS in their consolidated financial statements. The legislation came into effect in 2005 and applies to more than 8,000 companies in 30 countries, including countries such as France, Germany, Italy, Spain, and the United Kingdom. The adoption of IFRS in Europe means that IFRS has replaced national accounting standards and requirements as the basis for preparing and presenting group financial statements for listed companies in Europe, which is considered by many as a major milestone in the history of international accounting.

Outside Europe, many other countries also have been moving toward IFRS. By 2005, IFRS had become mandatory in many countries in Africa, Asia, and Latin America. In addition, countries such as Australia, Hong Kong, New Zealand, Philippines, and Singapore had adopted national accounting standards that mirror IFRS.

Today, IFRS are used in more than 100 countries. A significant number of Global Fortune 500 companies already use IFRS and this number is expected to increase by 2011 with further conversions to IFRS by major global players (most notably, Brazil, Canada, and India) and substantial convergence of local GAAPs in China and Japan to IFRS.

FAVORABLE AND HISTORIC BREAKTHROUGHS IN THE UNITED STATES

In the United States, since 2002, efforts have been underway to converge IFRS and U.S. GAAP; the earliest initiative was in the form of a well-known agreement entered into between the IASB and the U.S. standard setter (the FASB), referred to as the Norwalk Agreement. In the last few years, media reports are replete with news about the U.S. SEC developing an IFRS road map.

In November 2007, in a surprise move that is considered by some as the most significant nod of friendliness and an astounding move toward convergence in recent times, the U.S. SEC opened its doors to IFRS. This defining moment in the fast-tracked race of the IASB has helped gain global acceptance of the SEC's standards. In fact, this is the first time in the history of United States standard setting that a non-U.S. set of accounting standards were allowed to be used for listings on U.S. stock exchanges without requiring mandatory reconciliation to U.S. GAAP. Before this groundbreaking announcement was made by the U.S. SEC, all foreign private issuers (FPIs) were required to reconcile to U.S. GAAP the financial statements that they file with the U.S. SEC if the financial statements were prepared using any standards other than U.S. GAAP. While this exception to file financial statements without reconciliation to U.S. GAAP was made in a limited manner by the U.S. SEC, that is, only in the case of foreign private issuers (FPIs), such an exception to using U.S. GAAP for purposes of listing on the largest capital market of the world is undoubtedly a major breakthrough for the IFRS, the only non-U.S. GAAP standards that can boast of this special treatment.

In August 2008, the U.S. SEC went a step forward with its acceptance of IFRS and proposed to relax its rules further and permit the use of IFRS by U.S. issuers (i.e., domestic companies in the United States) provided certain *milestones* are achieved leading to mandatory use of IFRS by U.S. issuers starting for fiscal years ending on or after December 15, 2014. The milestones that need to be addressed before mandatory adoption of IFRS in the United States are

- Improvements in accounting standards, in accordance with a memorandum of understanding established between the IASB and FASB;
- Funding and accountability of the IASC Foundation;
- Improvement in the ability to use interactive data for IFRS reporting; and
- Education and training on IFRS in the United States.

According to this road map to convergence, in 2011, the U.S. SEC will assess the progress of the these milestones and will decide whether to mandate the use of IFRS for U.S. issuers. If, after assessment, the U.S. SEC is satisfied with the achievements of the milestones, then U.S. issuers may be allowed to make the transition to IFRS as early as 2014.

The other good news is that under this new friendly approach to convergence with IFRS (which some refer to as the sudden urge to merge or converge with IFRS in the United States), more specifically, under the U.S. SEC IFRS road map, limited early use of IFRS has also been permitted for eligible entities; *under this limited exception, certain U.S. issuers may even begin using IFRS soon. However, the final decisions in this regard are yet to be made as of this date.*

THE WAY FORWARD

IFRS are clearly emerging as a global financial reporting benchmark and most countries have already started using them as their benchmark standards for listed companies. With the recent issuance of IFRS for SMEs, a stand-alone set of standards for private entities that do not have public accountability, the global reach of the IASB is further enhanced. However, if these international standards are not applied uniformly across the world due to interpretational differences, then their effectiveness as a common medium of international financial reporting will be in question. If different entities within the region apply them differently based on their interpretation of the standards, it would make global comparison of published financial statements of entities using IFRS difficult. Debate still rages amongst accountants and auditors globally on many burning and contentious accounting issues that need a common stand based on proper interpretation of these standards.

According to one school of thought, IFRS are emerging as the much-awaited answer to the "billion-dollar question" on the minds of accountants, financial professionals, financial institutions, and regulators, that is, *which set of accounting standards would solve the conundrum of diversity in accounting practices worldwide by qualifying as a single or a common set of standards for the world of accounting to follow and rely upon?*

Undoubtedly, for years, U.S. GAAP was leading this much-talked about international race to qualify as the most acceptable set of accounting standards worldwide. However, due to several reasons, including the highly publicized corporate debacles such as that at Enron in the United States, the global preference (or choice) of most countries internationally has now clearly tilted in favor of IFRS as the most acceptable set of international accounting and financial reporting standards worldwide.

With the current acceptance of IFRS in more than 100 countries (and with several more expected to adopt IFRS in the coming years), one can probably argue that IFRS could possibly qualify as an Esperanto of international accounting (*Esperanto* refers to the well-known universal language). However, some people still believe that the race for global acceptance of IFRS is not over yet. While more than 100 countries have adopted IFRS as their national accounting standards, there are some important jurisdictions in the financial world (such as the United States) that have not yet fully accepted IFRS for financial reporting of their domestic companies. Therefore, unless the United States, the largest economic superpower of the world for years now, accepts IFRS as its national GAAP (replacing U.S. GAAP), it may be difficult to call IFRS the world's standards. There is, however, a strong possibility of the U.S. SEC's accepting IFRS ultimately. Judging from the amazing change in attitude of the U.S. SEC, which has already allowed use of IFRS by foreign private issuers for filings on U.S. stock exchanges, one may expect—that is, if the SEC's road map to convergence with IFRS goes through successfully without any glitches—that by the year 2014 (unless the date of convergence is extended further for whatever reason), the world of accounting may be rejoicing and celebrating under a strong common banner of a global set of accounting and financial reporting standards, namely, the IFRS. Some believe that the idea of a single set of standards for the world may be wishful thinking especially if the U.S. SEC's road map is amended adversely. As things stand presently, however, it may be expected that there is a strong possibility of allowing the use of IFRS in the United States in some form or another.

2 IASB *FRAMEWORK*

The IASB *Framework for the Preparation and Presentation of Financial Statements* (the *Framework*) sets out the concepts that underlie the preparation and presentation of financial statements (i.e., the objectives, assumptions, characteristics, definitions, and criteria that govern financial reporting). Therefore, the *Framework* is often referred to as the *conceptual framework*.

The *Framework* deals with

1. The objective of financial statements
2. Underlying assumptions
3. The qualitative characteristics that determine the usefulness of information in financial statements
4. The definition, recognition, and measurement of the elements from which financial statements are constructed
5. Concepts of capital and capital maintenance

The *Framework* is not a standard nor does it have the force of a standard. Instead, its importance can be judged from the following purposes for which it is made available to users of the standards:

- To assist and guide the International Accounting Standards Board (IASB) as it develops new or revised standards;
- To assist national standard setters in developing their national standards on a consistent basis with international principles; and
- To assist preparers of financial statements in applying standards and in dealing with topics that are not addressed by a standard.

Thus, in case of a conflict between the *Framework* and a specific standard, the standard prevails.

OBJECTIVE OF FINANCIAL STATEMENTS

The objective of financial statements is to provide information about the financial position, performance, and changes in financial position of an entity that is useful to a wide range of users in making economic decisions such as an investor deciding whether to sell or hold an investment in the entity, or employees assessing an entity's ability to provide benefits to them.

Users include present and potential investors, employees, lenders, suppliers, and other trade creditors, customers, governments and their agencies, and the public. Because investors are providers of risk capital, it is presumed that financial statements that meet their needs will also meet most of the needs of other users.

UNDERLYING ASSUMPTIONS

Two assumptions underlying the preparation and presentation of financial statements are: the accrual basis and going concern.

Accrual Basis

When financial statements are prepared on the *accrual basis of accounting*, the effects of transactions and other events are recognized *when they occur* (as opposed to when cash or its equivalent is received or paid), and they are recorded in the accounting records and reported in the financial statements of the periods to which they relate.

The accrual basis assumption is also addressed in IAS 1, *Presentation of Financial Statements*, which clarifies that when the accrual basis of accounting is used, items are recognized as assets, liabilities, equity, income, and expenses (the elements of financial statements) when they satisfy the definitions and recognition criteria for those elements in the *Framework*.

Going Concern

When financial statements are prepared on a *going concern* basis, it is presumed that the entity will continue in operation for the foreseeable future. In other words, it is assumed that the entity has neither the intention nor the need to liquidate or curtail materially the scale of its operations, in the *foreseeable future*, which, according to IAS1, *is at least a period of twelve months from the end of the reporting period.*

However, when significant doubts are cast on the ability of the entity to continue as a going concern, and thus such an assumption is not appropriate, the financial statements may need to be prepared on a different basis and, if so, that basis used is required to be disclosed.

The going concern assumption is also addressed in IAS 1, which requires management to make an assessment of an entity's ability to continue as a going concern when preparing financial statements.

Example 1

Company ABC is based in Nation XYZ and is under extreme pressure from recession and global financial difficulties. It is finding it quite difficult to meet the financial covenants given to banks (i.e., undertakings that it agreed with banks when it borrowed funds for working capital purposes from them). As per these financial covenants, Company ABC is required to maintain a healthy financial position. The terms of bank loans to Company ABC specifically require that Company ABC, which is highly leveraged, maintain a positive equity at all times during the year and also produce a positive cash flow from its operating activities as reflected in its cash flow statement for the most recent reporting period.

During the current financial period, Company ABC makes a substantial net loss for the year which erodes its equity, and thus the entity could not maintain a positive balance in shareholders' equity at the end of the financial period. Furthermore, as per the statement of cash flows for the current reporting period, it was unable to report a positive cash flow from operating activities. Such factors would normally raise doubts about the entity's ability to continue as a going concern, thereby requiring it to disclose the uncertainties.

QUALITATIVE CHARACTERISTICS OF FINANCIAL STATEMENTS

Qualitative characteristics are the attributes that make the information provided in a set of financial statements useful to users. According to the *Framework*, the four principal qualitative characteristics are

1. Understandability
2. Relevance
3. Reliability
4. Comparability

Understandability

Financial statements should provide information that is understood by users of financial statements. In other words, *understandability* refers to information being readily understandable by users of financial statements.

There are several end-users of financial statements. For instance, one of the users of information portrayed in a set of financial statements could be a layman who has invested in the shares of a public company (say, someone who is not a qualified financial professional and who has no knowledge of accounting and reporting standards). Another user of the financial statements could be a knowledgeable and trained financial analyst. Therefore, it would not be reasonable if the *Framework* required that financial statements need to be understandable by everyone. To put it differently, the requirement of the *Framework* is that the information contained in a set of financial statements should be

- Understandable by a user who has reasonable knowledge of business and economic activities and accounting; and
- A willingness to study the information with reasonable diligence.

Relevance

Information provided by a set of financial statements is considered relevant if it has the ability to influence users' economic decisions and is provided to users in a timely manner to influence their decisions. *Relevance* refers to information being relevant to the decision-making needs of users.

Information has the quality of relevance when it influences the economic decisions of users by helping them evaluate past, present, or future events, or confirming or correcting their past evaluations. In order to be relevant, information should at least have the following two characteristics:

1. *Predictive value:* Many users of financial statements use historic information provided by financial statements to predict the entity's future profitability and its cash flows.
2. *Confirmative value:* Many users of financial statements use the information provided by the financial statements to confirm their prior expectations of the entity's performance or stewardship of the management.

The concept of relevance is closely related to the concept of *materiality.* The *Framework* describes *materiality* as a threshold or cutoff point for information whose omission or misstatement could influence the economic decisions of users taken on the basis of the financial statements.

The concept of materiality is further addressed in IAS 1, which specifies that each material class of similar items shall be presented separately in the financial statements and that items of a dissimilar nature or function shall be presented separately unless they are immaterial. Under the concept of materiality, a specific disclosure requirement in a standard or an interpretation need not be met if the information is not material.

Reliability

Information provided by financial statements may be relevant, but if it not reliable then it is of little use. According to the *Framework,* to be reliable, information must be

- Free from material error;
- Neutral, that is, free from bias;

- Represent faithfully the transactions and other events it either purports to represent or could reasonably be expected to represent (representational faithfulness). If information is to represent faithfully the transactions and other events that it purports to represent, the Framework specifies that they need to be accounted for and presented in accordance with their substance and economic reality even if their legal form is different (substance over form); and
- Be complete within the bounds of materiality and cost.

Related to the concept of reliability is *prudence,* whereby preparers of financial statements should include a degree of caution in exercising judgments needed in making estimates, such that assets or income are not overstated and liabilities or expenses are not understated. However, the exercise of prudence does not justify the deliberate understatement of assets or income, or the deliberate overstatement of liabilities or expenses, because the financial statements would not be neutral and, therefore, not reliable.

Comparability

Comparability refers to information being comparable through time and across entities. To achieve comparability, like transactions and events should be accounted for similarly by an entity throughout an entity, over time for that entity, and by different entities.

Consistency of presentation is also addressed in IAS 1. It specifies that the presentation and classification of items in the financial statements, as a general rule, shall be retained from one period to the next, with specified exceptions.

CONSTRAINTS AND TRADE-OFFS BETWEEN DIFFERENT QUALITATIVE CHARACTERISTICS

In practice, there is often a trade-off between different qualitative characteristics of information. In these situations, an appropriate balance among the characteristics must be achieved in order to meet the objective of financial statements.

Example 2

Examples of trade-offs among qualitative characteristics of information are

1. There is a trade-off between reporting relevant information in a timely manner and taking time to ensure that the information is reliable. If information is not reported in a timely manner, it may lose its relevance. Therefore, entities need to balance relevance and reliability in determining when to provide information.
2. There is trade-off between benefit and cost in preparing and reporting information. In principle, the benefits derived from the information by users should exceed the cost for the preparer of providing it.
3. There is a trade-off between providing information that is relevant, but is subject to measurement uncertainty (e.g., the fair value of a financial instrument), and providing information that is reliable but not necessarily relevant (e.g., the historical cost of a financial instrument).

ELEMENTS OF FINANCIAL STATEMENTS

The *Framework* describes the elements of financial statements as broad classes of financial effects of transactions and other events. The elements of financial statements are

- **Assets.** An asset is a resource controlled by the entity as a result of past events and from which future economic benefits are expected to flow to the entity.
- **Liabilities.** A liability is a present obligation of the entity arising from past events, the settlement of which is expected to result in an outflow from the entity of resources embodying economic benefits.

- **Equity.** Equity is the residual interest in the assets of the entity after deducting all its liabilities.
- **Income.** Income is increases in economic benefits during the accounting period in the form of inflows or enhancements of assets or decreases of liabilities that result in increases in equity, other than those relating to contributions from equity participants.
- **Expenses.** Expenses are decreases in economic benefits during the accounting period in the form of outflows or depletions of assets or incurrences of liabilities that result in decreases in equity, other than those relating to distributions to equity participants.

According to the *Framework*, an item that meets the definition of an element should be recognized (i.e., incorporated in the financial statements) if

1. It is probable that any future economic benefit associated with the item will flow to or from the entity; and
2. The item has a cost or value that can be measured with reliability.

The *Framework* notes that the most common measurement basis in financial statements is historical cost, but that other measurement bases are also used, such as current cost, realizable or settlement value, and present value.

CONCEPTS OF CAPITAL AND CAPITAL MAINTENANCE

The *Framework* distinguishes between a *financial concept of capital* and a *physical concept of capital*. Most entities use a financial concept of capital, under which *capital* is defined in monetary terms as the net assets or equity of the entity. Under a physical concept of capital, capital is instead defined in terms of physical productive capacity of the entity.

Under the financial capital maintenance concept, a profit is earned if the financial amount of the net assets at the end of the period exceeds the financial amount of net assets at the beginning of the period, after excluding any distributions to, and contributions from, owners during the period.

Under the physical capital maintenance concept, a profit is instead earned if the physical productive capacity (or operating capability) of the entity (or the resources or funds needed to achieve that capacity) at the end of the period exceeds the physical productive capacity at the beginning of the period, after excluding any distributions to, and contributions from, owners during the period.

3 PRESENTATION OF FINANCIAL STATEMENTS (IAS 1)

INTRODUCTION

IAS 1 sets out overall requirements for the presentation of general purpose financial statements, prescribes guidelines for their structure, and lays out the minimum requirements for their content and disclosure.

OBJECTIVES

The objective of financial statements is to provide useful information when making economic decisions. The objectives of IAS 1 are to ensure comparability of presentation of that information with the entity's financial statements of previous periods and with the financial statements of other entities. Financial statements are prepared on a going concern basis, unless management either intends to liquidate the entity or to cease trading, or has no realistic alternative but to do so.

An entity prepares its financial statements, except for cash flow information, under the accrual basis of accounting.

Traditionally, a complete set of financial statements consist of a balance sheet, an income statement, a statement of changes in equity, a cash flow statement, and explanatory notes (including accounting policies). However, with the recent amendment to IAS 1, some of the titles of the components of the financial statements have been changed. For instance, a balance sheet may now be referred to as a *statement of financial position*. Furthermore, the revised IAS 1 has also introduced a new statement, the statement of comprehensive income. This statement combines income statement items with items that would have previously been presented in the statement of recognized income. Entities are *not required* to use the new titles in their financial statements. The revised IAS 1 is effective for annual periods beginning on or after January 1, 2009. (Early adoption was permitted.)

SCOPE

IAS 1 categorically states that an entity shall apply IAS 1 when preparing and presenting general purpose financial statements in accordance with IFRS. In other words, financial statements other than general purpose financial statements are scoped out. For instance, this standard does not apply to the structure and content of condensed interim financial statements (such financial statements are prepared in accordance with IAS 34, *Interim Financial Reporting*).

Furthermore, the requirements of IAS 1 apply equally to all entities, including those that present consolidated financial statements and those that present separate financial statements as defined in IAS 27, *Consolidated and Separate Financial Statements*. However, if entities with not-for-profit activities in the private sector or the public sector apply this standard, they may need to amend the descriptions used for particular line items in the financial statements and for the financial statements themselves. Similarly, entities such as some mutual funds, that do not have equity as defined in IAS 32, *Financial Instruments: Presentation*, and entities whose share capital is not equity (e.g., some cooperative entities) may need to adapt the financial statement presentation of member's or unit holder's interests.

KEY TERMS (AS PROVIDED IN IAS 1)

General purpose financial statements (referred to as financial statements). Statements that are intended to meet the needs of the users who are not in a position to require an entity to prepare reports tailored to their particular information needs.

Impracticable. When an entity cannot apply a requirement after making every reasonable effort to do so.

International Financial Reporting Standards (IFRS). Standards and interpretations issued by the International Accounting Standards Board (IASB). IFRS also include pronouncements issued by the previous standard-setting authorities, the IASC and the SIC. They comprise:

- International Financial Reporting Standards (IFRS)
- International Accounting Standards (IAS)
- Interpretations developed by the International Financial Reporting Interpretations Committee (IFRIC) or the former SIC

Other comprehensive income. Items of income and expenses (including reclassification adjustments) that are not recognized in profit or loss, as required or permitted by other IFRS.

Owners. Holders of instruments classified as equity.

Profit or loss. The total of income less expenses, excluding the components of other comprehensive income.

Total comprehensive income. The change in equity during a period resulting from transactions and other events, other than those changes resulting from transactions with owners in their capacity as owners.

COMPLETE SET OF FINANCIAL STATEMENTS

The components of a complete set of financial statements are

- A statement of financial position at the end of the period;
- A statement of comprehensive income for the period (presented as either a single statement or an income statement with a statement of recognized gains and losses);
- A statement of changes in equity for the period;
- A statement of cash flows for the period;
- Notes, including a summary of significant accounting policies and other explanatory information; and
- A statement of financial position at the beginning of the earliest comparative period when an entity applies an accounting policy retrospectively or makes a retrospective restatement of items in its financial statements.

While IAS 1 clarifies that an entity may use titles for statements, other than those used in this standard, it stresses that an entity shall present with equal prominence all of the components of financial statements in a complete set of financial statements.

GENERAL REQUIREMENTS OF IAS 1

- Financial statements shall present fairly the financial position, financial performance, and cash flows of an entity.
- An entity whose financial statements comply with IFRS shall make an explicit and unreserved statement of such compliance in the notes.

- An entity cannot rectify inappropriate accounting policies either by disclosure of the accounting policies used or by notes or explanatory material.
- In the extremely rare circumstances when the entity's management concludes that compliance with a requirement in an IFRS would be so misleading that it would conflict with the objective of financial statements set out in the IASB's *Framework*, the entity is required to depart from that requirement, provided the regulatory framework under which the entity operates requires, or does not prohibit, such a departure. It should be noted that invoking such a true and fair override (as this is sometimes referred to) is not expected to occur often in practice.
- *Going Concern:* An entity normally prepares financial statements on a going concern basis (explained in Chapter 2). However, if management either intends to liquidate the entity or to cease trading, or has no realistic alternative but to do so, it is not allowed to prepare financial statements using the going concern basis. Furthermore, when management is aware, in making its assessment, of material uncertainties related to events or conditions that may cast significant doubt upon the entity's ability to continue as a going concern, the entity shall disclose those uncertainties. Also, when an entity *does not* prepare financial statements on a going concern basis, it shall disclose that fact, together with the basis on which it prepared the financial statements and the reason why the entity is not regarded as a going concern.

    Example 1

    Destitute Inc. is a real estate developer. Since the subprime crisis, the real estate market has taken a sudden nosedive. As per the audited financial statements of Destitute Inc. for the year ended December 31, 20XX, the entity had a net loss of $10 million. At December 31, 20XX, its current assets aggregate $40 million and the current liabilities aggregate $55 million.

    However, due to unexpected major changes in government legislation relating to real estate, the industry is hoping to make profits in the coming year. Furthermore, the shareholders of the entity have arranged alternative/additional sources of finance for new investment opportunities they expect in the near future and also to support its working needs in the next 12 months.

    Under such circumstances, should Destitute Inc. prepare its financial statements under the going concern basis?

    The two factors that raise doubts about the entity's ability to continue as a going concern are: (1) the net loss for the year of $10 million; and (2) at the balance sheet date, the working capital deficiency (current liabilities of $55 million) exceed its current assets of $40 million by $15 million.

    However, there are two mitigating factors: (1) the shareholders' ability to arrange funding for the entity's expansion and working capital needs, and (2) projected future profitability due to unexpected changes in government legislation for the industry the entity is operating within.

    Based on these sets of factors—both negative and positive (mitigating) factors—it may be possible for the management of the entity to argue that the going concern assumption is appropriate and that any other basis of preparation of financial statements would be unreasonable at the moment. However, if matters deteriorate further, then in the future another detailed assessment would be needed to ascertain whether the going concern assumption is still valid.

- *Accrual Basis of Accounting:* An entity shall prepare its financial statements, except for cash flow information, using the accrual basis of accounting.
- *Materiality and Aggregation:* An entity shall present separately each material class of similar items. An entity shall present separately items of dissimilar nature or function unless they are immaterial.

- *Offsetting:* An entity shall not offset assets and liabilities or income and expenses, unless required or permitted by an IFRS.
- *Frequency of Reporting:* An entity shall present a complete set of financial statements at least annually.
- *Comparative Information:* Except when IFRS permits or requires otherwise, an entity shall disclose comparative information in respect of the previous period for all amounts reported in the current period's financial statements.
- *Changes in Presentation or Classification:* When the entity changes the presentation or classification of items in its financial statements, the entity shall reclassify comparative amounts unless reclassification is impracticable.

Identification of the Financial Statements

An entity shall clearly identify the financial statements and distinguish them from other information in the same published document.

The following line items, as a minimum, are to be presented on the face of the statement of financial position:

- *Assets:* Property, plant and equipment; investment property; intangible assets; financial assets; investments accounted for using the equity method; biological assets; deferred tax assets; current tax assets; inventories; trade and other receivables; and cash and cash equivalents
- *Equity:* Issued capital and reserves attributable to equity holders of the parent; and noncontrolling interest
- *Liabilities:* Deferred tax liabilities; current tax liabilities; financial liabilities; provisions; and trade and other payables
- *Assets and Liabilities Held for Sale:* The total of assets classified as held for sale and assets included in disposal groups classified as held for sale; and liabilities included in disposal groups classified as held for sale in accordance with IFRS 5, *Noncurrent Assets Held for Sale and Discontinued Operations.*

Further subclassifications of the line items presented in a statement of financial position, classified in the manner appropriate to the entity's operations, is required to be disclosed either in the statement of financial position, or in the notes.

How Information is Disclosed

- An entity shall disclose for each class of share capital: the number of shares authorized, issued and fully paid, and issued but not paid, par value per share, a reconciliation of the number of shares outstanding at the beginning and at the end of the period. An entity is also required to disclose the rights, preferences, and restrictions attaching to shares. Shares in the entity held by the entity or its subsidiaries or associates should also be disclosed. Furthermore, shares reserved for issue under options and contracts for the sale of shares along with their terms and conditions are also required to be disclosed.
- A description of the nature and purpose of each reserve within the equity.

Current/Noncurrent Distinction

Entities normally present a statement of financial position (also referred to as a balance sheet) that separates current assets and current liabilities from noncurrent assets and noncurrent liabilities respectively. Such a statement of financial position is usually referred to as a *classified* balance sheet. In practice, entities normally present current and noncurrent assets, and current and noncurrent liabilities, as separate classifications in their statements of financial position. However, when a presentation based on liquidity presents better (i.e., reliable and more relevant) information, the entity is required by IAS 1 to present all assets and liabilities in order of liquidity.

Current Assets

An entity shall classify an asset as current when

- It expects to realize the asset, or intends to sell or consume it, in its normal operating cycle;
- It holds the asset primarily for the purpose of trading;
- It expects to realize the asset within 12 months after the reporting period; or
- The asset is cash or a cash equivalent (as defined in IAS 7), unless the asset is restricted from being exchanged or used to settle a liability for at least 12 months after the reporting period.

Current Liabilities

An entity shall classify a liability as current when

- It expects to settle the liability in its normal operating cycle;
- It holds the liability primarily for the purpose of trading;
- The liability is due to be settled within 12 months after the reporting period; or
- The entity does not have an unconditional right to defer settlement of the liability for at least 12 months after the reporting period.

An amendment to IAS 1 as a result of the Annual Improvements Project recently clarified that liabilities held for trading and derivatives do not need to be classified as current.

STATEMENT OF COMPREHENSIVE INCOME

IAS 1 offers the choice of presenting all items of income and expense recognized in the period: *either* in a single statement, *or,* in two statements, that is, a statement displaying components of profit or loss, together with, another statement beginning with profit or loss and displaying components of other comprehensive income.

The standard prescribes, as a minimum, the following line items to be presented in a statement of comprehensive income:

- Revenue, finance costs, share of profit or loss from associates and joint ventures accounted using the equity method, tax expense, amounts required to be disclosed under IFRS 5 relating to discontinued operations;
- Profit or loss for the reporting period;
- Each component of other comprehensive income classified by nature;
- Share of other comprehensive income of associates and joint ventures accounted using the equity method; and
- Total comprehensive income.

Profit or loss for the reporting period as well as total comprehensive income for the period attributable to noncontrolling interests and owners of the parent are required to be disclosed separately.

Since the IAS 1 prescribes minimum line item disclosure, an entity is permitted to present additional line items, headings and subtotals in the statement of comprehensive income and the separate income statement (if the entity opts to present this statement). Such additional disclosures are allowed when such presentation is relevant to an understanding of the entity's financial performance.

Example 2: Single Statement Approach

Statement of Comprehensive Income

	20X9	20X8
Revenue	780,000	710,000
Expenses	(500,000)	(550,000)
Profit before tax	280,000	160,000
Income tax expense	(50,000)	(30,000)
Profit for the year from continuing operations	**230,000**	**130,000**
Loss for the year from discontinued operations	(61,000)	—
Profit for the year	**169,000**	**130,000**
Other comprehensive income:		
Exchange differences on translating foreign operations	10,000	20,000
Available-for-sale financial assets	4,800	7,000
Cash flow hedges	2,400	4,400
Gains on property revaluation	16,000	14,000
Actuarial (losses)/gains on defined benefit pension plans	(1,334)	2,666
Share of other comprehensive income of associates	800	(1,400)
Income tax relating to components of other comprehensive income	(8,000)	(7,800)
Other comprehensive income for the year, net of tax	24,666	38,866
Total comprehensive income for the year	**193,666**	**168,866**
Profit attributable to:		
Owners of the parent	152,542	117,780
Minority interest	16,458	12,220
	169,000	**130,000**
Total comprehensive income attributable to:		
Owners of the parent	173,208	150,246
Minority interest	20,458	18,620
	193,666	**168,866**

Example 3: Two Statements Approach

1. Income Statement

	20X9	20X8
Revenue	780,000	710,000
Expenses	(500,000)	(550,000)
Profit before tax	280,000	160,000
Income tax expense	(50,000)	(30,000)
Profit for the year from continuing operations	**230,000**	**130,000**
Loss for the year from discontinued operations	(61,000)	—
Profit for the year	**169,000**	**130,000**
Profit attributable to:		
Owners of the parent	152,542	117,780
Noncontrolling interest	16,458	12,220
	169,000	**130,000**

2. Statement of Comprehensive Income

	20X9	20X8
Profit for the year	169,000	130,000
Other comprehensive income:		
Exchange differences on translating foreign operations	10,000	20,000
Available-for-sale financial assets	4,800	7,000
Cash flow hedges	2,400	4,400
Gains on property revaluation	16,000	14,000
Actuarial (losses)/gains on defined benefit pension plans	(1,334)	2,666
Share of other comprehensive income of associates	800	(1,400)
Income tax relating to components of other comprehensive income	(8,000)	(7,800)
Other comprehensive income for the year, net of tax	24,666	38,866
Total comprehensive income for the year	**193,666**	**168,866**

Total comprehensive income attributable to:		
Owners of the parent	173,208	150,246
Noncontrolling interest	20,458	18,620
	193,666	**168,866**

Profit or Loss for the Period

An entity shall recognise all items of income and expense in a period in profit or loss unless an IFRS requires or permits otherwise. An entity shall present an analysis of expenses recognised in profit or loss using a classification based on either their nature or their function within the entity, whichever provides information that is reliable and more relevant.

Example 4

An example of a classification using the *nature of expense* method:

Revenue	x
Other income	x
Changes in inventories of finished goods and work in progress	x
Raw materials and consumable used	x
Employee benefits expenses	x
Depreciation and amortization expense	x
Other expenses	x
Total expenses	(x)
Profits before tax	x

Example 5

An example of a classification using the *function of expense* method:

Revenue	x
Costs of sales	(x)
Gross profits	x
Other income	x
Distribution costs	(x)
Administrative expenses	(x)
Other expenses	(x)
Profits before tax	x

An entity classifying expenses by function of expense method shall disclose additional information on the nature of expenses, including depreciation and amortization expense and employee benefits expense.

Statement of Changes in Equity

An entity is required to present a statement of changes in equity showing:

- Total comprehensive income for the period (separately disclosing amounts attributable to owners of the parent and to noncontrolling interests);
- For each component of equity, the effects of retrospective application or retrospective restatement required by IAS 8, *Accounting Policies, Changes in Accounting Estimates and Errors;* and
- For each component of equity, reconciliation between the carrying amount at the beginning and the end of period, separately disclosing changes resulting from profit or loss, each item of other comprehensive income, and transactions with owners, showing separately contributions by and distributions to owners and changes in ownership interests in subsidiaries that do not result in loss of control.

Statement of Cash Flows

IAS 7, *Statement of Cash Flows*, deals with the requirements for the presentation of the statement of cash flows.

Notes to the Financial Statements

The notes are a very important and integral part of the financial statements because they provide details about items presented in other components of the financial statements in addition to providing information about the basis of preparation of the financial statements and specific accounting policies used in the preparation of these financial statements.

DISCLOSURE OF ACCOUNTING POLICIES

An entity shall disclose in the summary of significant accounting policies:

- The measurement basis (or bases) used in preparing the financial statements, and, the other accounting policies used that are relevant to an understanding of the financial statements;
- The judgments, apart from those involving estimations that management has made in the process of applying the entity's accounting policies and that have the most significant effect on the amounts recognized in the financial statements; and
- The information about the assumptions it makes about the future, and other major sources of uncertainty at the end of the reporting period.

Other Disclosures

An entity shall disclose in the notes:

- The amount of dividends proposed or declared before the financial statements were authorized for issue but not recognized as a distribution to owners during the period, and the related amount per share;
- The amount of any cumulative preference dividends not recognized; and
- Information that enables users of its financial statements to evaluate the entity's objectives, policies, and processes for managing capital.

An entity shall disclose the following if not disclosed elsewhere in information published with the financial statements:

- The domicile and legal form of the entity, its country of incorporation, and the address of its registered office (or principle place of business, if different from the registered office);
- A description of the nature of the entity's operations and its principal activities; and
- The name of the parent and the ultimate parent of the group.

EXCERPTS FROM PUBLISHED FINANCIAL STATEMENTS

MARKS & SPENCERS GROUP PLC, Annual Report 2009

Notes to Financial Statements

Critical Accounting Estimates and Judgments

The preparation of consolidated financial statements requires the Group to make estimates and assumptions that affect the application of policies and reported amounts. Estimates and judgments are continually evaluated and are based on historical experience and other factors including expectations of future events that are believed to be reasonable under the circumstances. Actual results may differ from these estimates. The estimates and assumptions that have a significant risk of causing a material adjustment to the carrying amount of assets and liabilities are discussed here.

a. **Impairment of goodwill.** The Group is required to test, at least annually, whether good-will has suffered any impairment. The recoverable amount is determined based on value in use calculations. The use of this method requires the estimation of future cash flows and the choice of a suitable discount rate in order to calculate the present value of these cash flows. Actual outcomes could vary from those calculated. See note 13 for further details.

b. **Impairment of property, plant and equipment.** Property, plant, and equipment are re-viewed for impairment if events or changes in circumstances indicate that the carrying amount may not be recoverable. When a review for impairment is conducted, the recov-erable amount is determined based on value in use calculations prepared on the basis of management's assumptions and estimates. See note 14 for further details.

c. **Depreciation of property, plant, and equipment.** Depreciation is provided so as to write down the assets to their residual values over their estimated useful lives as set out above. The selection of these residual values and estimated lives requires the exercise of management judgment. See note 14 for further details.

d. **Postretirement benefits.** The determination of the pension cost and defined benefit ob-ligation of the Group's defined benefit pension schemes depends on the selection of certain assumptions that include the discount rate, inflation rate, salary growth, mortality and expected return on scheme assets. Differences arising from actual experiences or future changes in assumptions will be reflected in subsequent periods. See note 11 for further details.

e. **Refunds and loyalty scheme accruals.** Accruals for sales returns and loyalty scheme re-demption are estimated on the basis of historical returns and redemptions and these are recorded so as to allocate them to the same period as the original revenue is recorded. These accruals are reviewed regularly and updated to reflect management's latest best estimates, however, actual returns and redemptions could vary from these estimates.

4 INVENTORIES (IAS 2)

INTRODUCTION

IAS 2 prescribes the basis of determining and accounting for inventories as an asset until the related revenues are recognized. The standard also provides guidance on the valuation of inventories and their consequent write-down as an expense, and the treatment to be adopted on related revenues being recognized.

SCOPE

IAS 2 applies to all inventories except for the following cases that are governed by the provisions of other specific standards:

- Work-in-progress arising under construction contracts (IAS 11, *Construction Contracts*);
- Financial instruments (e.g., shares, debentures, bonds) held as inventory (IAS 32, *Financial Instruments: Presentation;* IAS 39, *Financial Instruments: Recognition* and *Measurement;* and IFRS 7, *Financial Instruments Disclosures;* and IFRS 9, *Financial Instruments*);
- Biological assets and produce that are related to agricultural activity (IAS 41, *Agriculture).*

The standard also does not apply to

- Producer's inventories such as livestock, agricultural and forest products, mineral oils, ores and gases, when such inventories are valued at net realizable value in accordance with well-established practices in those industries.
- Inventories held by commodity brokers-traders who measure their inventories at fair value less cost to sell.

KEY TERMS

Inventories. Assets that are

- Held for sale in the ordinary course of business (e.g., finished goods); or
- Used to produce goods for sale (e.g., raw material and work-in-progress); or
- Consumed in the production process or in the rendering of services (i.e., stores, spares, consumables).

Cost. Includes the purchase cost and all other costs incurred to bring the inventories to their present location and condition.

Net realizable value (NRV). The estimated selling price that is realizable in the normal course of business less the estimated cost required to complete and make the sale.

Fair value. The value at which an asset can be exchanged or a liability can be settled in an arm's-length transaction between two or more knowledgeable and willing parties.

BASIS OF VALUATION

Inventories should be valued at lower of cost and net realizable value. The following points should be considered when determining cost and net realizable value:

- *Cost* includes the cost of purchase of inventories and all other costs that are directly attributable to the acquisition of the inventories and bringing those inventories to their present location and condition, such as import duties and taxes that are not recoverable from the tax authority, or transport and handling charges.
- Cost of conversion includes costs that are directly related to production, such as direct labor and systematic allocation of fixed and variable production overheads that are incurred to convert the materials into finished goods. Unlike the fixed production overheads that remain constant irrespective of the volume of production, variable production overheads vary directly with the volume of production. In the case of joint products, when the cost of conversion of each product is not separately identified, the NRV of by-products is used to allocate costs on a rational and consistent basis. In the case of by-products, the NRV of the product is deducted from the cost of the main product to arrive at the cost of conversion.
- Costs do not include general and administrative costs, selling and distribution costs, abnormal wastage, and storage cost (unless these are related to the production process).
- Costs do not include interest and other borrowing costs, except if the inventory is a qualifying asset (see IAS 23, *Borrowing Costs*).
- The foreign exchange fluctuation on the inventories acquired in foreign currency is not included in the cost of purchase of inventories.
- The difference between the cost of purchase of inventories under normal credit terms and the amount payable under deferred settlement terms is not included as cost.

COST MEASUREMENT

The cost of inventories is measured using one of the following cost formulas:

- Specific identification method
- First-in, first-out (FIFO) method
- Weighted-average cost method

The specific identification method of measurement of inventories is used when the items purchased are not ordinarily interchangeable and are specifically segregated for a specific project. In the case of goods or services, they are produced and segregated for specific projects.

In all other cases, the cost of inventories should be measured using either the FIFO method or the weighted-average cost method. Inventories having a similar nature and use to the entity should be valued using the same cost formula. However, in the case of inventories with different nature or use, different cost formulas may be justified.

The FIFO method assumes that inventories purchased or produced first are sold first, thereby the items remaining at the end of the reporting period are those items of inventory that have been most recently purchased or produced.

Under the weighted-average cost method, the cost of each item is determined from the weighted average of the cost of similar items existing at the beginning of a period and the cost of those items purchased or produced during the period.

Example 1: First-In, First-Out (FIFO) Method

Odyssey Inc. is an international trading company. It commenced its operation on February 1, 2008. Odyssey Inc. imports goods from Singapore and sells them in the local market. It uses the FIFO method to value its inventory. Listed here are the company's purchases and sales during 2008:

Purchases

During the months of

February 2008	20,000 units @ $25 each
March 2008	25,000 units @ $30 each
August 2008	30,000 units @ $35 each

Sales

During the months of

June 2008	25,000 units
November 2008	30,000 units

Based on this information, with respect to the purchases and sales of Odyssey Inc., the valuation of inventory of Odyssey Inc. under the FIFO cost flow assumption at the following dates would be computed this way:

a. June 30, 2008
b. September 30, 2008
c. December 31, 2008

Inventory valuation on FIFO basis at June 30, 2008, September 30, 2008, and December 31, 2008

Step 1	February 2008	Purchase	+ 20,000 units @ $25	=	$500,000
	March 2008	Purchase	+ 25,000 units @ $30	=	$750,000
		Total			$1,250,000
Step 2	June 2008	Sales (25,000 units)	− 20,000 units @ $25	=	$(500,000)
			− 5,000 units @ $30	=	$(150,000)
					$(600,000)

a. Inventory valued on FIFO basis at June 30, 2008:

	20,000 units @ $30	=	**$600,000**

Step 3	August 2008	Purchase	+ 30,000 units @ $35	=	$1,050,000

b. Inventory valued on FIFO basis at September 30, 2008:

20,000 units @ $30	=	**$600,000**
30,000 units @ $35	=	**$1,050,000**
		$1,650,000

Step 4	November 2008	Sales (30,000 units)	− 20,000 units @ $30	=	$(600,000)
			− 10,000 units @ $35	=	$(350,000)
					$(700,000)

c. Inventory valued on FIFO basis at December 31, 2008:

20,000 units @ $35	=	**$700,000**

Example 2: Weighted-Average Cost Method

Steady LLC, a newly incorporated company, uses a software to cost and value its inventory. This popular software is programmed to value inventory using the weighted-average cost method only. The following are the purchases and sales made by Steady LLC during 2008 (as a newly set-up company, Steady LLC had no inventory carried forward from earlier periods):

Purchases		
January 15, 2008	200 units	@ $200 per unit
March 15, 2008	200 units	@ $300 per unit
September 25, 2008	200 units	@ $350 per unit

Sales	
March 25, 2008	100 units
December 15, 2008	175 units

Based on this information, the valuation of the inventory and the cost per unit of the inventory at March 31, 2008, September 30, 2008, and December 31, 2008, under the weighted-average cost method, would be

Month/date	Purchases/Sales/Balance		Rate per unit	Amount	Weighted-average cost per unit	Valuation date
January 15	Purchases	200 units	$200	$40,000		
March 15	Purchases	200 units	300	60,000		
March 15	Balance	400 units	250	$100,000		
March 25	Sales	(100) units	250	(25,000)		
March 31	**Balance**	**300 units**		**$75,000**	**$250**	**March 31, 2008**
September 25	Purchases	200 units	350	70,000		
September 30	**Balance**	**500 units**		**$145,000**	**$290**	**September 30, 2008**
December 15	Sales	(175) units	290	(50,750)		
December 31	**Balance**	**325 units**		**$94,250**	**$290**	**December 31, 2008**

NET REALIZABLE VALUE

Net realizable value (NRV) refers to estimated selling price in the ordinary course of business, less the estimated cost of completion and the estimated costs that are necessary to achieve the sale. NRV is estimated on the basis of the most reliable evidence at the time of valuation and it takes into account the purpose for which the inventory is held. The estimation of net realizable value should be made as at each balance sheet date. The value of inventory that is written down from cost is reversed if circumstances that previously caused the inventories to be written down below cost no longer exist or if there is clear evidence of an increase in the net realizable value because of changes in economic circumstances.

Measurement of Net Realizable Value

The NRV of the materials and other supplies held for use in production of finished goods is estimated this way:

- If the finished product in which raw material and supplies are used is sold at cost or above cost, then the estimated realizable value of the raw material and supplies is considered to be more than its cost.
- If the raw material and supplies used is sold below cost, then the replacement price of the raw material or supplies may be the best available measure of the net realizable value.

EXPENSE RECOGNITION

The carrying value of inventories should be recognized as an expense in the period that the inventories are sold and the related revenue is recognized (see IAS 18, *Revenue*).

When the cost of inventories at the reporting date is lower than its realizable value, or a loss of inventories occurs, the amount of write-down or loss of inventories should be recognized as an expense in the same period as the write-down or loss occurs. Similarly, when the net realizable value of inventories written down earlier rises over its stated value, the amount of reversal of write-down should be recognized as a reduction in the amount of inventories that is expensed in the period in which such reversal occurs.

Example 3

The following are the cost, estimated sales value, and the cost to complete for the items of inventory held by ABC LLC at December 31, 2008.

Item	Cost ($)	Estimated selling price ($)	Cost to complete ($)
A	2.00	2.50	0.50
B	4.00	4.00	0.80
C	6.00	10.00	1.00
D	5.00	6.00	2.00
E	1.00	1.20	0.25

Based on this information, the cost and/or the NRV that should be used in valuing the inventories is:

Item	Cost ($)	Estimated selling price less (−) cost to complete ($)	NRV ($)
A	2.00	2.50 − 0.50	2.00
B	4.00	4.00 − 0.80	3.20
C	6.00	10.00 − 1.00	9.00
D	5.00	6.00 − 2.00	4.00
E	1.00	1.20 − 0.25	0.95

The overall value of inventories of the above items will be as follows:

Item	Cost ($)	NRV ($)	Number of units	Total value* ($)
A	2.00	2.00	500	1,000
B	4.00	3.20	1,000	3,200
C	6.00	9.00	750	4,500
D	5.00	4.00	750	3,000
E	1.00	0.95	2,500	2,375
			Total	14,075

*At lower of cost or NRV.

Example 4

Tropical Blooms LLC purchased 1,000 units of inventories for $100,000 and incurred freight charges of $10,000. During the year, the company sold 750 units at $150 per unit. At the end of the year, Tropical Blooms LLC had 250 units of inventories out of which 50 units were damaged. It is estimated that the damaged units can be sold at $25 per unit and the balance 200 units, at $150 per unit.

The value of inventory at the end of year and the impact of the sale of damaged units on the income statement for the current financial reporting period will be

Cost of inventory

Total cost of purchase of inventory: $100,000 + $10,000 = $110,000
Cost per unit of inventory: $110,000/1,000 = $110 per unit

Net realizable value

Realizable value of damaged items: $25 per unit
Realizable value of undamaged items: $150 per unit

In the balance sheet, inventories are recorded at the lower of cost and NRV:

Damaged items	50 × $25 =	**$ 1,250**
Undamaged items	200 × $110 =	**$22,000**
Total value of inventories		**$23,250**

Impact of Sale

Sales revenue	750 × $150	**$112,500**
Cost of sold goods	750 × $110	**($82,500)**
Losses from damaged items:		
Net realizable value:	50 × $25	**$1,250**
Cost	50 × 110	**($5,500)**
Losses from damaged items:		**($4,250)**
Gross margin on sales	($112,500 − $82,500 − $4,250)	**$25,750**

DISCLOSURES

The financial statements should disclose the following:

- The accounting policies that are adopted for measuring inventories, including the cost measurement formula employed (FIFO, specific identification method or weighted-average cost method);

- The total carrying amount of inventories along with appropriate classifications (e.g., finished goods, work-in-progress, raw material, spare parts, etc.);
- The carrying amount of inventories carried at fair value less costs to sell (e.g., inventories of commodity broker-traders);
- The amount of inventories recognized as expense during the period (e.g., cost of sales);
- The amount of write-down of inventories if any, recognized as an expense in the period;
- The amount of any reversal of any previous write-down that is recognized as a reduction in the amount of inventories that is expensed in the period in which such reversal occurs and the circumstances or events that led to such reversal; and
- The carrying amount of inventories pledged as security for liabilities.

EXCERPTS FROM PUBLISHED FINANCIAL STATEMENTS

LECTRA, Annual Report 2008

Notes to Financial Statements

Accounting Policies

Inventories

Inventories of raw materials are valued at the lower of purchase cost (based on weighted-average cost, including related costs) and their net realizable value. Finished goods and works-in-progress are valued at the lower of standard industrial cost (adjusted at year-end on an actual cost basis) and their net realizable value. NRV is the probable sale price in the normal course of business, less the estimated cost of completion or upgrading of the product and unavoidable selling costs. Industrial cost does not include interest expense. A write-down is recorded if NRV is less than the book value. Write-downs on inventories of spare parts and consumables are calculated by comparing book value and probable NRV after a specific analysis of the rotation and obsolescence of inventory items, taking into account the utilization of items for maintenance and after-sales services activities, and changes in the range of products marketed.

BASF, Annual Report 2008

Notes to the Financial Statements

14. Inventories

In euros millions	2008	2007
Raw materials and factory supplies	1,769	1,800
Work-in-process finished goods and merchandise	4,924	4,708
Advance payments and services-in-process	70	70
	6,763	6,578

Work-in-process, finished goods, and merchandise are combined into one item due to the production conditions in the chemical industry. Services-in-process relate primarily to inventory not invoiced at the balance sheet date.

Price declines in the second half of 2008 led to an increase in the allowances for raw materials, intermediates, and end products. Overall, impairment losses on inventory amounted to €159 million in 2008 and €16 million in 2007. Of the total inventory, €1,343 million in 2008 and €1,444 million in 2007 was valued at NRV.

Reversals of impairment losses are made if the reasons for the impairment no longer apply. Reversals amounted to €5 million in 2008 and €4 million in 2007.

Inventories were valued using the weighted-average cost method.

BARLOWORLD

Notes to the Consolidated Annual Financial Statements for the Year Ended September 30

9. Inventories

In euros millions	*2008*	*2007*	*2006*
Raw materials and components		116	318
Work-in-progress	291	321	291
Finished goods	3,939	2,740	3,266
Merchandise	3,219	2,647	1,890
Consumable stores	26	17	112
Other inventories	20	28	10
Total inventories	7,495	5,869	5,907
Per business segment:			
Continuing operations			
Equipment	4,955	3,184	2,111
Automotive	1,870	1,711	1,449
Handling	769	602	1,140
Logistics	7	5	4
Corporate and other	11	5	6
Total continuing operations	7,612	5,507	4,710
Discontinued operations			
Car rental—Scandinavia			3
Cement			224
Coatings		362	498
Scientific		231	472
Steel tube	—	—	330
Total discontinued operations	—	593	1 527
Total group	7,612	6,100	6,237
Amounts classified as held for sale	(117)	(231)	(330)
Total per balance sheet	7,495	5,869	5,907
The value of inventories has been determined on the following bases:			
FIFO and specific identification	7,081	5,394	5,206
Weighted average	414	475	701
	7,495	5,869	5,907
Inventory pledged as security for liabilities	170	29	86
The secured liabilities are included under trade and other payables (note 18)			
Amount of write-down of inventory to net realizable value and losses of inventory	13	5	12
Amount of reversals of inventory previously written down	5	1	2
Amounts removed during the year from cash flow hedge reserve and included in the initial cost of inventory	(2)	2	(32)

5 STATEMENT OF CASH FLOWS (IAS 7)

INTRODUCTION

IAS 7 is one of the primary statements in financial reporting, along with the statement of financial position, the statement of comprehensive income, and the statement of changes in equity. The statement of cash flows presents the inflows and outflows of cash and cash equivalents by category (operating, investing, and financing activities) over a period of time. It provides users with a basis to assess the entity's ability to generate and utilize its cash.

KEY TERMS

Cash. Amount of cash on hand and demand deposits with banks.

Cash equivalents. Short-term, highly liquid investments that are readily convertible to known amounts of cash and that are subject to an insignificant amount of risk of changes in value.

Cash flows. Inflows and outflows of cash and cash equivalents.

Operating activities. Principal revenue-producing activities of the entity and other activities that are not investing or financing activities.

Investing activities. The acquisition and disposal of long-lived assets and other investments not included in cash equivalents.

Financing activities. Activities that result in changes in the size and composition of the contributed equity and borrowings of the entity.

This definition of cash *equivalents* signifies that it is held for meeting short-term commitments and not for investment purposes. To qualify as a cash equivalent, the investment must be short term in nature, must be readily convertible to known amount of cash, and must be subject to an insignificant risk of changes in value. Generally, *short term* means a period of three months or less from the date of acquisition.

Examples

1. A time or term deposit with a bank where the original maturity is six months will not qualify as a cash equivalent.
2. An investment made in equity shares generally will also not qualify as cash equivalents since they are subject to a risk of change in its values that can be significant.
3. An investment made in redeemable preference shares within a short period of its maturity and with a specified redemption date will qualify as a cash equivalent.

The amounts due on bank borrowings are generally considered as part of financing activities. However in some countries, where bank overdrafts are repayable on demand and they form an integral part of the entity's cash management system, they can be included as a component of cash equivalents. An important factor for such bank overdraft balances to be considered as cash equivalents is that the bank balance should fluctuate from being positive to overdrawn during the period for which the cash flow statement is prepared.

PRESENTATION OF A STATEMENT OF CASH FLOWS

The statement of cash flows shall categorize the information relating to cash receipts and cash payments under the following headings:

1. Operating activities;
2. Investing activities; and
3. Financing activities.

The entity must ensure that there is consistency in the classification of the cash flows. These classifications by activity assist the users to understand the impact of these activities on the financial position of the entity and on the amount of cash and cash equivalents.

In some cases, a single cash flow transaction may include components that have to be classified separately.

Example 1

In the case of cash repayment of a loan amount that includes principal and interest, the repayment made toward the principal amount is to be classified as a financing activity and that paid toward the interest amount is to be classified as an operating activity.

For the preparation of the cash flow statements, the movements within or between the items of cash equivalents are not to be considered since they are part of the cash management of the entity.

Example 2

When a one-month term deposit is foreclosed to acquire redeemable preference shares that mature within the next three months, the cash inflow or cash outflow are not considered for the purpose of preparing the cash flow statement since both activities are part of the entity's cash management and comprise movements between the components of cash equivalents.

Operating Activities

The amount of cash flows from operating activities indicates the extent of cash generated from operations to repay loans, pay dividends, make investments, and maintain the operational capability of the entity without obtaining any funds from external sources. This historical information is one of the important components that assist in forecasting future operating cash flows of the entity.

The cash flows from operating activities are mainly related to the revenue-producing activity of the entity. Therefore, the cash flows from sale and purchase of securities held for trading purposes by an investment company are classified as an operating activity, whereas the cash flows from sale and purchase of securities held for investment purposes by a manufacturing company are classified as an investing activity.

Examples of cash flows from operating activities.

1. Cash collections on sale of goods and rendering of services
2. Royalties, fees, commissions, and other revenue received in cash
3. Income tax refunds received, unless they can be specifically identified with financing or investing activities
4. Cash payments made to suppliers of goods and services
5. Cash payments made to and on behalf of employees
6. Income tax paid, unless the payments can be specifically identified with financing or investing activities

The cash flows from operating activities can be reported either by the direct method, wherein the major classes of gross cash receipts and cash payments are disclosed, or by the indirect method, wherein the profit or loss is adjusted for the effects of transactions of a noncash nature, any deferrals or accruals of past of future operating cash receipts or payments, and items of income or expense associated with investing or financing cash flows. IAS 7 encourages use of the direct method, but in practice, the vast majority of entities use the indirect method.

Example 3

Direct Method

In US dollars

Cash Flows from Operating Activities	*2008*	
Cash receipts from customers	$1,000,000	
Cash paid to suppliers	(700,000)	
Cash paid to employees	(100,000)	
Cash generated from operations	200,000	
Interest paid	(30,000)	
Income tax paid	(20,000)	
Cash from operating activities		$150,000

Indirect Method

In US dollars

Cash Flows from Operating Activities	*2008*
Profit before taxation	$1,000,000
Adjustments for:	
Depreciation	60,000
Income from investments	30,000
Interest expense	(40,000)
	1,050,000
Decrease in trade and other receivables	100,000
Increase in inventories	(200,000)
Decrease in trade and other payables	(150,000)
Cash from operating activities	$800,000

Investing Activities

The cash flows arising from investing activities represent the extent to which expenditure has been made for resources intended to generate future income and cash flows.

Examples.

Cash inflows:

- Proceeds from sale of property, plant, and equipment
- Proceeds from sale of investments
- Repayment of cash advances

Cash outflows:

- Purchase of property, plant, and equipment
- Purchase of investments
- Cash advances made to third parties

Financing Activities

Cash flows from financing activities include funds provided by and paid to owners and third parties.

Examples.

Cash inflows:

- Cash received on issue of shares
- Cash received on bank borrowings

Cash outflows

- Payment of dividends to shareholders
- Bank borrowings repayments

Noncash Transactions

When preparing the statement of cash flows, transactions that do not require cash or cash equivalents should be excluded. The required information on such transactions must be disclosed elsewhere in the financial statements.

Examples.

- Issue of shares against assets acquired
- Conversion of existing debt to equity

Foreign Currency Cash Flows

In regard to transactions in a foreign currency, the cash flows shall be recorded in the entity's functional currency and for this purpose, the exchange rate between the functional currency and the foreign currency at the date of the cash flow shall be applied to the related foreign currency amount.

Reporting Cash Flows on a Net Basis

Nonfinancial institutions generally consider the gross cash inflows and outflows for reporting cash flows. In this case, cash inflow (loan receipt) and cash outflow (loan repayment) are considered separately. However, in the following instances, the cash flows can be reported on a net basis:

1. Cash receipts and payments on behalf of customers reflect the activities of the customers rather than those of the entity
2. Cash receipts and payments for items where the turnover is quick, amounts are large and maturity periods are short

In addition, financial institutions are also permitted to report the cash flows from activities on a net basis in the following circumstances:

1. Cash receipts and payments for the acceptance and repayment of deposits with a fixed maturity date
2. Placing deposits with other financial institutions and withdrawing them during the period of reporting
3. Cash advances made by the financial institution to its customers and the repayment of those advances

Disclosures

Interest and dividends. The cash flow receipts and payments from interest and dividends should be disclosed separately. The classification of the receipts and payments under the respective activity of operating, investing, or financing must be consistently followed.

In the case of a financial institution, interest paid and interest received are usually classified as operating cash flows. However, in the case of entities other than financial institutions, there is no consensus on the classification of these cash flows as IAS 7 does not prescribe a specific classification.

Dividends are generally classified as a financing activity since they are a cost of obtaining financial resources.

Taxes on Income

As described previously, transactions that generate income on which taxes are levied are classified as operating, investing, or financing activities. The cash flows arising from taxes on income shall be separately disclosed and unless the tax can be specifically identified with financing and investing activities, it shall be classified as cash flows from operating activities.

Cash and Cash Equivalents

The components of cash and cash equivalents must be disclosed and a reconciliation of the amounts in the statement of cash flows with the cash and cash equivalent items reported in the statement of financial position (balance sheet) must be presented.

The management must also disclose the amount of significant cash and cash equivalent balances held by the entity that are not available for use by the group.

Example 4

Taj Express Inc.
Summary Cash Account
For the Year Ended December 31, 2008

In US dollars

Balance on 01/01/20X2	$50,000	Payment to suppliers	$2,000,000
Issue of equity shares	300,000	Purchase of property, plant, and equipment	200,000
Receipts from customers	2,800,000	Overhead expenses	200,000
Sale of property, plant, and equipment	100,000	Wages and salaries	100,000
		Taxation	250,000
		Dividends	50,000
		Repayment of bank loan	300,000
		Balance at 12/31/2008	150,000
	$3,250,000		$3,250,000

Based on this information, the statement of cash flows was prepared in accordance with IAS 7 under the direct method as follows:

Statement of Cash Flows
For the Year Ended December 31, 2008 (Direct Method)

In US dollars

Cash receipts from customers	$2,800,000	
Cash payments to suppliers	(2,000,000)	
Cash paid to employees	(100,000)	
Cash payments for overheads	(200,000)	
Cash generated from operations	500,000	
Income tax paid	(250,000)	
Net cash from operating activities		$250,000
Cash Flows from Investing Activities		
Payment for purchase of property, plant, and equipment	(200,000)	
Proceeds from sale of property, plant, and equipment	100,000	
Net cash (used in) investing activities		(100,000)
Cash Flows from Financing Activities		
Proceeds from issuance of equity share	300,000	
Bank loan repaid	(300,000)	
Dividend paid	(50,000)	
Net cash (used in) financing activities		(50,000)
Net increase in cash		100,000
Cash at the beginning of the year		50,000
Cash at the end of the year		$150,000

Example 5

Direct Inc.
Cash Flows
For the Year Ended December 31, 2008

In US dollars

Add:

Sale of investments	$700,000	
Depreciation on property, plant, and equipment	100,000	
Issue of preference shares	90,000	
Loan raised	45,000	
Decrease in inventories	120,000	
		1,055,000
		1,655,000
Less:		
Purchase of property, plant, and equipment	65,000	
Decrease in trade and other payables	60,000	
Increase in accounts receivable	80,000	
Exchange gain	80,000	
Profit on sale of investments	120,000	
Redemption of debentures	57,000	
Dividend paid	14,000	
Interest paid	9,500	
		485,500
		1,169,500
Add: opening cash and cash equivalents		15,500
Cash and cash equivalents, end of year		$1,185,000

The statement of cash flows prepared in accordance with IAS 7 under the indirect method will be as follows:

Direct Inc.
Statement of Cash Flows (Indirect Method)
For the Year Ended March 31, 2008

in US dollars

Cash Flows from Operating Activities

Net profit for the year		$600,000
Adjustments for:		
Exchange gain	($80,000)	
Profit on sale of investments	(120,000)	
Depreciation on property, plant, and equipment	100,000	
		(100,000)
		500,000
Increase in accounts receivable	(80,000)	
Decrease in inventories	120,000	
Decrease in trade and other payables	(60,000)	
		(20,000)
Net cash from operating activities		480,000
Cash Flows from Investing Activities		
Sale of investments	700,000	
Purchase of property, plant, and equipment	(65,000)	
Net cash from investing activities		635,000
Cash Flows from Financing Activities		
Issue of preference shares	90,000	
Loan raised	45,000	
Redemption of debentures	(57,000)	
Interest paid	(9,500)	
Dividend paid	(14,000)	
Net cash from financing activities		54,500
Net increase in cash and cash equivalents		1,169,500
Add: opening cash and cash equivalents		15,500
Cash and cash equivalents, end of year		$1,185,000

6 ACCOUNTING POLICIES, CHANGES IN ACCOUNTING ESTIMATES AND ERRORS (IAS 8)

INTRODUCTION

IAS 8 describes the basis for the selection of accounting policies and their amendment. Also, it prescribes the requirements and disclosures for any changes that are made in accounting estimates and corrections of prior period errors.

The objectives of this standard are to enhance the relevance and reliability of an entity's financial statements and to be able to compare the financial statements of an entity over time as well as with the financial statements of other entities.

KEY TERMS

Accounting policies. The specific principles, bases, conventions, rules, and practices applied by an entity in preparing and presenting financial statements.

Change in accounting estimate. An adjustment of the carrying amount of an asset or a liability, or the amount of the periodic consumption of an asset, which results from the assessment of the present status of, and expected future benefits and obligations associated with, assets and liabilities. Changes in accounting estimates result from new information or new developments and accordingly are not corrections of errors.

International Financial Reporting Standards (IFRS). The standards and interpretations adopted by the International Accounting Standards Board (IASB). They comprise:

- International Financial Reporting Standards (IFRS)
- International Accounting Standards (IAS)
- Interpretations developed by the International Financial Reporting Interpretations Committee (IFRIC) or the former Standing Interpretations Committee (SIC)

Prior period errors. Omissions from and misstatements in the entity's financial statements for one or more prior periods arising from a failure to use, or the misuse of, reliable information that

- Was available when financial statements for those periods were authorized for issue; and
- Could reasonably be expected to have been obtained and taken into account in the preparation and presentation of those financial statements.

Such errors include the effects of mathematical mistakes, mistakes in applying accounting policies, oversights or misinterpretations of facts, and fraud.

Retrospective application. The application of a new accounting policy to transactions, other events, or conditions as if that policy had always been applied.

Prospective application. A change in accounting policy and of recognizing the effect of a change in an accounting estimate, respectively, are

- Applying the new accounting policy to transactions, other events, or conditions occurring after the date when the policy is changed; and
- Recognizing the effect of the change in the accounting estimate in the current and future periods affected by the change.

Material. Misstatements or omissions are "material" if they can, either individually or cumulatively, influence the decisions of users of financial statements.

Impracticable. When an entity still cannot apply a requirement of a standard or interpretation after making every effort to do so. For a particular prior period, it is impracticable to apply a change in an accounting policy if

- The effects of the retrospective application are not determinable;
- The retrospective application requires assumptions about what management's intentions would have been at the time; or
- The retrospective application requires significant estimates of amounts, and it is impossible to distinguish objectively, from other information, information about those estimates that
  - Provides evidence of circumstances that existed at that time; and
  - Would have been available at that time.

Retrospective restatement. Correcting the recognition, measurement, and disclosure of the amounts of elements of financial statements as if a prior period error has never occurred.

SELECTION AND APPLICATION OF ACCOUNTING POLICIES

When selecting and applying an accounting policy, the standard or interpretation that applies to the relevant transaction, other event, or condition must be applied.

In case the standards or interpretations do not address a specific transaction, other event, or condition, the management must develop and use an accounting policy such that the information provided therein is relevant to decision-making needs of the users. Also, the financial statements must

- Represent faithfully the financial position, financial performance, and cash flows of the entity;
- Reflect the economic substance of transactions, other events, or conditions; and
- Be neutral, prudent, and complete in all material respects.

When making these judgments, the management must apply the following sources in *descending order:*

- The requirements in the standards and interpretations that deal with similar and related issues;
- The definitions, recognition criteria, and measurement concepts for assets, liabilities, income, and expenses as detailed in the IASB's Framework; and
- Most recent pronouncements of other standard-setting bodies that use a similar conceptual framework to develop standards, other accounting literature, and accepted industry practices, to the extent that these do not conflict with the sources mentioned earlier.

CONSISTENCY OF ACCOUNTING POLICIES

The accounting policies, once selected, must be applied consistently for similar transactions, other events, and conditions unless a standard or interpretation specifically requires or permits categorization of items for which different policies may be appropriate. When a standard or interpretation requires or permits such categorization, an appropriate accounting policy must be selected and applied consistently to each category.

Changes in Accounting Policies

An entity shall change an accounting policy only if the change

- Is required by a standard or interpretation; or
- Results in reliable and more relevant information being provided by the financial statements in regard to the effects of transactions, other events, or conditions on the entity's financial position, financial performance, or cash flows.

It may be noted that the following are *not* changes in accounting policies:

- The application of an accounting policy for transactions, other events, or conditions that differ in substance from those that occurred previously; and
- The application of a new accounting policy for transactions, other events, or conditions that did not occur previously or were immaterial.

Applying Changes in Accounting Policies

When an entity changes its accounting policy on the basis of a new or amended standard or interpretation, the transitional provisions that are specified therein must be followed in adopting the change. However, when no transitional provisions are specified, or if the entity changes its accounting policy voluntarily, the changes shall be applied retrospectively (as if the policy had always been applied).

When the change is applied retrospectively, the comparative (previous reporting period) figures that are presented in financial statements must be restated as if the new policy had always been applied. The impact of the new policy on the retained earnings prior to the earliest period presented should be adjusted against the opening balance of retained earnings. If it is impracticable to determine either the period-specific effects or the cumulative effect of the change, the entity shall apply the change prospectively from the start of the earliest period that is practically possible.

Example 1

In 2008, Advanced Lighting Limited changed its accounting policy relating to valuation of inventories. Before 2008, the inventories were valued under the weighted-average cost method. In 2008, the method was changed to the first-in, first-out (FIFO) method, because it was considered to more accurately reflect the usage and flow of inventories in the economic cycle. The impact on the inventory valuation was determined to be

December 31, 2006	an increase of $10,000
December 31, 2007	an increase of $15,000
December 31, 2008	an increase of $20,000

The income statements prior to adjustment are

	2008	2007
Revenue	$250,000	$200,000
Cost of sales	100,000	80,000
Gross profit	150,000	120,000
Administration costs	60,000	50,000
Selling and distribution costs	25,000	15,000
Net profit	$65,000	$55,000

The change in the accounting policy in the income statement and the statement of changes in equity, in accordance with requirements of IAS 8, will appear as follows:

Advanced Lighting Limited
Income Statement
For the Year Ended December 31, 2008

	2008	2007 (restated)
Revenue	$250,000	$200,000
Cost of sales	95,000	75,000
Gross profit	155,000	125,000
Administration costs	60,000	50,000
Selling and distribution costs	25,000	15,000
Net profit	70,000	60,000

Based on the change in accounting policy, the cost of sales will be reduced by $5,000 each year. The impact on the retained earnings included in the statement of changes in equity would be as follows (the shaded figures represent the situation if there had been no change in accounting policy):

Advanced Lighting Limited
Statement of Changes in Equity (Retained Earnings Columns Only)
For the Year Ended December 31, 2008

	Retained earnings	Retained earnings
At January 1, 2006, as originally stated	$300,000	$300,000
Change in accounting policy for valuation of inventory	10,000	
At January 1, 2007, as restated	310,000	
Net profit for the year, as restated	60,000	55,000
At December 31, 2007	370,000	355,000
Net profit for the year	70,000	65,000
At December 31, 2008	$440,000	$420,000

The cumulative impact at December 31, 2007, is an increase in retained earnings of $15,000 and at December 31, 2008, of $20,000.

Disclosure for Changes in Accounting Policies

Initial application of a standard or interpretation. When a new standard or interpretation is initially applied, the entity must disclose the change when it has an effect on current or prior periods or it would have an effect on future periods, but it is impracticable to determine the amount of adjustment required in current or prior periods or that will be required in the future period. The entity shall disclose

- The title of the standard or interpretation;
- When applicable, that the change is made in accordance with the transitional provisions;
- The nature of the change in the accounting policy;
- When applicable, a description of the transitional provisions;
- When applicable, the transitional provisions that might have an effect on future periods;
- For current and each prior period presented to the extent practicable, the amount of the adjustment for each financial statement line item;
- When applicable, the basic and diluted earnings per share for the current and each prior period presented to the extent practicable;
- The amount of the adjustment relating to periods before those presented, to the extent practicable; and
- When retrospective application is impracticable, the circumstances making it impracticable and the date from which the accounting policy has been applied.

Voluntary change in accounting policy. In the case of voluntary change in accounting policy, when the previous change has an effect on current or prior periods or would have an effect on future periods but it is impracticable to determine the amount of adjustment required in current or prior periods or that will be required in the future period, the entity shall disclose

- The nature of the change in the accounting policy;
- Reason for the new policy providing reliable and more relevant information;
- For the current and each prior period presented, to the extent practicable, the amount of the adjustment for each financial statement line item;
- If applicable, the basic and diluted earnings per share for the current and each prior period presented, to the extent practicable;
- The amount of the adjustment relating to periods before those presented, to the extent practicable; and
- If retrospective application is impracticable, the circumstances making it impracticable and the date from which the accounting policy has been applied.

When standards or interpretations have been issued but are not yet effective, the entity must disclose the fact that those standards or interpretations have been issued at the date of authorization of the financial statements but were not effective. Any known or reasonably estimable information relevant to assessing the possible impact of the new standard or interpretation must also be disclosed. The financial statements of subsequent periods need not repeat these disclosures.

Changes in Accounting Estimates

On account of uncertainties inherent in business activities, many items in the financial statements are estimated since they cannot be measured with accuracy. These accounting estimates may change on account of the business environment or as the management gains more experience. Such changes do not require restating the financial statements of a prior period, since they do not amount to a correction of an error.

Examples.

- Estimating allowance for doubtful debts
- Determining inventory obsolescence
- Estimating the useful lives of property, plant, and equipment
- Determining the fair values of financial assets or financial liabilities
- Estimating the amount of warranty obligations

The effect of a change in accounting estimate shall be recognized prospectively by including it in profit or loss in

- The period of change if the change affects that period only; or
- The period of the change and future periods, if the change affects both.

When a change in an accounting estimate gives rise to changes in assets and liabilities, or relates to an item of equity, the carrying amount of the related asset, liability, or equity item shall be adjusted in the period of the change.

Disclosure for Changes in Accounting Estimates

An entity should disclose amounts and nature of changes in accounting estimate that has an effect in the current period. Also, the entity must disclose the expected effect of the change on future periods, unless it is not practical to do so. In such cases, the entity must disclose the fact that it is impractical to estimate the effect of the accounting estimate change on future periods.

Errors. Errors in financial statements can arise on account of incorrect recognition, measurement, presentation, or disclosure of items in financial statements. When the financial statements contain errors that are material, they cannot be considered as complying with IFRS.

The entity shall correct material errors relating to prior periods, retrospectively in the first set of financial statements authorized for issue after their discovery by

- Restating the comparative amounts for the period(s) presented in which the error occurred; or
- If the error occurred before the earliest prior period presented, restating the opening balances of assets, liabilities, and equity for the earliest prior period presented.

Example 2

A limited company has been valuing its closing inventories under the weighted-average cost method. In 2008, management decided to change its accounting policy relating to the valuation of inventories to first-in, first-out (FIFO) method since it was considered to more accurately reflect the usage and flow of inventories in the economic cycle. Is the change in accounting policy justified?

Solution

As per IAS 8, an entity shall change an accounting policy only if the change

- Is required by an IFRS; or
- Results in the financial statements providing reliable and more relevant information about the effects of transactions, other events, or conditions on the entity's financial position, financial performance, or cash flows.

In this case, the company has changed its accounting policy in order to accurately reflect the usage and flow of inventories in the economic cycle. The change in accounting policy is justified.

Example 3

While carrying out the audit of Rainbow Trading Limited for 2008, it was noticed that the depreciation on property, plant, and equipment for 2007 was incorrectly recorded in the books of account at $30,000 instead of $50,000. The extract from the income statement for the years ended December 31, 2008 and 2007, before correction of this error is as follows:

	2008	2007
Gross profit	$400,000	$350,000
General and administrative expenses	(80,000)	(90,000)
Selling and distribution expenses	(50,000)	(20,000)
Depreciation	(50,000)	(30,000)
Net income before income taxes	220,000	210,000
Income taxes	(44,000)	(42,000)
Net profit	$176,000	$168,000

The retained earnings of Rainbow Trading Limited for 2008 and 2007 before correction of the error are as follows:

	2008	2007
Retained earnings, beginning of the year	$218,000	$50,000
Net profit for the year	$176,000	$168,000
Retained earnings, ending of the year	$394,000	$218,000

Rainbow Trading Limited pays income tax at 20% for both years.

Solution

The restated financial statements of Rainbow Trading Limited prepared in accordance with IAS 8 for the correction of the errors will be as follows:

Rainbow Trading Limited
Income Statement
For the Year Ended December 31, 2008

	2008	2007 (restated)
Gross profit	$400,000	$350,000
General and administrative expenses	(80,000)	(90,000)
Selling and distribution expenses	(50,000)	(20,000)
Depreciation	(50,000)	(50,000)
Net income before income taxes	220,000	190,000
Income taxes	(44,000)	(38,000)
	$176,000	$152,000

Rainbow Trading Limited
Statement of Changes in Equity (Retained Earnings Columns Only)
For the Year Ended December 31, 2008

	2008	2007 (restated)
Retained earnings, beginning, as reported previously	$218,000	$ 50,000
Correction of error, net of income taxes of $16,000 (see Note below) (16,000)		
Retained earnings, beginning, as restated	202,000	50,000
Net profit	176,000	152,000
Retained earnings, ending	$378,000	$202,000

Rainbow Trading Limited
Notes to the Financial Statements (Extract)
For the Year Ended December 31, 2008

Note XX: The company understated the depreciation on property, plant, and equipment to the extent of $20,000 in 2007. The financial statements for 2008 have been restated to correct this error.

Explanation

According to the revised IAS 8, the amount of correction of an error that relates to prior periods should be reported by adjusting the opening balance of retained earnings. Comparative information should be restated unless it is impracticable to do so. The steps in preparing the revised financial statements and related disclosures are

1. As presented in the statement of changes in equity (retained earnings columns only), the opening retained earnings was adjusted by $16,000, which represented the amount of error, $20,000.
2. The comparative amounts in the income statement have been restated to rectify the error.
3. The income tax liability is restated as follows:

Income taxes before correction	$ 42,000
Amount of correction	(4,000)
As restated	$ 38,000

Disclosures of Prior Period Errors

An entity shall disclose

- The nature of the prior period error;
- For each period presented, to the extent practicable, the amount of the correction;
- For each financial statement line item affected;
- Basic and diluted earnings per share for entities to which IAS 33 applies;
- The amount of the correction at the beginning of the earliest prior period presented; and
- If retrospective restatement is impracticable for a particular prior period, the circumstances that led to the existence of that condition and a description of how and from what date the error has been corrected.

The financial statements of subsequent periods need not repeat these disclosures.

EXCERPTS FROM PUBLISHED FINANCIAL STATEMENTS

Ahold, Annual Report 2008

Notes to Consolidated Financial Statements

3.   Significant Accounting Policies

Changes in Accounting Policies

As of 2008, Ahold has applied the revised IAS 1, *Presentation of Financial Statements*. The revised standard introduces requirements to present all changes in equity arising from transactions with owners in their capacity as owners separately from nonowner changes in equity and to disclose (1) income tax related to each component of other comprehensive income and (2) reclassification adjustments relating to components of other comprehensive income. In addition, when an entity applies an accounting policy retrospectively or makes a retrospective restatement or reclassification of items in its financial statements, IAS 1 requires the presentation of a third balance sheet as of the beginning of the earliest comparative period. The adoption of the revised IAS 1 did not have an impact on the company's financial results or position.

As of 2008, Ahold has early applied IFRS 8, *Operating Segments*. IFRS 8 introduces new disclosure requirements with respect to segment information. The adoption of IFRS 8 did not have an impact on Ahold's segment structure, consolidated financial results, or position; however, segment results no longer include intercompany royalties. Comparative information has been changed accordingly, with the effect that Giant-Carlisle's 2007 operating income increased by EUR 14 million and the Corporate Center's operating result decreased by the same amount.

7 EVENTS AFTER THE REPORTING PERIOD (IAS 10)

INTRODUCTION

The statement of financial position and the statement of comprehensive income reports on the financial position of an entity at a defined date (the reporting date) and the financial results of that entity for a period to that date (the reporting period). However, events that occur between the reporting date and the authorization date can have an influence on the financial position and financial results of the entity that are determined at the reporting date. It is, therefore, important that events after the reporting date are considered while preparing the financial statements at that date. While some events that occur can have an impact on the financial position and financial results of the reporting period, others may not have any financial impact, but will need to be disclosed in the financial statements for a better understanding.

IAS 10 deals with the situations under which the entity should adjust its financial statements for events after the reporting period and the disclosures that it should make about the authorization date and about the events after the reporting period.

IAS 10 also states that an entity should not prepare its financial statements on a going concern basis when events after the reporting period indicate that the going concern assumption is not appropriate.

KEY TERMS

Events after the reporting period. Favorable and unfavorable events that occur between the reporting date and the date when the financial statements are authorized for issue.

Adjusting events after the reporting period. Events that occur after the reporting date that provide evidence of conditions that existed at the end of the reporting period.

Nonadjusting events after the reporting period. Events that take occur after the reporting date that are indicative of conditions that arose after the reporting period.

Authorization date. The date on which the financial statements can be considered to be legally authorized for issue. An entity must disclose the date when the financial statements were authorized for issue and who gave that authorization.

Adjusting Events After the Reporting Period

In some cases, evidence that conditions existed at the reporting date may be available, irrespective of the fact that they were not known at that time. In such instances, the financial statements should be adjusted to reflect the adjusting events after the reporting date.

Example 1

Examples of events that could occur between the reporting date and the authorization date are:

1. The settlement of a court case that existed during the reporting period (any new provisions must also be recognized);

2. The finalization of the purchase/sale price of an asset that has been purchased/sold during the reporting period; or
3. The discovery of an error that has an impact on the financial position or financial results of the entity for the reporting period.

Nonadjusting Events After the Reporting Period

When conditions arise after the reporting period, an entity shall not adjust the amounts recognized in the financial statements to reflect its impact. However, when the nonadjusting events after the balance sheet date are significant and a nondisclosure can influence the evaluations and decisions that are taken by the users of financial statements, the entity must disclose the nature of the event and also provide an estimate of its financial effect or make a statement that such an estimate cannot be made.

Example 2

Examples of nonadjusting events that occur after the reporting period are

1. The market value of investments has declined (in this case, the decline in the market value relates to circumstances that arose after the reporting period and not to the condition of the investments at the reporting date); or
2. The destruction of a factory building by a fire after the reporting date.

In each of these cases, the events and the financial effects would be disclosed in the financial statements for the reporting period.

Dividends

If an entity declares dividends to the shareholders after the reporting period but before the date the financial statements are authorized to be issued, the entity shall not recognize the amount of dividends as a liability at the reporting date since no obligation or liability existed at that date. However a disclosure of such declaration must be made in the notes to the financial statements.

Going Concern

When the management decides to liquidate the entity or cease operations or has no other realistic option, it shall not prepare its financial statements on a going concern basis. In such cases, adequate disclosure of the facts must be made in the notes to the financial statements.

Example 3

Bloomingdale Inc. carries its inventory at the lower of cost and net realizable value (NRV). The value of inventory determined under the first-in, first-out (FIFO) method and reported in its financial statements at December 31, 2008, was US $10 million. On account of a negative economic trend in the market that developed subsequent to the reporting date, the company could not sell the inventory and therefore entered into an agreement on March 15, 2009, to sell the entire inventory for US $6 million. The financial statements were authorized for issue on March 30, 2009.

In this case, Bloomingdale Inc. must recognise the write-down of the value of inventory in the financial statements at December 31, 2008.

Example 4

On January 15, 2009, one of the trade debtors of Holiday Makers Limited filed for bankruptcy. The financial statements of the company for the year ended December 31, 2008 were authorized for issue on January 31, 2009.

In this case, although the debtor became insolvent after the reporting date on December 31, 2008, it can be presumed that a financial distress preceded the actual bankruptcy and, therefore, it provides evidence of the financial condition of the debtor on the reporting date. Thus, it is an adjusting event and an impairment provision against the debtor's balance on December 31, 2008, is justified.

Example 5

A severe fire on January 20, 2009 destroyed a significant portion of the building and the rolling mill of Steelmakers Inc. The financial statements of the company for the year ended December 31, 2008, were was authorized for issue on March 31, 2009.

In this case, the fire took place after the close of the reporting period and, therefore, does not impact conditions existing at the reporting date. It will have no effect on items appearing at the balance sheet date, and thus it is regarded as a nonadjusting event after the reporting period. However, an adequate disclosure of the nature of the event and an estimate of its financial effect must be disclosed in the financial statements.

If the damage is extensive and Steelmakers Inc. does not have the financial resources to replace the assets destroyed and this will seriously impact the continuing operations and solvency of the company, the going concern assumption may no longer be appropriate. Therefore, since Steelmakers Inc. may cease to be a going concern, the financial statements may have to be prepared using a liquidation basis.

EXCERPTS FROM PUBLISHED FINANCIAL STATEMENTS

BARLOWORLD

Notes to the Consolidated Annual Financial Statements for the Year Ended September 30, 2008

28. Dividends

	2008 Rm	2007 Rm	2006 Rm
Ordinary shares			
Final dividend No 158 paid on January 14, 2008: 200 cents per share (2007: No 155—450 cents per share; 2006: No 153—325 cents per share)	409	911	745
Special dividend paid on April 2, 2007: 500 cents per share		1,017	
Interim dividend (capital distribution) No 159 paid on June 9, 2008:			
100 cents per share (2007: No 157—175 cents per share; 2006: No 154—150 cents per share)	205	357	312
	614	2,285	1,057
Dividend attributable to treasury shares	—	—	(62)
Paid to Barloworld Limited shareholders	614	2,285	995
Paid to minorities	8	344	300
	622	2,629	1,295

On November 17, 2008, the directors declared dividend No 160 of 150 cents per share. This dividend has not been included as a liability in these financial statements. In compliance with the requirements of the JSE Limited, the following dates are applicable:

Date declared	Monday	November 17, 2008
Last day to trade cumulative dividend	Friday	January 9, 2009
Shares trade ex-dividend	Monday	January 12, 2009
Record date	Friday	January 16, 2009
Payment date	Monday	January 19, 2009

Share certificates may not be dematerialized or rematerialized between Monday, January 12, 2009, and Friday, January 16, 2009, both days inclusive.

Analysis of dividends declared in respect of current year's earnings shows:

	Cents	*Cents*	*Cents*
Ordinary Dividends Per Share:			
Interim dividend	100	175	150
Final dividend	150	200	450
	250	375	600

Six percent cumulative nonredeemable preference shares.
Preference dividends totaling R22 500 were declared on each of the following dates:

- April 25, 2008 (paid on May 26, 2008)
- October 10, 2007 (paid on November 5, 2007)
- April 26, 2007 (paid on May 28, 2007)
- September 29, 2006 (paid on October 30, 2006)
- March 29, 2006 (paid on April 24, 2006)
- October 30, 2005 (paid on October 31, 2005)

BALFOUR BEATTY PLC, Annual Report 2008

Notes to Financial Statements

12. Dividends on Ordinary Shares

	Per Share 2008 *(pence)*	*Amount* 2008 *(£m)*	*Per Share* 2007 *(pence)*	*Amount* 2007 *(£m)*
Proposed dividends for the year:				
Final—current year	5.1	24	4.6	20
Final—current year	7.7	37	6.9	30
	12.8	61	11.5	50
Recognized dividends for the year:				
Final—prior year	—	30	—	22
Interim—current year	—	24	—	20
		54		42

An interim dividend of 5.1 pence (p) (2007: 4.6p) per ordinary share was paid on December 10, 2008. Subject to approval at the Annual General Meeting on May 14, 2009, the final 2008 dividend will be paid on July 6, 2009 to holders of ordinary shares on the register on April 24, 2009 by direct credit or, where no mandate has been given, by check posted on July 3, 2009 payable on July 6, 2009. These shares will be quoted ex-dividend on April 22, 2009.

8 CONSTRUCTION CONTRACTS (IAS 11)

INTRODUCTION

The accounting for long-term construction contracts addresses the issue of when revenue and associated costs should be recognized and how these must be measured in the books of the contractor. The primary objective of IAS 11 is the allocation of contract revenue and contract cost to the accounting period in which construction work is performed.

IAS 11 is applicable in accounting for construction contracts in the contractor's financial statements. In other words, this standard does not apply to the customer (contractee).

KEY TERMS

Construction contract. A contract specifically negotiated for the construction of an asset or combination of assets that are closely interrelated or interdependent in terms of their design, technology, function, or use. Examples of such construction contracts are contracts for construction of a bridge, building, dam, pipeline, or road.

Contracts for the rendering of services that are directly related to the construction of assets, for example, services of an architect, and contracts for destruction or restoration of an asset and for the restoration of the environment following the demolition of an asset, are also included in the construction contract.

Fixed price contracts. Contracts wherein the contractor agrees on a fixed price or on a fixed rate per unit. In some cases, however, the contract price is subject to escalation.

Cost-plus contracts. Contracts in which the contractor is reimbursed the costs as defined in addition to a fixed percentage of the costs or a fixed fee.

CONTRACT OPTIONS

When the contract relates to the construction of more than one asset, it shall be treated as separate construction contracts if separate proposals for the construction of each asset were submitted, these proposals were subject to separate negotiation and finalization, and the revenue and costs related to the construction of each asset can be determined.

Similarly, a group contract with a single or multiple customers can be treated as a single construction contract if the group contract has been negotiated and finalized as a single package, the contracts are so interconnected that they form part of a single project, the contracts have to be performed sequentially or concurrently, and the revenue and costs related to each construction activity cannot be determined.

When a contract provides for the construction of an additional asset at the option of the customer, such construction of the additional asset should be treated as a separate construction contract if the nature of the asset differs significantly as compared to that mentioned in the original contract and the price of the additional asset is negotiated and finalized independent of the terms in the original contract.

CONTRACT REVENUE

Contract revenue shall comprise the amount of revenue initially agreed upon with the customer and the amount on account of variations from the agreed terms, claims made and incentives claimed, provided that it is probable that they will result in revenue and that they can be reliably measured.

Contract revenue is measured at the fair value of the consideration that is received or is receivable. This revenue measurement may have to be revised during the execution of the contract on account of uncertainties that may arise and are resolved.

Example 1

Contract revenues might include the

- Increase or decrease in revenue due to change or variation in scope of work that was initially agreed upon;
- Revenue increase on account of price escalation clauses that are mentioned in the initial contract;
- Increase or decrease in revenue due to increase or shortfall in units of output when the payment terms relate to a fixed rate per unit of output;
- Claims made as reimbursement of costs incurred on account of customer-caused delays in execution of the project that have been accepted or are likely to be accepted by the customer;
- Incentive payments received or receivable on an early completion of the contract; or
- Decrease in contract revenue due to penalties levied by the customer on account of delay in completion of the contract.

CONTRACT COST

Contract costs shall comprise all costs that are directly related to the specific contract, general costs related to the contract that can be allocated to the contract, and all other costs that can be specifically charged to the customer on the basis of the terms of the contract agreement.

The contract costs must relate to the period from the date of obtaining the contract to the final date of its completion. However, while calculating the contract cost incurred, the cost that relates to future activity on the contract such as cost of material delivered to site and the advance payment made to subcontractors must not be considered.

Some of the costs that can be directly related to the specific contract are

- Identifiable and measurable costs incurred to secure the contract;
- Labor cost, including supervision costs incurred at the site;
- Cost of material used in the contract;
- Depreciation on plant and equipment used on the contract;
- Mobilization and demobilization costs, like the cost incurred in moving materials and equipment to and from the site of the contract;
- Cost incurred on hiring of plant and equipment;
- Cost of design and technical assistance related to the contract;
- Claims from third parties; and
- Costs incurred on rectification work or work executed during a warranty period.

If any incidental income that is not related to contract revenue is generated (such as sale of scrap materials), these costs must be reduced by such income.

Some of the general costs that are related to the contract and can be allocated to the contract are

- Construction overheads, like payroll preparation charges;

- Insurance, like professional indemnity insurance; and
- Costs of design and technical assistance that are not directly related to the contract.

The above costs must be allocated to the contract in a systematic and rational manner that is consistent from year to year. Also, the allocation must be based on the assumption of a normal level of construction activity.

Some of the costs that can be specifically charged to the customer on the basis of the terms of the contract agreement are

- Some general administration cost for which reimbursement is agreed upon;
- Development cost agreed upon; and
- Reimbursement of any other cost that is agreed upon.

Recognition of Revenue and Costs

An important factor in the recognition of contract revenue and expenses is whether the outcome of the construction contract can be estimated reliably. When the outcome of a construction contract can be estimated reliably, the contract revenue and contract costs must be recognized with reference to the stage of completion of the construction activity at the end of the reporting period.

Outcome of Construction Contract Can Be Estimated Reliably

In accordance with paragraph 23 of IAS 11, the outcome of a fixed-price contract can be estimated reliably when

- The total contract revenue can be measured reliably;
- It is probable that the economic benefits associated with the contract will flow to the entity;
- Both the contract costs to complete the contract and the stage of contract completion at the end of the reporting period can be measured reliably; and
- The contract costs attributable to the contract can be clearly identified and measured reliably so that actual contract costs incurred can be compared with prior estimates.

Similarly, paragraph 24 of IAS 11 states that the outcome of a cost-plus contract can be estimated reliably when

- It is probable that the economic benefits associated with the contract will flow to the entity; and
- The contract costs attributable to the contract, whether specifically reimbursable, can be clearly identified and measured reliably.

Stage of Completion

Recognition of revenue and expenses by reference to the stage of completion of a contract is often known as the *percentage of completion method*. In accordance with this method, the contract revenue and contract costs to the stage of completion are matched so that only the revenue, expenses, and profit/loss attributable to the proportion of work completed is recognized. The contract revenue under this method is recognized as revenue in the reporting period in which the contract work is carried out. Similarly, contract costs are recognized as an expense in the reporting period to which the work performed relates to. However, any costs incurred that relate to a future activity must be considered as an asset when the costs are realizable.

There are different methods of determining the stage of completion of a contract. The progress payments and advances received from the customers is not a measurement of the contract work completed. Some of the methods that reliably measure the extent of work completed are

- Cost-to-cost method, which is the stage of completion or percentage of completion that would be estimated by comparing the total cost incurred to the reporting date with the total expected cost of the entire contract;
- By survey of work performed; or
- Completion of physical proportion of the contract work.

Example 2

Welldone Construction Company Limited signed a contract to construct a building for US $8.5 million. The company incurred contract costs of US $5.2 million up to December 31, 2008. It is estimated that the additional cost to complete the project will be US $2.5 million.

In this case, the revenue that should be recognized based on the stage of completion method is as follows:

Contract cost incurred till December 31, 2008	$5,200,000
Estimated cost to completion	$2,500,000
Estimated total cost of construction	$7,700,000
Estimated contract revenue	$8,500,000
Estimated profit	$1,200,000
The stage of completion of the contract	
(5,200,000 × 100)/7,700,000	67.5%
Revenue to be recognized based on stage of completion of the project	
(67.5% of US $8,500,000)	$5,737,500

Outcome of Construction Contract Cannot Be Estimated Reliably

When the outcome of a construction contract cannot be estimated reliably, the contract revenue shall be recognized only to the extent of the contract costs incurred, and the contract costs must be recognized as an expense in the reporting period that they are incurred.

In the early stages of a contract it might be difficult to reliably estimate the outcome of the contract. However, when there are existing conditions, it may be possible to estimate that the entity will recover in full the contract costs incurred to the reporting date. Therefore, in such circumstances, contract revenue is recognized only to the extent of costs incurred that are expected to be recoverable. That is, no profit is recognized.

Provision for Expected Losses

When it is expected that the total contract cost will exceed the total contract revenue, such excess must be recognized immediately, irrespective of

- Whether the contract work has commenced;
- The stage of completion of contract; or
- The amount of profits expected on other contracts that are not treated as a single contract.

Example 3

Bigtime Builders Limited undertook a contract for building a factory for US $15 million. The contractor incurred a cost of US $1 million on the construction up to December 31, 2008, and expects that the further cost to complete the construction will be US $15 million.

In this case, the construction is in the early stage of completion. However, since it is probable that the total contract cost of US $16 million will exceed the total contract revenue of US $15 million, the expected loss of US $1 million should be recognized as an expense in the reporting period ended at December 31, 2008.

Effect of Change in Estimate in Construction Contract

As the recognition of revenue and expenses in a construction contract is based on reliable estimates, they are bound to vary from one reporting period to another. The effect of the change in estimate of contract revenue or contract cost is accounted for as a change in accounting estimate in accordance with IAS 8, *Accounting Policies, Changes in Accounting Estimates and Errors.* The changed estimates are used to determine the contract revenue and contract expenses in the reporting period in which the change is made and in subsequent reporting periods.

Disclosures

In accordance with paragraph 39 of IAS 11, an entity (the contractor) shall disclose in the financial statements the following:

- The amount of contract revenue recognized in the contract period;
- The method used to determine the contract revenue recognized in the period;
- The method used to determine the stage of completion of contracts in progress;
- Total contract costs incurred and recognized profit (less recognized losses) up to the reporting date;
- Total advances received;
- Total amount of retentions;
- Gross amounts due from the customers for contract work, as an asset [(Cost incurred + Recognized profit) – (Recognized losses + Progress billing)];
- Gross amounts due to customers for contract work, as a liability [(Recognized losses + Progress billing) – (Cost incurred + Recognized profit)]; or
- Contingent liabilities or contingent assets that may arise on warranties, claims, and so on.

EXCERPTS FROM PUBLISHED FINANCIAL STATEMENTS

BALFOUR BEATTY PLC, Annual Report 2008

Notes to Financial Statements

Principal Accounting Policies

1.4 Revenue Recognition

Revenue from construction and service activities represents the value of work carried out during the year, including amounts not invoiced.

1.6 Construction and Service Contracts

When the outcome of individual contracts can be foreseen with reasonable certainty and can be estimated reliably, margin is recognized by reference to the stage of completion, based on the lower of the percentage margin earned to date and that forecast at completion. The stage of completion is normally measured by the proportion of contract costs incurred for work performed to date to the estimated total contract costs or the proportion of the value of work done to the total value of work under the contract, except where these would not be representative of the stage of completion. Full provision is made for all known or expected losses on individual contracts immediately once such losses are foreseen. Margin in respect to variations in contract work, claims, and incentive payments is recognized if it is probable they will result in revenue. Gross profit for the year includes the benefit of claims settled on contracts completed in prior years.

Precontract costs are expensed as incurred until it is virtually certain that a contract will be awarded, from which time further precontract costs are recognized as an asset and charged as an expense over the period of the contract. Amounts recovered in respect of precontract costs that have been written off are deferred and amortized over the life of the contract.

Notes to Accounts

2. Revenue

In £ millions	Group 2008	Group 2007	Company 2008	Company 2007
Revenue from contracting activities				
– construction	7,475	5,753	—	—
– services	643	602	—	—
Revenue from manufacturing activities	143	110	—	—
Proceeds from sale of development land	—	1	—	1
Dividends from subsidiaries	—	—	—	3
Dividends from joint ventures and associates	—	—	28	52
	8,261	6,466	28	56

19. Inventories

In £ millions	2008	2007
Unbilled work in progress	54	27
Development and housing land and work in progress	22	6
Manufacturing work in progress	9	12
Raw materials and consumables	33	22
Finished goods and goods for resale	7	5
	125	72

20. Construction Contracts

In £ millions	2008	2007
Contracts in progress at balance sheet date:		
Due from customers for contract work	383	338
Due to customers for contract work	(540)	(415)
	(157)	(77)

The aggregate amount of costs incurred plus recognized profits (less recognized losses) for all contracts in progress that had not reached practical completion at the balance sheet date was £13,061m (2007: £10,929m).

22. Trade and Other Receivables

In £ millions	Group 2008	Group 2007	Company 2008	Company 2007
Current				
Trade receivables	815	672	6	7
Less: Provision for impairment of trade receivables	(17)	(11)	—	—
	798	661	6	7
Due from subsidiaries	—	—	580	602
Due from joint ventures and associates	20	38	—	—
Due from jointly controlled operations	5	6	—	—
Contract retentions	224	127		
Accrued income	55	13	—	—
Prepayments	81	16	1	1
Due on acquisitions	10	—	—	1
	1,193	881	587	610

9 INCOME TAXES (IAS 12)

INTRODUCTION

IAS 12 prescribes the accounting treatment for income taxes. Income tax includes all domestic and foreign taxes that are based on taxable profits, as well as withholding and other taxes that are payable by subsidiaries on distributions to the reporting entity. Government grants that are dealt with by IAS 20, *Accounting for Government Grants and Disclosure of Government Assistance,* and investment tax credits are excluded from the application of this standard. However, the temporary differences that arise out of these grants and tax credits are considered.

The main basis of accounting for income taxes is the recognition of the current and future tax consequences of:

- The transactions that are recognized in the current period;
- Future recovery of assets in the entity's statement of financial position; and
- Future settlement of liabilities in the entity's statement of financial position.

It is assumed that the recovery of all assets and the settlement of all liabilities will have tax consequences, and that these consequences can be estimated reliably and cannot be avoided. It is also assumed that the entity will settle its liabilities and recover its assets over a period of time and that the consequences of tax will be determined at that point in time.

KEY TERMS

Accounting profit. The profit or loss for a period before deducting tax expense.

Taxable profit (Tax loss). The accounting profit (or loss) for a period that is adjusted for the rules of tax in the regime where the tax is charged.

Tax expense (Tax income). The aggregate amount of current and deferred tax included in the profit or loss for the period.

Current tax. The amount of income tax payable on taxable profit for the current period.

Deferred tax liabilities. The amount of income tax payable in future periods on taxable temporary differences.

Deferred tax assets. The amount of income tax recoverable in future periods on deductible temporary differences, unused tax losses carried forward, and unused tax credits carried forward.

Temporary differences. Differences between the carrying amount of an asset or liability in the statement of financial position and its tax base. Temporary differences may be either a taxable temporary difference or a deductible temporary difference.

Taxable temporary differences result in the payment of tax when the carrying amount of the asset or liability is settled. Therefore, a deferred tax liability will arise when the carrying value of the asset is greater than its tax base, or the carrying value of the liability is less than its tax base.

Deductible temporary differences occur when amounts that are deductible in terms of taxable profit or loss in future periods result in the carrying value of the asset or liability being recovered or settled. When the carrying value of the liability is greater than its tax base or the carrying value of the asset is less than its tax base, then a deferred tax asset may arise.

TAX BASE

The *tax base* is the amount that is attributed to an asset or liability for tax purposes. Some assets give rise to tax liabilities. If the asset is not taxed in the year of recognition, the tax liability is deferred giving rise to a *taxable temporary difference*. This temporary difference is reversed when the tax liability becomes due and it is recognized as an expense.

Similarly, some liabilities give rise to tax assets or reduce tax liabilities. If the tax asset is not deductible in the year of recognition, the tax asset is deferred giving rise to a *deductible temporary difference*. This temporary difference is reversed when the liability is reduced or a tax claim is made.

The tax base of an asset is the amount that is deductible for tax purposes against taxable income generated by the asset. For example, for an item of equipment, depreciation that has been charged in the current and earlier periods has already been considered as an expense, and the carrying value of the equipment will also be recognized as an expense in future years. When the income at the time the carrying amount of the asset is recovered is not taxable, the carrying value of the asset will be equal to the tax base. An example of this is the carrying amount of trade receivables. The revenue related to this trade receivable has already been considered as income for tax purposes and, therefore, there is no additional tax to be paid when the trade receivable is realized.

The tax base of a liability is its carrying amount less amounts that will be deductible for tax in the future. An example is the amount of a loan taken by an entity. The repayment of the loan will not have any tax consequences and, therefore, the tax base of the liability will be its carrying value. However, when interest is payable on the loan and the interest expense has already been considered as a deduction for tax purposes, the tax base for the liability will be the loan amount and the interest amount outstanding at the reporting date.

Some items with a tax base may not be recognized as an asset or as a liability. An example is the research costs incurred by an entity. If an entity has incurred $100,000 on research and development and 60% of the expenditure is an allowable deduction in the future period for computing taxable income, there will be a difference between the accounting profit and tax profit of $40,000. This difference, on account of the amount not being deductible, is called a *permanent difference*.

Example 1

First Choice Limited has the following assets and liabilities recorded in its financial statements at December 31, 2008:

In US dollars millions	Carrying value	Tax base
Property, plant, and equipment	$40,000	$25,000
Inventory	10,000	14,000
Trade receivables	6,000	8,000
Trade payables	16,000	16,000
Cash	5,000	5,000

First Choice Limited had made an allowance for inventory obsolescence of $4 million that is not allowable for tax purposes until the inventory is sold. It has also made an impairment charge against trade receivables of $2 million that will not be allowed in the current year for tax purposes but will be allowed in the future. The rate at which income tax liability is calculated is 30%.

Calculate the deferred tax provision at December 31, 2008.

Solution

	Carrying value	Tax base	Temporary difference
Property, plant, and equipment	$40,000	$25,000	$15,000
Inventory	10,000	14,000	(4,000)
Trade receivables	6,000	8,000	(2,000)
Trade payables	16,000	16,000	—
Cash	5,000	5,000	—
			9,000

The deferred tax provision will be $9,000 × 30% = $3,000.

The provision against inventory and the impairment charge for trade receivables will cause the tax base to be higher than the carrying value by the respective amounts.

Example 2

Research Inc. has spent $1 million developing a new product. These costs meet the definition of an intangible asset under IAS 38 and have been recognized in the statement of financial position as an intangible asset. Local tax legislation allows these costs to be deducted for tax purposes when they are incurred. Therefore, they have been recognized as an expense for tax purposes. At the end of the year, the intangible asset is deemed to be impaired by $500,000.

What would be the tax base of the intangible asset at the accounting year-end?

Solution

The tax base will be zero since the tax authority has already allowed the intangible asset costs to be deducted for tax purposes.

RECOGNITION AND MEASUREMENT OF CURRENT TAX LIABILITIES AND CURRENT TAX ASSETS

IAS 12 provides that an entity should recognize a liability in the statement of financial position to the extent of the unpaid current tax relating to the current and prior years. If the amount of tax already paid in respect of current and prior periods exceeds the amount due for those periods, the excess shall be recognized as an asset. An example of this is the amount claimed as a tax refund that is recognized as taxes receivable. Current tax should be recognized as income or expense and included in the net profit or loss for the period.

The current tax liabilities and current tax assets for the current and prior periods should be measured at the amount that is expected to be paid to, or recovered from, the tax authorities, using the tax rates and the tax laws that relate to the reporting period.

RECOGNITION OF DEFERRED TAX LIABILITIES AND DEFERRED TAX ASSETS

Deferred Tax Liability

A deferred tax liability arises out of taxable temporary differences. Therefore, a deferred tax liability is recognized on all taxable temporary differences other than those that arise on account of

- The initial recognition of goodwill. The value of goodwill, which is the residual amount after recognizing assets and liabilities at fair value, will only increase if a deferred tax liability is recognized.
- The initial recognition of assets and liabilities that do not affect the accounting of profit or loss or taxable profits or loss. Some assets and liabilities are not considered for tax purposes. Even though this will give rise to a taxable temporary difference, no deferred tax liability or asset is recognized when the carrying value of the item on initial recognition differs from its initial tax base.

- The initial recognition of assets and liabilities that are not part of business combinations;
- The possibility that the temporary difference associated with investments in subsidiaries, branches, associates, and joint ventures will not reverse in the future period and the parent, investor, or joint venture partner is able to control the timing of the reversal of the temporary difference. An example is when the joint venture partners have agreed that the profits will not be distributed.

Example 3

Productive Inc. acquired plant and equipment for $12 million on January 1, 2008. The asset is depreciated over four years on the straight-line basis, and the local tax code permits the management to depreciate the asset at 30% a year for tax purposes.

What would be the deferred tax liability, if any, that might arise on the plant and equipment at December 31, 2008, assuming a tax rate of 30%?

Solution

At December 31, 2008, the carrying value of the plant and equipment is $9 million and, using a 30% depreciation rate allowed by the local tax code, the tax written down value will be $8.4 million, giving a taxable temporary difference of $600,000. The deferred tax liability computed would be $180,000 (30% of the temporary difference of $600,000).

Deferred Tax Asset

Deferred tax assets arise from deductible temporary differences. A deferred tax asset is recognized on deductible temporary differences if it is probable that sufficient taxable profit will be available. However, no deferred tax asset is recognized on deductible temporary differences if it arises on account of

- The initial recognition of assets and liabilities that do not affect the accounting of taxable profit or loss;
- The initial recognition of assets and liabilities that are not part of business combinations; or
- The possibility that in regard to a deferred tax asset, the temporary difference is expected to continue into the foreseeable future and there are no taxable profits available against which the temporary difference can be offset.

Sufficient taxable profits to utilize the tax deductions will be available when the deductible temporary differences will reverse in the same accounting period or that loss can be carried forward or carried back. The deferred tax assets that will reverse in the future period must be ignored since they will relate to profits of the future period.

Tax-planning opportunities will create taxable profits in appropriate future periods to utilize the tax loss or tax credit.

At the end of each reporting period, an entity must assess unrecognized deferred tax assets. When it becomes probable that future taxable profit will allow the deferred tax asset to be recovered, the entity must recognize a previously unrecognized deferred tax asset to that extent.

Example 4

Capital Trading Limited has revalued its property and has recognized the increase in the revaluation in its financial statements. The carrying value of the property was $8 million and the revalued amount was $10 million. The tax base of the property was $6 million. In this country, the tax rate applicable to profits is 35% and the tax rate applicable to profits made on the sale of property is 30%. If the revaluation took place at the financial year end of December 31, 2008, calculate the deferred tax liability on the property as of that date.

Solution

Carrying value after revaluation	$10 million
Tax base	$6 million
Rate of tax applicable to the sale of property	30%
Deferred tax liability	$1.2 million
Calculated as	($10 million – $6 million) × 30%

ACCOUNTING FOR DEFERRED TAX

Deferred tax assets and liabilities should be measured at the tax rates that will apply to the period when the asset is realized or the liability is settled and must be based on tax rates and tax laws that relate to the reporting period. The deferred tax assets and liabilities shall not be discounted, since it is difficult to correctly determine the timing of the reversal of each temporary difference.

Temporary differences can also arise from adjustments on consolidation. Although the tax base of an item is often determined by the value in the separate financial statements, the deferred tax is determined on the basis of the consolidated financial statements. Therefore, the difference in the carrying value of an item in the consolidated financial statements and that in the separate financial statements gives rise to a temporary difference. IAS 12 does not directly prescribe how intergroup profits and losses should be measured for tax purposes. However, since the standard states that the expected manner of recovery or settlement of tax should be taken into account, the receiving company's tax rate should be used when calculating the provision for deferred tax as the receiving company would be taxed when the asset or liability is realized.

The process of accounting for deferred tax is to

- Prepare a statement of financial position that includes all the assets and liabilities and their tax base;
- Compare the carrying amounts in the balance sheet with the tax base. The differences, if any, will normally affect the deferred tax calculation;
- Identify the temporary differences that have not been recognized due to exemptions granted in this standard;
- Apply the tax rates to the temporary differences;
- Determine the movement between opening and closing deferred tax balances;
- Decide whether the offset of deferred tax assets and liabilities between different companies is acceptable in the consolidated financial statements; and
- Recognize the net change in deferred taxation.

Example 5

A subsidiary sold goods costing $25 million to its parent for $27 million, and all of these goods are still held as inventory at the year-end. Assume a tax rate of 30%. What are the deferred tax implications, if any?

Solution

The unrealized profit of $2 million will have to be eliminated from the consolidated statement of profit and loss and from the consolidated statement of financial position in group inventory. The sale of the inventory is a taxable event, and it causes a change in the tax base of the inventory. The carrying amount in the consolidated financial statements of the inventory will be $25 million, but the tax base is $27 million. This gives rise to a deferred tax asset of $2 million at the tax rate of 30%, which is $600,000 (assuming that both the parent and subsidiary are residents in the same tax jurisdiction).

DISCLOSURES

The disclosures under this standard can be categorized as that relating to the statement of profit and loss and that to the statement of financial position.

The required disclosures relating to the statement of profit and loss are

- Current tax expense or income;
- Any adjustments for prior period taxes;
- Deferred tax relating to temporary difference;
- Deferred tax relating to changes in tax laws or tax rates;
- Tax on changes in accounting policies and errors;
- Tax losses, credits or temporary difference of prior period to reduce

  - Current tax
  - Deferred tax expense; and

- Write-down of deferred tax assets.

In addition to these requirements, the following disclosures relating to the statement of financial position shall also be made:

- Current and deferred tax recognized directly in equity; and
- Amount of income tax relating to each component of other comprehensive income.

The following disclosures are made in the notes to the financial statements:

- The relationship between tax and accounting profit or loss as

  - A numerical reconciliation between tax expense or benefit and the product of accounting profit or loss and the applicable tax rate
  - A numerical reconciliation between the average effective tax rate and applicable rate;

- Note on changes in the applicable tax rates;
- Unrecognized deferred tax assets relating to deductible temporary differences and unused tax losses and tax credits;
- Unrecognized deferred tax liabilities relating to temporary differences associated with investments, proposed dividends and dividends declared before financial statements are authorized for issue;
- Regarding discontinued operations, the gain or loss on discontinuance; and the profit or loss from the ordinary activities of the discontinued operation for the current period and the previous period;
- Potential income tax consequences from payments of dividends; and
- Amount of deferred tax assets and the evidence supporting recognition when utilization is dependent upon future tax profit being more than the reversal of taxable temporary differences and a loss is incurred in the current or previous period in the same tax jurisdiction.

EXCERPTS FROM PUBLISHED FINANCIAL STATEMENTS

Ahold, Annual Report 2008

Notes to Consolidated Financial Statements

Significant Accounting Policies

Income Taxes

Income tax expense represents the sum of current and deferred tax. Income tax is recognized in the consolidated income statement except to the extent that it relates to items recognized directly in equity. Current tax expense is based on the best estimate of taxable income for the year, using tax rates that have been enacted or substantively enacted at the balance sheet date, and adjustments for current taxes payable (receivable) for prior years. Deferred tax is the tax expected to be payable or recoverable on differences between the carrying amounts of assets and liabilities and the corresponding tax basis used in the computation of taxable income. Deferred tax assets and liabilities are generally recognized for all temporary differences, except to the extent that a deferred tax liability arises from the initial recognition of goodwill. Deferred tax is calculated at the tax rates that are expected to apply in the period when the liability is settled or the asset is realized.

Deferred tax assets, including deferred tax assets for tax loss carryforward positions and tax credit carryforward positions, are recognized to the extent that it is probable that future taxable income will be available against which temporary differences, unused tax losses, or unused tax credits can be utilized. The carrying amount of deferred tax assets is reviewed at each balance sheet date and reduced to the extent that it is no longer probable that sufficient taxable income will be available to allow all or part of the asset to be recovered.

Deferred tax assets and liabilities are not discounted. Deferred income tax assets and liabilities are offset in the consolidated balance sheet when there is a legally enforceable right to offset current tax assets against current tax liabilities and when the deferred income taxes relate to income taxes levied by the same fiscal authority. Current income tax assets and liabilities are offset in the consolidated balance sheet when there is a legally enforceable right to offset and when the Company intends either to settle on a net basis, or to realize the asset and settle the liability simultaneously.

The ultimate tax effects of some transactions can be uncertain for a considerable period of time, requiring management to estimate the related current and deferred tax positions. The company recognizes liabilities for uncertain tax positions when it is more likely than not that additional taxes will be due. These liabilities are presented as current income taxes payable, except in jurisdictions where prior tax losses are being carried forward to be used to offset future taxes that will be due; in these instances, the liabilities are presented as a reduction to deferred tax assets.

Notes to Consolidated Financial Statements

Note 10. Income Taxes

Income Taxes Continuing Operations

The following table specifies the current and deferred tax components of income taxes on continuing operations in the consolidated income statement:

In € millions	2008	2007
Current Income Taxes		
Domestic taxes	(122)	(74)
Foreign taxes:		
United States	—	5
Europe—other	(12)	(19)
Total current tax expense	(134)	(88)

	2008	2007
Deferred Income Taxes		
Domestic taxes	(33)	(43)
Foreign taxes:		
United States	(59)	(27)
Europe—other	1	5
Total deferred tax expense	(91)	(65)
Total income taxes continuing operations	(225)	(153)

Effective income tax rate continuing operations. Ahold's effective tax rates in the consolidated income statement differ from the statutory income tax rate of the Netherlands of 25.5 % both 2008 and 2007. The following table reconciles these statutory income tax rates with the effective income tax rates in the consolidated income statement:

In € million	2008	%	2007	%
Income before income taxes	984		768	
Income tax expense at statutory tax rates	(251)	25.5	(196)	25.5
Adjustments to arrive at effective income tax rates:				
Rate differential (local statutory rates versus the statutory rates of the Netherlands)	(23)	2.4	1	(0.1)
Deferred tax income (expense) due to changes in tax rates	(4)	0.4	—	—
Deferred tax income (expense) related to movements of impairment of deferred tax assets	4	(0.4)	(16)	2.1
Financing and related costs	57	(5.8)	40	(5.2)
Reserves, (non-)deductibles, and discrete items	(8)	0.8	18	(2.4)
Reserves and discrete items	(225)	22.9	(153)	19.9

Financing and related costs include the result of Ahold's intercompany finance activities, which are carried out from the company's treasury center in Geneva, Switzerland.

Income Taxes Discontinued Operations

Income tax related to discontinued operations amounted to a benefit of 14 million in 2008 and an expense of EUR 85 million in 2007 and has been applied against income from discontinued operations. For further information, see Note 5.

Deferred Income Tax

The significant components of deferred income tax assets and liabilities as of December 28, 2008 and December 30, 2007 (including discontinued operations), as well as the deferred income tax benefit and expense recognized in income from continuing operations for 2008 and 2007, are as follows:

	Consolidated Balance Sheet		Consolidated Income Statement	
	December 28,	December 31,		
In € million	2008	2007	2008	2007
Leases and financings	188	167	10	10
Pensions and other postemployment benefits	108	136	(37)	(46)
Provisions	77	68	(22)	(9)
Derivatives and loans	16	—	(4)	—
Interest	32	21	11	16
Other	20	35	(51)	3
Total gross deferred tax assets	441	427	(93)	(26)
Unrecognized deferred tax assets	(21)	(17)	(3)	(2)
Total recognized deferred tax assets	420	410	(96)	(28)
Tax losses and tax credits	241	327	30	36
Unrecognized tax losses and tax credits	(207)	(279)	23	(92)
Total recognized tax losses and tax credits	34	48	53	(56)

	Consolidated Balance Sheet		Consolidated Income Statement	
	December 28, 2008	*December 31, 2007*	*2008*	*2007*
Total net tax assets position	454	458	(43)	(84)
Property, plant, and equipment and intangible assets	110	24	(31)	31
Inventories	88	74	(11)	(11)
Derivatives	—	3	—	—
Other	13	21	(96)	—
Total deferred tax liabilities	211	122	(48)	19
Deferred income tax expense	—	—	(91)	(65)
Net deferred tax assets	243	366		

Deferred income tax assets and liabilities are offset in the consolidated balance sheet when there is a legally enforceable right to offset current tax assets against current tax liabilities and when the deferred income taxes are levied by the same fiscal authority.

The deferred tax assets and liabilities are presented as noncurrent assets and liabilities in the consolidated balance sheet as follows:

In € million	*December 28, 2008*	*December 31, 2007*
Deferred tax assets	358	370
Deferred tax liabilities	(115)	(34)
Net deferred tax assets	243	336

As of December 28, 2008, Ahold had operating and capital loss carryforwards of a total nominal amount of EUR 2,406 million, expiring between 2009 and 2027 (December 30, 2007: EUR 3,364 million). The 2007 capital loss carryforward was adjusted to reflect the correct state capital loss on the sale of U.S. Foodservice. Future utilization of these losses is not considered probable to warrant recognition on the balance sheet. The following table specifies the years in which Ahold's operating and capital loss carryforwards are scheduled to expire:

In € million	*2009*	*2010*	*2011*	*2012*	*2013*	*2014–2018*	*2019–2023*	*After 2023*	*Total*
Operating and capital losses	44	40	354	1,311	19	15	193	430	2,406

Operating and capital loss carryforwards related to one jurisdiction may not be used to offset income taxes in other jurisdictions. Of the loss carryforwards, EUR 2,026 million relates to U.S. state taxes, for which a weighted-average tax rate of 4.1% applies.

The majority of the these deferred tax assets relate to tax jurisdictions in which Ahold suffered a loss in the current or preceding period. Significant judgment is required in determining whether deferred tax assets are realizable. Ahold determines this on the basis of expected taxable profits arising from the reversal of recognized deferred tax liabilities and on the basis of budgets, cash flow forecasts, and impairment models. Where utilization is not considered probable, deferred tax assets are not recognized.

Income Taxes in Equity

Income taxes recognized in and transferred from equity in 2008 and 2007 are as follows:

In € million	*2008*	*2007*
Derivatives	6	(3)
Share-based compensation	1	6
Share issuance costs	5	—
Other	—	3
	12	6

10 PROPERTY, PLANT, AND EQUIPMENT (IAS 16)

INTRODUCTION

IAS 16 sets out requirements for the recognition and measurement of property, plant, and equipment as well as prescribes financial statement disclosure requirements. This helps users of financial statements assess information about an entity's investment in its property, plant, and equipment and the changes in that investment.

SCOPE

IAS 16 describes the accounting treatment for property, plant, and equipment unless another standard requires or permits a different accounting treatment. This standard does not apply to

1. Property, plant, and equipment classified as held for sale under IFRS 5, *Noncurrent Assets Held for Sale and Discontinued Operations;*
2. Biological assets related to agricultural activity (see IAS 41, *Agriculture*);
3. The recognition and measurement of exploration and evaluation assets (see IFRS 6, *Exploration for and Evaluation of Mineral Resources*); or
4. Mineral rights and mineral reserves such as oil, natural gas, and nonrenewable resources.

KEY TERMS

Carrying amount. The amount at which an asset is recognized after deducting any accumulated depreciation and accumulated impairment losses.

Cost. The amount of cash or cash equivalents paid, or the fair value of the other consideration given, to acquire an asset at the time of its acquisition or construction or, where applicable, the amount attributed to that asset when initially recognized in accordance with the specific requirements of other IFRSs (for example, IFRS 2, *Share-Based Payment).*

Depreciable amount. The cost of an asset or other amount substituted for cost, less its residual value.

Depreciation. The systematic allocation of the depreciable amount of an asset over its useful life.

Fair value. The amount for which an asset could be exchanged, between knowledgeable, willing parties in an arm's-length transaction.

Impairment loss. The amount by which the carrying amount of an asset exceeds its recoverable amount.

Property, plant, and equipment. Tangible items that are held for use in the production or supply of goods or services, or for rental to others, or for administrative purposes and are expected to be used during more than one period.

Recoverable amount. The higher of an asset's net selling price and its value in use.

Residual value. The estimated amount that an entity would currently obtain from the disposal of the asset, after deducting the estimated costs of disposal, if the asset were already of the age and in the condition expected at the end of its useful life.

Useful life. (1) The period over which an asset is expected to be available for use by an entity; or (2) the number of production or similar units expected to be obtained from the asset by an entity.

RECOGNITION

The cost of an item of property, plant, and equipment shall be recognized as an asset only if it is probable that future economic benefits associated with the item will flow to the entity and the cost of the item can be measured reliably. IAS 16 applies only when these two basic recognition criteria to determine whether an expenditure qualifies as an asset are met and does not consider the increased utility or increased useful life criteria. During the course of their operations, an entity would acquire items that have individually insignificant value but will qualify as an asset under these two basic recognition criteria. Because it is very difficult for entities to account for every such item, this standard permits the aggregation of such individually insignificant value items, provided they are similar in nature (moulds, dies, etc.). However in practice, the entity adopts an accounting policy for the unit of measure for recognition of the expenditure as an expense or as an asset.

Although the two basic criteria can be applied to spare parts and servicing equipment, they are generally carried as inventory and are recognized in profit or loss as and when consumed. However, major spare part items and the spare parts and servicing equipment that can be used only in connection with an item of property, plant, and equipment, are treated as property, plant, and equipment.

Similarly, an entity may have to incur expenditure that will not directly enhance the future economic benefits of any particular asset but would, at the same time, ensure the flow of economic benefits of related property, plant, and equipment. An example of this expenditure is the installation of a system to prevent air pollution in accordance with the environmental regulations for setting up and operating a cement manufacturing plant. This item of expenditure qualifies as an asset since the air pollution system is a necessary requirement for operating the plant.

An entity might also incur inspection and replacement costs on items of property, plant, and equipment. An example of an inspection cost is the mandatory periodic expenditure that has to be incurred on inspection of ships and aircraft to certify their sea- and airworthiness. Also, a roll mill bearing that is a major item in a cement plant may have to be changed after a certain number of hours of running the plant. Such expenditure is considered an asset under this standard.

MEASUREMENT AT RECOGNITION

An item of property, plant, and equipment that satisfies the recognition criteria should be measured at its cost.

ELEMENTS OF COST

- Purchase price, including import duties and any nonrefundable purchase taxes, less of trade discounts and rebates granted by the supplier;
- Costs that are directly attributable to bringing the asset to the location and condition that is necessary for it to be used by the entity for the intended purpose. Examples of these costs are the cost of transportation of the asset to the site, cost of preparing the site, installation and assembly costs, remuneration, allowances and benefits paid to

employees who are involved in the setting up of the asset, and borrowing costs to the extent permitted by IAS 23, *Borrowing Costs*. Therefore, the costs that are not directly attributable, like advertising and promotion costs and training costs, should be expensed in the period they are incurred.

In the case of a self-constructed asset, the previous two principles that apply to an acquired asset will apply. If the entity manufactures similar items for sale, the cost of constructing the item to be included as property, plant, and equipment is determined the same way as for the items to be sold, except that the profit element is eliminated.

Example 1

Excellent Inc. is installing a new plant at its production facility and has incurred the following costs:

1.	Cost of the plant (cost per supplier's invoice plus taxes)	$10,500,000
2.	Initial delivery and handling costs	$500,000
3.	Cost of site preparation	$500,000
4.	Consultants used for advice on the acquisition of the plant	$650,000
5.	Interest charges paid to supplier of plant for deferred credit	$300,000
6.	Estimated dismantling costs to be incurred after six years	$1,000,000
7.	Operating losses before commercial production	$1,000,000

Which of these costs can be capitalized as part of the property, plant, and equipment in accordance with IAS 16?

Solution

According to IAS 16, these costs can be capitalized as directly attributable costs:

1.	Cost of the plant	$10,500,000
2.	Initial delivery and handling costs	500,000
3.	Cost of site preparation	500,000
4.	Consultants' fees	650,000
5.	Estimated dismantling costs to be incurred after six years	1,000,000
		$13,150,000

NOTE: The following costs cannot be capitalized:

- *Interest charges paid on deferred credit terms to the supplier of the plant (not being a qualifying asset as defined in IAS 23, **Borrowing Costs**) of $300,000; and*
- *Preoperating losses (operating losses before commercial production) amounting to $1 million.*

These costs are not considered directly attributable costs and, thus, cannot be capitalized. They should be written off to profit and loss in the period they are incurred.

MEASUREMENT OF COST

The cost of an item of property, plant, and equipment is measured at the date of its acquisition at the cash price equivalent. When the payment for the asset is deferred beyond normal credit terms, the difference between the cash price equivalent and the total payments made should be recognized as a finance cost. This finance cost must be expensed over the credit period unless the interest qualifies for capitalization in accordance with IAS 23, *Borrowing Costs*.

When an asset is acquired in exchange for another asset, the acquired asset must be measured at its fair value, unless the exchange transaction lacks commercial substance or the fair value cannot be reliably measured. In such cases, the acquired asset must be measured at the carrying value of the asset that was given up on the exchange transaction. The carrying value of the asset means the cost less accumulated depreciation and impairment losses. The exchange transaction will have commercial substance if there is an increase in the cash flow or the value of the entity's operation increases on account of the asset that is received on exchange.

When an entity receives grants or subsidies for the acquisition of an asset, the carrying value of the asset has to be reduced to that extent, in accordance with IAS 20, *Accounting for Government Grants and Disclosure of Government Assistance.*

MEASUREMENT AFTER RECOGNITION

IAS 16 provides an entity an accounting policy option of using the cost model or the revaluation model. Whichever model the entity adopts it shall apply that policy to an entire class of property, plant, and equipment. Examples of classes of property, plant, and equipment are land, land and buildings, plant and machinery, motor vehicles, office equipment, furniture, and fixtures.

Example 2

XYZ Inc. owns five ships that it uses in its business as property, plant, and equipment. Can the entity carry three ships under the cost model and the remaining two ships under the revaluation model?

Solution

IAS 16 permits an entity to choose between either the cost model or the revaluation model. It does not allow an entity to apply two different models for the same class of property, plant, and equipment. Therefore, XYZ Inc. is not allowed to carry three ships under the cost model while carrying two under the revaluation model, since the standard categorically prohibits such an accounting treatment.

Cost Model

This is a commonly used model. If an entity opts for the cost model then it is required to carry the item of property, plant, and equipment after its recognition at its cost less any accumulated depreciation and any accumulated impairment losses.

Depreciation. Each component of an item of property, plant, and equipment with a cost that is significant in relation to the total cost of the item shall be depreciated separately. This can result in the need for careful record keeping to separately identify those components of an item that have different useful lives, and therefore might be subject to different depreciation methods or rates. An entity may, however, choose to depreciate separately the parts of an item of property, plant, and equipment whose costs are not significant in relation to the total cost of the item.

The entity must commence depreciating the asset when it is at the location and condition and it is available for the intended use. The entity must also cease depreciating the asset when the asset is derecognized, or is reclassified as held for sale in accordance with IFRS 5, *Noncurrent Assets Held for Sale and Discontinued Operations.*

The depreciation charge for each period shall be recognized in profit and loss, unless it is included in the carrying amount of another asset. An example of this is the depreciation on an item of property, plant, and equipment used to generate a self-constructed asset. In this case, the depreciation will be added to the cost of the self-constructed asset in accordance with IAS 2, *Inventories.*

Depreciation shall be applied to the depreciable amount of an asset on a systematic basis over its expected useful life. Expected *useful life* is the period the asset is used, *not* the asset's *economic* life, which could be appreciably longer. Temporary idle time of the asset must be considered in determining the useful life, since the obsolescence on nonusage of the asset can also affect its life.

The depreciable amount takes account of the expected residual value of the assets. Both the useful life and the residual value shall be reviewed annually and the estimates revised as necessary in accordance with IAS 8, *Accounting Policies, Changes in Accounting Estimates and Errors.*

Depreciation method. An entity is permitted a choice of depreciation methods. It can use the *straight-line method*, the *diminishing balance method*, or *units of production method.* The depreciation method used shall reflect the pattern in which the asset's future economic benefits are expected to be consumed by the entity.

The depreciation method applied to an asset shall be reviewed at least at each financial year-end and, if there has been a significant change in the expected pattern of consumption of the future economic benefits embodied in the asset, the method shall be changed to reflect the changed pattern.

A change in depreciation method shall be accounted for as a change in an accounting estimate in accordance with IAS 8, *Accounting Policies, Changes in Accounting Estimates and Errors,* and is therefore accounted for prospectively (as opposed to retrospectively).

Revaluation Model

According to IAS 16, after recognition as an asset, an item of property, plant, and equipment, whose fair value can be measured reliably, may be carried at a revalued amount. This revalued amount will be the fair value at the date of the revaluation less any subsequent accumulated depreciation and subsequent accumulated impairment losses.

Entities that have initially measured them under the cost model may switch in later years to the revaluation model if the carrying values of the long-lived assets are no longer reflective of the fair value of the property, plant, and equipment in subsequent years. Once an entity uses the revaluation model the standard requires that revaluations of property, plant, and equipment shall be made with sufficient regularity to ensure that the carrying amount of the property, plant, and equipment does not differ materially from that which would be determined using fair value at the end of the reporting period. This standard also requires that when an asset is revalued, the entire class of the property, plant, and equipment to which the asset belongs must be revalued.

As a result of a revaluation of property, plant, and equipment in a subsequent period, if an asset's carrying amount is increased, the increase in the carrying amount is credited to other comprehensive income in the year of revaluation and is accumulated in equity under the heading of revaluation surplus. However, if the increase in carrying amount reverses a revaluation decrease of the same asset previously recognized in profit and loss then the increase in carrying amount is recognized in profit and loss to the extent that it offsets the previous decrease in carrying amount.

If an asset's carrying amount is decreased as a result of revaluation, the decrease is recognized in profit and loss. However, the decrease is recognized in other comprehensive income to the extent of any credit balance existing in the revaluation surplus in respect of that asset. The decrease recognized in other comprehensive income reduces the amount accumulated in equity under the heading of revaluation surplus.

According to IAS 16 (paragraph 35), when an item of property, plant, and equipment is revalued, an entity can treat *any accumulated depreciation* at the date of the revaluation in one of two ways:

1. "Restated proportionately with the change in the gross carrying amount of the asset so that the carrying amount of the asset after revaluation equals its revalued amount" (*according to the standard, this method is often used when an asset is revalued by means of applying an index to determine its depreciated replacement cost*); or

2. "Eliminated against the gross carrying amount of the asset and the net amount restated to the revalued amount of the asset" *(the standard states that this method is often used for buildings)*.

The revaluation surplus (included in equity) may be released to retained earnings in one of two ways:

1. When the asset is disposed of, or otherwise derecognized, the surplus can be transferred to retained earnings; or
2. The difference between the depreciation charged on the revalued amount and that based on cost can be transferred from the revaluation surplus to retained earnings. Under no circumstances are transfers from revaluation surplus to retained earnings recognized in profit and loss.

Example 3

XYZ Inc. purchased machinery at an initial cost of $2.5 million. After depreciating the machinery over a period of three years, XYZ Inc. decided to revalue this machinery. Since there was no other machinery owned by XYZ Inc. when it revalued this machinery, such a revaluation was that of the entire class of an item of property, plant, and equipment.

At the date of revaluation, accumulated depreciation amounted to $1 million.

The fair value of the asset, by reference to transactions in similar assets, is assessed to be $1.75 million.

Solution

The entries to be booked would be

Dr. Accumulated depreciation	$1,000,000	
Cr. Asset cost		$1,000,000

Being elimination of accumulated depreciation against the cost of the asset

Dr. Asset cost	250,000	
Cr. Revaluation Surplus		250,000

Being uplift of net asset value to fair value

The net result is that the asset has a carrying amount of

$1.75 million = $2.5 million – $1 million + $250,000.

DERECOGNITION

When an item of property, plant, and equipment is either disposed of, or when no future economic benefits are expected from its use or disposal, it shall be derecognized.

An entity that is engaged in the business of renting assets to third parties may sell the assets that are used in such rental activities in the ordinary course of its business. In such a case, the carrying value of these assets at the date when they cease to be rented and become held for sale must be transferred to inventories. The proceeds from the sale of these items included as inventories should be recognised as revenue in accordance with IAS 18, *Revenue*.

The gain or loss resulting from derecognition of an item of property, plant, and equipment is the difference between the net disposal proceeds, if any, and the carrying amount of the item of property, plant, and equipment. Such gain or loss resulting from derecognition of an item of property, plant, and equipment shall be included in profit and loss when the item is derecognized and is not to be classified as revenue.

DISCLOSURES

Disclosures with respect to each class of property, plant, and equipment are extensive and comprise:

- Measurement bases for determining gross carrying amounts;
- Depreciation methods;
- Useful lives or depreciation rates used;
- Gross carrying amount and accumulated depreciation (aggregated with accumulated impairment losses) at the beginning and end of the period;
- Additions;
- Assets classified as held for sale;
- Acquisitions through business combinations;
- Increases and decreases arising from revaluations and from impairment losses and reversals thereof;
- Depreciation;
- Net exchange differences recognized under IAS 21, *The Effects of Changes in Foreign Exchange Rates*;
- Other changes;
- Existence and amounts of restrictions on ownership title;
- Assets pledged as security for liabilities;
- Assets in the course of construction;
- Contractual commitments for the acquisition of property, plant, and equipment; and
- Compensation for assets impaired, lost, or given up.

If property, plant, and equipment are stated at revalued amounts, the following items must be disclosed:

- The effective date of the valuation;
- Whether an independent valuer was involved;
- Methods and significant assumptions used in assessing fair values;
- The extent to which fair values were measured by reference to observable prices in an active market, recent market transactions on an arm's-length basis, or were estimated using other techniques;
- For each class of asset revalued, the carrying amount that would have been recognized if the class had not been revalued; and
- The revaluation surplus, indicating the change for the period and any restrictions on distributions to shareholders.

EXCERPTS FROM PUBLISHED FINANCIAL STATEMENTS

Ahold, Annual Report 2008

Notes to Consolidated Financial Statements

Significant Accounting Policies

Property, Plant, and Equipment

Items of property, plant, and equipment are stated at cost less accumulated depreciation and impairment losses. Cost includes expenditures that are directly attributable to the acquisition or construction of an asset and includes borrowing costs incurred during construction. Where applicable, estimated asset retirement costs are added to the cost of an asset. Subsequent expenditures are capitalized only when it is probable that future economic benefits associated with the item will flow to the company and the costs can be measured reliably. All other subsequent expenditures represent repairs and maintenance and are expensed as incurred.

Depreciation is computed using the straight-line method based on the estimated useful lives of the items of property, plant, and equipment, taking into account the estimated residual value. Where an item of property, plant, and equipment comprises major components having different useful lives, each such part is depreciated separately. The assets' useful lives are reviewed, and adjusted if appropriate, at each balance sheet date.

The estimated useful lives of property, plant and equipment are

Land	Indefinite
Buildings	30–40 years
Building components	7–20 years
Machinery and equipment	5–12 years
Other	3–10 years

Depreciation of assets subject to finance leases and leasehold improvements is calculated on a straight-line basis over either the lease term (including renewal periods when renewal is reasonably assured) or the estimated useful life of the asset, whichever is shorter.

11. Property, Plant, and Equipment

Buildings and land include improvements to these assets. Other buildings and land mainly includes distribution centers. Other property, plant, and equipment mainly consist of trucks, trailers, and other vehicles, as well as office furniture and fixtures. Assets under construction mainly consist of stores.

In 2008, Ahold recognized impairment losses of EUR 10 million related to Stop & Shop/Giant-Landover (EUR 7 million), Albert Heijn (EUR 2 million), and Albert/Hypernova (EUR 1 million). The carrying amount of the affected assets exceeded the higher of the present value of their estimated future cash flows and fair value less costs to sell. The present value of estimated future cash flows has been calculated using discount rates ranging between 9.0–12.6 percent (2007: 8.4–12.5 percent).

Assets classified as held for sale or sold during 2008 mainly relate to the divestment of Schuitema.

The additions to property, plant, and equipment include capitalized borrowing costs of EUR 4 million (2007: EUR 6 million). Generally, the capitalization rate used to determine the amount of capitalized borrowing costs is a weighted average of the interest rate applicable to the respective operating companies. This rate ranged between 5.8–8.4 percent (2007: 4.3–6.7 percent). Other movements include transfers to and from investment property.

The carrying amount of land and buildings includes an amount of EUR 762 million and EUR 243 million (December 30, 2007: EUR 795 million and EUR 236 million) in respect of assets held under finance leases and financings, respectively. In addition, the carrying amount of machinery and equipment includes an amount of EUR 8 million (December 30, 2007: EUR 9 million) in respect of assets held under finance leases. Ahold does not have legal title to these assets. Company-owned property, plant, and equipment with a carrying amount of EUR 75 million (December 30, 2007: EUR 196 million) have been pledged as security for liabilities, mainly for loans.

11 LEASES (IAS 17)

INTRODUCTION

IAS 17 prescribes the accounting treatment for leases in the financial statements of lessees and lessors and shall be applied in accounting for all leases other than those to explore for or use nonregenerative resources like minerals and oil and to the licensing agreements for motion picture films, video recordings, plays, manuscripts, and so on. However, this standard cannot be used as a basis to measure any of the following:

- Properties held by lessees that qualify as investment property under IAS 40, *Investment Property*;
- Properties held by lessors that qualify as investment property under IAS 40, *Investment Property*, which are provided under operating leases;
- Biological assets in accordance with IAS 41, *Agriculture,* held by lessees under finance leases; or
- Biological assets in accordance with IAS 41, *Agriculture,* provided by lessors under operating leases.

KEY TERMS

Lease. An agreement whereby the lessor grants the lessee the right to use an asset for an agreed period of time in return for a payment.

Finance lease. A lease that transfers to the lessee substantially all the risks and rewards incidental to ownership of an asset, although title may or may not eventually be transferred.

Operating lease. A lease other than a finance lease.

Minimum lease payments. Payments that are guaranteed to be made under the lease agreement, other than those incurred by and reimbursed to the lessor. Minimum lease payments relating to a lessor are the residual value guaranteed either by the lessee, a related party, or a third party that is capable of discharging the financial obligations under the guarantee.

CLASSIFICATION OF LEASES

Leases can be classified as financing and operating in nature. The basis of classification of these two types of leases is the extent to which the risks and rewards related to the ownership of the assets are transferred to the lessee and lessor. Risks will include those on account of idle capacity and technological obsolescence.

A lease is classified as a finance lease if it transfers substantially all the risks and rewards of ownership to the lessee. If it does not transfer the risks and rewards of ownership, it is classified as an operating lease.

In determining whether a lease is a financing or operating lease, the substance of the agreement and the nature of the commercial transaction are very important factors besides the legal form. Some of the situations that would individually, or in combination, lead to a lease being classified as a finance lease are

- The ownership of the asset is transferred to the lessee at the end of the lease term;
- The lessee has the option to purchase the asset at a price that is expected to be less than the fair value;
- It is expected that the purchase option will be exercised;
- The term of the lease covers the major part of the economic life of the asset, even if title is not transferred at the end of the lease;
- The present value of the minimum lease payments is at least equal to substantially all of the fair value of the asset; or
- The leased assets are of a specialized nature that only the lessee can use them without major modification.

Similarly, the following situations, whether individually or in combination, can also lead to a lease being classified as a finance lease:

- The lessee can cancel the lease and the lessor's loss on account of such cancellation will be borne by the lessee;
- The gains or losses on changes in the fair value of the residual asset value will be to the lessee;
- The lessee has the option to continue the lease for a secondary term at a rent that is below the market rate.

The classification of a lease is made at the commencement of the lease. The lease will commence on the date of the agreement or on the date the parties to the lease agree to the provisions of the lease agreement. When the terms of the lease are later substantially altered such that the classification of the lease made at inception will change, it will be deemed that a new lease has been made.

A land lease is classified as an operating lease if title is not transferred. Therefore, in many cases, the leases of land and buildings will have to be treated differently, as the land lease can be an operating lease while the building lease could be a finance lease. In such cases there could be difficulties in allocating the minimum lease payments to land and the buildings. If an allocation cannot be reliably made, both the land and building leases should be recognized as either a finance lease or as an operating lease, depending on the suitability of the classification.

LEASES IN THE FINANCIAL STATEMENT OF LESSEES

Finance Leases

Initial recognition. The lessee should, at the commencement of the lease term, recognize the finance lease as an asset and a liability. This recognition must be made at the fair value of the leased asset or, if lower, at the present value of the minimum lease payments. The discount rate to be used in calculating the present value of the minimum lease payments is the interest rate implicit in the lease. If the implicit interest rate cannot be determined, the lessee's incremental borrowing rate must be used. The initial direct costs of the lessee, like negotiating and securing leasing arrangements, must be added to the amount recognized as an asset.

Subsequent measurement. Subsequent to the initial recognition, the lease payments should be apportioned between the amount paid to reduce the outstanding liability and the finance charges. The finance charge should be allocated over the period of the lease term so as to reflect a constant periodic rate of interest on the liability. Contingent rents should be charged as expenses in the periods in which they are incurred. This standard defines contingent rent, like that based on future market rates of interest or percentages of future sales, as that portion of the lease payments that is not fixed in amount but is based on the future amount of a factor that changes other than with the passage of time.

A finance lease gives rise to depreciation expense for depreciable assets, as well as finance expense for each accounting period. The depreciation policy for depreciable leased assets shall be consistent with that for depreciable assets that are owned, and the depreciation recognized shall be calculated in accordance with IAS 16, *Property, Plant, and Equipment,* and IAS 38, *Intangible Assets.* If there is no reasonable certainty that the lessee will obtain ownership by the end of the lease term, the asset shall be fully depreciated over the shorter of the lease term and its useful life.

Disclosures. The following minimum disclosures are required to be made in the financial statements:

- The net carrying value for each class of asset at the reporting date;
- Reconciliation between the total of the minimum lease payments and their present value;
- Total of the future minimum lease payments analyzed either as

  - Less than one year
  - Between one year and five years
  - More than five years

- Contingent rents;
- Total future minimum lease payments expected to be received under noncancelable subleases; and
- General description of the lessee's material leasing arrangements.

Example 1

Anthony Inc. has taken an asset on lease from Jack Inc. on April 1, 2010. The following information is given:

Lease term	4 years
Fair value at inception of lease	$1,600,000
Annual lease rent payable at the end of the year	$ 500,000
Guaranteed residual value (GRV)	$ 100,000
Expected residual value	$ 300,000
Implicit interest rate (DF)	14.97%

The lease has been classified as a finance lease.

You are required to calculate the amount at which Anthony Inc. will record a lease asset and lease liability at the inception of the lease, and the annual depreciation and finance charges.

Solution

In the case of a finance lease, the lessee records the leased asset and lease liability at fair value or present value (PV) of minimum lease payments (MLP), whichever is less.

MLP (lessee)	=	Lease rental + GRV by or on behalf of lessee
	=	($5000,000 × 4) + $100,000
	=	$2,100,000

Year	*DF @ 14.97*
1	0.8698
2	0.7565
3	0.6580
4	0.5724
	2.8567

PV of MLP (lessee)	=	($5000,000 × 2.8567) + ($100,000 × 0.5724)
	=	$1,485,590

Therefore, Anthony Inc. will record a leased asset and lease liability at the inception of lease at FV = $1,600,000 or PV of MLP = $1,485,590, whichever is less, that is, $1,485,590.

Also, a finance lease will give rise to depreciation and finance expenses.

Depreciation has been calculated on the straight-line method (SLM) over the lease period.

$$\text{Depreciation} = \frac{\$1,485,590}{4} = \$371,398$$

Finance expense will be recognized at a constant rate on the outstanding liability.

Year	Financial charges	Lease payment	Reduction in outstanding liability	Outstanding liability
April 1, 2008	—	—	—	1,485,590
March 31, 2009	222,393	500,000	277,607	1,207,983
March 31, 2010	180,835	500,000	319,165	888,818
March 31, 2011	133,056	500,000	366,944	521,874
March 31, 2012	78,126*	600,000	521,874	—

Adjusted for rounding.

Operating Leases

Lease payments under an operating lease shall be recognized as an expense on a straight-line basis over the lease term, unless another basis can be established that is more representative of the user's benefit. When the lessee receives any incentive or rebate, like a rent-free period, the total reduced lease rent that is to be paid over the lease term must be allocated over the entire period.

Disclosures. The following disclosures are required to be made in addition to those required by the financial instruments standards:

- Total future minimum lease payments under noncancelable operating leases for each of the following:
  - Less than one year
  - Between one year and five years
  - More than five years
- Total future minimum lease payments expected to be received under noncancelable subleases;
- Lease and sublease payments and contingent rents recognized as an expense; and
- A general description of the significant leasing arrangements.

LEASES IN THE FINANCIAL STATEMENT OF LESSORS

Finance Leases

Initial recognition. Lessors should recognize assets held under a finance lease as a receivable in their statements of financial position. The amount of receivable should be recognized at its net investment in the lease.

The net investment in the lease represents the aggregate of the minimum lease payments and any unguaranteed residual value (portion of the residual value of the leased asset on which there is no guarantee of realization) discounted at the interest rate implicit in the lease.

Lessors often incur costs like legal fees for negotiating and arranging a lease. In the case of lessors who are not manufacturers or dealers, such initial direct costs are included in the initial amount of the finance lease receivable, and the amount of income recognized over the lease term is reduced to that extent. However, when the lessor is a manufacturer or dealer, such initial direct costs are recognized as an expense when the profit on sale is accounted for.

Subsequent measurement. The recognition of finance income shall be based on a pattern reflecting a constant periodic rate of return on the lessor's net investment in the finance lease.

Manufacturer or dealer lessors shall recognize selling profit or loss in the period, in accordance with the policies used by the entity for the rest of direct sales. If artificially low interest rates have been quoted, the result from the sale will be reduced to that which would have been obtained had the entity used market interest rates. The costs incurred by manufacturer or distributor lessors, in connection with the negotiation or the hiring of the lease, are recognized as an expense when they recognize the result in the sale.

Disclosures. The following minimum disclosures are required:

- Reconciliation between the gross carrying amount of the investment in the lease and the present value of the future minimum lease payments receivable;
- Gross investment in the lease and the future minimum lease payments for each of the following:
    - Less than one year
    - Between one year and five years
    - More than five years
- Unearned finance income;
- Unguaranteed residual value;
- Doubtful recoverable lease payments;
- Contingent rents recognized as income; and
- A general description of the significant leasing arrangements.

Operating Leases

Lessors shall present assets subject to operating leases in their statements of financial position according to the nature of the asset.

Lease income from operating leases shall be recognized as income on a straight-line basis over the lease term, unless another basis is more representative of the nature of the benefit derived.

Initial direct costs, like negotiation costs, incurred by the lessors should be added to the asset cost and must be expensed over the lease term on the same basis as the lease income is recognized.

The depreciation on leased assets must be recognized as an expense. The amount of depreciation should be calculated in accordance with IAS 16, *Property, Plant, and Equipment* and IAS 38, *Intangible Assets*.

Disclosures. The following disclosures are required in addition to the requirements of the financial instruments standards:

- Total future minimum lease payments under noncancelable operating leases for each of the following:
    - Less than one year
    - Between one year and five years
    - More than five years
- Contingent rents recognized as income;
- A general description of the significant leasing arrangements.

Sale and leaseback transactions. A sale and leaseback transaction is a common financing transaction. It involves the owner selling an asset and the purchaser leasing the same asset back to the owner. In this transaction, the lease payment and the sale price are usually interdependent.

When the lease results in the lessee having to defer recognition of any profit on disposal over the lease term, the lease is in the nature of a finance lease. The income on a finance lease is amortized over the lease term.

If the leaseback is an operating lease and the entire transaction is at fair value, the gain or loss on disposal is recognized immediately. If the sale price is below the fair value, the profit or loss must be recognized immediately, unless the loss is compensated for by future lease payments at below market price. In this case, the profit or loss should be deferred and amortized over the lease term. If the sale price is above fair value, the excess over fair value should be deferred and amortized over the lease period.

Example 2

On March 31, 2008, Standfort Inc. sold equipment to Samsuns Inc. and immediately leased back the equipment for 12 years. The lease was classified as a finance lease in accordance with the provisions contained in IAS 17. Following is the information for the year ended March 31, 2008:

Sale price	$4.8 million
Carrying amount	$3.6 million
Estimated remaining useful life	15 years

The provisions of IAS 17 are relevant in this context. Accordingly, the excess or deficiency of sale proceeds over the carrying amount should not be immediately recognized as profit or loss in the financial statement of Standfort Inc. Instead, it should be deferred or amortized over the lease term in proportion to the depreciation of the leased asset.

For the financial year 2007–2008, the deferred gain of Standfort Inc. from the sale of equipment is $1.2 million. This will be amortized over the lease term (which is 12 years) in proportion to the depreciation of the asset.

Example 3

Tom Inc. leased a machine to Jerry Inc. on the following terms:

	($ million)
Fair value of the machinery	20.00
Lease term	5 years
Lease rental per annum	5.00
Guaranteed residual value (GRV)	1.00
Expected residual value	2.00
Internal rate of return	15%

Depreciation is provided on the straight line method at 10% per annum. Ascertain the unearned financial income and necessary entries to be recorded in the books of Jerry Inc. (the lessee) in the first year.

Solution

Computation of unearned finance income

According to IAS 17, *unearned finance income* is the difference between (a) the gross investment in the lease and (b) the present value of minimum lease payments under a finance lease from the standpoint of the lessor, and any unguaranteed residual value accruing to the lessor, at the interest rate implicit in the lease.

Where

1. Gross investment in the lease is the aggregate of (a) minimum lease payments from the standpoint of the lessor and (b) any unguaranteed residual value accruing to the lessor.

Gross investment = Minimum lease payments + Unguaranteed residual value

= (Total lease rent + Guaranteed residual value) + Unguaranteed residual value

= [($5 million × 5 years) + $1 million] + $1 million

= $27 million (a)

2. Table showing present value of (i) Minimum lease payments (MLP) and (ii) Unguaranteed residual value (URV).

Year	MLP Inclusive of URV ($ million)	Internal rate of return (Discount factor 15%)	Present value ($ million)	
1	5	.8696	4.3480	
2	5	.7561	3.7805	
3	5	.6575	3.2875	
4	5	.5718	2.8590	
5	5	.4972	2.4860	
	1 million (guaranteed residual value)	.4972	0.4972	
			17.2582	(i)
	1 million (unguaranteed residual value)	.4972	0.4972	(ii)
		(i) + (ii)	**17.76**	(b)

Unearned finance income = (a) – (b)

= $27 million – $17.76 million

= $9.24 million (approx.)

Journal Entries in the books of Jerry Inc.

In million $

At the inception of lease:

Dr Machinery account	17.2582	
Cr To Tom Inc. account		17.2582

Being lease of machinery recorded at present value of MLP

At the end of the first year of lease:

Dr. Finance charges account (refer working note)	2.58873	
Cr. To Tom Inc. account		2.58873

Being the finance charges for first year due

Dr. Tom Inc. account	5	
Cr. Bank account		5

Being the lease rent paid to the lessor, which includes outstanding liability of $2.41127 and a finance charge of $2.58873

Dr. Depreciation account	1.72582	
Cr. Machinery account		1.72582

Being the depreciation provided at 10% p.a. on straight-line method

Dr. Profit and loss account	4.31455	
Cr. Depreciation account		1.72582
Cr. Finance charges account		2.58873

Being the depreciation and finance charges transferred to profit and loss account

As per IAS 17, the lessee should recognize the lease as an asset and a liability at an amount equal to the fair value of the leased asset at the inception of the lease. However, if the fair value of the leased asset exceeds the present value of minimum lease payments from the standpoint of the lessee, the amount recorded should be the present value of these minimum lease payments. Therefore, in this case, as the fair value of $20 million is more than the present value amount of $17.2582, the machinery has been recorded at $17.2582 in the books of Jerry Inc. (the lessee) at the inception of the lease.

Working note. The following table shows apportionment of lease payments to Tom Inc.— the finance charges and the reduction of outstanding liability.

Year	Outstanding liability (opening balance)	Lease rent	Finance charge	Reduction in outstanding liability	Outstanding liability (closing balance)
1	$17.2582	$5.0	2.58873	$2.41127	$14.84693
2	14.84693	5.0	2.22704	2.77296	12.07397
3	12.07397	5.0	1.8111	3.18890	8.88507
4	8.88507	5.0	1.33276	3.67324	5.21783
5	5.21783	5.0	0.78267	5.21183	1.0005*
			8.7423	**17,25,820**	

NOTE: Figures in $ million.

*The difference between this figure and guaranteed residual value ($1 million) is due to approximation in computing the interest rate implicit in the lease.

Example 4

Alpha Inc. has sold an asset to Beta Inc. and has taken it back on lease on the same day. The leased term is five years. The lease rentals are as follows:

Year	Lease rental
1	$1,000
2	$1,500
3	$2,000
4	$2,500
5	$3,000

Alpha Inc. has classified the lease as an operating one in accordance with the provisions of IAS 17. How will Alpha Inc. account for the profit/loss on the sale of the asset under each of the following options?

  A. Sale value = Fair value = $10,000
  B. Sale value = $11,000 and Fair value = $10,000
  C. Sale value = $9,000 and Fair value = $10,000

Given that carrying amount is

  1. $10,000
  2. $ 9,000
  3. $11,000

Solution

NOTE: All amounts shown are in dollars

A.1.	10,000	10,000	10,000	No profit or loss.
2.	10,000	10,000	9,000	Recognize profit of 1,000 immediately.
3.	10,000	10,000	11,000	Recognize loss of 1,000 immediately.
B.1.	11,000	10,000	10,000	Defer profit of 1,000 in the ratio of lease.
2.	11,000	10,000	9,000	Recognize profit of 1,000 immediately and defer profit of 1,000 in the ratio of lease rent.
3.	11,000	10,000	11,000	Recognize loss of 1,000 immediately and defer profit of 1,000 in the ratio of lease rent.
C.1.	9,000	10,000	10,000	Recognize loss of 1,000 immediately or defer in the ratio of lease rent if the loss is compensated by future lease payments at below market price.
2.	9,000	10,000	9,000	No profit or loss. A profit cannot be recognized immediately and a loss deferred. However, as done in (B.3.), a loss can be recognized immediately and profit deferred, even though there was no profit/loss.
3.	9,000	10,000	11,000	Recognize loss of 1,000 immediately. Recognize future loss of 1,000 immediately.

EXCERPTS FROM PUBLISHED FINANCIAL STATEMENTS

Barloworld Annual Report 2008

Notes to the Consolidated Annual Financial Statements for the Year Ended September 30

30. Commitments

	Long term > 5 years Rm	Medium term 2–5 years Rm	Short term < 1 year Rm	2008 Total Rm	2007 Total Rm	2006 Total Rm
Lease commitments:						
Operating lease commitments						
Land and buildings	575	935	340	1,850	1,638	1,955
Motor vehicles	1	180	127	308	261	488
Other	—	81	39	120	40	66
	576	1,196	506	2,278	1,939	2,509

Land and building commitments include the following items:

- Commitments for the operating and administrative facilities used by the majority of business segments. The average lease term is five years. Many lease contracts contain renewal options at fair market rates.
- Properties used for office accommodation and used car outlets in the major southern African cities. Rentals escalate at rates which are in line with the historical inflation rates applicable to the southern African environment. Lease periods do not exceed five years.
- Properties at airport locations. The leases are in general for periods of five years and the rental payments are based on a set percentage of revenues generated at those locations subject to certain minimums.
- Motor vehicle commitments are mainly for vehicles in use in the offshore operations. The average lease term is four years.

	Long term > 5 years Rm	Medium term 2—5 years Rm	Short term < 1 year Rm	2008 Total Rm	2007 Total Rm	2006 Total Rm
Finance lease commitments						
Present value of minimum lease payments						
Land and buildings	365	214	21	600	436	394
Motor vehicles		49	25	74	99	79
Rental fleets		188	82	270	341	382
Other	—	—	—	—	1	195
	365	451	128	944	877	1,050
Minimum lease payments						
Land and buildings	541	458	83	1,082	849	766
Motor vehicles		56	28	84	123	87
Rental fleets		208	95	303	382	441
Other	—	—	—	—	1	251
Total including future finance charges	541	722	206	1,469	1,355	1,545
Future finance charges				(525)	(478)	(495)
Present value of lease commitments (Note 15)				944	877	1,050

Land and building commitments are for certain fixed-rate leases in the automotive division for trading premises with an average term of twelve years including a purchase option at the end of the term.

Rental fleet commitments arise in Barloworld Finance in the United Kingdom, which has financed certain rental units under capital leases with various institutions. These expire at the same time as the related lease with the customer.

Other commitments for the prior years mainly relate to Cement and include the following items:

- A suspensive sale agreement in PPC between RTA Leasing (Proprietary) Limited and BOE Bank, interest was payable biannually at the end of March and September of each year. The effective interest rate was 12.5% per annum with capital repayments of R98 million in 2007.
- Plant and equipment leased by the Cement division from Saldanha Steel (Proprietary) Limited with fixed payment terms. The agreement matures in April 2013.

12 REVENUE (IAS 18)

INTRODUCTION

The term *income* that encompasses both revenue and gains is defined in the *Framework for the Preparation and Presentation of Financial Statements*. Income is the increase in economic benefits during the accounting period in the form of inflows or enhancements of assets, or decreases of liabilities that result in increases in equity, other than those relating to contributions from equity participants.

Revenue arises from an entity's ordinary course of activities. Revenue can arise from such sources as sales of goods, provision of services, royalty fees, franchise fees, management fees, dividends, interest, and subscriptions. Gains do not arise out of the core business operations and include such items as profit on disposal of noncurrent assets, retranslating balances in foreign currencies, or fair value adjustments to financial and nonfinancial assets.

SCOPE

The provisions of IAS 18 are to be applied in accounting for revenue arising from the

- Sale of goods;
- Rendering of services; and
- Use of the entity's assets by third parties that yields interest, royalties, or dividends.

However the standard does not deal with revenue that arises from the following, since they are dealt with by other standards:

- Lease agreements (IAS 17)
- Dividends from investments that are accounted for under the equity method (IAS 28)
- Insurance contracts (IFRS 4)
- Changes in fair values of financial instruments (IAS 39)
- Changes in the values of current assets
- Initial recognition and changes in value of biological assets (IAS 41)
- Initial recognition of agricultural produce (IAS 41)
- Extraction of mineral ores

KEY TERMS

Revenue. The gross inflow of economic benefits during the period arising in the course of ordinary activities of an entity when those inflows result in increases in equity other than increases relating to contributions from equity participants.

Fair value. The amount for which an asset could be exchanged, or a liability settled between knowledgeable, willing parties in an arm's-length transaction.

MEASUREMENT OF REVENUE

The amount of revenue arising on a transaction is usually determined by the terms of the agreement between the entity and the buyer or the user of the asset. It is measured at the fair value of the consideration received or receivable, taking into account the amount of any trade discounts and volume rebates allowed by the entity.

Example 1

Under the terms of the arrangement that Trident Limited has with a customer, the customer gets a 2% discount on the total purchases that they make over a 12-month period, provided the total purchases exceed $1 million per year. During the 9 month financial period from April 1, 2008, to December 31, 2008, the sales to the customer were $900,000.

How much revenue should Trident Limited recognize?

Solution

During the 9-month period, Trident Limited made a sale of $900,000. On a pro rata basis, Trident Limited will make sales to its customer of $1.2 million ($900,000 × 12/9). Therefore, Trident Limited should accrue a retrospective rebate of 2% on $900,000 and recognize revenue of $882,000.

In the case of exchange of goods or services, no revenue must be recognized if the goods or services exchanged are similar in nature. However, when the goods or services exchanged are dissimilar in nature, revenue is recognized at the fair value of the goods or services received. If such fair value is not readily determinable, revenue is recognized at the fair value of the goods given up or services provided. In both cases, revenue is adjusted for any cash or cash equivalents transferred.

IDENTIFICATION OF A TRANSACTION

In general conditions, the recognition criteria of the standard are applied to each transaction. However, in certain more complex transactions, the criteria need to be applied to the components of a transaction.

Example 2

Full Service Co. sells equipment for $140,000, which includes a commitment to service the equipment for a period of two years. The same equipment is sold for $100,000 without the service warranty.

Solution

In this case, Full Service Co. should recognize revenue on sale of goods of $100,000. The balance of $40,000 must be recognized over two years as service revenue.

REVENUE ON SALE OF GOODS

Revenue from sale of goods must be recognized only when all the following conditions have been satisfied:

- The significant risks and rewards of ownership of the goods has been transferred by the entity to the buyer;
- The entity does not have effective control over the goods sold, nor does the entity retain any continuing managerial involvement to a degree that is usually associated with ownership;
- The amount of revenue can be measured reliably;
- It is probable that the economic benefits associated with the transaction will flow to the entity; and
- The costs incurred or that will be incurred, in respect of the transaction, can be measured reliably.

Under general terms of a transaction, the transfer of significant risks and rewards of ownership takes place when title passes to the buyer or at the time that the buyer receives possession of the goods. However, in some cases, the transfer of risks and rewards of ownership does not coincide with the transfer of legal title or the passing of possession, as in the case of sale of a building that is still under construction.

IFRIC 15, *Agreements for the Construction of Real Estate,* has standardized the practice of recognition of revenue by real estate developers in respect of the sales of units before construction is complete (off-plan sales). In case the developer is selling the completed unit, revenue must be recognized at delivery, as it is similar to selling a product. Similarly, when the buyer does not, under the terms of the agreement for the construction of real estate, have the authority to specify major changes in the structure or design, revenue must be recognized at delivery. However, when the buyer has the authority (whether exercised) to specify major changes in the structure or design, either before or during the construction period, revenue must be recognized in accordance with IAS 11, *Construction Contracts*, and under this standard.

Similarly, in many instances, the sale of goods is made subject to conditions. In all instances, if the seller retains significant risks of ownership, the transaction is not regarded as a sale for the purposes of recognizing revenue.

In the case of a sale transaction, revenue must not be recognized unless it is probable that the future economic benefits will flow to the entity. In some instances, where the receipt of the consideration is in doubt, revenue must not be recognized. However, when the collection of revenue accounted for in the previous reporting period is in doubt, the amount equivalent to the uncollectible amount must be recognized as an expense in the current reporting period.

At the time revenue is recognized, the costs that relate to the same transaction must be recognized simultaneously. When the costs cannot be measured reliably, the related revenue must not be recognized.

Example 3

1. **Sales made with a condition to install the equipment.** If the installation is a simple process and it forms an insignificant part of the sales contract, revenue can be recognized on delivery.
2. **Sales made on consignment.** In this case revenue is recognized only when the consignee has sold the goods.
3. **Sale is completed but goods are delivered on payment of the last installment.** In such cases, revenue can be recognized when a significant amount is received, the goods are on hand and ready for delivery, and the full payment is normally received.
4. **Sale is made and the buyer accepts the title and billing but the delivery of goods is delayed at the buyer's request.** In this case revenue is recognized when the buyer takes title, provided it is probable that the delivery will be made, the item is on hand, identified and ready for delivery to the buyer at the time the sale is recognized, the buyer specifically acknowledges the deferred delivery instructions; and the usual payment terms apply.

Example 4

Big Ben Electronics, which is a retailer in consumer goods, grants its customers a right to return the goods in case of a defect in the product sold.

In such a case, the mere fact that the customer has a right to return the goods cannot be considered as a significant retention of risks and rewards on the ownership of the goods sold to the customers. The risk that is not transferred is the risk of the goods that are sold being returned by customers. Therefore, in such cases, revenue is recognized at the time of sale, provided the seller can reliably estimate the returns of goods in the future and recognize a provision under IAS 37, *Provisions, Contingent Liabilities, and Contingent Assets.*

Example 5

Anthony Publishers Inc. is engaged in publishing books for medical professionals. It invoices its distributors at list price less 50% discount. The distributors are also entitled to commission of

5% on the list price of the books actually sold by them. Unsold books are returned to the publisher at the end of the period.

In this case, the publisher-distributor relationship can be considered as of principal and agent. Revenue can be recognized by Anthony Publishers Inc. only when the books are finally sold by the distributor to the customers.

REVENUE FROM RENDERING OF SERVICES

Revenue from rendering services shall be recognized by reference to the stage of completion of the transaction at the end of the reporting period when

- The amount of revenue can be measured reliably;
- It is probable that the economic benefits associated with the transaction will flow to the entity;
- The stage of completion of the transaction at the end of the reporting period can be measured reliably; and
- The costs incurred for the transaction and the costs to complete the transaction can be measured reliably.

When the outcome of the transaction involving the rendering of services cannot be estimated reliably, revenue shall be recognized only to the extent of the expenses recognized that are recoverable.

Example 6

- Subscription income is recognized on a straight-line basis over the subscription period;
- Professional fees for development of software are recognized on the basis of the stage of completion of the development; and
- Installation fees are recognized over the period of installation by reference to the stage of completion.

In accordance with IFRIC 15, when a developer of real estate is selling a construction service (and not construction goods) to the buyer, revenue from rendering services must be recognized on a percentage-of-completion basis as construction progresses. However, if the developer is required to provide services together with construction materials in order to perform their contractual obligation to deliver the real estate to the buyer, the revenue must be accounted for as the sale of goods under IAS 18.

When services of similar nature and value are exchanged or swapped, the exchange is not regarded as a transaction that generates revenue. When services are rendered in exchange for dissimilar services, the revenue is measured at the fair value of the services received, adjusted by the amount of any cash or cash equivalents transferred. When the fair value of the goods or services received cannot be measured reliably, the revenue is measured at the fair value of the goods or services given up, adjusted by the amount of any cash or cash equivalents transferred.

In the case of barter transactions involving advertising services, SIC 31, *Revenue— Barter Transactions Involving Advertising Services*, states that revenue from a barter transaction cannot be measured reliably at the fair value of advertising services received. However, a seller can reliably measure revenue at the fair value of the advertising services it provides in a barter transaction by reference only to nonbarter transactions that

- Involve advertising similar to the advertising in the barter transaction;
- Occur frequently;
- Represent a predominant number of transactions and amount, when compared to all transactions, to provide advertising that is similar to the advertising in the barter transaction;

- Involve cash and/or another form of consideration (such as marketable securities, nonmonetary assets, and other services) that has a reliably measurable fair value; and
- Do not involve the same counterparty as in the barter transaction.

IFRIC 13, *Customer Loyalty Programmes,* addresses accounting for loyalty award credits (such as points or travel miles) that entities grant to customers who buy other goods or services. Such entities should

- Allocate some of the proceeds of the initial sale to the award credits as a liability. The amount of proceeds allocated to the award credits is measured by reference to their fair value; that is, the amount for which the award credits could have been sold separately; and
- Recognize the deferred portion of the proceeds as revenue only when it has fulfilled its obligations.

If at any time the expected costs of meeting the obligation exceed the consideration received, the entity must recognize a liability (IAS 37).

INTEREST, ROYALTIES, AND DIVIDENDS

Revenue that arises from the use of the entity's assets by third parties and yields interest, royalties, and dividends shall be recognized when

- It is probable that the economic benefits associated with the transaction will flow to the entity; and
- The amount of revenue can be measured reliably.

The revenue shall be recognized on the following bases:

- Interest shall be recognized using the effective interest method (IAS 39);
- Royalties shall be recognized on an accrual basis in accordance with the terms of the relevant agreement; and
- Dividends shall be recognized when the shareholder has the right to receive payment.

Example 7

Total sales of a company included a sum of $183 million representing royalties receivable for supply of know-how to a company in Southeast Asia. According to the royalty agreement, the amount is to be received in U.S. dollars. However, exchange permission was denied to the company in Southeast Asia for remitting the same. How should this be treated in the books?

Solution

In accordance with IAS 18, royalties are recognized on an accrual basis in accordance with the terms of the relevant agreement. Since the royalty receivable is already included in sales, it can be assumed that it has accrued. However, IAS 18 also states that recognition should be postponed if there is reasonable uncertainty of ultimate collection. In the given case, royalties receivable is in U.S. dollars and the company has been denied permission for remitting the same. Therefore, revenue recognition must be postponed until such time as remittance is received or it becomes reasonably certain that it will be received. However, if revenue has already been recognized in the books of the earlier reporting period, a separate provision must be made for the amount equivalent to the uncertainty.

Example 8

Highend Publication has received one million subscriptions during the current year under its new scheme whereby customers are required to pay a sum of $3.00, for which they will be entitled to receive STARDUST magazine for a period of 3 years. Can Highend Publication treat the entire amount as revenue for the current year?

Solution

Revenue received should be deferred and recognized, either (1) on a straight-line basis over time, or (2) based on the sales value of the item delivered in relation to the total sales value of all the items covered by the subscription. Highend Publication cannot treat the entire amount as revenue for the current year. The revenue should be recognized on a straight-line basis.

DISCLOSURES

The following disclosures shall be made:

- The accounting policies adopted for the recognition of revenue, including the methods adopted to determine the stage of completion of transactions involving the rendering of services;
- The amount of each significant category of revenue recognized during the period, including revenue arising from:
  - Sale of goods
  - The rendering of services
  - Interest
  - Royalties
  - Dividends; and
- The amount of revenue arising from exchanges of goods or services included in each significant category of revenue.

EXCERPTS FROM PUBLISHED FINANCIAL STATEMENTS

Balfour Beatty PLC, Annual Report 2008

Notes to the Accounts

1.   Principal Accounting Policies

1.4 Revenue Recognition. Revenue is measured at the fair value of the consideration received or receivable for goods and services provided, net of trade discounts, value added and similar sales-based taxes, after eliminating sales within the group. Revenue is recognized as follows:

- Revenue from construction and service activities represents the value of work carried out during the year, including amounts not invoiced;
- Revenue from manufacturing activities is recognized when title has passed; and
- Interest income is accrued on a time basis, by reference to the principal outstanding and the effective interest rate applicable, which is the rate that exactly discounts estimated future cash receipts through the expected life of the financial asset to that asset's net carrying amount.

Dividend income is recognized when the shareholder's right to receive payment is established.

Ahold, Annual Report 2008

Notes to the Consolidated Financial Statements

3.   Significant Accounting Policies

Net Sales

Ahold generates and recognizes net sales to retail customers at the point of sale in its stores and upon delivery of groceries to Internet customers. Ahold also generates revenues from the sale of products to retail franchisees, which are recognized upon delivery. Ahold recognizes franchise fees as revenue when all material services relating to the contract have been substantially performed. Discounts earned by customers, including those provided in connection with bonus or loyalty cards, are recognized as a reduction of sales at the time of the sale.

Generally, net sales and cost of sales are recorded based on the gross amount received from the customer for products sold and the amount paid to the vendor for products purchased. However, for certain products or services, such as the sale of lottery tickets, third-party prepaid phone cards, stamps, and public transportation tickets, Ahold acts as an agent, and consequently records the amount of commission income in its net sales. Net sales exclude sales taxes and value-added taxes.

The Lectra Group, Annual Report 2008

Notes to the Consolidated Financial Statements

Revenues

Revenues from sales of hardware are recognized when the significant risks and benefits relating to ownership are transferred to the purchaser.

For hardware or for software, in cases where the company also sells the computer equipment on which the software is installed, these conditions are fulfilled upon physical transfer of the hardware in accordance with the contractual sale terms.

For software not sold with the hardware on which it is installed, these conditions are generally fulfilled at the time of installation of the software on the customer's computer (either by CD-ROM or downloading).

Revenues from software evolution contracts and recurring services contracts are booked monthly over the duration of the contracts.

Revenues from the billing of services not covered by recurring contracts are recognized at the time of performance of the service or, where appropriate, on a percentage-of-completion basis.

13 EMPLOYEE BENEFITS (IAS 19)

INTRODUCTION

IAS 19 prescribes the accounting treatment and disclosure by employers for employee benefits. In accordance with this standard, an employer should recognize a liability when service has been provided by an employee in exchange for the benefits to be paid in the future. Similarly, an employer should recognize an expense when the economic benefits are received by the employer from the services provided by the employee.

SCOPE

IAS 19 shall be applied by an employer in accounting for all employee benefits except those relating to IFRS 2, *Share-Based Payment*. This standard also does not deal with reporting by employee benefit plans. These are dealt with by IAS 26, *Accounting and Reporting by Retirement Benefit Plans*.

The employee benefits that are provided may be consequent to formal plans or formal agreements that are entered into between the employer and employees (individually or groups), on account of mandatory legislative or industry practices, or on account of informal practices that give rise to a constructive obligation to grant such benefits.

All benefits paid to full-time, part-time, permanent, casual, or temporary employees, and to directors and other managerial personnel of the entity are covered under this standard. The settlement of the benefits to the employee or their dependants (their spouses and children) or others, like an insurance company, may be made either through payments or by provision of goods and services.

KEY TERMS

Multiemployer plans. Contribution or defined benefit plans that pool the assets that are contributed by many entities that are not under common control and utilize those assets to provide benefits to employees of more than one entity without identifying the entity that employs them.

Current service cost. The increase in the present value of the defined benefit obligation that arises as a result of the employee services in the current period.

Interest cost. The increase in the present value of the defined benefit obligation that arises because the benefits payable are within one year of the settlement of the scheme.

Return on plan assets. The interest, dividends, and other income that is derived from the plan assets, which includes any realized or unrealized gains or losses on those assets, less the administration cost of the plan, and any tax payable by the plan.

TYPES OF EMPLOYEE BENEFITS

Employee benefits can be categorized as follows:

- Short-term benefits, like salaries or wages paid periodically;
- Postemployment benefits like pension payments or insurance payments;

- Other long-term employee benefits, like long-term disability benefits; and
- Termination benefits, like severance pay or gratuities.

SHORT-TERM EMPLOYEE BENEFITS

Short-term employee benefits are monetary benefits that are payable within 12 months after the end of the period in which services are rendered and the nonmonetary benefits for current employees. Monetary benefits include salaries, wages, social security contributions, paid annual leave, paid sick leave, profit sharing, and bonuses. Nonmonetary benefits include perquisites to employees like housing, medical care, use of motor vehicles, and subsidized goods or services.

Recognition and Measurement

Short-term employee benefit obligations are measured on an undiscounted basis since they are due to be paid within 12 months of the reporting date. This undiscounted amount of the employee benefits that is to be paid to an employee who has rendered service during the reporting period must be recognized as a liability (accrued expense) and the associated costs as an expense. When the payment made exceeds the amount of benefits that is to be paid, the excess must be recognized as an asset (prepaid expense).

It is very common that an employer grants an employee compensation for short-term absences from work. This compensation for short-term absence can be either accumulating or nonaccumulating in nature.

Payments for accumulating compensated absences, such as unutilized paid annual leave to the credit of the employee at the end of the reporting period, are carried forward and the employee is entitled to either take the leave or to cash in the entitlement. In this case, the employer must make an accrual for the amount that is expected to be paid as a result of the unsettled or unutilized entitlement at the reporting date.

Payments for nonaccumulating compensated absences, such as eligible maternity leave, are not carried forward to be used in future periods and also cannot be cashed in. Therefore, in such cases, the liability and cost are not recognized until the event has occurred.

When an employer has entered into an agreement with employees to share profits or to make incentive payments at the end of the reporting period, the cost and liability thereof must be recognized as there is a constructive or legal obligation to make the payment and the amount that is expected to be paid can be reliably estimated.

The amount that is expected to be paid can be reliably estimated if the plan has formal terms which contain the basis for calculating the amount of the benefit or the past practices and trends provide a good evidence of the amount that is to be paid under such constructive or legal obligations.

Disclosure

There are no specific disclosure requirements regarding short-term employee benefits. However, other standards, like IAS 24, *Related-Party Disclosures*, require that disclosures relating to remuneration and benefits paid to key management personnel be disclosed. Similarly, IAS 1, *Presentation of Financial Statements*, requires that employee benefits be disclosed as an expense.

POSTEMPLOYMENT BENEFIT PLANS

Postemployment benefit plans are the formal or informal arrangements under which the employer provides postemployment benefits to the employees. This will include retirement benefits such as pensions, life insurance cover, and postemployment medical insurance facilities.

Postemployment benefit plans can either be defined contribution plans or defined benefit plans.

Under a *defined contribution plan*, the employer enters into an arrangement to make a fixed contribution to a fund for a certain period of time, under the condition that the employer is not obligated to make further payments, even in a case where the assets of the fund are insufficient to pay all the employee benefits. An example of this plan is the contribution that the employer makes to an employee pension fund, wherein the benefits that are paid to the employee are solely based on the asset and income generation of the fund. Therefore, under this plan, the employees assume the risk that the benefits will be less than what is expected in the future (actuarial risk) and that the assets invested by the fund will not earn enough returns to meet the expected benefits (investment risk).

Defined benefit plans are those postemployment benefit plans that are not defined contribution plans. Under this plan, the employer assumes the responsibility and related risk of meeting the obligation to the current and former employees.

Recognition and Measurement

In the case of a multiemployer plan, where a number of unrelated employers pool their contributions under an agreement and utilize the assets to provide benefits to all their employees, the terms and conditions of such an agreement will determine whether the plan is to be accounted for as a defined contribution plan or a defined benefit plan. When adequate information is not available to account for this plan as a defined benefit plan, it should be treated as a defined contribution plan.

DEFINED CONTRIBUTION PLANS

The obligation of the employer under this plan for the reporting period is limited to the amount of contribution that is required to be made during that period. Therefore, there is no requirement for an actuarial valuation to be carried out to measure the obligation or the expense and account for the gain or loss that may arise on such an actuarial valuation. Similarly, for measurement purposes, the contribution that is due does not have to be discounted unless it is due beyond a period of 12 months from the reporting date. In such cases, the contributions that are due have to be discounted using a rate that has reference to the market yield on good quality corporate bonds.

As in the case of short-term employee benefit obligations, the contribution to a defined contribution plan should be recognized as a liability (accrued expense) and the associated costs as an expense. When the payment made exceeds the amount of contribution that is due to be paid at the reporting date, such excess must be recognized as an asset (prepaid expense).

Disclosure

The amount that is recognized as an expense for defined contribution plans should be disclosed in the financial statements. Similarly contributions made to defined contribution plans for key management personnel must also be disclosed, as required by IAS 24, *Related-Party Disclosures*.

In the case of a multiemployer plan, the entity must disclose the fact that the plan is a defined benefit plan and explain the reason why it is accounted for as a defined contribution plan.

DEFINED BENEFIT PLANS

Unlike in defined contribution plans, the benefits payable to employees under a defined benefits scheme are based on the terms of the plan and not on the amount of the contributions. This means that the employer undertakes the risks of providing the required funds to meet the obligations relating to the benefits to current and former employees. Therefore, the measurement and recognition for defined benefit plans is more complex than that of defined contributions plans.

Example 1

Under the terms of a pension plan, the employer contributes 10% of the employees' salary per month and the employees contribute 5% of their salary per month. The employer guarantees a payment to the employee equivalent to 103% of the amount of the contributions made.

This pension scheme will be a defined benefit plan since the employer has guaranteed a fixed rate of return and therefore assumes the risk.

Recognition and Measurement

In many cases, the contributions in defined benefit plans are made to funds that are independent of the employer. The contributions to these funds are made either by the employer or by the employer and employee jointly. The benefits to the employees are paid at a future date from asset and income generation of the fund; therefore there is no guarantee that the assets of the fund will be sufficient to meet the future benefit obligations. Since the employer undertakes this risk of shortfall, the expense recognized in a defined benefit plan is not equal to the contribution made for the period.

The accounting for a defined benefit plan is complex because the actuarial assumptions made in the actuarial techniques for the valuation of the benefits payable in the future might change over time. In addition, the obligations have to be recognized at the reporting date by discounting, since the benefits are settled several years after the employee renders the services.

In accounting for the defined benefits, the employer must determine the following key information:

- A reliable estimate of the amount of the benefit that the employees have earned in the current and prior period for service rendered;
- The present value of the defined benefit obligation and the current service cost, by discounting the benefit using the projected unit credit method;
- The fair value of any plan assets;
- The total amount of actuarial gains and losses and the amount of those actuarial gains and losses that are to be recognized;
- The past service costs, in cases of a change in a plan or the introduction of a plan; and
- The resulting gain or loss, in cases where a plan has been curtailed, changed, or settled (an example is a restructuring on account of reduction in the number of employees).

The employer must account for its legal obligation and any constructive obligation that arises from any informal practices. For example, there may be a case where, under the government intervention, the entity has no alternative but to pay employee benefits, even though the terms of the defined benefit plan permit the employer to terminate its obligations. When an entity has more than one defined benefit plan, the entity should apply these calculations for each plan separately.

Accounting for assets or liabilities of the defined benefit plan. The asset or liability on account of the defined benefit plan that is recognized in the statement of financial position shall be the net total of the following:

- The present value of the defined benefit obligation, plus or minus
- Any actuarial gains less losses not yet recognized because the gains and losses fall outside the limits of the corridor (10% of the fair value of the plan assets), minus
- Past service cost not yet recognized, minus
- The fair value of the plan assets at the reporting date.

When the net total is a positive amount, a liability is recorded in the statement of financial position. When the net total amount is negative, an asset is recognized at the lower of the amounts calculated above and the net total of any unrecognized net actuarial losses and past service costs, and the present value of any benefits available in the form of refunds or reductions in future employer contributions to the plan.

It is often difficult to determine the benefits that are available in the form of refunds or reductions in future employer contributions. Similarly, in some government controlled pension and benefit plans, refunds of overfunded amounts, or reductions in the premium payments, are not granted to the employers. In such cases, a proper disclosure must be made.

The *present value of a defined benefit obligation* is the discounted value of the expected future payments that is required to settle the obligation from past and current employee services. This present value is based on the future salaries payable, application of applying the projected unit credit actuarial method, and attributing the benefits to the periods of service under the plan's benefit formula.

The *projected unit credit actuarial method* looks at each period of service, which creates an additional increment of benefit entitlement and measures each unit of benefit entitlement separately to determine the final obligation. The whole postemployment benefit obligation is then discounted. The use of this method involves a number of actuarial assumptions, like mortality rates, retirement age, and discount rates, which are some of the factors that go into determining the final cost of the postemployment benefits provided. The rate used for discounting the obligations is the market yield of high-quality corporate bonds with terms similar to the obligations at the reporting date.

The *actuarial gains and losses* represent the adjustments that are made on account of the differences between the previous actuarial assumptions and the actual occurrence and the effect of any changes in actuarial assumptions.

The *past service cost* is the increase or decrease in the present value of a defined benefit obligation for employee service in previous periods that arises on account of changes in the postemployment, or long-term employee benefits, plan. Any benefit paid to employees during the period under the plan will reduce the liability.

Plan assets are those assets that are held by a long-term employee benefit fund and any qualifying insurance policies. The assets in a long-term employee benefit fund are held by separate legal entities that exist only to pay or fund employee benefits. The assets in these funds are not returned to the reporting entity, other than as a reimbursement of the employee benefit payments and when the value of the assets is in excess of all of the employee benefit obligations. Similarly, *qualifying insurance policies* are issued by an insurer who is not a related party (IAS 24, *Related-Party Disclosures*), and the proceeds of the policy are not returned to the reporting entity other than as a reimbursement of the employee benefit payments and when the value of the assets is in excess of all of the employee benefit obligations.

The *fair value of plan assets* at the end of the reporting period is the total of the following amounts:

- Fair value of the plan assets at the beginning of the reporting period, plus
- Contributions from employer or employee during the reporting period, plus or minus
- The actual return on plan assets during the reporting period (interest income, dividend income), minus
- The benefits paid under the plan during the reporting period.

The assets and liabilities from the different employment benefit plans that an employer may have are presented separately in the statement of financial position. The assets and liabilities can be offset only if there is a legally enforceable right to use the surplus in one plan to settle the obligation in another and the employer intends to use this right. When one entity acquires another entity, the purchasing entity must recognize the assets and liabilities arising from the selling entity's postemployment benefits at the present value of the defined benefit obligation, less the fair value of any plan assets.

Example 2

An entity has the following balances relating to its defined benefit plan:

- Present value of the obligation: $33 million
- Fair value of plan assets: $37 million
- Actuarial losses: $3 million unrecognized
- Past service cost: $2 million unrecognized
- Present value of available future refunds and reduction in future contributions: $1 million

Calculate the value of the net plan asset.

Solution

The negative amount (asset) determined under the standard will be

Present value of the obligation	$33 million
Fair value of plan assets	($37 million)
Unrecognized actuarial losses	($3 million)
Unrecognized past service cost	($2 million)
	($9 million)

The limit under this standard will be

Unrecognized actuarial losses	$3 million
Unrecognized past service cost	$2 million
Present value of available future refunds and reduction in future contributions	$1 million
	$6 million

The entity recognizes an asset of $6 million and discloses the fact that the limit has reduced the carrying amount of the asset by $3 million.

Accounting for expense or income of the defined benefit plan. An entity shall recognize the net total of the following amounts in the statement of profit and loss, except to the extent that another standard requires or permits their inclusion in the cost of an asset:

- Current service cost;
- Interest cost for the reporting period;
- The expected return on any plan assets;
- Actuarial gains and losses amortized in the reporting period; and
- Past service cost recognized in the reporting period.

The *current service cost*, that is, the increase in the present value of the defined benefit obligation arising from employee service in the current period, is affected by variables that are key in determining the defined benefit obligation and how these benefits are attributed to the period of service.

The *actuarial gains and losses* are the excess of the net cumulative unrecognized actuarial gains and losses at the end of the previous reporting period over the greater of

- 10% of the present value of the defined benefit obligation at the beginning of the reporting period; and
- 10% of the fair value of the plan assets at the same date.

The excess determined by the above method (corridor approach) is then divided by the expected average remaining lives of the employees in the plan. An entity can recognize the whole amount of the actuarial gains and losses in other comprehensive income in the reporting period in which they occur and include it under retained earnings. However, when they do so the same treatment must be applied to all defined benefit plans and for all actuarial gains or losses.

Past service cost arises when an entity introduces a defined benefit plan or changes the benefits payable under an existing defined benefit plan. In measuring its defined benefit liability, an entity should recognize past service cost as an expense on a straight-line basis over the average period until the benefits become vested. To the extent that the benefits are already vested immediately following the introduction of, or changes to, a defined benefit plan, an entity should recognize past service cost immediately. In addition, the effects of settlements and curtailments and adjustments to the benefit asset recognized in the statement of the financial position may also affect the employee benefit expense recognized in the statement of income.

The employee benefit expense that is measured is recognized in the profit or loss for the reporting period unless other standards require or allow cost to be added to an asset.

Example 3

A chief executive officer (CEO) of an entity receives a retirement benefit of 10% of his final annual salary for his contractual period of three years. The CEO does not contribute to the scheme. His anticipated salary over the three years is Year 1 $100,000, Year 2 $120,000, and Year 3 $144,000. Assume a discount rate of 5%.

What would be the current service cost, the pension liability, and the interest cost for the three years?

Solution

Year	Annual salary ($)	Current service cost ($)	Discounted current service cost ($)	Interest cost (5%×Liability) ($)	Liability brought forward ($)	Liability at year-end ($)
1	100,000	14,400	13,061	—	—	13,061
2	120,000	14,400	13,714	653	13,061	27,428
3	144,000	14,400	14,400	1,372	27,428	43,200
Total		43,200	41,175	2,025		

Disclosure

The following major disclosures are required for postemployment defined benefit plans by this standard:

- Description of type of plan;
- Accounting policy for recognizing actuarial gains or losses;
- Reconciliation of the opening balance of the present value of defined benefit obligation to the closing balance, disclosing each item that has been affected;
- Reconciliation of difference between the employee benefit asset or liability reported on the statement of financial position to the funded status of the plans;
- Total expense reported in the statement of profit or loss;
- Amounts recognized in the statement of comprehensive income;

- Information about investments held as plan assets, actual return on the plan assets, and how the expected return is determined; and
- Details of actuarial assumptions used and sensitivity analysis in relation to changes in key estimates.

OTHER LONG-TERM EMPLOYEE BENEFITS

Other long-term employee benefits will include the share of profits payable after 12 months of the reporting date, benefits payable on long-term disability of employees, and so on.

The liability on account of other long-term employee benefits that is recognized in the statement of financial position shall be the net total of the following:

- The present value of the defined benefit obligation at the reporting date, minus
- The fair value of the plan assets at the reporting date.

An entity shall recognize the net total of the following amounts in the statement of income, except to the extent that another standard requires or permits their inclusion in the cost of an asset:

- Current service cost;
- Interest cost for the reporting period;
- The expected return on any plan assets;
- Actuarial gains and losses amortized in the reporting period;
- Past service cost recognized in the reporting period; and
- Effect of any curtailments or settlements.

Disclosure

There are no specific disclosures required for other long-term employee benefits. However, IAS 1, *Presentation of Financial Statements*, and IAS 24, *Related-Party Disclosures*, may have to be applied.

TERMINATION BENEFITS

Termination benefits are those benefits payable to an employee on account of the employer's decision to terminate the individual's services before the normal agreed period, or on account of an employee's decision to opt for voluntary retirement in exchange for these benefits.

An entity should recognize the termination benefits as a liability and an expense only when the entity is committed either to terminate the employment of an employee or group of employees before the normal agreed period or provide termination benefits as a result of an offer made in order to encourage voluntary withdrawal from the entity.

Under this standard, the commitment of the employer is demonstrated by the employer drawing up a detailed plan for termination, which cannot be withdrawn under normal circumstances. The plan must include the location, function, approximate number of employees to be terminated, termination benefits to be provided and implementation schedule of the plan.

The termination benefits can be paid as a lump sum amount or paid over a period of time as enhanced retirement benefits or continued salary payments for a period of time. At the time that the termination plan is announced, it will be difficult for the employer to determine how many employees will avail of the offer. In this case, the employer must estimate the expense and corresponding liability.

This cost of termination must be expensed in full as the employer does not benefit from the employee's future service.

Disclosure

There are no specific disclosures required for termination benefits. However, IAS 1, *Presentation of Financial Statements*, and IAS 24, *Related-Party Disclosures*, may have to be applied.

EXCERPTS FROM PUBLISHED FINANCIAL STATEMENTS

Holcim Ltd., Annual Report 2008

Accounting Policies

Employee Benefits—Defined Benefit Plans

Some group companies provide defined benefit pension plans for employees. Professionally qualified independent actuaries value the funds on a regular basis. The obligation and costs of pension benefits are determined using the projected unit credit method. The projected unit credit method considers each period of service as giving rise to an additional unit of benefit entitlement and measures each unit separately to build up the final obligation. Past service costs are recognized on a straight line basis over the average period until the amended benefits become vested. Gains or losses on the curtailment or settlement of pension benefits are recognized when the curtailment or settlement occurs.

Actuarial gains or losses are amortized based on the expected average remaining working lives of the participating employees, but only to the extent that the net cumulative unrecognized amount exceeds 10% of the greater of the present value of the defined benefit obligation and the fair value of plan assets at the end of the previous year. The pension obligation is measured at the present value of estimated future cash flows using a discount rate that is similar to the interest rate on high-quality corporate bonds where the currency and terms of the corporate bonds are consistent with the currency and estimated terms of the defined benefit obligation.

A net pension asset is recorded only to the extent that it does not exceed the present value of any economic benefits available in the form of refunds from the plan or reductions in future contributions to the plan and any unrecognized net actuarial losses and past service costs.

Employee Benefits—Defined Contribution Plans

In addition to the defined benefit plans described, some group companies sponsor defined contribution plans based on local practices and regulations. The group's contributions to defined contribution plans are charged to the income statement in the period to which the contributions relate.

Employee Benefits—Other Long-Term Employment Benefits

Other long-term employment benefits include long-service leave or sabbatical leave, medical aid, jubilee or other long-service benefits, long-term disability benefits, and, if they are not payable wholly within 12 months after the year-end, profit sharing, and variable and deferred compensation.

The measurement of these obligations differs from defined benefit plans in that all actuarial gains and losses are recognized immediately and no corridor approach is applied.

Employee Benefits—Equity Compensation Plans

The group operates various equity-settled share-based compensation plans. The fair value of the employee services received in exchange for the grant of the options or shares is recognized as an expense. The total amount to be expensed is determined by reference to the fair value of the equity instruments granted. The amounts are charged to the income statement over the relevant vesting periods and adjusted to reflect actual and expected levels of vesting (Note 33).

HOLCIM Annual Report 2008

Notes to the Financial Statements

32. Employee Benefits

Personnel Expenses

CHF million	2008	2007
Production and distribution	3,079	3,068
Marketing and sales	458	450
Administration	960	**1,040**
Total	**4,497**	**4,558**

Personnel Expenses and Number of Personnel

The Group's total personnel expenses, including social charges, are recognized in the relevant expenditure line by function of the consolidated statement of income and amounted to CHF 4,497 million (2007: 4,558). As of December 31, 2008, the group employed 86,713 people (2007: 89,364).

Defined Benefit Pension Plans

Some Group companies provide pension plans for their employees, which under IFRS are considered as defined benefit pension plans. Provisions for pension obligations are established for benefits payable in the form of retirement, disability, and surviving dependent's pensions. The benefits offered vary according to the legal, fiscal, and economic conditions of each country. Benefits are dependent on years of service and the respective employee's compensation and contribution. A net pension asset is recorded only to the extent that it does not exceed the present value of any economic benefits available in the form of refunds from the plan or reductions in future contributions to the plan and any unrecognized actuarial losses and past service costs. The obligation resulting from the defined benefit pension plans is determined using the projected unit credit method. Unrecognized gains and losses resulting from changes in actuarial assumptions are recognized as income (expense) over the expected average remaining working lives of the participating employees, but only to the extent that the net cumulative unrecognized amount exceeds 10% of the greater of the present value of the defined benefit obligation and the fair value of plan assets at the end of the previous year.

Other Postemployment Benefits

The Group operates a number of other postemployment benefit plans. The method of accounting for these provisions is similar to the one used for defined benefit pension schemes. A number of these plans are not externally funded, but are covered by provisions in the balance sheets.

Group Companies

The following table reconciles the funded, partially funded, and unfunded status of defined benefit plans and other postemployment benefit plans to the amounts recognized in the balance sheet.

Reconciliation of Retirement Benefit Plans to the Balance Sheet

CHF million	2008	2007
Net liability arising from defined benefit pension plans	245	311
Net liability arising from other postemployment benefit plans	79	**81**
Net liability	**324**	**392**
Reflected in the balance sheet as follows:		
Other assets net (Note 24)	(10)	(24)
Defined benefit obligations	334	416
Net liability	**324**	**392**

Retirement Benefit Plans

Reconciliation of Retirement Benefit Plans to the Balance Sheet

CHF millions	Defined benefit pension plans		Other postemployment benefit plans	
	2008	*2007*	*2008*	*2007*
Present value of funded obligations	**2,530**	**3,074**	**0**	**12**
Fair value of plan assets	(2,375)	(3,068)	0	(12)
Plan deficit of funded obligations	**155**	**6**	**0**	**0**
Present value of unfunded obligations	**201**	**218**	**95**	**100**
Unrecognized actuarial losses	(167)	(22)	(16)	(18)
Unrecognized past service costs	(15)	(6)	0	(1)
Unrecognized plan assets	71	115	0	0
Net liability from funded and unfunded plans	**245**	**311**	**79**	**81**
Amounts recognized in the income statement are as follows:				
Current service costs	102	93	2	2
Interest expense on obligations	152	161	6	6
Expected return on plan assets	(161)	(170)	0	0
Amortization of actuarial losses (gains)	33	(34)	1	1
Past service costs	2	(5)	(1)	0
Gains (losses) on curtailments and settlements	4	(2)	(2)	0
Limit of asset ceiling	(21)	52	0	0
Others	1	1	0	0
Total (included in personnel expenses)	**112**	**96**	**6**	**9**
Actual return on plan assets	**(183)**	**188**	**0**	**0**
Present value of defined benefit obligations				
Opening balance as per January 1	**3,292**	**3,435**	**112**	**143**
Current service costs	102	93	2	2
Employees' contributions	25	26	0	0
Interest cost	152	161	6	6
Actuarial (gains) losses	(173)	(176)	1	(3)
Currency translation effects	(449)	(67)	(9)	(7)
Benefits paid	(225)	(180)	(8)	(8)
Past service costs	2	(5)	(1)	0
Change in structure	5	17	(3)	(21)
Curtailments	2	(4)	(5)	0
Settlements	(2)	(8)	0	0
Closing balance as per December 31	**2,731**	**3,292**	**95**	**112**
Fair value of plan assets				
Opening balance as per January 1	3,068	2,939	12	28
Expected return on plan assets	161	170	0	0
Actuarial (losses) gains	(345)	16	0	0
Currency translation effects	(444)	(76)	0	0
Contribution by the employer	115	145	7	8
Contribution by the employees	25	26	0	0
Benefits paid	(203)	(167)	(7)	(8)
Change in structure	0	19	(12)	(16)
Settlements	(2)	(4)	0	0
Closing balance as per December 31	**2,375**	**3,068**	**0**	**12**
Plan assets consist of:				
Equity instruments of Holcim Ltd. or subsidiaries	1	3	0	0
Equity instruments of third parties	745	1,315	0	0
Debt instruments of Holcim Ltd. or subsidiaries	24	34	0	0
Debt instruments of third parties	958	1,161	0	12
Land and buildings occupied or used by third parties	308	362	0	0
Other	339	193	0	0
Total fair value of plan assets	**2,375**	**3,068**	**0**	**12**

CHF millions	Defined benefit pension plans		Other postemployment benefit plans	
	2008	2007	2008	2007
Principal actuarial assumptions used at balance sheet date				
Discount rate	5.3%	5.0%	6.0%	6.2%
Expected return on plan assets	5.4%	5.6%	—	3.0%
Future salary increases 2.8% 3.0%	2.8%	3.0%		
Medical cost trend rate 8.2% 8.3%			8.2%	8.3%

The overall expected rate of return on plan assets is determined based on the market prices prevailing on that date applicable to the period over which the obligation is to be settled.

Experience Adjustments

CHF million	Defined benefit pension plans				Other postemployment benefit plans			
	2008	2007	2006	2005	2008	2007	2006	2005
Present value of defined benefit obligation	2,731	3,292	3,435	3,085	95	112	143	162
Fair value of plan assets	(2,375)	(3,068)	(2,939)	(2,470)	0	(12)	(28)	(12)
Deficit	**356**	**224**	**496**	**615**	**95**	**100**	**115**	**150**
Experience adjustments:								
On plan liabilities	24	(17)	57	112	(3)	3	0	1
On plan assets	(341)	13	76	150	0	0	0	0

Change in Assumed Medical Cost Trend Rate

A 1 percentage point change in the assumed medical cost trend rate would have the following effects:	Increase CHF million 2008	Increase CHF million 2008	Decrease CHF million 2007	Decrease CHF million 2007
– On the aggregate of the current service cost and interest cost components of net periodic postemployment medical costs	1	1	1	1
– On the accumulated postemployment benefit obligations for medical costs	5	5	4	4

Expected contributions by the employer to be paid to the postemployment benefit plans during the annual period beginning after the balance sheet date are CHF 103 million (2007: 139).

14 ACCOUNTING FOR GOVERNMENT GRANTS AND DISCLOSURE OF GOVERNMENT ASSISTANCE (IAS 20)

INTRODUCTION

IAS 20 prescribes the accounting treatment and disclosure of government grants and the disclosure of other forms of government assistance. The standard, however, does not deal with the following:

- Special problems that arise from reflecting the effects of changing prices on financial statements or similar supplementary information;
- Government assistance provided in the form of tax benefits (including income tax holidays, investment tax credits, accelerated depreciation allowances, and concessions in tax rates);
- Government participation in the ownership of the entity; and
- Government grants covered by IAS 41.

KEY TERMS

Government. Government, government agencies, and similar bodies, whether local, national, or international.

Government grants. Government assistance in the form of transfers of resources by government to an entity in return for past or future compliance by the entity with certain conditions relating to the operating activities of the entity. They exclude those forms of government assistance that cannot reasonably be valued and transactions with government that cannot be distinguished from other normal trading transactions of the entity. Government grants are sometimes referred to as subsidies, subventions, and premiums.

Government assistance. The action taken by government to provide an economic benefit specific to an entity or group of entities qualifying under certain criteria. It excludes benefits provided indirectly through actions affecting general trading conditions, such as the provision of infrastructure in development areas or the imposition of trading constraints on competitors.

Fair value. The amount for which an asset could be exchanged between a knowledgeable, willing buyer and a knowledgeable, willing seller in an arm's length transaction.

RECOGNITION OF GOVERNMENT GRANTS

Government grants, including nonmonetary grants at fair value, shall not be recognized until there is reasonable assurance that

- The entity will comply with the conditions attaching to them, and
- The grants will be received.

In respect of government loans received in periods beginning on or after January 1, 2009, the benefit of a government loan received at a rate below the market rate of interest should be considered as a government grant. While the loan shall be recognized and measured in accordance with IAS 39, *Financial Instruments: Recognition and Measurement*, the benefit of the below market rate of interest shall be measured as the difference between the initial carrying value of the loan determined in accordance with IAS 39 and the proceeds received.

PRESENTATION OF GRANTS RELATED TO ASSETS

Government grants are those grants whose primary condition is that an entity qualifying for them should acquire (either purchase or construct) a long-term asset or assets. Subsidiary conditions may also be attached to such grants. Examples of these subsidiary conditions include specifying the type of long-term assets, location of long-term assets, or periods during which the long-term assets are to be acquired or held. Such government grants related to assets, including nonmonetary grants at fair value, shall be presented in the statement of financial position, either by setting up the grant as deferred income or by deducting the grant in arriving at the carrying amount of the asset.

IAS 20 prescribes two methods of presentation in financial statements of grants (or the appropriate portions of grants) related to assets as acceptable alternatives. One method sets up the grant as deferred income, which is recognized as income on a systematic and rational basis over the useful life of the asset. The other method deducts the grant in arriving at the carrying amount of the asset. The grant is recognized as income over the life of a depreciable asset by way of a reduced depreciation charge.

Example 1

XYZ Inc. built a township in an economically backward suburb of the city in which its headquarters are located. It constructed buildings costing $500 million in this township on which investment XYZ Inc. received a government grant of $50 million (based on 10% of the cost of construction). The conditions attached to the grant were that XYZ Inc. should support the township by employing laborers from the suburban area and paying them a minimum wage of $50 per day during the construction of the buildings in the township. The building is depreciated over its useful life of 10 years.

How is this government grant treated in the books of XYZ Inc.?

Solution

IAS 20 prescribes the accounting treatment of government grants that meet the two criteria for recognition, that is, there is reasonable assurance that the entity will comply with the conditions of the grant and the grant is received. The standard lays down two methods of presentation of a government grant relating to assets in the financial statements of the entity that is the recipient of the grant:

1. Under the first method, the grant is presented as a deduction from the gross value of the assets in arriving at its book value. Thus, in this case, only 90% of the cost of the assets (after adjusting the grant against the asset's cost) will be presented as an item of property, plant, and equipment on the financial statements of XYZ Inc.. Therefore, the asset is shown at $450 million ($500 million less $50 million), and the $450 million is depreciated over the period of 10 years at $45 million per annum.
2. Alternatively, under the second method, the government grant can be shown as deferred income on the financial statements of XYZ Inc. and is recognized as income on a systematic and rational basis over the useful life of the asset. In this case, the asset at $500 million and deferred income at $50 million is shown. Each year one-tenth of the asset ($50 million) and the deferred income ($5 million) is drawn down, with the same net effect on income statement at $45 million.

PRESENTATION OF GRANTS RELATED TO INCOME

Grants related to income are sometimes presented as a credit in the statement of comprehensive income, either separately or under a general heading, such as "other income," or they are deducted in reporting the related expense. Both methods are regarded as acceptable for the presentation of grants related to income. Disclosure of the grant may be necessary for a proper understanding of the financial statements. Disclosure of the effect of the grants on any item of income or expense, which is required to be separately disclosed, is usually appropriate.

REPAYMENT OF GOVERNMENT GRANTS

A government grant that becomes repayable shall be accounted for as a change in accounting estimate (see IAS 8, *Accounting Policies, Changes in Accounting Estimates and Errors*). Repayment of a grant related to income shall be applied first against any unamortized deferred credit set up in respect of the grant. To the extent that the repayment exceeds any such deferred credit or where no deferred credit exists, the repayment shall be recognized immediately as an expense. Repayment of a grant related to an asset shall be recorded by increasing the carrying amount of the asset or reducing the deferred income balance by the amount repayable. The cumulative additional depreciation that would have been recognized to date as an expense in the absence of the grant shall be recognized immediately as an expense.

Example 2

MM Ltd. received a government grant of $300 million for acquiring plant and machinery costing $1,500 million during 1999–2000 and having a useful life of 10 years. The grant received was credited to deferred income in the balance sheet, but during 2002–2003, due to noncompliance of the conditions laid down for the grant, the company had to refund the grant to the government. Balance in deferred income in 2002–2003 was $270 million and the written down value of plant and machinery was $1,080 million.

What should be the appropriate treatment of the refund of the grant, the effect on the cost of the plant and machinery, and the amount of depreciation that is charged during the year 2002–2003 in MM Ltd.'s financial statements?

Solution

According to IAS 20, if a government grant becomes refundable (say, due to nonfulfillment of a condition attached to the grant), then the treatment for the refund depends on the treatment accorded to the government grant when it was initially received. In this instance, the grant received was treated as deferred income. Therefore, the refund amount is adjusted against the balance in the deferred income and the balance, if any, left thereafter should be charged to income or loss. In this case, the refund will be charged to deferred income to the extent of the balance remaining; that is, $270 million and the balance refund of $30 million will be charged to profit and loss. There will be no effect on the cost of the plant and machinery and the amount of depreciation charged will be the same as earlier years.

Disclosures

The entity receiving the government grant shall disclose the following:

- The accounting policy adopted for government grants, including the methods of presentation adopted in the financial statements;
- The nature and extent of government grants recognized in the financial statements and an indication of other forms of government assistance from which the entity has directly benefited; and

- Unfulfilled conditions and other contingencies attaching to government assistance that has been recognized.

EXCERPTS FROM PUBLISHED FINANCIAL STATMENTS

Acerinox, S.A., Annual Report 2008

Notes to Financial Statements

Accounting Policies

2.12 Deferred Income

Deferred income includes government grants. Government grants are recognized in the balance sheet as the original amount awarded when there is reasonable assurance they will be received and the group will comply with the conditions attached.

The Group has only received grants in respect of the acquisitions of intangible assets and property, plant and equipment. These are included under noncurrent liabilities and recognized in the income statement on a straight-line basis over the expected lives of the assets for which the grants were received, expect for those relating to CO_2 emission rights which are taken to income in line with the recognition of the corresponding greenhouse gas emission expense.

14. Deferred Income

Movement in outright government grants, which include emission rights received free of charge (see Note 2.6.d) and other capital grants, is as follows:

In thousands of euros	2008	2007
Balance at January 1	**1,350**	1,774
Grants awarded	**8,119**	2,829
Taken to income	**(6,249)**	(3,133)
Translation differences	**55**	(120)
Balance at December 31	**3,275**	1,350

Deferred income includes grants received by North American Stainless, Inc. for investments in fixed assets, as well as amounts in respect of emission rights assigned free of charge in accordance with the national allocation plan which have not been consumed in the present year (see Note 7).

The group considers that it has met or will meet all the conditions for receipt of these grants in the period stipulated and, therefore, no significant contingencies exist in connection with the grants obtained.

16.1 Ordinary Revenues

Details of ordinary revenues in 2008 and 2007 are as follows:

In thousands of euros	2008	2007
Sales of goods	**5,043,991**	6,895,661
Services rendered	**6,580**	6,320
Self-constructed assets	**28,323**	5,256
Operating lease revenue	**446**	447
Revenue from grants and subsidiaries	**691**	**851**
Revenue from disposal of property, plant, and equipment	**451**	2,221
Revenue from subsidies of emission rights	**5,145**	2,282
Other income	**13,756**	6,039
Total	**5,099,383**	6,919,077

15 THE EFFECTS OF CHANGES IN FOREIGN EXCHANGE RATES (IAS 21)

INTRODUCTION

An entity may have foreign operations, deal in foreign currencies, and also present its financial statements in a foreign currency. IAS 21 prescribes the methodologies of (1) translation of foreign currency transactions into functional currency; (2) inclusion of financial elements of foreign operations in the financial statements of an entity; and (3) translation of financial statements into a presentation currency. The primary issues involved are selection of exchange rate(s) and reporting the effects of changes in exchange rates in the financial statements.

SCOPE

The provisions of IAS 21 apply to the following:

- In accounting for transactions and balances in foreign currencies except for those derivative transactions and balances that are within the scope of IAS 39;
- In translating the results and financial position of foreign operations that are included in the financial statements of the entity by consolidation, proportionate consolidation, or the equity method; and
- In translating an entity's results and financial position into a presentation currency.

IAS 39 applies in accounting for currency derivatives and hedge accounting for foreign currency transactions. Moreover, IAS 21 does not apply to the presentation in a statement of cash flows of the cash flows arising from transactions in a foreign currency or to the translation of cash flows of a foreign operation. In these cases, IAS 7 applies.

KEY TERMS

Exchange rate. The ratio of exchange for two currencies.

Closing rate. The spot exchange rate at the end of the reporting period.

Spot exchange rate. The exchange rate for immediate delivery.

Exchange difference. Results from translating a given number of units of one currency into another currency at different exchange rates.

Functional currency. The primary economic environment in which the entity operates.

Presentation currency. The currency in which the financial statements are presented.

Monetary items: Units of currency held and assets and liabilities to be received or paid in a fixed or determinable number of units of currency.

IDENTIFICATION OF FUNCTIONAL CURRENCY

The *functional currency* is the currency of the primary economic environment in which an entity operates. It is identified based on the primary indicators and other indicators as described below. IAS 21, paragraph 9, describes the primary indicators of the functional currency as

1. The currency that mainly influences sales prices for goods and services (this will often be the currency in which sales prices for its goods and services are denominated and settled) and of the country whose competitive forces and regulations mainly determine the sales prices of its goods and services;
2. The currency that mainly influences labor, material, and other costs of providing goods or services (this will often be the currency in which such costs are denominated and settled).

Paragraph 10 in IAS 21 describes the other indicators of the functional currency as

1. The currency in which funds from financing activities, such as issuing debt and equity instruments are generated; and
2. The currency in which receipts from operating activities are usually retained.

Additional factors used to judge if the functional currency of a foreign operation is the same as of the reporting entity can be found in paragraph 1q of IAS 21, which states

1. The activities of the foreign operation are carried out as an extension of the reporting entity rather than being carried out with a significant degree of autonomy;
2. Transactions with the reporting entity are a high proportion of the foreign operation's activities;
3. Cash from operating activities of the foreign operation directly affect the cash flow of the reporting entity and are readily available for remittance; or
4. Cash flows from the activities of the foreign operation are sufficient to service existing and normally expected debt obligations without funds being made available by the reporting entity.

If there is a mixed result arising out of this evaluation, then management would give priority to the indicators stated in paragraph 9 of IAS 21.

An entity's functional currency reflects the underlying transactions, events, and conditions that are relevant to it. Therefore, an entity has to determine its functional currency, and once it is determined the functional currency is not changed unless there is a change in those underlying transactions, events, and conditions.

NET INVESTMENT IN A FOREIGN OPERATION

A *foreign operation* is an entity that is a subsidiary, associate, joint venture, or branch of a reporting entity, the activities of which are based or conducted in a country or currency other than those of the reporting entity.

An entity often has amounts due from foreign operations in the form of loans or receivables. An item for which settlement is neither planned nor likely to occur in the foreseeable future is, in substance, a part of the entity's net investment in that foreign operation. It includes long-term loans granted by another subsidiary of the entity to the foreign operation, but it excludes trade receivables or trade payables.

Translation of Foreign Currency Transactions into the Functional Currency

The steps to be taken for currency translation under IAS 21 are as follows:

1. Identify the functional currency; and
2. Translate all foreign currency transactions into the functional currency as explained here:

a. All foreign currency transactions of buying/selling of goods and services, other operating income or expense, money borrowed or repaid, assets purchased or sold are translated into the functional currency of the entity by applying the spot exchange rate at the date of the transaction.

   For practical reasons, a rate that approximates the actual rate at the date of the transaction is often used, for example, an average rate for a week or a month might be used for all transactions in each foreign currency occurring during that period. But in periods of highly volatile exchange rates, use of an average rate is inappropriate.

b. The translation subsequent to the previous initial recognition is carried out at the end of each reporting period as follows:

   •   Monetary items in foreign currency are translated applying the closing rate;
   •   Nonmonetary items in foreign currency, which are carried at cost, are translated applying the exchange rate of the date of the transaction; and
   •   Nonmonetary items in foreign currency, which are carried at revalued amount (fair value), are translated applying the exchange rate of the date of revaluation (fair value determination).

   The carrying amount of a nonmonetary item is determined in accordance with the appropriate standard. For example, according to IAS 16, the carrying amount of property, plant, and equipment may be determined at cost or revalued amount. For the purpose of this standard, irrespective of the method of measurement adopted, if the value of the asset is determined in a foreign currency, it must be translated into the functional currency in accordance with the provisions of IAS 21. Similarly, for some other nonmonetary items, like inventories, the carrying amount is decided by applying IAS 2, *Inventories*, which requires the lower of the cost and net realizable value. In this case also, the carrying amount of such nonmonetary assets is first determined applying the appropriate standard and then the provisions of IAS 21 are applied. (See example 3.)

In the case of monetary items, except those that are part of net investments in foreign operations, the gain or loss on settlement or translation at the end of each reporting period is recognized in the profit or loss of the period.

Translation Principles for Financial Assets and Liabilities of a Foreign Operation

In the above case, the following occurs:

•   The monetary financial assets and liabilities are initially measured at fair value, amortized cost, or cost in the functional currency of the foreign operation. These are then translated applying the closing exchange rate; and
•   The nonmonetary financial assets (such as investment in equity instruments) are translated using the closing rate if it is carried at fair value in the foreign currency. In case it is not carried at fair value in accordance with IAS 39, it is translated at a historical rate, since its fair value cannot be reliably measured (such as investment in unlisted equity shares).

An exception to this principle is the exposure to changes in foreign currency rates under IAS 39 in the case of the translation of a financial asset or financial liability, which is designated as a hedged item in a fair value hedge.

Exchange differences arising because of a net investment in a foreign operation are accounted for in the profit or loss in the separate or individual financial statements of the investor, whereas it is charged to other comprehensive income in the consolidated financial statements (the financial statements that include the foreign operation).

When several exchange rates are available, the rate used is that at which the future cash flows represented by the transaction or balance could have been settled if those cash flows had occurred at the measurement date. If exchangeability between two currencies is temporarily lacking, the rate used is the first subsequent rate at which exchanges could be made.

Example 1: Currency Transaction That Is Settled During the Same Accounting Period

XYZ Limited, whose functional currency is €, buys raw materials invoiced at US $10,000 on January 1, 2008. This is a credit transaction. Exchange rate €1 = US $1.47.

XYZ Limited records this transaction as follows:

Dr. Purchases   6,803
    Cr. Creditors   6,803
To record transaction for US $10,000 at exchange rate of €1 = US $1.47.

Now suppose that the entity pays to the creditors US $10,000 on March 1, 2008. Exchange rate € 1 = US $1.52.

Dr. Creditors   6,803
    Cr. Bank   6,579
    Cr. Exchange gain   224
To record payment of US $10,000 at exchange rate €1 = US $1.52.

Exchange gain/loss is credited/charged to profit or loss.

Example 2: Mark to Market Valuation of Outstanding Monetary Item on the Reporting Date

XYZ Limited, whose functional currency is €, buys raw materials invoiced at US $10,000 on April 1, 2008. This is a credit transaction. Exchange rate €1 = US $1.58.

XYZ Limited records this transaction as follows:

Dr. Purchases   6,329
    Cr. Creditors   6,329
To record transaction for US $10,000 at exchange rate of €1 = US $1.58.

Now suppose that the entity did not settle the creditors of US $10,000 on June 30, 2008, which is the second quarter reporting date. At June 30, 2008, the exchange rate is €1 = US $1.52. XYZ Limited has to value the amount due to the creditors, which is a monetary item, by applying the closing exchange rate of the reporting date.

Dr. Exchange fluctuation loss   250
    Cr. Creditors   250

By this, the creditor is valued at US $10,000/1.52, or €6,579.

To record exchange rate fluctuation to June 30, 2008, (10,000/1.52) –6,329
Exchange fluctuation gain/loss is credited/charged to profit or loss.

Example 3: Valuation of Inventories

The cost of inventories of the foreign operation of an Indian company is US $10,000. Based on the exchange rate on the date of purchase of inventories (US $1 = Rs. 50.00), the cost of inventories in functional currency is Rs. 500,000.

The net realizable value (NRV) is US $10,100, which is translated at the closing exchange rate of US $1 = Rs. 48.00 as Rs. 484,000.

In the foreign currency valuation, cost in US$ is lower than the net realizable value; therefore, the inventories are valued at cost $10,000, even though, if cost and NRV are compared after translation, NRV is lower in the functional currency, that is, Rs. 484,000.

Cost information is translated using the exchange rate on the date of a transaction whereas NRV is translated at the closing exchange rate. NRV may be lower than the cost after translation because the exchange rate falls below the exchange rate on the date of the transaction.

According to paragraph 24 of IAS 21, the carrying amount of a nonmonetary asset is first determined applying the appropriate standard then IAS 21 is applied. In this case, the translated value of the inventories should be Rs. 500,000.

The difference of Rs. 16,000 is accounted for as an impairment loss, recognized in the functional currency.

Interaction Between IAS 21 and IAS 39: Segregation of Fair Value Gain/Loss from Translation Difference

Paragraphs 32 and 48 of IAS 21 require that all exchange differences resulting from translating the financial statements of a foreign operation are recognized in other comprehensive income until disposal of the net investment. Exchange differences arising from financial instruments carried at fair value are also part of such translation difference. Financial assets/liabilities classified as at fair value through profit or loss (FVTPL) and financial assets that are available for sale are the financial instruments that need discussion here. This is because there exists a fair value gain or loss component that, according to paragraph 55 of IAS 39, should be recognized in profit or loss, so far as financial instruments designated as at fair value through profit or loss, or held for trading are concerned. Changes in fair value of available-for-sale investments should be recognized in other comprehensive income.

This accounting is illustrated in paragraph E.3.3 of guidance on implementing IAS 39.

Example 4

X Limited is a U.S. subsidiary of ABC Limited, an Indian company. As on December 31, 2007, X Limited had fair value through profit and loss (FVTPL) account financial assets of US $2,000 and the closing exchange rate was US $1 = Rs. 39.44. ABC Limited has translated these assets applying the spot exchange rate. FVTPL account financial assets were carried at Rs. 78,880.

As on December 31, 2008, the exchange rate was US $1 = Rs. 49.72. Meanwhile, the fair value of the FVTPL account financial assets has declined to US $1,000.

According to paragraph E3.3 of the guidance on implementing IAS 39

Fair value loss	=	US $1,000 × Average exchange rate (44.58)
	=	Rs. 44,580 to be charged to profit or loss
Translation difference	=	[US $1,000 × 49.72 – Rs. 78,800] – (–44,580)
	=	+ Rs. 15,420 to be credited to other comprehensive income
Total difference	=	Translated value as on December 31, 2008

$$\text{US } \$1,000 \times 49.72 = 49{,}720$$

Translated value as on December 31, 2007 $= \underline{78{,}880}$

$$-29{,}160$$

Of which:

Fair value loss	=	– Rs. 44,580
Translation gain	=	+ Rx. 15,420

Use of Presentation Currency Other Than Functional Currency

The presentation currency is the currency in which financial statements are presented. An entity may present its financial statements in any currency (or currencies).

The three steps for translation of functional currency into presentation currency are as follows:

1. Assets and liabilities for each statement of financial position presented (including comparatives) shall be translated at the closing rate at the date of that statement of financial position;
2. Income and expenses for each statement of comprehensive income or separate income statement presented (including comparatives) shall be translated at exchange rates at the dates of the transactions; and
3. All resulting exchange differences shall be recognized in other comprehensive income.

However, when the financial statements of the foreign operation are translated into the presentation currency, exchange differences on monetary items (other than those representing the net investment in foreign operation) are accounted for in profit or loss.

Change in Functional Currency

When there is a change in the entity's functional currency, the entity shall translate all the items into the new functional currency using the exchange rate at the date of the change. The resulting translated amounts are then treated as their historical costs. The exchange differences that have arisen from translation of foreign operations and have been previously recognized in other comprehensive income must not be reclassified from equity to profit or loss until such time as the operations are disposed.

Disposal of Foreign Operations

When foreign operations are disposed of entirely, the total amount of exchange differences relating to that foreign operation that is recognized in other comprehensive income and included in the separate component of equity must be reclassified from equity to the profit or loss at the time the gain or loss on disposal is recognized.

If the entity loses control or significant influence over a former subsidiary, associate, or joint controlled operation that has a foreign operation, the above accounting treatment is adopted, even if the entity continues to retain an interest in the subsidiary, associate, or joint controlled operations.

When the subsidiary that has foreign operations is disposed of partially, the proportionate share of the total amount of exchange differences that is recognized in other comprehensive income must be allocated to the noncontrolling interests in that foreign operation. In other cases of partial disposal of a foreign operation, the proportionate share of the total amount of exchange differences recognized in other comprehensive income must be allocated to profit or loss.

Disclosures

The disclosures relating to currency translation are set out in paragraphs 51–57 of IAS 21:

Disclosures regarding current translation difference charged to income statement and other comprehensive income

- The amount of exchange differences recognized in profit or loss except for those arising on financial instruments measured at fair value through profit or loss in accordance with IAS 39; and
- Net exchange differences recognized in other comprehensive income and accumulated in a separate component of equity and a reconciliation of the amount of such exchange differences at the beginning and end of the period.

Disclosures when presentation currency is different from functional currency

• Disclose the fact together with disclosure of the functional currency and the reason for using a different presentation currency.

Disclosures when an entity presents financial statements in a currency other than the functional currency

• The entity has to disclose the fact that the financial statements comply with requirements of IFRS after ensuring the compliance of all the provisions of IFRS, including the translation methods that are detailed in paragraphs 39 and 42 of IAS 21.

Disclosures when an entity displays financial statement or statements in a currency other than the functional currency or presentation currency and does not comply with the requirements of IFRS as required in paragraph 55 of IAS 21

• The entity has to clearly identify the information as supplementary information to distinguish it from the information that complies with IFRS;
• The entity must disclose the currency in which such supplementary information is displayed; and
• The entity must also disclose the functional currency and the method of translation used to determine the supplementary information.

EXCERPTS FROM PUBLISHED FINANCIAL STATEMENTS

Holcim, Annual Report 2008

Notes to Financial Statements

Accounting Principles and Policies

Foreign Currency Translation

Income statements of foreign entities are translated into the group's reporting currency at average exchange rates for the year and balance sheets are translated at exchange rates ruling on December 31.

Goodwill arising on the acquisition of a foreign entity is expressed in the functional currency of the foreign operation and is translated at the closing rate.

Foreign currency transactions are accounted for at the exchange rates prevailing at the date of the transactions; gains and losses resulting from the settlement of such transactions and from the translation of monetary assets and liabilities denominated in foreign currencies are recognized in the income statement, except when deferred in equity as qualifying cash flow hedges.

Exchange differences arising on monetary items that form part of an entity's net investment in a foreign operation are reclassified to equity (currency translation adjustment) in the consolidated financial statements and are only released to the income statement on the disposal of the foreign operation. The individual financial statements of each of the group's entities are measured using the currency of the primary economic environment in which the entity operates (the functional currency).

Lectra Group, Annual Report 2008

Notes to the Consolidated Financial Statements

Accounting Principles and Policies

Translation Methods

Translation of Financial Statements of Foreign Subsidiaries

Most subsidiaries' functional currency is the local currency, which corresponds to the currency in which the majority of their transactions are denominated.

Accounts of foreign companies are translated as follows:

- Assets and liabilities are translated at the official year-end closing rates;
- Reserves and retained earnings are translated at historical rates;
- Income statement items are translated at the average monthly exchange rates for the year for revenues and cost of products and services sold, and at the annual average rate for all other income statement items, other than in the case of material transactions;
- Items in the cash flow statement are translated at the annual average exchange rate. Thus, movements in short-term assets and liabilities are not directly comparable with the corresponding balance sheet movements, due to the currency translation impact, which is shown under a separate heading in the cash flow statement "Effect of changes in foreign exchange rates"; and
- Gains or losses arising from the translation of the net assets of foreign consolidated subsidiaries and those derived from the use of average exchange rates to determine income or loss, are recognized under currency translation adjustment in shareholders' equity, and therefore have no impact on earnings unless all or part of the corresponding investments are divested. They are adjusted to reflect long-term unrealized gains or losses on internal group positions.

Translation of Balance Sheet Items Denominated in Foreign Currencies

Third Party Receivables and Payables. Foreign currency receivables and payables are booked at the average exchange rate for the month in which they are recorded and may be hedged.

Receivables and payables denominated in foreign currencies are translated at the December 31 exchange rate. Unrealized differences arising from the translation of foreign currencies appear in the income statement. Where a currency has been hedged forward, the translation adjustment reflected on the income statement is offset by the variation in fair value of the hedging instrument.

Intercompany Receivables and Payables. Translation differences on short-term receivables and payables are included in net income using the same procedure as for third party receivables and payables.

Unrealized translation gains or losses on long term assets and liabilities, whose settlement is neither scheduled nor probable in the foreseeable future, are recorded as a component of shareholders' equity under the heading "Currency translation adjustment" and have no impact on net income, in compliance with the paragraph "Net Investment in a Foreign Operation" of IAS 21.

Exchange rate for major currencies (equivalent value in euros)

	2008	2007
U.S. dollar		
Annual average rate	1.47	1.37
Closing rate	1.39	1.47
Japanese yen (100)		
Annual average rate	1.52	1.61
Closing rate	1.26	1.65
British pound		
Annual average rate	0.80	0.68
Closing rate	0.95	0.73
Canadian dollar		
Annual average rate	1.56	1.47
Closing rate	1.70	1.44
Hong Kong dollar		
Annual average rate	11.45	10.69
Closing rate	10.78	11.48
Chinese yuan		
Annual average rate	10.22	10.42
Closing rate	9.50	10.75

16 BORROWING COSTS (IAS 23)

INTRODUCTION

The objective of IAS 23 is to prescribe the accounting treatment for borrowing costs. This standard does not deal with the actual or imputed cost of owners' equity, including preferred capital that is not classified as a liability.

KEY TERMS

Borrowing costs. Interest and other costs incurred by an entity in connection with the borrowing of funds.

Qualifying asset. An asset that takes a substantial period of time to get ready for its intended use or sale.

RECOGNITION

Borrowing costs that are directly attributable to the acquisition, construction, or production of a qualifying asset should be capitalized as part of the cost of that asset.

Examples of Borrowing Costs

- Interest and charges on bank borrowings and other short-term and long-term borrowings
- Finance charges in respect of assets acquired under finance leases or under other similar arrangements
- Exchange differences arising from foreign currency borrowings to the extent that they are regarded as an adjustment to interest costs

Borrowing costs are capitalized as part of the cost of a qualifying asset when it is probable that they will result in future economic benefits to the entity and the costs can be measured reliably. Other borrowing costs are recognized as an expense in the period in which they are incurred.

The main qualifying criterion for a qualifying asset is that it requires a substantial period of time to set up and get ready for its intended sale or use. Therefore, the cost of the asset is not a factor for consideration. Assets that are already ready for their intended use or sale, or that can be purchased readily, are *not* qualifying assets.

Examples of Qualifying Assets

- Manufacturing plants
- Power generation facilities
- Investment properties

Generally, inventories that are manufactured or produced during the course of regular operations over a short period of time are not qualifying assets. However, inventories that require a substantial period of time to bring them to a saleable condition can be regarded as qualifying assets for the purposes of this standard.

BORROWING COSTS ELIGIBLE FOR CAPITALIZATION

Borrowing costs can be incurred for specific or general purposes. The borrowing costs that are eligible for capitalisation are based on the direct relationship that can be established between the borrowings and the qualifying asset.

Specific Borrowing

When an entity specifically borrows funds for the purpose of obtaining a particular qualifying asset, the borrowing costs that are directly related to that qualifying asset can be readily identified. Therefore, when funds are borrowed specifically for the purpose of obtaining a qualifying asset, the amount of borrowing costs that are eligible for capitalization should be the amount of actual borrowing costs incurred on such borrowing during the period, less any income earned on the temporary investment of those borrowings.

General Borrowing

When the financing activity of an enterprise is coordinated centrally or a range of debt instruments are used to borrow funds at varying rates of interest, such borrowings cannot be readily identifiable with a specific qualifying asset. As a result, the exercise of judgment is required to determine the amount of borrowing costs that are directly attributable to the acquisition, construction, or production of that qualifying asset.

To the extent that funds are borrowed generally and are used for the purpose of obtaining a qualifying asset, the amount of borrowing costs eligible for capitalization should be determined by applying a capitalization rate to the expenditure on that asset. The capitalization rate in such cases should be the weighted average of the borrowing costs applicable to the borrowings of the enterprise that are outstanding during the period, other than borrowings made specifically for the purpose of obtaining a qualifying asset. However, the amount of borrowing costs capitalized during a period should not exceed the actual amount of borrowing costs incurred during that period.

Treatment of Excess of Carrying Amount over Recoverable Amount

When the carrying amount or the expected ultimate cost of the qualifying asset exceeds its recoverable amount or net realizable value (NRV), the carrying amount should be written down or written off in accordance with the requirements of other standards (IAS 36, *Impairment of Assets*).

COMMENCEMENT OF CAPITALIZATION

The capitalization of borrowing costs as part of the cost of a qualifying asset should commence when all the following conditions are satisfied:

- Expenditure for the acquisition, construction, or production of a qualifying asset is being incurred;
- Borrowing costs are being incurred; and
- Activities that are necessary to prepare the asset for its intended use or sale are in progress.

The activities necessary to prepare the asset for its intended use or sale can exceed the period of the physical construction of the asset. They include technical and administrative work prior to the commencement of the physical construction, such as obtaining permits and so on. However, such activities exclude the holding of an asset when no production or development that changes the asset's condition is taking place.

Example 1

Borrowing cost may be incurred while land is under development during the period in which activities related to development are being undertaken.

In such cases, borrowing costs incurred include the cost of obtaining permits, since the land acquired for building purposes is held without any associated development activity taking place.

SUSPENSION OF CAPITALIZATION

The capitalization of borrowing costs should be suspended during extended periods in which active development is interrupted. This will depend on the facts of each situation.

Example 2

Borrowing costs may be incurred during an extended period in which the construction activity of a building is stopped because of an economic downturn. In such cases, the capitalization of borrowing costs should be suspended.

Borrowing costs may be incurred during a period in which the construction activity of a building is stopped because of substantial technical and administrative work being carried out. In such cases, the capitalization of borrowing costs should not be suspended.

Borrowing costs may be incurred during a period in which the construction activity of a bridge is stopped because of high water levels that are common during the construction period in the geographic region. In such cases, the capitalization of borrowing costs should not be suspended.

CESSATION OF CAPITALIZATION

Capitalization of borrowing costs should cease when substantially all the activities necessary to prepare the qualifying asset for its intended use or sale are complete. An asset is normally ready for its intended use or sale when its physical construction or production is complete even though routine administrative work might still continue. If minor modifications, such as the decoration of a property to the user's specification, are all that are outstanding, this indicates that substantially all the activities are complete.

When the construction of a qualifying asset is completed in parts and a completed part is capable of being used while construction continues for the other parts, capitalization of borrowing costs in relation to a part should cease when substantially all the activities necessary to prepare that part for its intended use or sale are complete.

Disclosures

The financial statements should disclose the following:

- The amount of borrowing costs capitalized during the period; and
- The rate of capitalization used to determine the amount of borrowing costs that are eligible for capitalization.

Example 3

Concorde Inc. obtained a term loan during the year ended December 31, 2008, amounting to $650 million for modernization and development of its factory. During the year, buildings costing $120 million were completed and plant and machinery amounting to $350 million were installed. A sum of $70 million has been given as a capital commitments advance for assets, the installation of which is expected in the following year. The amount of $110 million has been utilized for working capital requirements.

Interest incurred on the loan of $650 million during the year ended December 31, 2008, amounted to $58.5 million.

How should the interest amount of $58.5 million be treated in the financial statements of XYZ Inc.?

Solution

Interest incurred amounting to $58.5 million should be apportioned using the amounts of loan utilized for various purposes. Except for the portion of the loan that was used for working capital requirements ($110 million), the rest was utilized for the construction of qualifying assets, and therefore the borrowing costs eligible for capitalization will be calculated as $(650 − 110)/650 × 58.5 million = $48.6 million.

Example 4

During May 2007, Hitech Trading Limited obtained a bank loan to be used for the purposes of the construction of a new office tower. The construction was completed in September 2008 and the building was placed in service immediately thereafter. Interest on the actual amount used for construction of the building until its completion was $20 million, whereas the total interest incurred on the bank loan for the period ended December 31, 2008, amounted to $25 million.

Can it be argued that the entire $25 million be treated as eligible borrowing costs that can be capitalized along with the cost of the office tower building since the loan was specifically taken for the purposes of construction of the building?

Solution

According to IAS 23, *Borrowing Costs*, capitalization of borrowing costs should cease when substantially all the activities necessary to prepare the qualifying asset for its intended use or sale are complete. Therefore, interest on the amount that has been used for the construction of the building up to the date of its completion (September 2008) amounting to $20 million alone can be capitalized.

EXCERPTS FROM PUBLISHED FINANCIAL STATEMENTS

Ahold, Annual Report 2008

Notes to Consolidated Financial Statements

3.   Significant Accounting Policies

Items of property, plant, and equipment are stated at cost less accumulated depreciation and impairment losses. Cost includes expenditures that are directly attributable to the acquisition or construction of an asset and includes borrowing costs incurred during construction. Where applicable, estimated asset retirement costs are added to the cost of an asset. Subsequent expenditures are capitalized only when it is probable that future economic benefits associated with the item will flow to the company and the costs can be measured reliably. All other subsequent expenditures represent repairs and maintenance and are expensed as incurred.

11.   Property, Plant, and Equipment (Extract)

The additions to property, plant, and equipment include capitalized borrowing costs of EUR 4 million (2007: EUR 6 million). Generally, the capitalization rate used to determine the amount of capitalized borrowing costs is a weighted average of the interest rate applicable to the respective operating companies. This rate ranged between 5.8–8.4% (2007: 4.3–6.7%). Other movements include transfers to and from investment property.

17 RELATED-PARTY DISCLOSURES (IAS 24)

INTRODUCTION

While related-party transactions are a normal and common feature of business and commerce, in some cases, entities may enter into transactions with related parties at terms that unrelated parties might not enter into under normal circumstances. In order to ensure transparency in financial reporting, most accounting standards around the world prescribe disclosures of transactions with related parties.

The objective of IAS 24 is to ensure that an entity's financial statements contain the disclosures necessary to draw attention to the possibility that its financial position and profit or loss may have been affected by the existence of related parties and by transactions and outstanding balances with such parties.

KEY TERMS

Related parties. Parties are considered to be related if one party has the ability to control the other party or to exercise significant influence or joint control over the other party in making financial and operating decisions. A party is related to an entity if

1. The party, directly or indirectly through one or more intermediaries, does the following:

    a. Controls, is controlled by, or is under common control with the entity (this includes parents, subsidiaries, and fellow subsidiaries);
    b. Has an interest in the entity that gives it significant influence over the entity; or
    c. Has joint control over the entity;

2. The party is an associate (as defined in IAS 28, *Investments in Associates*) of the entity;
3. The party is a joint venture in which the entity is a venturer (see IAS 31, *Interests in Joint Ventures*);
4. The party is a member of the key management personnel of the entity or its parent;
5. The party is a close member of the family of any individual referred to in (1) or (4);
6. The party is an entity that is controlled, jointly controlled or significantly influenced by or for which significant voting power in such entity resides with, directly or indirectly, any individual referred to in (4) or (5); or
7. The party is a post-employment benefit plan for the benefit of employees of the entity or of any entity that is a related party of the entity.

Close members of the family of an individual. Family members who may be expected to influence, or be influenced by, that individual in their dealings with the entity. They include the individual's domestic partner and children, children of individual's domestic partner, and dependents of the individual or the individual's domestic partner.

Related-party transaction. A transfer of resources, services, or obligations between related parties, regardless of whether a price is charged.

Key management personnel. Persons who have the authority and responsibility for planning, directing, and controlling the activities of the entity, directly or indirectly, including all directors (whether executive or otherwise).

Compensation. All employee benefits (as described in IAS 19, *Employee Benefits*, and IFRS 2, *Share-Based Payment*) and also includes all forms of consideration paid, payable or provided by or on behalf the entity in return for services rendered to the entity.

SUBSTANCE OVER FORM

IAS 24 stresses that in considering possible related-party transactions, particular attention should be given to substance of the relationship and not merely its legal form. It is in this context that the standard notes that the following are not necessarily related-party transactions despite their legal form. In other words, the standard scopes out certain related parties and categorically identifies the following as not to be related parties:

- Two entities simply because they have a director or key manager in common;
- Two venturers who share joint control over a joint venture;
- Providers of finance, trade unions, public utilities, government departments, and agencies in the course of their normal dealings with an entity; and
- A single customer, supplier, franchiser, distributor, or general agent with whom an enterprise transacts a significant volume of business merely by virtue of the resulting economic dependence.

Disclosures

Relationships between parents and subsidiaries. Regardless of whether there have been transactions between a parent and a subsidiary, an entity must disclose the name of its parent and, if different, the ultimate controlling party. If neither the entity's parent nor the ultimate controlling party produces financial statements available for public use, the name of the next most senior parent that does so must also be disclosed.

Management compensation. Disclose key management personnel compensation in total and for each of the following categories:

- Short-term employee benefits
- Post-employment benefits
- Other long-term benefits
- Termination benefits
- Equity compensation benefits

Related-party transactions. If there have been transactions between related parties, disclose the nature of the related party relationship as well as information about the transactions and outstanding balances necessary for an understanding of the potential effect of the relationship on the financial statements.

These disclosures would be made separately for each category of related party and would include the following:

- The amount of the transactions;
- The amount of outstanding balances, including terms and conditions and guarantees;
- Provisions for doubtful debts related to the amount of outstanding balances; and
- Expense recognized during the period in respect of bad or doubtful debts due from related parties.

Examples of Transactions That Are Disclosed If They Are with a Related Party

- Purchases or sales of goods
- Purchases or sales of property and other assets
- Rendering or receiving of services
- Leases
- Transfers of research and development
- Transfers under license agreements
- Transfers under finance arrangements (including loans and equity contributions in cash or in kind)
- Provision of guarantees or collateral
- Settlement of liabilities on behalf of the entity or by the entity on behalf of another party

A statement that related party transactions were made on terms equivalent to those that prevail in arm's length transactions should be made only if such terms can be substantiated.

Example 1

Exuberance Inc. made sales amounting to $180 million to Hush Hush Inc. during the financial year ended December 31, 2008. The Chief Executive Officer (CEO) of Exuberance Inc. is the sole owner of Hush Hush Inc.. The sales were made to Hush Hush Inc. at normal selling prices without any preferential treatment given to it by Exuberance Inc. vis-à-vis its other customers.

The Chief Financial Officer (CFO) of Exuberance Inc. is of the view that since these sales were on normal selling prices, there is no need for any disclosure under IFRS. Is the contention of the CFO in line with requirements of IAS 24?

Solution

According to IAS 24, *Related-Party Disclosures*, entities over which a key management personnel is able to exercise significant influence are related parties. This would therefore cover transactions with entities owned by the CEO, who is one of the key management personnel. Hence, disclosure of this transaction is required, irrespective of whether the transaction was done at normal selling price. Therefore, the contention of the CFO of Exuberance Inc. is not in line with IAS 24.

Example 2

Restless Inc. is a listed company and believes in full transparency and accurate disclosure of related-party transactions in its financial statements prepared under IFRS. The company is concerned that, compared to its peers, it may be perceived as having paid too much to its CEO. However, the board of directors, in line with their company's clean reputation, decide to disclose all transactions with the CEO.

Remuneration and other payments made to the entity's CEO during the year 20XX were

- An annual salary of $3 million
- Share options and other share-based payments valued at $2 million
- Contributions to retirement benefit plan amounting to $3 million
- Reimbursement of his travel expenses for business trips totalling $2.5 million

Which transactions, if any, are to be disclosed under IAS 24?

Solution

For the year ended December 31, 20XX, transactions with the CEO, a key management personnel member, that should be disclosed under IAS 24 are as follows:

Short term benefits (salary)	$3 million
Post-employment benefits (retirement benefit plan contribution)	$3 million
Share-based payments (e.g., stock options)	$2 million
Total	$8 million

Reimbursement of his travel expenses for business trips totalling $2.5 million need not be disclosed, as it is not part of his compensation.

RECENT AMENDMENTS TO THE STANDARD (NOVEMBER 2009)

The following amendments have been recently made to the definition of a related party and to the disclosure requirements for government-related entities:

- In the definition of a *related party*, an associate includes subsidiaries of the associate and a joint venture includes subsidiaries of the joint venture. Therefore, for example, an associate's subsidiary and the investor that has significant influence over the associate are related to each other.

The following additional terms have been defined in the amendment:

- *Government* refers to government, government agencies, and similar bodies, whether local, national, or international.
- A *government-related entity* is controlled, jointly controlled, or significantly influenced by a government.

Contrary to the present requirements, an entity is exempt from the disclosure requirements in relation to related-party transactions, outstanding balances, and commitments with the following:

- A government that has control, joint control, or significant influence over the reporting entity; and
- Another entity that is a related party because the same government has control, joint control, or significant influence over both the reporting entity and the other entity.

In such cases, the reporting entity shall disclose the following about the transactions and related outstanding balances:

- The name of the government and the nature of its relationship with the reporting entity;
- The nature and amount of each individually significant transaction in required detail that will enable users of the entity's financial statements to understand the effect of related party transactions on its financial statements; and
- For other transactions that are collectively but not individually significant, a qualitative or quantitative indication of their extent.

For the purpose of determining the level of details to be disclosed, the reporting entity should consider the closeness of the related party relationship and the following relevant factors to establish the level of significance of the transaction:

- Significant in terms of size
- Carried out on nonmarket terms
- Outside normal day-to-day business operations, such as the purchase and sale of businesses
- Disclosed to regulatory or supervisory authorities
- Reported to senior management
- Subject to shareholder approval

These revisions in this standard are effective for annual periods beginning on or after January 1, 2011, with earlier application permitted.

EXCERPTS FROM PUBLISHED FINANCIAL STATEMENTS

Barloworld, Annual Report 2008

Notes to the Consolidated Annual Financial Statements for the Year Ended September 30

41. Related-Party Transactions

Various transactions are entered into by the company and its subsidiaries during the year with related parties. Unless specifically disclosed, these transactions occurred under terms that are no less favorable than those entered into with third parties. Intragroup transactions are eliminated on consolidation.

The following is a summary of other transactions with related parties during the year and balances due at year-end.

R million	Associates of the group	Joint ventures in which the group is a venturer
2008		
Goods and services sold to		
Bartrac Equipment		87
The Used Equipment Company (Pty) Limited		9
Vostochnaya Technica UK		7
Energyst B.V.	3	
Barloworld Heftruck Verhuur B.V.		12
PhakisaWorld Fleet Solutions		101
	3	216
Goods and services purchased from		
The Used Equipment Company (Pty) Limited		94
Barloworld Heftruck Verhuur B.V.		29
		123
Other transactions		
Management fees received from joint ventures		11
		11
Amounts due from related parties as at end of year		
Vostochnaya Technica Siberia loan		275
PhakisaWorld Fleet Solutions loan		221
Other loans to joint venturers		10
		506
2007		
Goods and services sold to		
Barzem Enterprises (Pty) Limited	26	
Du Pont Barloworld (Pty) Limited (Herberts)	89	
International Paints (Pty) Limited	38	
NMI Durban South Motors (Pty) Limited		8
Sizwe Paints (Pty) Limited	20	
The Used Equipment Company (Pty) Limited		34
PhakisaWorld Fleet Solutions	39	
Other sales to related parties	6	
	218	42
Goods and services purchased from		
NMI Durban South Motors (Pty) Limited		4
Du Pont Barloworld (Pty) Limited (Herberts)	4	
	4	4

Other transactions

Management fees received from associates	4	—
	4	—

Amounts due to/from related parties as at end of year

Barzem Enterprises (Pty) Limited	(15)	
Du Pont Barloworld (Pty) Limited (Herberts)	9	
International Paints (Pty) Limited	10	
NMI Durban South Motors (Pty) Limited		1
PhakisaWorld Fleet Solutions	22	
PhakisaWorld Fleet Solutions loan	184	
The Used Equipment Company (Pty) Limited		127
Vostochnaya Technica Siberia loan		100
Other loans to associates	19	—
	229	228

2006

Goods and services sold to

Barzem Enterprises (Pty) Limited	25	
Du Pont Barloworld (Pty) Limited (Herberts)	76	
International Paints (Pty) Limited	31	
Mine Support Products (Pty) Limited	31	
NMI Durban South Motors (Pty) Limited		7
Sizwe Paints (Pty) Limited	18	
The Used Equipment Company (Pty) Limited		4
Umndeni Circon (Pty) Limited	78	
Other sales to related parties	3	1
	262	12

Goods and services purchased from

NMI Durban South Motors (Pty) Limited		5
Umndeni Circon (Pty) Limited	11	
The Used Equipment Co (Pty) Limited		2
International Paints (Pty) Limited	1	—
	12	7

Other transactions

Management fees received from associates	8	—
	8	—

Amounts due to/from related parties as at end of year

Barzem Enterprises (Pty) Limited	(11)	
Du Pont Barloworld (Pty) Limited (Herberts)	11	
Finaltair Barloworld SA		98
International Paints (Pty) Limited	18	
Mine Support Products (Pty) Limited	5	
Sizwe Paints (Pty) Limited	3	
The Used Equipment Company (Pty) Limited		139
Umndeni Circon (Pty) Limited	18	
Loans and other trade-related amounts due from related parties	2	—
	46	237

Terms on other outstanding balances

- Unless otherwise noted, all outstanding balances are payable within 30 days, unsecured and not guaranteed.
- Except for the impairment of the Finaltair loan, there are no doubtful debt provisions raised in respect of amounts due to/from related parties and no bad debts incurred during the year on these balances.

Associates and joint ventures

- The loans to associates and joint ventures are repayable on demand and bears interest at market related rates.
- The loan to Finaltair was fully impaired during 2007 as per note 5.
- Details of investments in associates and joint ventures are disclosed in notes 5, 39, and 40.

Subsidiaries

- Details of investments in subsidiaries are disclosed in note 37.

Directors

- Details regarding directors' remuneration and interests are disclosed in note 36 and share options are disclosed in note 34.

Transactions with key management and other related parties (excluding directors)

- There were no material transactions with key management or close family members of related parties.

Shareholders

- The principal shareholders of the company are disclosed within this Web site.

Barloworld Medical Scheme

- Contributions of R73 million were made to the Barloworld Medical Scheme on behalf of employees (2007: R92 million; 2006: R83 million).

18 ACCOUNTING AND REPORTING BY RETIREMENT BENEFIT PLANS (IAS 26)

INTRODUCTION

IAS 26 prescribes accounting and reporting requirements for retirement benefit plans. In other words, this standard is applicable to the retirement benefit plans and affects participants of a retirement benefit plan as a group but does not address reports that might be made to individuals about their particular retirement benefits. It sets out the form and content of the general purpose financial reports of retirement benefit plans. IAS 26 applies to

- *Defined contribution plans* where benefits are determined by contributions to the plan together with investment earnings thereon;
- *Defined benefit plans* where benefits are determined by a formula usually based on employees' earnings and/or years of service.

SCOPE

The retirement benefit plan is a separate entity, distinct from the employer of the plan's participants; the standard treats it as such. IAS 26 also applies to retirement benefit plans that have sponsors other than an employer (for example, trade associations or groups of employers). Whether there are formal retirement benefit plans or informal retirement benefit arrangements, the standard prescribes the same accounting for both. It is also worthy of mention that this standard applies whether a separate fund is created and regardless of whether there are trustees. The requirements of this standard also apply to retirement benefit plans with assets invested with an insurance company, unless the contract with the insurance company is in the name of a specified participant or a group of participants, and the responsibility is solely of the insurance company.

KEY TERMS

Actuarial present value of promised retirement benefits. The present value of the expected future payments by a retirement benefit plan to existing and past employees, attributable to the service already rendered.

Defined benefit plans. Retirement benefit plans whereby retirement benefits to be paid to plan participants are determined by reference to a formula, usually based on employees' earnings and/or years of service.

Defined contribution plans. Retirement benefit plans whereby retirement benefits to be paid to plan participants are determined by contributions to a fund together with investment earnings thereon.

Funding. The transfer of assets to a separate entity (distinct from the employer's enterprise), called the fund, to meet future obligations for the payment of retirement benefits.

Net assets available for benefits. The assets of a retirement benefit plan less its liabilities, other than the actuarial present value of promised retirement benefits.

Participants. The members of a retirement benefit plan and others who are entitled to benefits under the plan.

Retirement benefit plans. Formal or informal arrangements based on which an entity provides benefits for its employees on or after termination of service, which usually are referred to as termination benefits. These could take the form of annual pension payments or lump-sum payments. Such benefits, or the employer's contributions toward them, should, however, be determinable or possible of estimation in advance of retirement from the provisions of a document (that is, based on a formal arrangement) or from the entity's practices (which is referred to as an informal arrangement).

Vested benefits. Entitlements, the rights to which, under the terms of a retirement benefit plan, are not conditional on continued employment.

DEFINED CONTRIBUTION PLANS VERSUS DEFINED BENEFIT PLANS

Retirement benefit plans can either be defined contribution plans or defined benefit plans. When the amount of the future benefits payable to the participants of the retirement benefit plan is determined by the contributions made by the participants' employer, the participants, or both, together with investment earnings thereon, such plans are defined contribution plans. Defined benefit plans guarantee certain defined benefits, often determined by a formula that takes into consideration factors such as number of years of service of employees and their salary level at the time of retirement, irrespective of whether the plan has sufficient assets; thus the ultimate responsibility for payment (which may be guaranteed by an insurance company, the government, or some other entity, depending on local law and custom) remains with the employer. In rare cases, a retirement benefit plan may contain characteristics of both defined contribution and defined benefit plans; for the purposes of this standard, such a hybrid plan is deemed to be a defined benefit plan.

DEFINED CONTRIBUTION PLANS

According to IAS 26, the report of a defined contribution plan should contain a statement of net assets available for benefits and a description of the funding policy. In preparing the statement of net assets available for benefits, the plan investments should be carried at fair value, which in the case of marketable securities would be their market value. If an estimate of fair value is not possible, the entity must disclose why fair value has not been used.

Example 1

The following is an example of a statement of net assets available for plan benefits for a defined contribution plan:

Worker Friendly Corp. Defined Contribution Plan
Statement of Net Assets Available for Benefits
December 31, 2008

In thousands of US $
Assets
Investments at fair value

U.S. government securities	10,000
U.S. municipal bonds	13,000
U.S. equity securities	13,000
EU equity securities	13,000
U.S. debt securities	12,000
EU corporate bonds	12,000
Others	11,000
Total investments	84,000

Receivables

Amounts due from stockbrokers on sale of securities	25,000
Accrued interest	15,000
Dividends receivable	12,000
Total receivables	52,000

Cash	15,000
Total assets	151,000

Liabilities
Accounts payable

Amounts due to stockbrokers on purchase of securities	20,000
Benefits payable to participants (due and unpaid)	21,000
Total accounts payable	41,000
Accrued expenses	21,000
Total liabilities	62,000
Net assets available for benefits	89,000

DEFINED BENEFIT PLANS

Defined benefit plans are those plans where the benefits are guaranteed amounts, and amounts to be paid as retirement benefits are determined by reference to a formula, usually based on employees' earnings and/or number of years of service. The critical factors are thus the retirement benefits that are fixed or determinable, without regard to the adequacy of assets that may have been set aside for payment of the benefits. This, clearly, is different from the way defined contribution plans work—they provide the employees, upon retirement, amounts that have been set aside, plus or minus investment earnings or losses that have been accumulated thereon, however great or small that amount may be.

IAS 26 requires that the report of a defined benefit plan should contain either

1. A statement that shows the following:

    a. The net assets available for benefits;
    b. The actuarial present value of promised retirement benefits, distinguishing between vested and nonvested benefits; and
    c. The resulting excess or deficit.

or

2. A statement of net assets available for benefits including either of the following:

    a. A note disclosing the actuarial present value of promised retirement benefits, distinguishing between vested and nonvested benefits; or
    b. A reference to this information in an accompanying actuarial report.

IAS 26 recommends, but does not mandate, that for defined benefit plans, a report of the trustees in the nature of a management or directors' report and an investment report may also accompany the statements.

IAS 26 does not make it incumbent upon the plan to use annual actuarial valuations. If an actuarial valuation has not been prepared on the date of the report, the most recent valuation should be used as the basis for preparing the financial statement. The standard does, however, require that the date of the actuarial valuation used should be disclosed. Actuarial present values of promised benefits should be based either on current or projected salary levels; *whichever basis is used should also be disclosed.* Furthermore, the effect of any changes in actuarial assumptions that had a material impact on the actuarial present value of promised retirement benefits should also be disclosed. The report should explain the relationship between actuarial present values of promised benefits, the net assets available for benefits, and the policy for funding the promised benefits.

As in the case of defined contribution plans, investments of a defined benefit plan should be carried at fair value, which for marketable securities would be market values.

Example 2

Examples of the alternative types of reports prescribed for a defined benefit plan are as follows:

Forward-Looking Inc. Defined Benefit Plan
Statement of Net Assets Available For Benefits, Actuarial Present Value
of Accumulated Retirement Benefits and Plan Excess or Deficit
December 31, 2008

Statement of Net Assets Available for Benefits

In thousands of US $
Assets
Investments at fair value

U.S. government securities	155,000
U.S. municipal bonds	35,000
U.S. equity securities	35,000
EU equity securities	35,000
U.S. debt securities	25,000
EU corporate bonds	25,000
Others	15,000
Total investments	325,000

Receivables

Amounts due from stockbrokers on sale of securities	155,000
Accrued interest	55,000
Dividends receivable	25,000
Total receivables	235,000

Cash	55,000
Total assets	615,000

Liabilities
Accounts payable

Amounts due to stockbrokers on purchase of securities	150,000
Benefits payable to participants (due and unpaid)	150,000
Total accounts payable	300,000

Accrued expenses	120,000
Total liabilities	420,000
Net assets available for benefits	195,000

Actuarial present value of accumulated plan benefits

Vested benefits	120,000
Nonvested benefits	30,000
Total	150,000

Excess of net assets available for benefits over actuarial present value of accumulated plan benefits	45,000

Forward-Looking Inc. Defined Benefit Plan
Statement of Changes in Net Assets Available for Benefits
December 31, 2008

In thousands of US $

Investment income	
Interest income	45,000
Dividend income	15,000
Net appreciation (unrealized gain) in fair value of investments	15,000
Total investment income	75,000
Plan contributions	
Employer contributions	55,000
Employee contributions	50,000
Total plan contributions	105,000
Total additions to net asset value	180,000
Plan benefit payments	
Pensions (annual)	25,000
Lump-sum payments on retirement	35,000
Severance pay	10,000
Commutation of superannuation benefits	15,000
Total plan benefit payments	85,000
Total deductions from net asset value	85,000
Net increase in asset value	95,000
Net assets available for benefits	
Beginning of year	100,000
End of year	195,000

ADDITIONAL DISCLOSURES REQUIRED BY THIS STANDARD

In the case of both defined benefit plans and defined contribution plans, IAS 26 requires that the reports of a retirement benefit plan should also contain the following information:

- A statement of changes in net assets available for benefits;
- A summary of significant accounting policies; and
- A description of the plan and the effect of any changes in the plan during the period.

Reports provided by retirement benefits plans also include the following, if applicable:

- A statement of net assets available for benefits disclosing:

  - Assets at the end of the period suitably classified;
  - The basis of valuation of assets;
  - Details of any single investment exceeding either 5 percent of the net assets available for benefits or 5 percent of any class or type of security;
  - Details of any investment in the employer; and
  - Liabilities other than the actuarial present value of promised retirement benefits;

- A statement of changes in net assets available for benefits showing:

  - Employer contributions;
  - Employee contributions;

- Investment income, such as interest and dividends;
- Other income;
- Benefits paid or payable (analyzed, for example, as retirement, death, and disability benefits, and lump-sum payments);
- Administrative expenses;
- Other expenses;
- Taxes on income;
- Profits and losses on disposal of investments and changes in value of investments; and
- Transfers from and to other plans;

- A description of the funding policy;
- For defined benefit plans, the actuarial present value of promised retirement benefits (which may distinguish between vested benefits and nonvested benefits) based on the benefits promised under the terms of the plan, on service rendered to date, and using either current salary levels or projected salary levels. This information may be included in an accompanying actuarial report to be read in conjunction with the related information; and
- For defined benefit plans, a description of the significant actuarial assumptions made and the method used to calculate the actuarial present value of promised retirement benefits.

According to IAS 26, since the report of a retirement benefit plan contains a description of the plan, either as part of the financial information or in a separate report, it may contain:

- The names of the employers and the employee groups covered;
- The number of participants receiving benefits and the number of other participants, classified as appropriate;
- The type of plan—defined contribution or defined benefit;
- A note as to whether participants contribute to the plan;
- A description of the retirement benefits promised to participants;
- A description of any plan termination terms; or
- Changes in previous items during the period covered by the report.

Furthermore, it is not uncommon to refer to other documents that are readily available to users in which the plan is described, and to include in the report only information on subsequent changes.

EXCERPTS FROM PUBLISHED FINANCIAL STATEMENTS

Eurocontrol Pension Fund, Annual Report 2008

2.2 Pension Fund Accounts

Balance Sheet

	Notes	2008	2007
Assets			
Net assets available for benefits			
Securities	5	334,759,452.39	255,884,853.74
Cash and short-term deposits	6	18,492,329.26	3,829,404.41
Accrued income	7	183,386.14	509,697.00
Total		353,435,167.79	260,223,955.15
Liabilities			
Defined Benefit Obligation	8	962,703,376.94	781,187,673.22
Deficit	10	−609,268,209.15	520,963,718.07
Total		353,435,167.79	260,223,955.14

Statement of Changes in Net Assets Available for Benefits

	Notes	2008	2007
Net assets available for benefits			
January 1		**260,223,955.14**	**173,437,142.78**
Employer contributions	12	68,125,280.67	68,512,553.34
Employee contributions	12	15,873,713.74	16,302,576.53
Investment income	13	–4,268,727.28	5,008,912.21
Transfer from other pension schemes	14	26,443,017.01	6,952,753.91
Internal transfers		0.00	–11,679.14
Settlement of benefits	15	–12,881,657.87	–9,914,420.84
Transaction costs		–80,413.62	–64,553.68
Net assets available for benefits			
December 31		**353,435,167.79**	**260,223,285.11**

Changes in the Present Value of the Defined Benefit Obligation (DBO)

	Notes	2008	2007
Present value of obligation,			
January 1		**–781,187,673.22**	**–784,872,118.01**
Interest cost	8	–46,073,226.15	–41,524,164.96
Current service cost	8	–43,863,987.16	–50,089,974.36
New vested past service cost	8	–22,627,719.01	
Actual benefits paid	15	12,881,657.87	9,925,429.95
Internal transfers	8	–2,940,481.75	9,717,762.60
External transfers	14	–30,822,324.23	—
Actuarial gain/loss during the year	8	–48,069,623.29	75,655,391.55
Present value of obligation,			
December 31		**–962,703,376.94**	**781,187,673.22**

Accounting Principles

Investments in Securities

Investments in securities are recorded at market value by reference to official prices quoted on the day of valuation.

Benefit Obligations

The agency actuary consultant performs valuations of the defined benefit obligation. The actuarial valuations in the balance sheet were carried out using the projected unit credit method. An actuarial valuation according to the accumulated benefit obligation method is presented in Note 9.

Notes to Pension Fund Accounts

Note 5. Investments in Securities

Investment Strategy

In 2005, the pension fund supervisory board approved an initial investment strategy for a period of three years. The assets were invested in a passive management style, in two investment funds from Vanguard Investments Europe, with a target allocation of 80% in Euro government bonds and 20% in global equities.

In 2008, the pension fund supervisory board approved a revised strategy aiming at investing 45% of the fund's assets in equities, 44% in bonds, 10% in real estate, and 1% in cash. The board decided to spread the transition to this new strategy over 24 months, starting in September 2008. Due to the financial crisis, the board also took some measures to protect the assets, which explains the assets allocation at December 31, 2008 (80% bonds, 15% equities, 5% cash).

As at December 31, 2008, the market value of the fund's investments was evaluated using quoted market prices, as shown in the following table.

Value of Investments

Statement of Investments for December 31, 2008 Compared to December 31, 2007 (in €)

Subaccount	Vanguard Fund Name	Number of Units 12/31/2008	Last Published Net Asset Value (NAV) 12/31/2008	Market Value 12/31/2008	Market Value 12/31/2007
PBO subaccount	Euro government bonds	782.217,89	154,4571	120.819.106,86	85.283.334,56
PBO subaccount	Global stock index instit Euro hedged	2.775.620,35	74,922	20.795.502,79	21.196.164,13
PBO subaccount	Euro investment grade bonds	41.493,73	140,1161	5.813.939,62	—
PBO subaccount	Euro zone equities	27.021,16	88,1000	2.380.564,20	—
Future services subaccount	Euro government bonds	928.389,66	154,4571	143.396.374,55	112.458.361,49
Future services subaccount	Global stock index instit Euro hedged	3.304.228,40	7,4922	24.755.940,02	27.976.994,14
Future services subaccount	Euro investment grade bonds	52.468,37	140,1161	7.351.663,38	—
Future services subaccount	Euro zone equities	49.881,38	88,1000	4.394.549,58	—
Maastricht ATC subaccount	Euro government bonds	26.507,20	154,4571	4.094.225,24	3.666.642,48
Maastricht ATC subaccount	Global stock index instit Euro hedged	94.048,05	7,4922	704.626,80	912.660,99
Maastricht ATC subaccount	Euro investment grade bonds	1.406,09	140,1161	197.015,85	—
Maastricht ATC subaccount	Euro zone equities	635,00	88,1000	55.943,50	—
CEATS subaccount	Euro government bonds				3.482.884,71
CEATS subaccount	Global stock index instit Euro hedged				907.811,24
TOTAL				**334.759.452,39**	**255.884.853,74**

Note 8. Actuarial Evaluation of the Defined Benefit Obligation

The actuary has evaluated the DBO by using the projected unit credit method, in accordance with IAS. The principal financial and actuarial assumptions used are disclosed in the following table:

Financial Assumptions

Valuation date	December 31, 2008	December 31, 2007
Discount rate	5.40%	5.55%
Salary increase	Rate of salary increases due to grade or step changes on top of inflation	Rate of salary increases due to grade or step changes on top of inflation
Inflation	2%	2%
Cost of living adjustment	4%	4%

In the actuarial study at December 31, 2008, as prescribed by IFRS, the rate used for discounting the liabilities of the fund is based on their duration of 19 years and reflects the rate for high quality corporate bonds of this duration. As of December 31, 2008, this rate amounted to 5.40 percent.

Based on these financial assumptions, on the demographic assumptions, and on the plan characteristics, the DBO has been evaluated, as at December 31, 2008, as follows:

Evaluation of the DBO Financed by the Pension Fund at 12/31/2008 and 12/31/2007 (in €)

	2008	*2007*
DBO relating to past service up to December 31, 2004 (PBO subaccount)	698.398.439	588.210.677
DBO relating to service as from January 1, 2005 (Future services subaccount)	257.725.465	182.340.421
DBO relating to Maastricht ATC allowances subaccount	6.579.473	5.512.806
DBO relating to CEATS subaccount	—	5.123.769
Total	**962.703.377**	**781.187.673**

Note 9. Accumulated Benefit Obligation (ABO)

The ABO represents the actuarial present value of benefits attributed by the pension benefit formula to employee services rendered before a specified date and is based on the employee service and compensation prior to that date. The ABO differs from the projected benefit obligation (PBO) in that it includes no assumption about future compensation levels.

Comparison of ABO 2008 and 2007 (in €)

	ABO December 31, 2008	*ABO December 31, 2007*
PBO	439.376.746	371.509.188,79
Future services	155.034.156	110.856.416,41
ATC	4.155.140	3.461.622,34
CEATS	—	2.986.865,41
Total	**598.566.042**	**488.814.092,95**

Comparison of ABO 2008 and PBO 2008 (in €)

	ABO December 31, 2008	*PBO December 31, 2008*
PBO	439.376.746	698.398.439
Future services	155.034.156	257.725.465
ATC	4.155.140	6.579.473
Total	**598.566.042**	**962.703.377**

Note 10. Deficit

Table 9 shows a breakdown of the total deficit per subaccount and is followed by an explanation on how the deficits are expected to be covered.

Breakdown of the Deficit by Subaccount (in €)

	2008	*2007*
PBO	540.355.945	477.803.388
Future services	67.435.674	41.507.993
ATC	1.476.590	927.053
CEATS	—	725.284
Total	609.268.209	520.963.718

PBO. Pursuant to the EUROCONTROL Commission Measure No. 04/107 dated November 5, 2004, the following has been decided:

> The past service liabilities, as fixed at 1 January 2005 relating to the services of staff in post at that date, shall represent the legal commitment of the Organization and shall be paid into the Eurocontrol Pension Fund by Member States in the form of yearly installments, over a period of 20 years as from 1 January 2005. The yearly installments shall be annually updated in accordance with the results of the actuarial studies. This measure shall enter into force on 1 January 2005 together with the establishment of the "EUROCONTROL Pension Fund."

Consequently, past liabilities related to pension rights accrued before January 1, 2005, by staff in post at that date were recognized as the responsibility of the member states. They are committed to financing pension rights accrued before January 1, 2005 through special contributions, in annual installments over 20 years. The amount of these installments will be reviewed periodically, in light of the conclusions of the actuarial studies.

As at December 31, 2008, the commitment from member states was calculated as shown in Table 15.10 as follows:

Member States Commitment to Reconstitute the PBO Subaccount

Total benefit obligation relating to the PBO subaccount	698.398.439
Fair value of assets relating to the PBO subaccount	–158.042.494
Commitment of member states to PBO	540.355.945

Future services and ATC. The deficit is explained by the use of the projected unit credit method to calculate the DBO, which is a PBO based on career progression assumptions while the assets reflect the contributions accumulated based on past salaries and make no assumptions about future return on assets and future increases of contributions due to career progression. Reference is made to Note 9, presenting the ABO and comparing it to the PBO, and to Note 11, showing the funding ratio based on the ABO instead of the PBO. Note 11 shows that for the future services and ATC subaccounts, the ABOs are covered by the assets of the fund.

The deficit under the projected unit credit method will be funded with the future employer and employee contributions and with the expected return on investments. In addition, in Article 83 of the staff regulations, member states jointly guarantee the payment of the pensions.

Note 12. Contributions to the Plan

In 2008, contributions were made up of the following elements:

Member States Annual Installment and Contributions

At its 26th session in November 2006, the provisional council agreed with the recommendation of the pension fund supervisory board to increase the annual PBO contributions of all member states by 1.2 percent per year over the remaining amortization period. The annual installment for 2008 to the PBO subaccount was therefore set at €36.337.000 as approved in the permanent commission measure No. 07/136.

The agency contribution rate to the future services and ATC subaccounts is currently set at 20% of salary.

In total, the member states contributed for an amount of €68.125.281 in 2008, which is broken down by subaccount in Table 13.

Member States/Agency Contributions

	2008	2007
PBO	36.337.000	35.907.440
Future services	31.356.285	31.604.358
ATC	431.996	523.387
CEATS	—	477.368
Total	**68.125.281**	**68.512.553**

Staff Contributions

The staff contribution rate is currently set up at 10 percent of salary. In 2008, an amount of €15.873.714 was deducted from the staff remuneration and transferred into the pension fund, as detailed in Table 14.

Staff Contributions

	2008	2007
Future services	15.657.725	15.802.162
ATC	215.988	261.730
CEATS	—	238.684
Total	**15.873.714**	**16.302.577**

19 CONSOLIDATED AND SEPARATE FINANCIAL STATEMENTS (IAS 27)

INTRODUCTION

IAS 27 prescribes the circumstances under which consolidated financial statements are required to be prepared, and is applied in the preparation and presentation of consolidated financial statements for a group of entities under the control of a parent. This standard must also be applied to account for investments in subsidiaries, jointly controlled entities, and associates when an entity presents separate financial statements (by choice or to comply with local regulations). However, it does not deal with accounting for business combinations. That is dealt with in IFRS 3, *Business Combinations*.

KEY TERMS

Consolidated financial statements. The financial statements of a group of entities that are presented as those of a single economic activity.

Control. The power to govern financial and operating policies of an entity for economic gains.

Noncontrolling interest (formerly known as minority interest). The part of the equity in a subsidiary that is not directly or indirectly owned by a parent.

Parent. An entity that has one or more subsidiaries.

Subsidiary. An entity that is controlled by a parent.

PRESENTATION AND SCOPE OF CONSOLIDATED FINANCIAL STATEMENTS

A parent that has one or more subsidiaries should present consolidated financial statements unless all the following conditions are satisfied:

- The parent is a subsidiary and the owner of the parent has no objection to the parent not presenting consolidated financial statements;
- The parent's debt or equity is not traded in the public market;
- The parent has neither filed, nor is in the process of filing, the financial statements with any regulatory or similar authority for the purpose of issuing any instruments to the public; and
- The ultimate or intermediate parent prepares consolidated financial statements in accordance with the IFRSs and makes them available for public use.

The requirement that all of the above conditions are met means that consolidated financial statements are being presented by the ultimate parent or an intermediate parent. In this case, the parent can elect to prepare and present only separate financial statements.

In preparing and presenting consolidated financial statements, all of the parent's subsidiaries must be considered. Subsidiaries are determined based on control exercised by the parent. Control is presumed to exist when the parent acquires more than half of the voting rights of another enterprise. However, in cases like the following, the parent may control a subsidiary even if the parent has less than half of the voting rights:

- The parent has command over more than one-half of the voting rights because of an agreement with other investors;
- The parent can govern the financial and operating policies under the provisions of law;
- A statute or an agreement allows the parent to govern the financial and operating policies of the subsidiary; or
- The parent has the authority to appoint or remove a majority of the members of the board of directors or has power to cast the majority of votes at a meeting of the board of directors.

To determine whether control exists, the parent should also consider the potential voting rights that are currently exercisable or convertible because of the parent owning instruments like share warrants, share call options, convertible debt, or equity instruments.

A subsidiary cannot be excluded from consolidation because the parent is a mutual fund or venture capital organization, or because the business of the subsidiary is dissimilar from that of the other entities within the group. However, the subsidiary need not be consolidated under the following conditions:

- The parent loses control over the subsidiary, which can occur when the parent loses the power to govern the financial and operating policies of the subsidiary. This can arise because of governmental control, a legal or contractual agreement, or the operation of the subsidiary under severe long-term restrictions that impairs its ability to transfer funds to the parent; or
- The control of the parent over the subsidiary is intended to be temporary. This should be evidenced by the fact that the subsidiary has been acquired with the intention to dispose of it within the forthcoming 12-month period and management of the parent is actively seeking a buyer. In this case, the provisions of IFRS 5, *Noncurrent Assets Held for Sale and Discontinued Operations,* will apply.

PROCESS OF CONSOLIDATION

In preparing the consolidated financial statements, the items of assets, liabilities, equity, income and expenses of the independent financial statements of the parent and its subsidiaries are combined line by line.

During the process of consolidation, the following occur:

- The carrying amount of the parent's investment in each subsidiary and that portion of equity of the subsidiary that relates to the parent's investment should be eliminated, and the resultant goodwill, if any, must be accounted for in accordance with IFRS 3, *Business Combinations*;
- The minority interest in the profit or loss of the subsidiaries being consolidated should be identified;
- The minority interests in the net assets of the subsidiaries being consolidated should be identified, which will comprise the amount of noncontrolling interest at the original combination date (IFRS 3, *Business Combinations*) and the noncontrolling interest's share of changes in equity since the date of combination;
- Intragroup balances, transactions, income, expenses, and dividends must be eliminated in full. In this process, the profits and losses resulting from intragroup transactions that have been recognized in assets, such as inventory, must also be eliminated;
- The financial statements of both the parent and the subsidiary that are used in the preparation of the consolidated financial statements should all be prepared as of the same reporting date. When the financial periods do not end on the same reporting

date and it is not practical to prepare the subsidiary's financial statements for the additional period to end on the parent's reporting date, adjustments must be made for any significant transactions or events that have occurred between the reporting dates The difference between the end of the reporting period of the subsidiary and that of the parent must not be more than three months. The length of the reporting periods and the difference between the end of the reporting periods should be the same over the years;

- The accounting policies adopted by the subsidiaries and the parent must be the same when the transactions and events occur in similar circumstances. When the accounting policies are not uniform, appropriate adjustments should be made to the financial statements of the subsidiaries so as to be in line with that of the parent; and
- Minority interests should be presented separately from the parent's equity, although shown within equity. The amount of net income or loss and each component of other comprehensive income that relates to the minority interests should be allocated, even if it results in the minority interests having a deficit balance.

When there is a change in the parent's ownership interest in a subsidiary that does not result in a loss of control, such changes should be accounted for as equity transactions. An example of such a change would be the parent increasing its shareholding in the subsidiary after control was established.

Example 1

The trial balances of the holding company Bond Holdings Limited and its 75%-owned subsidiary, Coat Trading Limited, at December 31, 2008, are as follows:

	Bond Holdings Limited (US $)	*Coat Trading Limited (US $)*
Property, plant, and equipment	200,000	100,000
Investments	75,000	—
Current assets	250,000	400,000
Current liabilities	(15,000)	(250,000)
Share capital	(300,000)	(100,000)
Reserves	(75,000)	(150,000)
Revenue	(500,000)	(800,000)
Direct costs	300,000	550,000
Administration expenses	125,000	100,000

The separate and consolidated financial statements of the holding and subsidiary companies will be as follows:

Statement of Financial Position at December 31, 2008

	Bond Holdings Ltd. *(US $)*	Coat Trading Ltd. *(US $)*	Consolidated *(US $)*
Property, plant, and equipment	200,000	100,000	300,000
Investments	70,000	—	—
Current assets	250,000	400,000	650,000
Current liabilities	(150,000)	(250,000)	(400,000)
Net assets	**370,000**	**250,000**	**550,000**
Share capital	300,000	100,000	300,000
Noncontrolling interest	—	—	75,000
Reserves	70,000	150,000	175,000
	370,000	**250,000**	**550,000**

Noncontrolling interest in subsidiary will comprise the following:

Share capital (30%)	US $30,000
Share of profit	US $45,000
	US $75,000

Statement of Income for Year Ended December 31, 2008

	Bond Holdings Limited (US $)	Coat Trading Limited (US $)	Consolidated (US $)
Revenue	500,000	800,000	1,300,000
Direct costs	**(300,000)**	(550,000)	(850,000)
Administration expenses	(125,000)	(100,000)	(225,000)
Net profit	75,000	150,000	225,000
Noncontrolling interest	—	—	(45,000)
Profit for the year	75,000	150,000	180,000

Example 2

At December 31, 2008, Delta Holdings Limited has a 75% shareholding interest in its subsidiary, Acra Trading Limited. The fair market value of the net identifiable assets (tangible and intangible, other than goodwill) of Acra Trading Limited at December 31, 2008, is US $1 million against the book value of US $800,000. The fair market value of Acra Trading Limited as a whole is US $1.2 million.

In this case, the parent company's share of the subsidiary is 75% and the noncontrolling interest is 25%. The amount of the subsidiary included in the consolidated financial statements of Delta Holdings Limited will be as follows:

Subsidiary	100% value (US $)	Parent company share (75%) (US $)	Noncontrolling interest (25%) (US $)	Consolidated (US $)
Net book value of net identifiable assets (A)	800,000	600,000	200,000	800,000
Fair market value increment of net identifiable assets (B – A)	200,000	150,000	50,000	200,000
Fair market value of net assets (B)	1,000,000	750,000	250,000	1,000,000
Goodwill (C – B)	200,000	150,000	—	150,000
Fair market value of subsidiary (C)	1,200,000	900,000	250,000	1,150,000

LOSS OF CONTROL

One of the most common circumstances under which a parent can lose control over a subsidiary is through disposal of a part of its investment. However, a parent can also lose control of a subsidiary without a change in the ownership levels. An example of this is the subsidiary being placed under the management of a receiver appointed by a court because of an ongoing litigation.

The loss of control over a subsidiary can occur as a result of a single or multiple transactions. In some cases, like where transactions are interdependent, the parent should account for these multiple transactions as a single transaction.

When there is a loss of control, the parent must

- Derecognize the assets, liabilities, and goodwill of the subsidiary at their carrying amounts on the date of losing control;
- Derecognize the carrying amount of the minority interest on the date of losing control;
- Recognize the fair value of any consideration received and the distribution if any of the shares of the erstwhile subsidiary;
- Recognize any investment retained in the erstwhile subsidiary at its fair value on the date of losing control;
- Reclassify to profit or loss, or transfer directly to retained earnings, if required in accordance with other IFRS, the amounts to account for all items recognized in other

comprehensive income in relation to that subsidiary on the same basis as would be required if the parent had directly disposed of the related assets or liabilities; and

• Recognize any resulting difference in profit or loss, attributable to the parent.

Example 1

At April 1, 2008, Ezmaa Holdings Limited, which held a 60% ownership interest in Sonic Limited at a carrying value of $800,000, sold 50% of its holding (a 30% ownership interest) for $500,000. At the date of sale, the carrying value of the minority interest is $350,000 and the carrying value of the net assets of Sonic Limited is $1,000,000.

The profit or loss of Ezmaa Holdings Limited on loss of control is calculated as follows:

Sale proceeds of 50% of the investment	$ 500,000
Fair value of retained 50% of the investment	$ 500,000
Carrying value of minority interest on date of sale	$ 350,000
	$ 1,350,000
Less carrying value of the net assets of Sonic Limited	$(1,000,000)
Profit to be recognized by Ezmaa Holdings Limited	$ 350,000

Upon losing control, the provisions of IAS 28, *Investments in Associates*, IAS 31, *Interests in Joint Ventures*, or IAS 39, *Financial Instruments: Recognition and Measurement,* whichever are the most appropriate, are applied to the balance holding of 30%.

ACCOUNTING FOR INVESTMENTS IN SEPARATE FINANCIAL STATEMENTS

When an entity prepares separate financial statements, the investments made in subsidiaries, jointly controlled entities, and associates should be accounted for either at cost or in accordance with the provisions of IAS 39, *Financial Instruments: Recognition and Measurement.*

For the purpose of consistency, the same method of accounting should be applied for all categories of investments. Investments that are held for sale and are accounted for at cost should be accounted for in accordance with the provisions of IFRS 5, *Noncurrent Assets Held for Sale and Discontinued Operations.* However, investments that are accounted for in accordance with the provisions of IAS 39 are excluded from the measurement requirements of IFRS 5. This will mean that the measurement principles of IAS 39 will continue to apply even when the investments are classified as held for sale.

Example 2

Sertex Holdings Limited acquired 100% shareholding of Unicorn Limited on July 1, 2008, with the intention of disposing of it within one year. At the date of acquisition, the fair value of the assets of Unicorn Limited was $26 million and the fair value of the liabilities was $6 million. At the end of the reporting date on December 31, 2008, the fair value of assets of Unicorn Limited was $23 million and the fair value of the liabilities was $5 million.

In this case, Sertex Holdings Limited, which acquired Unicorn Limited on July 1, 2008, should account for the investments under IFRS 5, *Noncurrent Assets Held for Sale and Discontinued Operations*, since it meets the criteria as being held for sale.

Initially, the fair value of the assets would be recorded at $26 million. The fair value of the liabilities would be recorded at $6 million. At the reporting date on December 31, 2008, Sertex Holdings Limited should remeasure the investment in Unicorn Limited at the lower of its cost and fair value less cost to sell, which will be $23 million – $5 million = $18 million. The assets and liabilities will have to be presented separately in the consolidated financial statements from any other assets and liabilities. The total assets at December 31, 2008, will be shown separately as $23 million and the total liabilities will be shown separately as $5 million.

Similarly, when investments in jointly controlled entities and associates are accounted for in accordance with IAS 39 in the consolidated financial statements, the subsidiary should continue to account for those investments in the same manner in its separate financial statements.

Dividends from a subsidiary, jointly controlled entity, or associate should be recognized in profit or loss in the entity's separate financial statements when the entity's right to receive the dividend is established.

When an entity applies the IFRSs for the first time, the provisions of IFRS 1, *First-Time Adoption of International Financial Reporting Standards*, allow the entity the option to measure the initial cost of investments in subsidiaries, jointly controlled entities, and associates in the separate financial statements at either the fair value or at the carrying amount under the previous accounting practices.

When a parent reorganizes the shareholding structure of the group by establishing a new entity to act as the holding company of the parent, that holding company (the new parent) should, in its separate financial statements, measure the cost of its investment in the previous parent at the carrying amount of its share of the equity items of the previous parent at the date of the reorganization. However, this is subject to the following conditions being satisfied:

- The new parent must obtain control of the previous parent by issuing equity instruments in exchange for existing equity instruments of the previous parent;
- The assets and liabilities of the new parent after reorganization are the same as that of the previous parent before the date of reorganization; and
- On reorganizing, the owners of the previous parent continue to have the same level of interest in the group as before reorganization.

Disclosures

The disclosures that are required under this standard can be categorized as follows:

Disclosures required in the consolidated financial statements.

- Basis of establishing control when the parent does not directly or indirectly own more than half of the voting power;
- Basis of ownership not constituting control, even though an entity directly or indirectly owns more than half of the voting or potential voting power of an investee;
- The reporting period of a subsidiary, when the reporting date or period is different from that of the parent, along with the reasons for using different dates;
- The nature and extent of significant restrictions, if any, for a subsidiary to transfer funds to the parent in the form of cash dividends or for repayments of loans or advances;
- A schedule disclosing the effect of ownership changes that do not result in a loss of control over the subsidiary on the portion of the equity that is attributable to owners of the parent; and
- Specific details on the gain or loss if the parent loses control of a subsidiary.

Disclosures required in separate financial statements. When a parent is not required under this standard to prepare consolidated financial statements, the following disclosures are required for the separate financial statements:

- The fact that the financial statements are separate, the exemption option from consolidation has been exercised, the name and country of incorporation or residence of the ultimate or intermediate parent whose consolidated financial statements have been prepared under the IFRSs for public use, and the address where those consolidated financial statements are available;
- A list of significant investments in subsidiaries, jointly controlled entities, and associates, including the name, country of incorporation or residence, proportion of own-

ership interest, and proportion of voting power held if this is different from the ownership interest; and
- The method used to account for the investments disclosed.

When a parent, who is not required under this standard to prepare consolidated financial statements, and the entity have an interest in a joint venture or are investors in an associate and prepare separate financial statements, the following disclosures are required:

- The statements are separate financial statements and the reasons why those statements are prepared;
- A list of significant investments in subsidiaries, jointly controlled entities, and associates, including the name, country of incorporation or residence, proportion of ownership interest, and proportion of voting power held if this is different from the ownership interest; and
- The method used to account for the investments disclosed, identifying the consolidated financial statements that have been prepared in accordance with this standard or IAS 28, *Investments in Associates*, or IAS 31, *Interests in Joint Ventures*, as the case may be.

EXCERPTS FROM PUBLISHED FINANCIAL STATEMENTS

Balfour Beatty PLC, Annual Report 2008

Notes to the Accounts

1. Principal Accounting Policies

1.2 Basis of Consolidation

The group accounts include the accounts of the company and its subsidiaries together with the group's share of the results of joint ventures and associates drawn up to December 31 each year.

a) Subsidiaries

Subsidiaries are entities over which the group has control, being the power to govern the financial and operating policies of the investee entity so as to obtain benefits from its activities. The results of subsidiaries acquired or sold in the year are consolidated from the effective date of acquisition or to the effective date of disposal, as appropriate.

The purchase method of accounting is used to account for the acquisition of subsidiaries by the group. On acquisition, the assets, liabilities, and contingent liabilities of a subsidiary are measured at their fair values at the date of acquisition. Any excess of the fair value of the cost of acquisition over the fair values of the identifiable net assets acquired is recognized as goodwill. Any deficiency of the cost of acquisition below the fair values of the identifiable net assets acquired (discount on acquisition) is credited to the income statement in the period of acquisition. The interest of minority shareholders is stated at the minority's proportion of the fair value of the assets and liabilities recognized.

Accounting policies of subsidiaries are adjusted where necessary to ensure consistency with those used by the group. All intragroup transactions, balances, income, and expenses are eliminated on consolidation.

b) Joint Ventures and Associates

Joint ventures are those entities over which the group exercises joint control through a contractual arrangement. Associates are entities over which the group is in a position to exercise significant influence, but not control or joint control, through participation in the financial and operating policy decisions of the investee. The results, assets, and liabilities of joint ventures and associates are incorporated in the financial statements using the equity method of accounting, except when classified as held for sale.

The equity return from the military housing joint ventures of Balfour Beatty Communities is contractually limited to a maximum preagreed level of return, beyond which Balfour Beatty Communities does not share in any increased return. Investments in joint ventures and associates are initially carried in the balance sheet at cost (including goodwill arising on acquisition) and adjusted by postacquisition changes in the group's share of the net assets of the joint venture or associate, less any impairment in the value of individual investments. Losses of joint ventures and associates in excess of the group's interest in those joint ventures and associates are only recognized to the extent that the group is contractually liable for or has a constructive obligation to meet the obligations of the joint ventures and associates.

Unrealised gains and losses on transactions with joint ventures and associates are eliminated to the extent of the group's interest in the relevant joint venture or associate.

Any excess of the cost of acquisition over the group's share of the fair values of the identifiable net assets of the associate or joint venture entity at the date of acquisition is recognized as goodwill. Any deficiency of the cost of acquisition below the group's share of the fair values of the identifiable net assets of the joint venture or associate at the date of acquisition (discount on acquisition) is credited to the income statement in the period of acquisition.

c)　**Jointly Controlled Operations**

The group's share of the results and net assets of contracts carried out in conjunction with another party are included under each relevant heading in the income statement and balance sheet.

Ahold, Annual Report 2008

Notes to the Consolidated Financial Statements

3.　Significant Accounting Policies

Consolidation

The consolidated financial statements incorporate the financial statements of the company and its subsidiaries. Subsidiaries are entities over which the company has control. Control is the power to govern the financial and operating policies, generally accompanying a shareholding of more than one-half of the voting rights. The existence and effect of potential voting rights that are currently exercisable or convertible are considered when assessing whether the company controls another entity. Subsidiaries are fully consolidated from the date control commences until the date control ceases. All intragroup transactions, balances, income, and expenses are eliminated upon consolidation. Unrealized losses on intragroup transactions are eliminated unless the transaction provides evidence of an impairment of the assets transferred.

Noncontrolling interests are recorded in the consolidated balance sheet, the consolidated income statement for the noncontrolling shareholders' share in the net assets, and the income or loss of subsidiaries, respectively. The interest of noncontrolling shareholders in an acquired subsidiary is initially measured at the noncontrolling interest's proportion of the net fair value of the assets, liabilities, and contingent liabilities recognized.

5.　Assets Held for Sale and Discontinued Operations

Discontinued Operations

Income from discontinued operations per segment, consisting of results from discontinued operations and results on divestments, was as follows:

€ million		2008	2007
Giant-Carlisle	Tops	7	33
Albert/Hypernova	Poland	(5)	249
Schuitema	Schuitema	161	—
U.S. Foodservice	U.S. Foodservice	13	1,750
Various	Various	2	2
Results on divestments of discontinued operations		**178**	**2,039**

Results on Divestments of Discontinued Operations

2008 Divestments

On April 23, 2008, Ahold announced that it had reached an agreement with Schuitema and CVC on the divestment of its 73.2% in Schuitema to CVC. The sale was completed on June 30, 2008, for proceeds of EUR 515 million. At the same time, Ahold, Schuitema, and CVC entered into a store purchase agreement for the transfer of 56 Schuitema stores, including owned real estate, for a total purchase price of EUR 208 million, valuing Ahold's previously owned 73.2% interest in these stores at EUR 153 million. Taken together, the net consideration for the sale of Ahold's 73.2% interest in Schuitema (that is, net of the 56 stores retained) amounted to EUR 362 million, resulting in a gain on divestment of EUR 161 million, as summarized by the following:.

€ million	Total Schuitema	56 stores retained	Total sold
Fair value (100%)	703	208	495
Noncontrolling interest (26.8%)	(188)	(55)	(133)
Fair value of Ahold's 73.2% interest	**515**	**153**	**362**

The retained stores were transferred to Albert Heijn in several tranches during the second half of 2008 and in early 2009. Until the date of transfer, the stores were operated by Schuitema under its trading name and for its benefit. Following the transfer, the stores were converted into Albert Heijn stores.

Schuitema's results for 2008 and prior years have been classified as results from discontinued operations in their entirety. The assets and liabilities related to the stores that were transferred to Albert Heijn (primarily land and buildings and finance lease assets and liabilities) have been retained in Ahold's consolidated balance sheet at their carrying amounts. The 26.8% noncontrolling interest related to the 56 retained stores has effectively been acquired by Ahold as part of the transaction. The excess of the fair value paid over the existing carrying amount of the noncontrolling interest related to the retained stores amounted to EUR 54 million and was recognized directly in equity. In addition to the assets and liabilities retained, Ahold also acquired real estate related to certain of the retained stores from a third party for EUR 51 million.

The following table presents the reconciliation between cash received and result on divestments of discontinued operations:

€ million	2008	2007
Cash received (net of cash divested of EUR 16 million and EUR 288 million, respectively)	321	5,435
Net assets divested	(173)	(3,441)
Changes in accounts receivable/payable (net)	11	(49)
Cumulative exchange rate differences transferred from equity	—	120
Income taxes	19	(26)
Result on divestments of discontinued operations	**178**	**2,039**

Holcim, Annual Report 2008

Consolidated Financial Statements

Accounting Policies

Adoption of Revised and New IFRSs and New Interpretations

In 2010, group Holcim will adopt the following revised standards relevant to the group:

IAS 27 (revised), *Consolidated and Separate Financial Statements*; and
IFRS 3 (revised), *Business Combinations*.

According to IAS 27 (revised), changes in the ownership interest of a subsidiary that do not result in a loss of control will be accounted for as an equity transaction. The amendment to IFRS 3 (revised) introduces several changes, such as the choice to measure a noncontrolling interest in the acquiree either at fair value or at its proportionate interest in the acquiree's identifiable net assets, the accounting for step acquisitions requiring the remeasurement of a previously held interest to fair value through profit or loss as well as the expensing of acquisition costs directly to the income statement.

Scope of Consolidation

The consolidated financial statements comprise those of Holcim Ltd. and of its subsidiaries, including joint ventures. The list of principal companies is presented in the section "Principal Companies of the Holcim Group."

Principles of Consolidation

Subsidiaries, which are those entities in which the group has an interest of more than one-half of the voting rights or otherwise has the power to exercise control over the operations, are consolidated. Subsidiaries are consolidated from the date on which control is transferred to the group and are no longer consolidated from the date that control ceases. All intercompany transactions and balances between group companies are eliminated.

The group's interest in jointly controlled entities is consolidated using the proportionate method of consolidation. Under this method, the group records its share of the joint ventures' individual income and expenses, assets and liabilities, and cash flows in the consolidated financial statements on a line-by-line basis. All transactions and balances between the group and joint ventures are eliminated to the extent of the group's interest in the joint ventures.

Investments in associated companies are accounted for using the equity method of accounting. These are companies over which the group generally holds between 20 and 50% of the voting rights and has significant influence but does not exercise control. Goodwill arising on the acquisition is included in the carrying amount of the investment in associated companies. Equity accounting is discontinued when the carrying amount of the investment together with any long-term interest in an associated company reaches zero, unless the group has, in addition, either incurred or guaranteed additional obligations in respect of the associated company.

Minority Interests

Minority interests represent the portion of profit or loss and net assets not held by the group and are presented separately in the consolidated statement of income and within equity in the consolidated balance sheet.

Notes to the Consolidated Financial Statements

1.   Changes in the Scope of Consolidation

The scope of consolidation has been affected mainly by the following deconsolidations made during 2008 and 2007:

Deconsolidated in 2008	*Effective as at*
Holcim Venezuela	December 31, 2008
Egyptian Cement Company	January 23, 2008

Deconsolidated in 2007	*Effective as at*
Group Holcim South Africa	June 5, 2007

At December 31, 2008, Holcim Venezuela was deconsolidated. Immediately thereafter, it was accounted for as an associate and classified as held for sale (Note 19).

The impact of the above resulted in group Holcim derecognizing assets and liabilities amounting to CHF 313 million and CHF 96 million respectively, including the derecognition of attributable goodwill of CHF 3 million and the recognition of an investment in an associate of CHF 220 million.

On January 23, 2008, a competitor acquired 100% of the outstanding shares of Orascom Cement, an affiliated company of Orascom Construction Industries (OCI). Orascom Cement owns 53.7% of the shares in Egyptian Cement Company. As a result of a joint venture agreement with OCI, Holcim proportionately consolidated its 43.7% interest in Egyptian Cement Company. Given the acquisition of Orascom Cement by a competitor, the joint venture agreement between OCI and Holcim became void and Holcim applies equity accounting in accordance with IAS 28 to its investment as of this date. Since Holcim's stake remains unchanged, the above event will have no impact on consolidated net income.

The impact of the above resulted in group Holcim derecognizing its proportionate interest of total assets and liabilities amounting to CHF 933 million and CHF 605 million respectively including the derecognition of attributable goodwill of CHF 80 million and the recognition of an investment in an associate of CHF 223 million.

On June 5, 2007, Holcim disposed of 85% of its direct interest in the parent of the group Holcim South Africa in the context of a black economic empowerment transaction.

Since the date of the disposal, group Holcim South Africa has been accounted for as an associate based on its 15% interest in accordance with IAS 28 using the equity method of accounting due to significant influence.

Assets and Liabilities of Group Holcim South Africa at the Date of Disposal

CHF million	
Cash and cash equivalents	66
Other current assets	165
Property, plant, and equipment	298
Other assets	30
Short-term liabilities	(169)
Long-term provisions	(54)
Other long term liabilities	(62)
Net assets	**274**
Minority interest	(154)
Net assets disposed	**120**
Total selling price	**1,278**
Cash	713
Loan notes	565

During 2008, the outstanding loan notes relating to the sale of group Holcim South Africa were fully repaid.

The sale of the shareholding resulted in a capital gain of CHF 1,110 million. Additionally, a special dividend of CHF 150 million net was received from the group Holcim South Africa.

Business combinations individually not material are included in aggregate in note 38. If the acquisitions had occurred on January 1, 2008, group net sales and net income would have remained substantially unchanged.

An overview of the subsidiaries, joint ventures, and associated companies is included in section "Principal Companies of the Holcim Group" on pages 178 to 180.

5.   Change in Consolidated Net Sales

CHF million	*2008*	*2007*
Volume and price	1,157	1,933
Change in structure	(303)	759
Currency translation effects	(2,749)	391
Total	**(1,895)**	**3,083**

21.   Investments in Associates

CHF million	*2008*	*2007*
January 1	809	727
Share of profit of associates	229	259
Dividends earned	(196)	(228)
Acquisitions net	402	62
Reclassifications net	203	0
December 31	1,341	809

In 2008, the item Acquisitions net includes the subscription to the private placement of shares amounting to USD 282 million (CHF 305) in its associated company Huaxin Cement Co., Ltd. which resulted in an increase in its participation from 26.1% to 39.9%.

In 2008, the item Reclassification net mainly includes an increase of CHF 223 million relating to the deconsolidation of Egyptian Cement Company when the joint venture agreement between OCI and Holcim became void and Holcim applied equity accounting to its investment (Note 1).

Sales to and purchases from associates amounted to CHF 202 million (2007: 137) and CHF 18 million (2007: 32), respectively.

The following amounts represent the group's share of assets, liabilities, net sales, and net income of associates:

Aggregated Financial Information—Associates

CHF million	2008	2007
Total assets	2,685	1,906
Total liabilities	(1,403)	(1,097)
Net assets	**1,282**	**809**
Net sales	1,528	1,201
Net income	207	70

Net income and net assets also reflect the unrecognized share of losses of associates.

Ahold, Annual Report 2008

Notes to the Parent Company Financial Statements

1. Significant Accounting Policies

Basis of Preparation

The parent company financial statements of Ahold have been prepared in accordance with Part 9, Book 2 of the Netherlands Civil Code. In accordance with subsection 8 of section 362, Book 2 of the Netherlands Civil Code, the measurement principles applied in these parent company financial statements are the same as those applied in the consolidated financial statements (see Note 3 to the consolidated financial statements).

As the financial data of Koninklijke Ahold N.V. (the parent company) are included in the consolidated financial statements, the income statement in the parent company financial statements is presented in condensed form (in accordance with section 402, Book 2 of the Netherlands Civil Code).

Investments in Subsidiaries, Joint Ventures and Associates

Investments in subsidiaries, joint ventures and associates are accounted for using the net equity value. Ahold calculates the net equity value using the accounting policies as described in Note 3 to the consolidated financial statements. The net equity value of subsidiaries comprises the cost, excluding goodwill, of Ahold's share in the net assets of the subsidiary, plus Ahold's share in income or losses since acquisition, less dividends received. Goodwill paid upon acquisition of an investment in a joint venture or associate is included in the net equity value of the investment and is not shown separately on the face of the balance sheet.

20 INVESTMENT IN ASSOCIATES (IAS 28)

INTRODUCTION

IAS 28 prescribes the accounting treatment that is to be adopted for investments in associates. However, it excludes investments in associates that are held by venture capital entities or mutual funds, unit trusts, and other similar entities if they are held for trading financial assets in accordance with IAS 39, *Financial Instruments: Recognition and Measurement.*

KEY TERMS

Associates. Entities in which the investor has significant influence, but not control or joint control. This includes unincorporated entities like a partnership, over which the investor has a significant influence, but it is neither a subsidiary nor a joint venture.

Significant influence. The power to participate in the financial and operating policy decision-making process of an entity, but without having control or joint control over those policies. The policy-making processes will include participation in decisions about dividend declarations and other distributions.

Control. The power to govern the financial and operating policy of an entity so as to obtain economic benefits.

Joint control. The contractually agreed sharing of control over an economic activity. This will exist only when unanimous consent of all parties who are sharing the control is required in the financial and operating policy decision-making process of the entity.

Equity method. A method of accounting by which an investment in an associate is initially recorded at cost and subsequently adjusted to reflect the investor's share of the net assets of the associate. The profit or loss relating to the investment in the associate is included in the investor's statement of income.

SIGNIFICANT INFLUENCE

When an investor holds a 20% or more share in the voting power (directly or indirectly) of the associate, it is presumed that there is significant influence unless it can be demonstrated otherwise. Similarly, if the holding is less than 20%, the investor will be presumed not to have significant influence unless such influence can be clearly demonstrated.

The following circumstances will indicate the existence of significant influence:

- The investor has a representation on the board of directors or an equivalent governing body of the associate;
- The investor has a participation in the policy-making process of the associate;
- There are material transactions between the investor and the associate;
- There is movement of management between the investor and the associate; or
- There is provision of essential technical information between the investor and the associate.

An important factor in determining whether an investor has significant influence is the existence and the effect of potential voting rights that are held by the investor that are currently exercisable or convertible. Potential voting rights will include warrants, call options, and debt instruments that can increase or reduce voting power if they are exercised or converted. The term *currently exercisable* means that the potential voting rights can be exercised or converted immediately by the investor.

Significant influence is considered to be lost when the investor loses the power to participate in the financial and operating policy decision making process of the associate. This can occur either because of a change in ownership levels through a contractual agreement with other parties, or the associate becoming subject to the control of government or a court, administrator, or regulator.

EQUITY METHOD

Under the equity method, the investment in the associate is initially carried at cost. The aforesaid value of the investment is then increased or decreased to recognize the investor's share of the profit or loss of the associate after the date of acquisition. The distributions that are received from the associate will reduce the carrying amount of the investment. Adjustments to the carrying value of the investment may also have to be made because of the changes in the investor's interest in the associate. Changes that arise from changes in the associate's other comprehensive income could be due to revaluation of property, plant, and equipment, or from foreign exchange translation differences. The investor's share of these changes should be recognized in other comprehensive income by the investor in accordance with IAS 1, *Presentation of Financial Statements*.

Example 1

Encon Limited acquired 30 percent of the equity shares, and thereby voting rights, of Eagle Inc. on January 1, 2008, for a purchase consideration of $15 million. The retained earnings of Eagle Inc., over which Encon Limited has significant influence, was $20 million at the date of acquisition and $25 million at December 31, 2008. Calculate the carrying value of the investment in Eagle Inc. in the financial statements of Encon Limited at December 31, 2008.

Solution

The carrying value of the investment will be

Cost of investment	$15.0 million
Share in post-acquisition profits–30% of ($25m – 20m)	$ 1.5 million
	$16.5 million

The share of the post-acquisition profits of $1.5 million will be credited to the retained earnings of Encon Limited. Goodwill in an associate is not separately recognized. The entire carrying amount of $16.5 million will be tested for impairment at December 31, 2008.

When the investor holds potential voting rights, for the purpose of determining the share of the investor's profit or loss or share of changes in the associate's equity, the present ownership interest is considered. This will mean that the effect of the option to exercise or convert the potential voting rights must not be considered.

METHOD OF ACCOUNTING

An investor should account for investments in associates under the equity method, except under the following three circumstances:

1. The investments are classified as held for sale under IFRS 5, *Noncurrent Assets Held for Sale and Discontinued Operations*. Under this standard, investments are classified as held for sale if the significant influence is intended to be temporary in nature

because the associate has been acquired and held exclusively with a view to its disposal within 12 months from acquisition and the management of the associate is actively seeking a buyer;

2. The parent entity that has investments in associates is exempted under IAS 27, *Consolidated and Separate Financial Statements*, from preparing consolidated financial statements; and

3. All of the following conditions are fulfilled by the investor:

   a. The investor is a wholly owned subsidiary or is a partially owned subsidiary of another entity and its owners have been informed about and do not object to the investor not applying the equity method. In this case, the owners are all those who are entitled to vote;

   b. The investor's debt or equity instruments are not traded in a public market;

   c. The investor did not file and is not in the process of filing its financial statements with a securities commission or other regulatory body for the purpose of issuing any class of financial instrument in a public market; and

   d. The ultimate or any intermediate parent of the investor produces consolidated financial statements that are available for public use and comply with the IFRS.

The investor's share of profits or losses under the equity method should be determined on the basis of the most recently available financial statements of the associate. When the financial statements of the investor and the associate are prepared to different reporting dates, adjustments for significant transactions or events that have taken place between the date of the associate's financial statements and the date of the investor's financial statements should be made. However, the difference between the reporting dates should not be more than three months.

When the accounting policies adopted by the associate are different from those of the investor, adjustments, if any, to the associate's financial statements should be made so that they are in line with the accounting policies adopted by the investor.

At the time the investor makes the initial investment in an associate, the difference, if any, between the cost of the investment and the investor's share of the net fair value of the associate's net assets and liabilities is accounted for in accordance with IFRS 3, *Business Combinations*. Therefore, any goodwill that arises because the cost of the investment is more than the investor's share of the net fair value of the associate's net assets and liabilities will be included in the carrying value of the investment. The provisions of IFRS 3 do not allow amortization of the goodwill. Any negative goodwill that arises because the investor's share in fair value of associate's net assets exceeds the cost of investment should be included as income in determination of the investor's share of associate's profit or loss, in the period in which the investment is acquired.

Subsequent to the acquisition of the investment in the associate, the carrying value of the investment should be tested for impairment under IAS 36, *Impairment of Assets*, and any adjustments should be made to the investor's share of the associates' profits or losses. The impairment test must be carried out on each investment unless the associate does not generate independent cash flows.

If the investor's share of loss in an associate exceeds the carrying value of the investment in the associate, such excess of the loss should not be recognized by the investor unless the investor has a legal or constructive obligation or has made payments on behalf of the associate. When the associate reports profits, the investor should first adjust the share of the losses that have not yet been recognized, and only then recognize its share of those profits.

The carrying value of the investment in the associate is the amount determined under the equity method and the amount of any long term interests that form part of the investor's net investment in the associate. Long term interests will mean those interests that are not planned or likely to be settled in the near future. An example of this is preferred shares and long term receivables. However, this does not include trade receivables, trade payables, and any secured long term receivables or loans.

The losses that are recognized under the equity method in excess of the investor's investment in ordinary shares are applied to the other components of the investor's interest in reverse order of their priority in liquidation.

The investor should not account for the investments in associates if the investor ceases to have significant influence over the associate. In such cases, the investment should be accounted for under IAS 39, *Financial Instruments: Recognition and Measurement*, provided that the associate does not become a subsidiary or joint venture.

On loss of significant influence, the investor shall determine the fair value of the investment in the associate. The difference between the fair value of the retained and disposed investment and the carrying value of the investment is recognized as a profit or loss by the investor. For accounting for the investment as a financial asset under IAS 39, the carrying amount at the date when the investment ceases to be considered as an associate shall be treated as cost on its initial measurement as a financial asset.

Accounting for Investments in Separate Financial Statements

When the investor or its parent prepares consolidated financial statements, investments in associates should be accounted for in the separate financial statements of the investor at cost or in accordance with IAS 39, *Financial Instruments: Recognition and Measurement*. This accounting treatment must be applied consistently to each category of investments.

Example 2

During the reporting period ended December 31, 2008, Buffalo Limited has sold inventory costing $250,000 to its 25% owned associate, Citizen Inc. for $350,000. Buffalo Limited has also, during the previous reporting period, purchased inventory from Citizen Inc. at $150,000. The cost of the inventory sold by Citizen Inc. is $100,000.

The items purchased by both entities are held as inventories at the year-end. How will the intercompany profit on these transactions be dealt with in the financial statements?

Solution

Sales from Buffalo Limited to Citizen Inc.

Intercompany profit on sales ($350,000 – $250,000)	$100,000
Profit to be reported ($100,000) × 75/100	$75,000

The profit of $25,000 will be deferred until the inventory is sold.

Sales from Citizen Inc. to Buffalo Limited

The profit made by Citizen Inc. on sales to Buffalo Limited ($150,000 – $100,000)	$50,000
Profit to be eliminated in carrying value ($50,000) × 25/100	$12,500

Example 3

Easy Investments Limited acquired 25% of the equity shares in Leader Limited at December 31, 2007, for a fair value of $3 million. The statement of financial position of Leader Limited at December 31, 2007, is as follows:

Share capital	$5,000,000
Reserves and surplus	$5,000,000
	$10,000,000
Property, plant, and equipment	$5,000,000
Investments	$2,000,000
Current assets	$3,000,000
	$10,000,000

During the year ended December 31, 2008, Leader Limited made a profit of $700,000. Leader Limited also declared a dividend at 40% of its reserve and surplus at December 31, 2007.

Required

- Calculate the goodwill, if any, on acquisition of shares in Leader Limited;
- Determine the value of Easy Investments Limited's investment in Leader Limited in its consolidated financial statements; and
- Explain what disclosures are required in Easy Investments Limited's financial statements.

Solution

In accordance with IAS 28, Leader Limited is an associate of Easy Investments Limited since it holds more than 20% of the shares of Leader Limited.

Calculation of Goodwill

Cost of the investments	$3,000,000
Share in value of Leader Limited at the date of investment (25% of $10,000,000)	$2,500,000
Goodwill	$ 500,000

Calculation of Share of Profits and Dividends Received

Share of profits for year ended December 31, 2008 (25% of $700,000)	$175,000
Share of dividends declared (25% of (40% of $5,000,000)	$500,000

The share of profits of $175,000 is recognized in the statement of income and the share of dividends of $500,000 is adjusted to the investment account in the statement of financial position.

Carrying Value of Investments at December 31, 2008

Share in value of Leader Limited at the date of investment on December 31, 2007 (25% of $10,000,000)	$2,500,000
Less dividends received	$ (500,000)
	$2,000,000
Add share of profit for year ended December 31, 2008	$ 175,000
Add goodwill on acquisition*	$ 500,000
	$2,675,000

Share of dividends declared [25% of (40% of $ 5,000,000)]

DISCLOSURES

Under IAS 28, the following disclosures are required to be made by the investor:

- Fair value of investments in associates for which there are published price quotations;
- Summarized financial information of associates that must include the aggregated amounts of assets, liabilities, revenues, and profit or loss;
- Explanations when investments of less than 20% are accounted for by the equity method or when investments of more than 20% are not accounted for by the equity method;
- The reporting date of the financial statements of an associate that is different from that of the investor, and the reason for considering the same;
- Nature and extent of any significant restrictions on the ability of associates to transfer funds to the investor in the form of cash dividends or repayment of loans or advances;

- Unrecognized share of losses of an associate, both for the period and cumulatively, if an investor has discontinued recognition of its share of losses of an associate;
- Explanation of any associate that is not accounted for using the equity method; and
- Summarized financial information of associates, either individually or in groups that are not accounted for using the equity method, including the amounts of total assets, total liabilities, revenues, and profit or loss.

Additionally, the following disclosures relating to contingent liabilities are required:

- Investor's share of the contingent liabilities of an associate incurred jointly with other investors; and
- Contingent liabilities that arise because the investor is severally liable for all or part of the liabilities of the associate.

If separate financial statements of the associate are prepared, the following disclosures are required:

- The fact that separate financial statements are prepared and reasons for such preparation;
- A list of significant investments in subsidiaries, associates, and jointly controlled entities with details of name of associate, country of incorporation, proportion of ownership, and share of interest (or voting power held, if different); and
- A description of the method used to account for the above investments.

EXCERPTS FROM PUBLISHED FINANCIAL STATEMENTS

Siemens AG, Annual Report 2008

Notes to Consolidated Financial Statements (in millions of €, except where otherwise stated and per share amounts)

2. Summary of Significant Accounting Policies

Associated Companies

Companies in which Siemens has the ability to exercise significant influence over operating and financial policies (generally through direct or indirect ownership of 20 to 50% of the voting rights) are recorded in the consolidated financial statements using the equity method of accounting and are initially recognized at cost. The excess of Siemens' initial investment in associated companies over Siemens' ownership percentage in the underlying net assets of those companies is attributed to certain fair value adjustments with the remaining portion recognized as goodwill. Goodwill relating to the acquisition of associated companies is included in the carrying amount of the investment and is not amortized but is tested for impairment as part of the overall investment in the associated company. Siemens' share of its associated companies' postacquisition profits or losses is recognized in the income statement, and its share of postacquisition movements in equity that have not been recognized in the associates' profit or loss is recognized directly in equity. The cumulative postacquisition movements are adjusted against the carrying amount of the investment in the associated company. When Siemens' share of losses in an associated company equals or exceeds its interest in the associate, Siemens does not recognize further losses, unless it incurs obligations or makes payments on behalf of the associate. Material intercompany results arising from transactions between Siemens and its associated companies are eliminated to the extent of Siemens' interest in the associated company.

8. Income/Loss from Investments Accounted for Using the Equity Method, Net

	Year ended September 30	
	2008	*2007*
Share of profit, net	259	75
Gains/losses on sales, net	1	35
Impairment	═══	(2)
	260	108

The net share of profit in fiscal years 2008 and 2007, respectively, includes €(119) and €(429) from NSN (see also Note 4). For further information on the company's principal investments accounted for under the equity method, see Note 19.

19. Investments Accounted for Using the Equity Method

As of September 30, 2008, NSN (see Note 4), BSH Bosch und Siemens Hausgeräte GmbH (BSH), and AREVA NP S.A.S., France (Areva), which are all unlisted, were the principal investments accounted for using the equity method. Summarized financial information for NSN, BSH and Areva, not adjusted for the percentage of ownership held by Siemens, is presented below. See Note 4 for additional information on EN.

	September 30	
	2008	*2007*
Total assets*	27,300	26,457
Total liabilities*	18,642	17,355

*Balance sheet information for BSH and Areva as of June 30, for NSN as of September 30.

	Year Ended September 30	
	2008	*2007*
Revenue**	27,871	18,631
Net income /loss**	(24)	(628)

** Income statement information for NSN for the twelve months ended September 30, 2008 and the six months ended September 30, 2007; for BSH and Areva for the twelve months ended June 30, 2008 and 2007.

By the end of September 2008, the investment in FSC has been classified as assets held for disposal and accounting under the equity method has been ceased from that date on. Summarized financial information for FSC, not adjusted for the percentage of ownership held by Siemens, is presented below:

	September 30	
	2008	*2007*
Total assets	3,063	3,352
Total liabilities	2,771	2,960

	Year Ended September 30	
	2008	*2007*
Total assets	6,169	6,895
Net income/loss	(23)	68

For further information see also Note 8.

21 FINANCIAL REPORTING IN HYPERINFLATIONARY ECONOMIES (IAS 29)

INTRODUCTION

In a hyperinflationary economy, money loses purchasing power at a high rate making the comparison of amounts from transactions and other events that have occurred at different times or even within the same accounting period misleading. IAS 29 has instituted a methodology of restatement of accounting information using suitable price indices to make the financial statements of different periods comparable and the accounting indicators for the same accounting period useful for users' decision making.

SCOPE

IAS 29 is applicable to the financial statements, including the consolidated financial statements, of any entity whose functional currency is the currency of a hyperinflationary economy. An entity shall apply this standard from the beginning of the reporting period in which it identifies the existence of hyperinflation in the country in whose currency it reports.

IAS 29 requires presentation of financial statements restated in accordance with the measuring unit current at the end of the reporting period. The restated financial statements are not to be presented as a supplement to unrestated financial statements. Moreover, separate presentation of the financial statements before restatement is discouraged.

KEY TERMS

Hyperinflationary economy. An economy that is *inter alia* characterized by the following:

1. The general population prefers to keep its wealth in nonmonetary assets or in a relatively stable foreign currency. Amounts of local currency held are immediately invested to maintain purchasing power;
2. The general population regards monetary amounts not in terms of the local currency but in terms of a relatively stable foreign currency. Prices may be quoted in that currency;
3. Sales and purchases on credit take place at prices that compensate for the expected loss of purchasing power during the credit period, even if the period is short;
4. Interest rates, wages, and prices are linked to a price index; and
5. The cumulative inflation rate over three years is approaching, or exceeds, 100%.

Monetary items. Assets and liabilities expressed in terms of money held and items to be received or paid in money.

RESTATEMENT OF FINANCIAL STATEMENTS

Conversion Unit

All financial statement elements, whether they are based on a historical cost approach or a current cost approach, are stated in terms of the measuring unit current at the end of the reporting period.

The corresponding figures for the previous period required by IAS 1, *Presentation of Financial Statements*, and any information in respect of earlier periods, shall also be stated in terms of the measuring unit current at the end of the reporting period.

For the purpose of presenting comparative amounts in a different presentation currency, paragraphs 42(b) and 43 of IAS 21, *The Effects of Changes in Foreign Exchange Rates*, are also applied.

The measuring unit current at the end of the reporting period is determined using a general price index that reflects changes in general purchasing power. IAS 29 prefers that all entities belonging to the same hyperinflationary economy should use the same general index. Therefore, a hyperinflationary economy that follows IFRSs should notify a general price index to be followed by the entities for the purpose of presentation of financial statements.

The measuring unit current at a particular measurement date is determined by applying a conversion factor:

$$\frac{\text{Index on the reporting date}}{\text{Index on the measurement date}}$$

This means the conversion factor for all items measured using the currency of hyperinflationary economy on the reporting date is 1. Items measured using the currency of a hyperinflationary economy at a date earlier than the reporting date are converted applying a conversion factor that is greater than 1.

Example 1

Delta Corporation, Zimbabwe (Annual Report 2008) has worked out the measuring unit current at the end of the reporting period as described here:

The restatement has been calculated by means of conversion factors derived from the consumer price index (CPI) prepared by the Zimbabwe Central Statistical Office. The conversion factors used to restate the financial statements at March 31, 2008, using a 2001 base year, are as follows:

	Index	*Conversion factor*
March 31, 2008	8,395,791,848.8	1.0
March 31, 2007	2,008,932.1	4,179.2
March 31, 2006	87,337.5	96,130.4

Restatement of Statement of Financial Position

1. *Monetary items.* Items of assets and liabilities that are already expressed in terms of the measuring unit current at the end of the reporting period are not restated. Examples include monetary items like debtors, creditors, and bank deposits.
2. *Assets and liabilities linked by agreement to changes in prices.* Examples are index-linked bonds and loans. They are adjusted in accordance with the agreement in order to ascertain the amount outstanding at the end of the reporting period. For these kinds of assets and liabilities, a specific index is used for the measuring unit current at the end of the reporting period.
3. *Nonmonetary items carried at current price.* Nonmonetary items that are carried at amounts current at the end of the reporting period, such as net realizable value and fair value, are not restated.
4. *Other nonmonetary items.* All other nonmonetary assets and liabilities are restated.

5. *Nonmonetary items carried at cost.* Many nonmonetary assets are carried at cost or cost less depreciation; hence, they are expressed at amounts current at their date of acquisition. They are restated as explained in Example 2.

6. *Nonmonetary items that are revalued.* When nonmonetary assets are revalued, they are restated based on the conversion factor of the date of revaluation.

7. *Reduction to recoverable amount.* Restated amounts of property, plant, and equipment, goodwill, patents and trademarks are reduced to recoverable amount and restated amounts of inventories are reduced to net realizable value (NRV).

Example 2

Bizar, a trader of fast-moving consumer goods, is identified as having a reporting currency of a hyperinflationary economy. It follows the cost model for measuring property, plant, and equipment as per IAS 16:

	December 31, 2007	*December 31, 2008*
Acquisition cost		
(Date of acquisition 2001)	CU 2000	CU 2000
Accumulated depreciation	CU 500	CU 600

Index on the date of acquisition is 110; 1,200 on December 21, 2007, and 2,000 on December 31, 2008.

In the statement of financial position on December 31, 2007, Bizar would restate property, plant, and equipment as

	Historical cost	*Conversion factor*	*Restated*
Acquisition cost	2,000	1,200/110=10.91	21,820
Less accumulated depreciation	500	10.91	5,455
Net			16,365

In the statement of financial position on December 31, 2008, Bizar would restate property, plant, and equipment as

	Restated 2007 measuring unit current	*Conversion factor*	*Restated 2008 measuring unit current*	
			2007	*2008*
Acquisition cost	21,820	2,000/1,200 = 1.67	36,440	36,440
Less accumulated depreciation	5,455	1.67	9,110	9,110
Depreciation for 2008		2,000/110 = 18.18		1,818
Net	16,365		27,330	25,512

If the entity does not have a record of the date of acquisition of the asset, then it would make a professional valuation of the asset for the first-time application of IAS 29.

8. *Equity method associates or joint ventures.* Profit or loss of the equity-method associate or joint venture is included in the consolidated financial statement of the investor. The statement of financial position and statement of comprehensive income of such an investee are restated for calculating the investor's share of its net assets and profit or loss. When the restated financial statements of the investee are expressed in a foreign currency, they are translated at closing rates.

9. *Capitalization of borrowing costs.* It is not appropriate both to restate the capital expenditure financed by borrowing and to capitalize that part of the borrowing costs that compensates for the inflation during the same period. This part of the borrowing costs is recognized as an expense in the period in which the costs are incurred.

10. *Conversion of equity.* The components of owners' equity, except retained earnings and any revaluation surplus, are restated by applying a general price index from the dates the components were contributed or otherwise arose. Any revaluation surplus that arose in previous periods is eliminated. Restated retained earnings are derived from all the other amounts in the restated statement of financial position.

RESTATEMENT OF COMPREHENSIVE INCOME

The restatement of items of income and expense (other than depreciation and amortization) are carried out applying the change in the general price index from the dates when the items of income and expenses were initially recorded in the financial statements. This means an entity has to keep records of indices against every transaction relating to income and expense and restate on the reporting date once the closing index becomes available. A practical difficulty that arises in applying this clause is nonavailability of general price indices on a daily basis. For example, Delta Corporation, Zimbabwe, has restated all items in the income statements applying the relevant monthly conversion factors.

Example 3

Entity E, which belongs to a hyperinflationary economy, has prepared a historical cost based trial balance as on December 31, 2008, as shown here, along with guidance on converting various elements of the financial statements.

Trial balance

	CU	CU	Conversion
Sales		8,080	Monthly index
Purchases	4,460		Monthly index
Expenses	2,597		Monthly index
Accumulated depreciation	0	400	Index of the acquisition month of related property, plant, and equipment
Opening inventory	200		Index of the acquisition month
Interest	150		Monthly index
Equity share capital	0	200	Index of the contribution month
Retained earnings		4,000	Residual
15% bank loan		1,000	No conversion
Property, plant, and equipment	3,000		Index of the acquisition month
Debtors	400		No conversion
Creditors		200	No conversion
Bank deposit	2,900		No conversion
Cash	173		No conversion
	13,880	**13,880**	

Further information:

Depreciation for 2008—CU 200; Closing inventory—CU 250

Acquisition date index: Opening inventory 12,800; Property, plant, and equipment 6,000; Owners' contribution to equity 2,000; Closing inventories were acquired in November 2008.

Understanding the Restatement Process

Step 1: Conversion of Sales, Purchases, Expenses, and Interest

2008	Index	Sales	Purchases	Expense	Interest	Restated Sales	Purchases	Expense	Interest
Jan	13,000	200	110	80		1,462	804	585	0
Feb	14,500	230	128	92		1,507	839	603	0
Mar	17,000	270	150	110		1,509	838	615	0
Apr	27,000	400	292	125		1,407	1,027	440	0
May	36,000	540	320	150		1,425	844	396	0
Jun	40,000	600	360	190	75	1,425	855	451	178
Jul	45,000	650	380	230		1,372	802	486	0
Aug	57,000	810	420	260		1,350	700	433	0
Sep	60,000	840	500	290		1,330	792	459	0
Oct	65,000	900	550	320		1,315	804	468	0
Nov	75,000	1,140	600	350		1,444	760	443	0
Dec	95,000	1,500	650	400	75	1,500	650	400	75
		8,080	**4,460**	**2,597**	**150**	**17,046**	**9,715**	**5,778**	**253**

Note: Items of income and expense (except depreciation and amortization) are converted applying the index of the date of the transactions. Since indices are not available on a daily basis, they are converted using the index of the appropriate month.

Step 2: Finding Out Gain or Loss on Net Monetary Items

An entity loses the purchasing power during inflation for holding monetary assets, whereas it gains purchasing power for carrying monetary liabilities. This means holding net monetary assets means purchasing power loss.

Monetary assets	*CU*	*Weighted-average conversion factor*	*At current purchasing power*
Debtors	400	0.789474	316
Bank deposit	2,900	0.263158	763
Cash	173	0.894737	155
Total monetary assets	3,473		1,234
Monetary liabilities			
Creditors	200	0.789474	158
15% bank loan	1,000	0.126316	126
Total monetary liabilities	1,200		284
Net monetary assets	2,273		950
Purchasing power loss on monetary assets			−1,323

This purchasing power loss on net monetary asset is deducted from profit or loss.

Step 3: Finding Restated Retained Earnings. This is the net restatement difference of all items of income, expense, assets, liabilities, and equity adjusted for purchasing power gain or loss on net monetary items.

	Prestatement CU	*CU*	*Restated*		*Difference*
Sales		8,080		17,046	−8,966
Purchases	4,460		9,715		5,255
Expenses	2,597		5,778		3,181
Accumulated depreciation		400		6,967	−6,567
Opening inventory	200		1,484		1,284
Interest	150		253		103
Equity share capital		200		9,500	−9,300
Retained earnings		4,000		34,813 *	
15% bank loan		1,000		1,000	0
Property, plant, and equipment	3,000		47,500		44,500
Debtors	400		400		0
Creditors		200		200	0
Bank deposit	2,900		2,900		0
Cash	173		173		0
Purchasing power loss on net monetary assets			1,323		1,323
	13,880	13,880	69,526	69,526	30,813

*Total difference 30,813 + Prestatement balance 4,000 = 34,813.

Step 4: Restated Statement of Comprehensive Income

	Prestatement CU	*Restated*
Sales	8,080	17,046
Cost of goods sold		
Opening inventory	200	1,484
Purchases	4,460	9,715
Less closing inventory	250	317
	4,410	**10,883**
Expenses	2,597	5,778
Depreciation	200	3,167
Interest	150	253
	7,357	20,081
Profit/loss before charging purchasing power loss on net monetary items	723	−3,035
Purchasing power loss on net monetary items		−1,323
Net loss		−4,358

Note: This presentation is made for preliminary understanding only. IAS 29 prefers that comparative prerestated income statement data are not presented.

Step 4: Statement of Financial Position

	Prestatement	Restated
Noncurrent assets		
Property, plant, and equipment	3,000	47,500
Less accumulated depreciation	–600	–10,134
	2,400	37,366
Current assets		
Inventory	250	317
Debtors	400	400
Bank deposit	2,900	2,900
Cash	173	173
	3,723	3,790
Total assets	6,123	41,156
Liabilities and equity		
Noncurrent liabilities		
Bank loan	1,000	1,000
Current liability		
Creditors	200	200
Equity		
Equity share capital	200	9,500
Retained earnings	4,723	30,455*
	6,123	41,155

Retained Earnings = 34,813 – 4,358.

STATEMENT OF CASH FLOWS

IAS 29 requires that all items in the statement of cash flows are expressed in terms of the measuring unit current at the end of the reporting period.

Taxes

The restatement of financial statements in accordance with IAS 29 may give rise to differences between the carrying amount of individual assets and liabilities in the statement of financial position and their tax bases. Deferred tax asset or liabilities are worked out in accordance with IAS 12, *Income Taxes*.

Consolidation

When the parent and subsidiary both have reporting currencies that are currencies of a hyperinflationary economy, the financial statements of the subsidiary are restated first; then consolidation is carried out in accordance with IAS 27.

Economy Ceases to Be a Hyperinflationary Economy

When an economy ceases to be hyperinflationary, an entity will discontinue the preparation and presentation of financial statements as per IAS 29. The entity shall treat the amounts expressed in the measuring unit current at the end of the previous reporting period as the basis for the carrying amounts in its subsequent financial statements.

EXCERPTS FROM PUBLISHED FINANCIAL STATEMENTS

Massmart, Annual Report 2008

Notes to the Annual Financial Statements for the Year Ended June 30, 2008

6.   Hyperinflation

In the 2007 financial year, the decision was made to prospectively deconsolidate the results of the Zimbabwean Makro operations.

In terms of IAS 27, *Consolidated and Separate Financial Statements*, control is defined as "the power to govern the financial and operating policies of an entity so as to obtain benefits from its activities." It is evident from the current social, political, and economic developments within Zimbabwe that control does not exist. This has been evidenced through the forcing of retailers to sell goods at predetermined prices and the inability of the Massmart Group to repatriate monies. It is Massmart's view that, throughout the 2008 financial year, it did not have control over the Zimbabwean operations and as such the results remain deconsolidated. This will be assessed on a yearly basis going forward.

On deconsolidation, the investment in Makro Zimbabwe has been reflected as an available-for-sale financial asset in line with the requirements of IAS 39, *Financial Instruments: Recognition and Measurement*. At year-end, the fair value of this asset has been determined to be zero. Details can be found in Note 14 on page 130.

14. Investments

Reconciliation of available-for-sale investments

	2008 Rm	2007 Rm
Opening balance	—	—
Deconsolidation of Makro Zimbabwe	—	13.2
Fair value adjustment of investment in Makro Zimbabwe	—	(13.2)
Closing balance	—	—

Makro Zimbabwe was deconsolidated in the prior year and the investment has been carried as an available-for-sale financial asset. At the prior year-end, the fair value of this asset has been determined to be zero and the adjustment taken to equity as a reserve.

22 INTERESTS IN JOINT VENTURES (IAS 31)

SCOPE

IAS 31 sets out the requirements for accounting for "interests in joint ventures." Joint ventures are widely used in conducting business, particularly in the investment property sector and in extractive industries.

IAS 31 shall be applied

- In accounting for interests in joint ventures, *and*
- In reporting joint venture assets, liabilities, income, and expenses in the financial statements of joint venturers and the investors.

IAS 31 scopes out venturers' share in jointly controlled entities held by

- Venture capital organizations; or
- Mutual funds, unit trusts, and similar entities including investment-linked insurance funds that upon initial recognition are designated at *fair value through profit and loss account* or are classified as held for trading in accordance with IAS 39. However, the venturer is required to make disclosures in accordance with IAS 31.

Furthermore, a venturer with an interest in a jointly controlled entity is exempted from proportionate consolidation and applying the equity method when it meets the following conditions:

1. The interest is classified as held for sale in accordance with IFRS 5;
2. The exception in IAS 27 allowing a parent that has interest in a jointly controlled entity not to present consolidated financial statements is applicable; or
3. When all the following conditions apply:

   a. The venturer is a 100% owned or a partially owned subsidiary of another entity and its owners have no objection to the venturer not applying the proportionate consolidation or the equity method;

   b. The venturer's debt or equity is not traded in a public market;

   c. The venturer did not file, nor is it in the process of filing, its financial statements with a regulator or securities commission for the purpose of issuing any class of instruments in a public market; and

   d. The ultimate or intermediate parent of the venturer produces consolidated financial statements available for public use that comply with IFRS.

KEY TERMS

Joint venture. A contractual arrangement whereby two or more parties (the "venturers") undertake an economic activity that is subject to "joint control."

Joint control. The contractually agreed sharing of control over an economic activity and exists only when strategic financial and operating decisions relating to activities require unanimous consent of the parties sharing control.

Venturer. A party to a joint venture who has control over the joint venture.

TYPES OF JOINT VENTURES

Joint ventures can be formed or structured in several ways. IAS 31 identifies the following three types of joint ventures that are commonly described as, and meet the definition of, a *joint venture*:

1. Jointly controlled operations
2. Jointly controlled assets
3. Jointly controlled entities

The standard emphasizes that all joint ventures have the following common features:

- There exists a contractual arrangement whereby two or more joint venturers are bound; and
- The contractual arrangement establishes joint control.

JOINTLY CONTROLLED OPERATIONS

Some joint ventures involve the use of the assets and resources of the venturers as opposed to the formation of a corporation, a partnership, or other entity, or a financial structure that is separate from the venturers themselves. In such cases, each venturer uses its own assets and incurs its own expenses and raises its own financing. The joint venture arrangement in such cases provides a means of sharing the revenues derived from the joint venture activities.

Example 1

X Inc. and Y Ltd. are two venturers that have entered into an arrangement to combine their resources and expertise in building a ship. Different parts of the ship are built by X Inc. and Y Ltd. Each venturer bears its own costs; however, they share in the revenues from the sale of the ship and their shares are determined according to their contractual arrangement (i.e., the joint venture arrangement). This arrangement is a jointly controlled operation.

JOINTLY CONTROLLED ASSETS

Some joint venture arrangements involve joint control by the venturers of one or more assets contributed to, or acquired for the purpose of the joint venture and dedicated to the purposes of the joint venture. The venturers share in the revenues derived from the joint venture in their agreed-upon shares in accordance with the joint venture arrangement.

Example 2

ABC Inc. and XYZ Corporation enter into a joint venture arrangement whereby they jointly control and operate an oil pipeline. Each venturer uses the pipeline to transport its own product. As per the terms of the joint venture arrangement, both ABC Inc. and XYZ Corporation have agreed to bear an equal share of the operating costs of the pipeline (i.e., each venture bears one-half of the total costs of operating the pipeline). The net profits from the joint venture business are also shared equally by the venturers. This arrangement is a jointly controlled asset.

JOINTLY CONTROLLED ENTITIES

This type of a joint venture involves the establishment of a corporation, partnership, or other entity (i.e., the jointly controlled entity) wherein each venturer has an interest. In this form of a joint venture, a contractual arrangement between the venturers establishes the joint control over the economic activity of the joint venture.

The jointly controlled entity controls the assets of the joint venture, incurs liabilities and expenses, and recognizes the revenues from the activities of the joint venture arrangement. Each venturer is entitled to share in the profits (in some cases the output) of the jointly controlled entity.

Such joint ventures maintain their own accounting records and prepare, and usually present, their own financial statements.

Example 3

Excellent Inc. and Good Ltd. enter into a joint venture arrangement whereby they establish a corporation called Great Corporation. The venturers participate equally in the share capital of the corporation and have agreed to share equally in the profits and losses of the corporation. Both the venturers have equal representation on the Board of the corporation and the management of the corporation is run jointly by their representatives. This is an example of a joint controlled entity wherein both venturers jointly own and control the joint venture business and assets.

FINANCIAL STATEMENTS OF THE VENTURER

In accounting for the interest in the joint venture, IAS 31 allows a choice between either the proportionate consolidation method or the equity method. However, it should be noted that the IASB is proposing to amend IAS 31 so that the proportionate consolidation method would no longer be available (see "Proposed Amendments to IAS 31," later in this chapter).

Proportionate Consolidation Method

The proportionate consolidation method is a method by which a venturer's financial statements reflect

- Its share of assets that it controls jointly;
- Its share of liabilities for which it is jointly responsible;
- Its share of income; and
- Its share of expenses of the jointly controlled entity.

There are two reporting formats.

Format 1: Under this method of reporting, the venturer may combine, *line by line,* its share of each of the assets, liabilities, income, and expenses.

Format 2: Under this method of reporting, the venturer may include *separate line items* for its share of the assets, liabilities, income, and expenses.

Equity Method

The equity method is a method by which an interest in a jointly controlled entity is initially recorded at cost and adjusted thereafter for the postacquisition change in the venturer's share of net assets of the jointly controlled entity. The profit or loss of the venturer includes the venturer's share of the profit or loss of the jointly controlled entity.

Exceptions to the proportionate consolidation and equity methods.

1. Interests in jointly controlled entities that are classified as held for sale in accordance with IFRS 5 should be accounted in accordance with IFRS 5. If the interest in a jointly controlled entity no longer meets the classification criteria under IFRS 5 after some time, then the interest shall be accounted for using the proportionate consolidation or equity method as from the date of its classification as held for sale. Financial

statements for the periods since classification as held for sale are amended accordingly.

2. If an investor ceases to have joint control over an entity then it shall account for any remaining investment in accordance with IAS 39 from that date (provided the former jointly controlled entity does not become a subsidiary or an associate).
3. From the date when a jointly controlled entity becomes a subsidiary of an investor, the investor should account for it in accordance with IAS 27 and IFRS 3.
4. From the date when a jointly controlled entity becomes an associate, the investor shall account for its interest in accordance with IAS 28 from the date on which the jointly controlled entity becomes an associate.

Transactions between a venturer and a joint venture. When a venturer enters into a transaction with the joint venture, say, it contributes or sells assets to the joint venture, the recognition of any portion of a gain or loss from the transaction should reflect the substance of the transaction.

The standard mandates that the venturer recognizes only that portion of the gain or loss that is attributable to the interests of the other venturers. However, IAS 31 requires that the venturer shall recognize the full amount of loss when the contribution or sale provides evidence of a reduction in the net realizable value (NRV) of the current assets. (This is also clarified by SIC 13, *Jointly Controlled Entities—Nonmonetary Contributions by Venturers.*)

DISCLOSURES

A venturer shall disclose a listing and description of the following:

1. Interests in significant joint ventures; and
2. Proportion of ownership interest held in jointly controlled entities.

A venturer that uses a line-by-line reporting format for proportionate consolidation or the equity method, while recognizing its interest held in jointly controlled entities, has to disclose the aggregate amount of each of the following:

- Current assets
- Current liabilities
- Long-term assets
- Long-term liabilities
- Income and expenses related to its interest in joint ventures

A venturer shall disclose the method it has used to recognize its interest in the jointly controlled entities. A venturer shall also disclose its share of contingent liabilities and commitments.

PROPOSED AMENDMENTS TO IAS 31

The IASB has issued an Exposure Draft (ED 9) proposing to replace the proportionate consolidation method of accounting for jointly controlled entities with the equity method and require additional disclosures about such arrangements.

The following comprise the principal differences between the proposals in ED 9 and IAS 31:

- ED 9 uses the term *joint arrangement* to describe all arrangements in which the parties have shared decision making. The term *joint venture* is used for one type of joint arrangement—one that involves a jointly controlled entity such that the venturers do not have rights to individual assets or obligations for liabilities of the venture. Rather, each venturer is entitled to a share of the outcome (e.g., profit or loss) of the activities of the joint venture. IAS 31 uses the term *joint venture* for all contractual arrangements in which two or more parties have joint control.

- ED 9 requires equity accounting for those joint arrangements meeting the new definition of a joint venture. For other types of joint arrangements (joint operations and joint assets), an entity accounts for its interest in the individual assets, liabilities, revenues, and expenses, or financing of the joint arrangement. This produces a similar result to proportionate consolidation, although the underlying principle is different. IAS 31 permits proportionate consolidation for all types of joint ventures (jointly controlled operations, jointly controlled assets, and jointly controlled entity).
- ED 9 has more extensive disclosure requirements than IAS 31.

EXCERPTS FROM PUBLISHED FINANCIAL STATEMENTS

Ahold Annual Report 2008

Notes to the Consolidated Financial Statements

3. Significant Accounting Policies

Investments in Joint Ventures and Associates

A joint venture is a contractual arrangement whereby Ahold and other parties undertake an economic activity through a jointly controlled entity. Joint control exists when strategic financial and operating policy decisions relating to the activities require the unanimous consent of the parties sharing control. Associates are entities over which Ahold has significant influence but not control, generally accompanying a shareholding of between 20% and 50% of the voting rights. Significant influence is the power to participate in the financial and operating policy decisions of the entity but is not control or joint control over those policies.

Joint ventures and associates are accounted for using the equity method. Under the equity method, investments in joint ventures and associates are measured at cost as adjusted for post-acquisition changes in Ahold's share of the net assets of the investment (net of any accumulated impairment in the value of individual investments). Where necessary, adjustments are made to the financial statements of joint ventures and associates to ensure consistency with the accounting policies of the company.

Unrealized gains on transactions between Ahold and its joint ventures and associates are eliminated to the extent of Ahold's stake in these investments. Unrealised losses are also eliminated unless the transaction provides evidence of an impairment of the assets transferred.

14. Investments in Joint Ventures

Ahold owns 60% of the outstanding common shares of ICA, a food retailer operating in Sweden, Norway and the Baltic states. The 60% shareholding does not entitle Ahold to unilateral decision-making authority over ICA due to the shareholders agreement with the joint venture partner, which provides that strategic, financial, and operational decisions will be made only on the basis of mutual consent. On the basis of this shareholders agreement, the company concluded that it has no control over ICA and, consequently, does not consolidate ICA's financial statements. For condensed financial information on ICA, see Note 6.

Ahold also has a 49% stake in JMR, which is classified as held for sale and discontinued operation (see Note 5), and is a partner in various smaller joint ventures. Changes in investments in joint ventures are as follows:

In € million	2008	2007
Beginning of the year	869	799
Investments and increases in existing shareholdings	6	1
Share in income of joint ventures	109	138
Dividend	(70)	(66)
Classified as held for sale or sold	(4)	(2)
Exchange rate differences	(109)	(1)
Other changes	1	—
End of the year	802	869

Effective January 1, 2009, the tax legislation in Sweden concerning intercompany loans has been changed. ICA estimates that this will result in approximately SEK 300 million (EUR 27 million) higher income tax charges annually for the ICA Group.

23 FINANCIAL INSTRUMENTS: PRESENTATION (IAS 32)

INTRODUCTION

A *financial instrument* is a contract that gives rise to a financial asset to one entity, and a financial liability or equity instrument to another entity. Financial instruments include primary financial instruments like receivables, payables, loans and advances, debentures and bonds, and derivative instruments like options, futures, forwards, swaps, caps, collars, floors, forward rate agreements (FRA), and so on. A derivative with a positive value is a financial asset and one with a negative value is a financial liability. A contract to buy or sell a nonfinancial item may give rise to a financial asset or financial liability.

Example 1

Hiace Manufacturing Corporation has made investments in equity and debentures/bonds of another company as well as investments in government bonds and Treasury bills. Also, it has receivables against credit sales made and has bank deposits and cash in hand. The company has taken loans from banks and has issued debentures for financing its various projects. It has also issued 8% redeemable preference shares that are to be redeemed after five years.

These transactions give rise to the following financial assets and financial liabilities:

Financial assets

- Investments in equity shares, debentures/bonds, government bonds and Treasury bills
- Trade receivables
- Cash and cash equivalents

Financial liabilities

- Debentures
- Loans
- Redeemable preference shares

Accounting for financial instruments is covered by three standards:

- IAS 32, *Financial Instruments: Presentation*
- IAS 39, *Financial Instruments: Recognition and Measurement*
- IFRS 7, *Financial Instruments: Disclosures*

A new standard, IFRS 9, *Financial Instruments,* was issued in November 2009 to simplify the classification and measurement of financial instruments. Upon completion of the different phases of the IASB's financial instrument project and completion of the new standard, IAS 39, *Financial Instruments: Recognition and Measurement,* will be withdrawn. Although IFRS 9, *Financial Instruments,* will come into effect for the accounting periods beginning on or after January 1, 2013, an early application is permitted. This simplified version standard on financial instruments is an attempt to rationalize the accounting norms based on the recent experience of global recession. IAS 32 covers the presentation issues of financial instruments.

SCOPE

IAS 32, *Financial Instruments,* sets out principles for

- Distinguishing financial liabilities and equity instruments;
- Recognition of compound financial instruments;
- Presentation of Treasury shares;
- Recognition of interest, dividend, losses or gains; and
- Offsetting financial assets and financial liabilities.

Financial instruments that are not covered under IAS 32 are

- Investments in equity shares of subsidiary, associate, or joint venture. They are covered respectively by IAS 27, *Consolidated and Separate Financial Statements*; IAS 28, *Investments in Associates;* and IAS 31, *Interests in Joint Ventures.* However, all derivatives linked to interests in subsidiaries, associates, or joint ventures are within the scope of this standard.
- Employers' rights and obligations arising from employee benefit plans. IAS 19, *Employee Benefits,* applies to these assets and liabilities.
- Financial instruments, contracts, and obligations under share-based payment transactions to which *IFRS 2, Share-Based Payment,* applies, except for
    - Certain share-based payment transactions are entered into to buy or sell nonfinancial items. When these transactions contain net settlement clauses, or net settlement is customary although not explicit in the contract, IAS 32 applies to those contracts.
    - Other examples are a category of share-based payment transactions that the reporting entity takes delivery of but sells within a short period after delivery for the purpose of generating a profit from short-term fluctuations in price or a dealer's margin.
    - When the nonfinancial item that is the subject of the contract of a share-based payment is readily convertible to cash.
    - Treasury shares purchased, sold, issued, or canceled in connection with employee share option plans, employee share purchase plans, and all other share-based payment arrangements.
- Rights and obligations under insurance contracts except (1) financial guarantee contracts that an insurer elects to account for as financial instruments, and (2) embedded derivatives in host insurance contracts that are to be separated in accordance with IAS 39, *Financial Instruments: Recognition and Measurement.*

FINANCIAL ASSETS

Financial assets are

- Cash (e.g., currency, cash and bank deposits; bank deposits reflect a contractual right to receive cash; but gold bullion is a commodity);
- An equity instrument of another entity (e.g., investment in equity shares of another company);
- A contractual right
    - To receive cash or another financial asset from another entity; or
    - To exchange financial assets or financial liabilities with another entity for terms which are potentially favorable to the entity; and
- A contract that will or may be settled in the entity's own equity instruments and is

- A nonderivative for which the entity is or may be obliged to receive a variable number of the entity's own equity instruments; or
- A derivative that will or may be settled other than by exchange of a fixed amount of cash or another financial asset for a fixed number of entity's own equity instruments

The following Examples (2 to 4) illustrate the situation when a financial asset arises out of

- Exchange of financial assets or liabilities in potentially favorable terms;
- Nonderivative-based contracts as financial asset when an entity is obliged to receive a variable number of the entity's own equity instruments;
- Derivative-based contracts as financial asset when an entity is obliged to receive a fixed number of the entity's own equity instruments.

Example 2

X Ltd. has entered into a contract with its lender bank to pay off 4.5% of the €10 million loan due in five years against 3.5% of €10 million loan of the same maturity. Current market yield is 3.5%.

In this case, the entity has exchanged its existing financial liability for a potentially favorable term that decreases in the value of an existing financial liability, that is, 4.5% of the €10 million loans.

This type of transaction occurs in a declining interest rate scenario. There will arise a situation at the end of reporting period that the lender agrees to reduce the interest rate, which is effectively a new low-interest-rate loan in exchange of old high-interest-rate loan. The borrower would exchange a financial liability in favorable term. To give effect to this agreement which is not yet effected, the borrower will recognize a financial asset and the lender will recognize a financial liability.

Valuation

PV of annuity at 3.5% for five years = 4.5151 and PV at 3.5% at fifth year = 0.842.

(a) Fair value of 3.5% €10 million loan = PV of interest + PV of repayment

$$= €0.35 \text{ million} \times 4.5151 + €10 \text{ million} \times 0.842 = €10 \text{ million}.$$

(b) Fair value of 4.5% €10 million loan at market yield of 3.5%

$$= €0.45 \text{ million} \times 4.5151 + €10 \text{ million} \times 0.842$$

$$= €10.4515 \text{ million}.$$

As this is a contract to exchange an existing financial liability (4.5% €10 million loan) with a potentially favorable term with 3.5% €10 million loan, the entity will recognize a gain of €0.4515 million and create a financial asset arising out of the contract to pay off the old loan that is not yet effected.

Example 3

When an entity buys back its own shares at a fixed price, it is an equity transaction. On the contrary, if a company enters into a contract (as on December 1, 2009) to set off trade receivables of €100 million (a fixed amount) due from a customer who is also a shareholder of the company against receiving such number of common shares that will be determined based on the share price after three months (February 28, 2010). This becomes a financial instrument as the company will be obliged to receive variable quantities of its own equity shares. If the quantity of common shares to be bought back was fixed, then this contract would have been treated as a fixed price share buy-back transaction

Gain/loss will arise out of this contract based on the price of the common share of the company as on the reporting date. There will arise a financial asset in case of gain or a financial liability in case of a loss. In effect, it is a forward-buy contract, which is a derivative.

Example 4

Company E entered into a futures contract to buy its 100,000 common shares (as on December 1, 2009) at a price to be determined based on price of the common share after three months (as on February 28, 2010). This contract in effect is no different from the nonderivative-based contract discussed in Example 3, except that quantity of common shares to be bought back is fixed. The resultant gain or loss arising out of change in price of the common shares of the company as on the reporting date will create a financial asset or financial liability respectively.

FINANCIAL LIABILITIES

Financial liabilities are

- A contractual obligation

  - To deliver cash or any other financial asset to another enterprise; or
  - To exchange financial instruments with another enterprise for terms which are potentially unfavorable.

- A contract that will or may be settled in the entity's own equity instruments and is a nonderivative for which the entity is or may be obliged to receive a variable number of the entity's own equity instruments, or a derivative that will or may be settled other than by exchange of a fixed amount of cash or another financial asset for a fixed number of the entity's own equity instruments.

Examples of liabilities are accounts payable, bills payable, loans and advances payable, bank overdraft, and debentures payable.

A financial instrument that contains a nonfinancial obligation that can be avoided only by making a transfer of cash or other financial asset is also classified as a financial liability. For example, a reporting entity borrows $1 million from a bank for five years which can be settled by transferring to the bank either its branch building or by repaying the loan by paying $1 million plus rolled-up interest at market rates. Since there is an option to repay the advance in cash, the transaction becomes a financial liability of the reporting entity and financial asset of the bank.

EQUITY INSTRUMENTS

An *equity instrument* is any contract that evidences a residual interest in the assets of an entity after deducting all of its liabilities. Examples of equity instruments are

1. Nonputtable equity shares
2. Certain types of preference shares
3. Warrants or written call options that allow the holder to subscribe for or purchase a fixed number of nonputtable equity shares in the issuing entity in exchange for a fixed amount of cash or another financial asset

Example 5

Identify the nature of the following financial instruments from the standpoint of the issuer (X Ltd.):

1. X Ltd. issues 10 million equity shares of face value Euros 10 each at Euros 120 for cash.
2. X Ltd. entered into a contract to buy back 1 million of its own equity shares from Y Ltd. at Euros 120 each in cash.
3. X Ltd. entered into a contract to buy back 1 million of its own equity shares from Y Ltd. against Loans and Advances of Euros 120 million due from Y Ltd. Number of shares to be delivered by Y Ltd. will be decided based on the price of the equity shares after six months (to be precise on November 30, 2009).

4. X Ltd. entered into a contract to surrender a business unit for Euros 2000 million to Y Ltd. for which it will receive its own equity shares. The number of equity shares to be surrendered by Y Ltd. will be decided by the average price of the equity over next three months.

Solution

Items (1) and (2) are equity instruments. They are contracts to issue or buy own equity shares at a fixed price. Items (3) and (4) are financial liabilities. The entity will receive a variable number of the entity's own equity instruments.

PRESENTATION OF LIABILITIES AND EQUITY

IAS 32 requires that an issuer of a financial instrument shall classify at the time of initial recognition the instrument or its component parts into

- Equity; or
- Financial liability; or
- Financial assets.

This is to be done based on the substance of the transaction and definitions of the terms. A critical feature of a financial liability is the existence of

- A contractual obligation of the issuer of the financial instrument to deliver cash or other financial asset to the holder under conditions that are potentially unfavorable to the issuer; or
- Contractual obligation of the issuer to exchange financial asset or financial liability with the holder.

Although dividends are often paid for equity instruments, there is no obligation to pay such dividends. When an issuer has an obligation to pay dividends or to repay the capital, like in the case of redeemable preference shares without a coupon payment obligation or irredeemable preference shares with a coupon payment obligation, the instrument is classified as a liability.

Example 6

On liquidation the residual value left after meeting all other liabilities is payable to the holders of the equity instruments. If an entity under liquidation prepares financial statements after the amount available to equity shareholders is determined, the equity becomes a financial liability of the entity—it would present amount due to shareholders as a financial liability, and cash and cash equivalents as financial assets.

Example 7

An entity offers rights shares to existing shareholders to buy one share for every 10 shares held at $70 when the market price was $250. There is a fixed date for exercise of the right, or right renouncement or transfer. On the cut-off date, January 7, 2009, the entity received payment for 1 million right shares. The reporting date of the entity was December 31, 2008, on which date it received application for 10,000 right shares. How should the entity account for the rights issue?

Solution

The rights issue obligation is an obligation to issue equity instruments. The issuer has made an offer to the shareholders. The equity issue obligation will arise once the entity receives the right exercise form. There is no financial liability. Of course, the entity shall disclose the rights attached to the particular class of equity stating the figure of rights already accepted.

Example 8

In Example 7, if the rights issues are denominated in a currency other than the functional currency of the issuer, the current practice appears to require such issues to be accounted for as derivative liabilities.

The proposed amendment to this standard states that if such rights are issued *pro rata* to an entity's existing shareholders for a fixed amount of currency, they should be classified as equity regardless of the currency in which the exercise price is denominated.

The amendment, which has been issued in October 2009, applies on a retrospective basis and is effective for annual periods beginning on or after February 1, 2010, with earlier application permitted.

Example 9

Should a bonus issue be classified as an equity transaction?

Solution

Yes. The issuer assumes an obligation to distribute additional equity shares by making adjustment to another component of equity, say retained earnings. Thus issue of bonus shares results in an equity transaction. The entity shall debit retained earnings to create additional common stock.

COMPOUND FINANCIAL INSTRUMENTS

A compound financial instrument is a nonderivative financial instrument that contains a financial liability component and an equity component. Examples of a compound financial instrument are convertible debentures or convertible and redeemable preference shares.

The issuer of a nonderivative financial instrument is required to evaluate the terms of the instrument to determine if it contains a financial liability component and equity component. Such components should be separated and classified appropriately in the balance sheet (IAS 32, paragraph 28). This is the position from the perspective of the issuer. IAS 39 explains the separation of embedded derivative from the perspective of holders of compound financial instruments that contain debt and equity features.

Convertible debentures or bonds in which the holder gets the option to convert into equity shares of the issuer have two components, namely (1) a bond with early redemption option and (2) attached share warrants (a call option on shares). For this type of compound instrument, the issuer should separate the liability and equity components for the purpose of presentation in the financial statements. The liability component is accounted for as per IAS 39, *Financial Instruments: Recognition and Measurement.* However, IFRS 9, *Financial Instruments* (which will eventually replace IAS 39) does not require separation of embedded derivative if the host contract is a financial instrument.

The value of any derivative features, such as a call option, embedded in the compound financial instrument other than the equity component (such as an equity conversion option) is included in the liability component. The sum of the carrying amounts assigned to the liability and equity components on initial recognition is always equal to the fair value that would be ascribed to the instrument as a whole. No gain or loss arises from initially recognizing the components of the instrument separately.

TREASURY SHARES

When an entity reacquires its own equity instruments, those instruments (termed as treasury shares) are deducted from equity. An entity does not recognize any gain or loss in profit or loss on the purchase, sale, issue, or cancellation of an entity's own equity instruments. Such treasury shares may be acquired and held by the entity or by other members of the consolidated group. Consideration paid or received is recognized directly in equity.

Example 10

An entity enters into a forward contract to buy back its shares from 10 holders amounting to US $50 million after three months.

Based on the constructive obligation, the entity shall deduct the treasury stock under contract from equity and classify it as a liability. It is a forward contract to buy back own shares at a fixed and determinable price on a forward date falling within the ambit of paragraph 27(a) of IAS 32.

PURCHASED AND WRITTEN OPTION TO BUY/SELL OWN EQUITY

An entity may enter into an option contract on its own equity. Options may be traded or nontraded. Of course, in almost all jurisdictions, trading in own shares is not permitted. Therefore, generally, this can take the form of a nontraded option.

A purchased option on own shares signifies that the entity has entered into a contract to buy back own shares. On the other hand, a written option signifies that the entity has to issue its own shares (may be a reissue of treasury stock).

From the definition of a financial asset and financial liability, derivatives on own shares are qualified as equity only when they involve an "exchange of a fixed amount of cash or another financial asset for a fixed number of the entity's own equity instruments."

Analysis of the settlement characteristics of a purchased option/written option to buy/sell own shares is important in classifying whether it is a derivative or nonderivative. Normally, there are four kinds of settlement:

1. Cash settled in which the buyer of the call option takes cash payment instead of taking delivery of own shares on expiry and settlement.
2. Cash settlement in the context of a written option implies that the call writer will make cash payment instead of giving delivery of own shares on expiry and settlement.
3. Cash settlement in the context of a purchased put option implies that the put buyer will take cash payment instead of giving delivery of own shares on expiry and settlement.
4. Cash settlement in the context of a written put option implies that the put writer will make cash payment instead of taking delivery of own shares on expiry and settlement.

Cash-settled options are derivatives even if they involve own shares, as there is no buying/selling of own shares.

The entity (issuer of the equity instrument) can also settle net. This means the issuer will buy or sell shares at the current market price to the extent of payoff. Here, although buying/selling is involved, it was not a contract to buy/sell a fixed quantity of equity in exchange for a fixed amount of cash or other financial asset. The amount depends on the market price as on the settlement date. Thus, it is a derivative contract that involves buying/selling of a variable number of equity shares. This results in a financial asset or liability depending on the value of the derivative on the date of the contract.

PUTTABLE INSTRUMENTS

A *puttable instrument* is a financial instrument that gives the holder the right to put the instrument back to the issuer for cash or another financial asset or is automatically put back to the issuer on the occurrence of an uncertain future event or the death or retirement of the instrument holder. An example is a contractual obligation for the issuer to repurchase or redeem that instrument for cash or another financial asset on exercise of the put.

Generally, a puttable instrument is classified as a financial liability, not as equity. However, when a puttable instrument contains all of the following five features, it is classified as equity:

1. The holder is entitled to a pro rata share of the entity's net assets in the event of the entity's liquidation;
2. The instrument is subordinate to all other instruments;
3. All instruments falling within the subordinate class have similar features;
4. The instrument contains only redemption or repurchase obligation—there is no other obligation to any other entity;
5. Total expected cash flows attributable to the instrument over the life of the instrument are based substantially on the profit or loss, the change in the recognized net assets, or the change in the fair value of the recognized and unrecognized net assets of the entity over the life of the instrument.

In addition, no other instruments (other than the puttable instrument) may have expected cash flows attributable to that instrument over the life of the instrument that are based substantially on the profit or loss. Existence of any other instrument will have the effect of substantially restricting or fixing the residual return to the puttable instrument holders.

Example 11

An open-ended mutual fund issues units to the unit holders that contain a repurchase feature. As these unit holders can offer their units for repurchase, these units are puttable instruments. Can they be classified as equity?

Solution

It is to be verified that whether

1. The open-ended mutual fund can issue only one class of units that ensures pro rata distribution of its net assets in the eventuality of liquidation of the fund, in which case all units will then carry same features;
2. Such units are subordinated to all other liabilities of the fund;
3. The obligation of the issuer relates to only to repurchase or redeem the units; and
4. Expected return on units depends on the profit/loss of the funds.

If all the above-mentioned conditions are fulfilled, then by virtue of IAS 32, paragraphs 16A and 16B, units of mutual funds having repurchase feature can be classified as equity instruments.

OFFSETTING FINANCIAL ASSETS AND LIABILITIES

Paragraph 42 of IAS 32 sets out principles for offsetting financial assets and financial liabilities and for net presentation. A financial asset and a financial liability shall be offset and the net amount presented in the statement of financial position only when an entity currently has a legally enforceable right to set off the recognized amounts and intends either to settle on a net basis, or to realize the asset and settle the liability simultaneously.

In accounting for a transfer of a financial asset that does not qualify for derecognition, the entity shall not offset the transferred asset and the associated liability

However, offsetting is not carried out based on the existence of the right only. There should be the intention to exercise the right or to settle simultaneously, so that the amount and timing of an entity's future cash flows are not affected. Intention to settle simultaneously without having a legal right does not justify offsetting.

In the following cases offsetting is inappropriate:

- Several different financial assets and financial liabilities (having different kinds of risks) are combined to emulate a single instrument;

- Financial assets and liabilities have the same type of risk but counterparties are different;
- Financial or other assets are pledged as collateral for nonrecourse financial liabilities;
- Financial assets are set aside in trust by a debtor for the purpose of discharging an obligation and the creditor has not accepted these assets in settlement of the obligation; or
- Obligations incurred are recoverable from a third party.

INTEREST, DIVIDENDS, LOSSES, AND GAINS

Interest and dividends relating to financial assets or financial liabilities are recognized as income or expense in profit or loss. Gain or loss on distributions to holders of an equity instrument is recognized directly in equity, net of any related income tax benefit.

Gains and losses associated with redemptions or refinancings of financial liabilities are recognized in profit or loss. But redemptions or refinancings of equity instruments are recognized as changes in equity. Changes in the fair value of an equity instrument are not recognized in the financial statements.

TRANSACTION COSTS OF AN EQUITY ISSUE

Transaction costs of an equity transaction are accounted for as a deduction from equity, net of any related income tax benefit. Those costs might include registration and other regulatory fees; amounts paid to legal, accounting, and other professional advisers; printing costs; and stamp duties.

EXCERPTS FROM PUBLISHED FINANCIAL STATEMENTS

The Volvo Group, Annual Report 2008

Notes to the Consolidated Financial Statements

Amounts in SEK M unless otherwise specified. The amounts within parentheses refer to the preceding year, 2007.

Gains, Losses, Interest Income and Expenses Related to Financial Instruments

The table that follows shows how gains and losses as well as interest income and expense have affected income after financial items in the Volvo Group divided on the different categories of financial instruments.

	Gains/ losses	Interest income	2007 Interest expenses	Gains/ losses	2008 Interest income	Interest expenses
Financial assets and liabilities at fair value through profit and loss						
Marketable securities	898	0	0	864	0	0
Derivatives for financial exposure	(403)	0	0	(924)	0	0
Loans receivable and other receivables	0	37	0	0	11	0
Financial assets available for sale						
Shares and participations for which a market value can be calculated	8	—	—	42	—	—
Shares and participations for which a market value cannot be calculated	98	—	—	60	—	—

	Gains/ losses	Interest income	2007 Interest wxpenses	Gains/ losses	2008 Interest income	Interest expenses
Cash and cash equivalents	—	249	0	0	362	0
Financial liabilities valued at amortized cost	3	0	(4,048)	(1)	0	(5,083)
Effect on income	604	286	(4,048)	41	373	(5,083)

Barclays Bank, Annual Report 2008

Accounting Policies

Issued Debt and Equity Securities

Issued financial instruments or their components are classified as liabilities when the contractual arrangement results in the group having a present obligation to either deliver cash or another financial asset to the holder, to exchange financial instruments on terms that are potentially unfavorable, or to satisfy the obligation otherwise than by the exchange of a fixed amount of cash or another financial asset for a fixed number of equity shares. Issued financial instruments, or their components, are classified as equity when they meet the definition of equity and confer on the holder a residual interest in the assets of the company. The components of issued financial instruments that contain both liability and equity elements are accounted for separately with the equity component being assigned the residual amount after deducting from the instrument as a whole the amount separately determined as the fair value of the liability component.

Financial liabilities, other than trading liabilities and financial liabilities designated at fair value, are carried at amortized cost using the effective interest method as set out in policy 6. Derivatives embedded in financial liabilities that are not designated at fair value are accounted for as set out in policy 7. Equity instruments, including share capital, are initially recognized as net proceeds, after deducting transaction costs and any related income tax. Dividend and other payments to equity holders are deducted from equity, net of any related tax.

Share Capital

Share Issue Costs

Incremental costs directly attributable to the issue of new shares or options including those issued on the acquisition of a business are shown in equity as a deduction, net of tax, from the proceeds.

Dividends on Ordinary Shares

Dividends on ordinary shares are recognized in equity in the period in which they are paid or, if earlier, approved by the Barclays PLC (the Company) shareholders.

Treasury Shares

Where the company or any member of the group purchases the company's share capital, the consideration paid is deducted from shareholders' equity as treasury shares until they are canceled. Where such shares are subsequently sold or reissued, any consideration received is included in shareholders' equity.

24 EARNINGS PER SHARE (IAS 33)

INTRODUCTION

The objective of IAS 33 is to describe the methodology for the determination and presentation of earnings per share (EPS). This would improve interentity performance comparisons in the same period and intraperiod performance for the same entity. Of course, the earnings-per-share data have limitations since different entities may follow different accounting policies and, therefore, may not have consistency in determining "earnings." IAS 33 establishes methodologies for determining the outstanding shares, which is the denominator that enhances comparability of the financial reporting. Thus, the focus of IAS 33 is on the denominator of the earnings-per-share calculation.

SCOPE

IAS 33 is applicable to separate or consolidated financial statements of the issuer

- Whose *ordinary shares* or *potential ordinary* shares are traded in a public market; or
- That files, or is in the process of filing, its financial statements with a securities commission or other regulatory organization for the purpose of issuing ordinary shares in a public market.

Public market means a domestic or foreign stock exchange or an over-the-counter market, including local and regional markets. Examples of potential ordinary shares are convertible debentures or preference shares, warrants, rights, options, and shares that would be issued upon the satisfaction of conditions resulting from contractual arrangements, such as the purchase of a business or other assets.

If an entity publishes both separate and consolidated financial statements, EPS disclosures would be required only for consolidated financial statements.

KEY TERMS

Antidilution. An increase in earnings per share or a reduction in loss per share resulting from the assumption that convertible instruments are converted, that options or warrants are exercised, or that ordinary shares are issued upon the satisfaction of specified conditions.

Dilution. A reduction in earnings per share or an increase in loss per share resulting from the assumption that convertible instruments are converted, that options or warrants are exercised, or that ordinary shares are issued upon the satisfaction of specified conditions.

Ordinary share. An equity instrument that is subordinate to all other classes of equity instruments.

Potential ordinary share. An equity instrument or other contract that may entitle its holder to ordinary shares.

MEASUREMENT

Basic Earnings Per Share and Diluted Earnings Per Share

An entity that discloses EPS should present both *basic earnings per share* and *diluted earnings per share* amounts for profit or loss attributable to ordinary equity holders of the parent entity and, if presented, profit or loss from continuing operations attributable to those equity holders in the income statement component of the statement of comprehensive income.

The profit or loss attributable to the parent entity means profit or loss of the consolidated entity after adjusting for noncontrolling interests.

An entity shall calculate basic EPS by dividing profit or loss attributable to ordinary equity holders of the parent entity and, if presented, profit or loss from continuing operations attributable to those equity holders, by the weighted average number of ordinary shares outstanding during the period. For the purposes of calculating diluted EPS, an entity shall adjust the profit or loss attributable to ordinary equity holders of the parent, and the weighted average number of shares outstanding for the effects of all dilutive potential ordinary shares.

Example 1: Computation of Basic Earnings Per Share

Equity share information and net profit of Entity X follows.

In millions	*Number of Shares*
Equity share capital as on January 1, 2008	100
New issue of shares on July 1, 2008	100

Consolidated net profit for 2008 € 600 million
Noncontrolling interest 30%

The basic EPS is computed in accordance with paragraph 10 of IAS 33

$$\text{Basic EPS} = \frac{\text{Earnings attributable to equity holders of the parent entity}}{\text{Weighted-average number of ordinary shares outstanding during the period}}$$

Weighted Average Number of Shares

Number of shares (million)	*Weighting*[*]	*Weighting number*
100	1	100
100	0.5	50
		150

*Weighting refers to the time for which the shares were outstanding.

$$\text{Basic EPS} = \frac{\text{€600 million} \times 70\%}{150} = \text{€2.80}$$

DILUTED EARNINGS PER SHARE

The following financial instruments may have the effect of diluting basic EPS (dilution implies reduction in EPS or increase in loss per share) and, therefore, analyzed for computing dilutive potential shares:

- Convertible debentures
- Convertible preference shares
- Contingently issuable shares
- Contracts that require the entity to repurchase its own shares, such as written put options and forward purchase contracts, are reflected in the calculation of diluted earnings per share if the effect is dilutive

Purchased call options and purchased put options are not included as they have an antidilutive effect.

Example 2: Computation of Diluted Earnings Per Share

Entity A has 500 million equity shares on January 1, 2008, as well as on December 31, 2008. Its net profit for the year 2008 is € 600 million. Effective tax rate of the entity is 30%. It has 100 million 5% convertible debentures of € 40, which is convertible into five equity shares. Noncontrolling interest is 30%.

$$\text{Basic EPS} = \frac{€600 \text{ million} \times 70\%}{500} = €0.84$$

On the other hand, diluted EPS is computed by adjusting the possible effect of full conversion of all of the convertible debentures into equity shares from the beginning of the reporting period. Net profit for the period is adjusted for the interest effect, net of tax, since the conversion would result in cessation of interest payments, with increased tax expense.

Adjusted net profit	= Net profit for the period	=	€	600 million
	+ Interest on convertible debentures	=		200 million
	– Tax effect @ 30%	=		60 million
		=	€	740 million
Weighted-average number of shares	=			
	Issued shares	=		500 million
	Potential shares	=		500 million
		=		1,000 million

$$\text{Diluted EPS} = \frac{€740 \text{ million} \times 70\%}{1,000} = €0.518$$

EPS has the effect of reduction because of potential conversion—so it is termed as *diluted earning per share*. (The number of equity shares that will be issued on full conversion of convertibles or rights are termed *potential equity shares*).

ANTIDILUTION

Potential equity shares may not have the effect of reducing the EPS or increasing the loss per share. In that case it is called *antidilution*.

Example 3: Understanding Antidilutive Effect

Let us reconsider the data given in Example 2 except that only one ordinary share will be issued against each debenture.

EPS is worked out to be € 0.86 taking into account the potential ordinary shares, which is higher than the basic EPS. This is antidilutive as the potential conversion should not reduce the basic EPS.

$$\text{EPS} = \frac{€740 \text{ million} \times 70\%}{500 + 100} = €0.86$$

BONUS ISSUE

In the case of a bonus issue, the comparative EPS presented is restated assuming the bonus issue in those periods as well.

Example 4

Equity share information and net profit of Entity B follows.

	Number of shares (million)	Face value Rs. in million)
Equity share capital as on Jan 1, 2007	100	100
New issue as on Jan 1, 2008	50	50
Net profit for 2007 €400 million		
Net profit for 2008 €500 million		

The company issues 1:5 bonus shares effective November 1, 2008—one share for every five shares held

Weighted-Average Number of Shares (Million)

2007	2008	2007 Adjusted	2008 Adjusted
100	150	120	180

Basic EPS Computation

	2007 as already presented	2007 restated	2008
400/100			
400/120	€4.00	€3.33	
500/180			€2.77

According to IAS 33, paragraph 28, the number of ordinary shares outstanding before the event is adjusted for the proportionate change in the number of ordinary shares outstanding as if the event had occurred at the beginning of the earliest period presented.

RIGHTS ISSUE

IAS 33 further explains that in a rights issue the exercise price is often less than the fair value of the shares. In such a rights issue a bonus element is included. If a rights issue is offered to all existing shareholders, the number of ordinary shares to be used in calculating basic and diluted EPS for all periods before the rights issue is the number of ordinary shares outstanding before the issue, multiplied by the following factor:

$$\frac{\text{Fair value per share immediately before the exercise of rights}}{\text{Theoretical ex-rights fair value per share**}}$$

**The theoretical ex-rights fair value per share =

$$\frac{\textit{Aggregate market value of the shares immediately before the exercise of the rights + Proceeds from the exercise of the rights}}{\textit{Number of share outstanding after the exercise of the rights}}$$

Where the rights are to be publicly traded separately from the shares before the exercise date, fair value for the purposes of this calculation is established at the close of the last day on which the shares are traded together with the rights.

Example 5

Entity M has issued one right share for every five shares held on May 1, 2008. The relevant information relating to basic EPS computation is

	2007	2008
Number of ordinary shares (million)	500	600
Net profit for the year (€million)	800	900
Share price as on April 30, 2008 (€)	20	
Exercise price of the right (€)	12	

Theoretical ex-right value per share: $\dfrac{(500 \times 20) + (100 \times 12)}{500 + 100} = €18.67$

Right adjustment factor: $20/18.67 = 1.07$

Computation Basic EPS for 2008 and Restatement of Basic EPS for 2007

2007

Basic EPS (€)	(800/500)	= 1.60
Basic EPS restated (€)	[800/(500 × 1.07)]	= 1.50

2008

Basic EPS (€)	900/[(500 × 1.07) × 4/12 + 600 × 8/12]	= 1.56

INCREASING RATE PREFERENCE SHARES

Sometimes an entity issues preference shares at a low initial dividend and it is compensated by the issuer by issuing at a discount. Alternatively, such a low rate of dividend may be compensated by a redemption premium. These are referred to as *increasing rate preference shares.* Any original issue discount or premium on increasing rate preference shares is amortized to retained earnings using the effective interest method and treated as a preference dividend for the purposes of calculating earnings per share.

Example 6: Effect of Increasing Rate Preference Shares

Equity share information and net profit of X Ltd. follows, which is used to calculate its basic EPS in accordance with paragraph 10 of IAS 33.

	Number of shares (million)	*Amount (€ million)*
Ordinary shares as on January 1, 2008	100	
New issue of shares on July 1, 2008	100	
Nonredeemable noncumulative preference shares		
Rate of dividend 4% market		
Face value €10 per share		
Issue price €7.8 per share	10	100
Net profit for 2008 = €400 million		

How should the company calculate net profit attributable to equity shareholders and compute basic EPS?

Solution

The company has increasing rate preference shares, which are classified as equity under IAS 32 in its capital structure. They are recorded at €78 million. The dividend should be imputed to the extent if the discount on preference shares is over three years:

Year	*Cash flows (in € million)*	*Imputed dividend (€ million)*	*Imputed carrying amount (€ million): amortized to retained earnings*
0	78		
1	0	6.74	84.74
2	0	7.32	92.05
3	−100	7.95	100.00
	8.63%		

Net profit attributable to equity shareholders	=	
Net profit	=	€ 400.00 million
– Preference dividend paid	=	4.00 million
– Preference dividend imputed	=	6.74 million
		€ 389.24 million

$$\text{Basic EPS} = \frac{€389.24 \text{ million}}{150 \text{ million}} = €2.60$$

PRESENTATION

As per IAS 33, paragraph 66, an entity should present basic and diluted EPS:

- For profit or loss from continuing operations attributable to the ordinary equity holders of the parent entity, and
- For profit or loss attributable to the ordinary equity holders of the parent entity for the period for each class of ordinary shares that has a different right to share in profit for the period presented.

An entity has to present basic and diluted EPS with equal prominence for all periods presented. Also, loss per share (basic and diluted) must be presented.

If basic and diluted earnings per share are equal, the entity can present both of them in one line in the statement of comprehensive income.

An entity that reports a discontinued operation has to disclose the basic and diluted amounts per share for the discontinued operation either in the statement of comprehensive income or in the notes.

DISCLOSURES

According to IAS 33, paragraph 70, the following disclosure requirements for EPS must be included:

- The amounts used as the numerators in calculating basic and diluted EPS, and a reconciliation of those amounts to profit or loss attributable to the parent entity for the period.

  The reconciliation shall include the individual effect of each class of instruments that affects EPS.
- The weighted-average number of ordinary shares used as the denominator in calculating basic and diluted EPS, and a reconciliation of these denominators to each other.

  The reconciliation shall include the individual effect of each class of instruments that affects EPS.
- Instruments (including contingently issuable shares) that could potentially dilute basic EPS in the future, but were not because they are antidilutive for the period(s) presented.
- A description of *ordinary share* transactions or *potential ordinary share* transactions, other than those accounted for in accordance with *paragraph 64* of IAS 33 (which deals with retrospective adjustments of EPS) that occur after the reporting period and that would have changed significantly the number of ordinary shares or potential ordinary shares outstanding at the end of the period if those transactions had occurred before the end of the reporting period. (Also known as the *possible effect analysis*.)

EXCERPTS FROM PUBLISHED FINANCIAL STATEMENTS

Adidas Group, Annual Report 2008

Notes to the Consolidated Financial Statements

29. Earnings Per Share

Basic earnings per share (EPS) are calculated by dividing the net income attributable to shareholders by the weighted average number of shares outstanding during the year.

Dilutive potential shares arose under the Management Share Option Plan (MSOP) of Adidas AG, which was implemented in 1999 (see Note 33). As the required performance criteria for the exercise of the stock options of all tranches of the share option plan have been fulfilled, dilutive potential shares impact the diluted EPS calculation.

It is also necessary to include dilutive potential shares arising from the convertible bond issuance in October 2003 in the calculation of diluted EPS as at December 31, 2008 and 2007, respectively, as the required conversion criteria were fulfilled at the balance sheet date (see Note 15). As a result, the convertible bond is assumed to have been converted into ordinary shares and the net income is adjusted to eliminate the interest expense less the tax effect.

Earnings Per Share

	Year Ending December 31	
	2008	*2007*
Net income attributable to shareholders (€million)	642	551
Weighted average number of shares	197,562,346	203,594,975
Basic earnings per share (€)	3.25	2.71
Net income attributable to shareholders (€million)	642	551
Interest expenses on convertible bond (net of taxes) (€million)	13	12
Net income used to determine diluted earnings per share (€million)	655	563
Weighted-average number of shares	197,562,346	203,594,975
Weighted share options	86,542	187,887
Weighted assumed conversion convertible bond	15,684,315	15,684,315
Weighted-average number of shares for diluted earnings per share	213,333,203	219,467,177
Diluted earnings per share (€)	3.07	2.57

Unilever Group, Annual Report 2008

Notes to the Consolidated Accounts

7.   Combined Earnings Per Share

Combined Earnings Per Share From Continuing Operations	*2008*	*2007*	*2006*
Basic earnings per share	**€1.79**	€1.32	€1.19
Diluted earnings per share	**1.73**	1.28	1.15
From Discontinued Operations			
Basic earnings per share	—	0.03	0.46
Diluted earnings per share	—	0.03	0.45
From Total Operations			
Basic earnings per share	**1.79**	1.35	1.65
Diluted earnings per share	**1.73**	1.31	1.60

Basis of Calculation

The calculations of combined EPS are based on the net profit attributable to ordinary capital divided by the average number of share units representing the combined ordinary share capital of NV and PLC in issue during the year, after deducting shares held as treasury stock. Earnings per share are calculated on the basis of the revised nominal share values which have been applied since May 22, 2006, and which resulted in a one-to-one equivalence of ordinary shares of NV and PLC as regarding their economic interest in the Group. For further information please refer to note 22.

The calculations of diluted EPS are based on (1) conversion into PLC ordinary shares of the shares in a group company that are convertible in the year 2038, as described in corporate governance; and (2) the effect of share-based compensation plans, details of which are set out in note 29.

Calculation of Average Number of Share Units (million)	*2008*	*2007*	*2006*
Average number of shares: NV	**1,714.7**	1,714.7	1,714.7
PLC	**1,310.2**	1,310.2	1,310.2
Less shares held by employee share trusts and companies	**(215.3)**	(150.3)	(141.6)
Combined average number of share units for all bases except diluted earnings per share	**2,809.6**	2,874.6	2,883.3
Add shares issuable in 2038	**70.9**	70.9	70.9
Add dilutive effect of share-based compensation plans and forward equity contract	**25.4**	30.6	18.3
Adjusted combined average number of share units for diluted earnings per share basis	**2,905.9**	2,976.1	2,972.5

Calculation of earnings (€ million)	2008	2007	2006
For earnings per share from total operations:			
Net profit attributable to ordinary capital for total operations	**5,027**	3,888	4,745
For earnings per share from continuing operations:			
Net profit from continuing operations	**5,285**	4,056	3,685
Minority interest in continuing operations	**(258)**	(248)	(266)
Net profit attributable to ordinary capital for continuing operations	**5,027**	3,808	3,419

The numbers of shares included in the calculation of EPS is an average for the period. These numbers are influenced by the share buyback programmes that we undertook during 2007 and 2008. During those periods, the following movements in shares took place:

Share units (million)	2008	2007
Number of shares at 1 January (net of treasury stock)	**2,853.1**	2,889.9
Net movements in shares under incentive schemes	**11.4**	29.7
Share buyback	**(75.4)**	(66.5)
Number of shares at December 31	**2,789.1**	2,853.1

25 INTERIM FINANCIAL REPORTING (IAS 34)

INTRODUCTION

IAS 34 prescribes the minimum content of an interim financial report and the principles for recognition and measurement in complete or condensed financial statements for an interim financial report.

SCOPE

IAS 34 does not prescribe the periodicity of an interim financial report (i.e., quarterly or half-yearly). Normally, the securities regulators and stock exchanges require an entity whose debt or equity securities are publicly traded to publish interim financial reports. If an entity is required or elects to publish an interim financial report, it shall follow IAS 34. Of course, release of quarterly financial information as per guidelines of the stock exchange does not qualify as an interim financial report.

IAS 34 encourages publicly traded entities

- To provide interim financial reports at least at the end of the first half of its financial year; and to make available such an interim report within 60 days from the end of the financial period.

If an entity has not published an interim financial report or has published an interim financial report that does not conform to IAS 34, this does not debar it from becoming IFRS-compliant. Paragraph 19 of IAS 34 requires a special disclosure that the interim financial report of the entity complies with IAS 34.

An interim financial report is not described as complying with IFRS unless it complies with all of the requirements.

KEY TERMS

Interim period. A period that is less than a full financial year.

Interim financial report. A financial report containing either a complete set of financial statements (as described in IAS 1, *Presentation of Financial Statements*) or a set of condensed financial statements (as described in IAS 34) for an interim period.

CONTENTS OF AN INTERIM FINANCIAL REPORT

An entity can present either a complete set of financial statements or a condensed set of financial statements for interim reporting purposes. The following table summarizes the requirements under IAS 34 of a complete and a condensed interim financial report.

Contents of an Interim Financial Report

Complete Interim Financial Report	Condensed Interim Financial Report
Components	**Components**
1. A statement of financial position as at the end of the period. 2. A statement of comprehensive income for the period 3. A statement of changes in equity for the period 4. A statement of cash flows for the period 5. Notes, comprising a summary of significant accounting policies and other explanatory information 6. A statement of financial position as at the beginning of the earliest comparative period when an entity applies an accounting policy retrospectively or makes a retrospective restatement of items in its financial statements, or when it reclassifies items in its financial statements	1. Condensed statement of financial position 2. A condensed statement of comprehensive income, presented as either • A condensed single statement or • A condensed separate income statement and a condensed statement of comprehensive income 3. A condensed statement of changes in equity 4. A condensed statement of cash flows 5. Selected explanatory notes
	When an entity prepares a separate statement of income If an entity presents components of profit or loss in a separate income statement (i.e., separately from components of other comprehensive income), then condensed separate income statement information is to be taken from that separate statement.
Minimum Content	**Minimum Content**
1. To follow IAS 1 in totality.	1. Each of the headings and subtotals that were included in its most recent annual financial statements would be included, and 2. Selected explanatory notes as required under IAS 34. Additional line items or notes are included if their omission would make the condensed interim financial statements misleading.
Disclosure Basic and Diluted EPS	**Disclosure Basic and Diluted EPS**
An entity shall present basic and diluted earnings per share for that period when the entity is within the scope of IAS 33, *Earnings Per Share.*	An entity shall present basic and diluted earnings per share for that period when the entity is within the scope of IAS 33, *Earnings Per Share.*

Example 1

Entity E prepares interim financial statements containing financial statements complying fully with IAS 1, but provides only selected explanatory notes in accordance with paragraph 16 of IAS 34. Has the company published a complete set of financial statements for interim financial reporting purposes?

Solution

To be qualified as a complete set of financial statements under IAS 34, an entity has to follow IFRS in full. Since it has published selected explanatory notes, its financial statements can qualify as a condensed set only.

PERIODS FOR WHICH INTERIM FINANCIAL REPORTS ARE REQUIRED

1. Statement of financial position as of the end of current interim period and a comparative statement of financial position as of the end of the immediately preceding financial year.
2. Statement of comprehensive income for the current interim period and cumulatively for the current financial year to date, with the comparative statements of comprehensive income for the comparable interim periods (current and year-to-date) of the immediately preceding financial year. As permitted by IAS 1, an interim report may present for each period either (a) a single statement of comprehensive income, or (b) a statement displaying components of profit or loss (i.e., a separate income statement) and a second statement beginning with profit or loss and displaying components of other comprehensive income (i.e., statement of comprehensive income).
3. Statement of changes of equity cumulatively for the current financial year to date, with a comparative statement for the comparable year-to-date period of the immediately preceding financial year.
4. Statement of cash flows cumulatively for the current financial year to date, with a comparative statement for the comparable year-to-date period of the immediately preceding financial year.

Example 2

Here are examples of the periods for which the various components of the interim financial report, along with comparatives, are to be presented:

1. **Statement of Financial Position**

    a. Suppose an entity prepares Quarterly Interim Financial Reports. At the end of the first quarter, its statement of financial position is required at the following dates:

       Solution

For current interim period	*Comparative statement of financial position as of the end of the immediately preceding financial year*
As on March 31, 2009	As December 31, 2008

    b. Suppose an entity prepares half-yearly interim financial reports. At the end of the half-year its statement of financial position is required at the following dates:

       Solution

For current interim period	*Comparative statement of financial position as of the end of the immediately preceding financial year*
As on June 30, 2009	As December 31, 2008

2. **Statement of Comprehensive Income**

    a. Suppose an entity prepares a quarterly interim financial report. At the end of the first quarter its statement of comprehensive income is required at the following dates:

Solution

For the current _interim period_	Cumulatively for the current finan- _cial year to date_	Comparative statements of comprehensive income for the compar- _able interim period_	Comparative statements of comprehensive income for the comparable immediately preceding _financial year of column 2_
For the quarter ended on March 31, 2009		For the period ended on March 31, 2008	

b. Suppose an entity prepares a quarterly interim financial report. At the end of the second quarter its statement of comprehensive income is required at the following dates:

Solution

For the current _interim period_	Cumulatively for the current finan- _cial year to date_	Comparative statements of comprehensive income for the compar- _able interim period_	Comparative statements of comprehensive income for the comparable immediately preceding _financial year of column 2_
For the quarter ended on June 30, 2009	For the half-year ended on June 30, 2009	For the quarter ended on June 30, 2008	For the half-year ended on June 30, 2008

c. Suppose an entity prepares a quarterly interim financial report. At the end of the third quarter its statement of comprehensive income is required at the following dates:

Solution

For the current _interim period_	Cumulatively for the current finan- _cial year to date_	Comparative statements of comprehensive income for the compar- _able interim period_	Comparative statements of comprehensive income for the comparable immediately preceding _financial year of column 2_
For the quarter ended on September 30, 2009	For nine months ended on September 30, 2009	For the quarter ended on September 30, 2008	For nine months ended on September 30, 2009

d. Suppose an entity prepares a half-yearly interim financial report. At the end of first half its statement of comprehensive income is required at the following dates:

Solution

For the current _interim period_	Cumulatively for the current finan- _cial year to date_	Comparative statements of comprehensive income for the compar- _able interim period_	Comparative statements of comprehensive income for the comparable immediately preceding _financial year of column 2_
For the half-year ended on June 30, 2009		For the half-year ended on June 30, 2008	

3. **Statement of Changes in Equity**

a. Suppose an entity prepares a quarterly interim financial report. At the end of the first quarter its statement of changes in equity is required at the following dates:

Solution

For current interim period	Comparative statement of financial position as of the end of the immediately _preceding financial year_
As on March 31, 2009	As December 31, 2008

b. Suppose an entity prepares a half-yearly interim financial report. At the end of the half-year its statement of changes in equity is required at the following dates:

Solution

For current interim period As on June 30, 2009	*Comparative statement of financial position as of the end of the immediately preceding financial year* As December 31, 2008

4.   Statement of Cash Flows

a.   Suppose an entity prepares a quarterly interim financial report. At the end of the first quarter its statement of cash flows is required at the following dates:

Solution

For current interim period For the period ended on March 31, 2009	*Comparative statement of financial position as of the end of the immediately preceding financial year* For the period ended on December 31, 2008

b.   Suppose an entity prepares half-yearly interim financial report. At the end of the half-year its statement of cash flows is required at the following dates:

Solution

For current interim period For the period ended on June 30, 2009	*Comparative statement of financial position as of the end of the immediately preceding financial year* For the period ended on December 31, 2008

A parent company would prepare an interim financial report on a consolidated basis. For the first interim financial report comparatives shall also be provided. In case of a new entity, no comparatives are required of the first financial year.

SELECTED EXPLANATORY NOTES

The idea of accepting disclosure of only *selected explanatory notes* in the interim financial report is justifiable because the financial statement users have access to the most recent annual financial statements wherein detailed notes are available concerning various elements of financial statements. Notes to the interim financial report are therefore regarded as updates from the previous annual financial report. Therefore, an explanation of events and transactions that are significant to an understanding of the changes in financial position and performance of the entity since the end of the last annual reporting period is more useful. The interim financial report should reflect changes only if an entity elects to prepare a condensed set of financial statements. Paragraph 16 of IAS 34 specifies the following selected explanatory notes:

1. Statement of compliance with same accounting policies and method since most recent annual financial statements: The statement notes that the same accounting policies and methods of computation are followed in the interim financial statements as compared with the most recent annual financial statements.

    In the interim financial report, a full set of accounting policies are not required to be disclosed. Those are available in the most recent financial statements.

    In case there is a change in accounting policy, a description of the nature and effect of the change is to be disclosed.

2. Explanatory comments about the seasonality or cyclicality of interim operations.

3. The nature and amount of any unusual items affecting assets, liabilities, equity, net income, or cash flows because of their nature, size, or incidence.

4. The nature and amount of changes in estimates of amounts reported in prior interim periods of the current financial year or changes in estimates of amounts reported in

prior financial years, if those changes have a material effect in the current interim period.

5. Issuances, repurchases, and repayments of debt and equity securities.
6. Dividends paid (aggregate or per share) separately for ordinary shares and other shares.
7. If the entity is required to prepare segment information as per IFRS 8, they must disclose

   - Revenues from external customers;
   - Intersegment revenues;
   - A measure of segment profit or loss;
   - Total assets for which there has been a material change from the amount disclosed in the last annual financial statements;
   - A description of differences from the last annual financial statements in the basis of segmentation or in the basis of measurement of segment profit or loss; and
   - A reconciliation of the total of the reportable segments' measures of profit or loss to the entity's profit or loss before tax expense (tax income) and discontinued operations (of course, if an entity allocates tax income or expense to reportable segments, it may reconcile profit or loss after tax).

8. Material events that occurred after the interim period.
9. Effect of changes in the composition of the entity such as business combinations, obtaining or losing control of subsidiaries and long-term investments, restructurings, and discontinued operations. In the case of a business combination, an entity has to provide disclosures as per IFRS 3 as well.
10. Changes in contingent liabilities or contingent assets since the end of the last annual reporting period.

An entity shall provide comparative information in the explanatory notes as well. But there is no explicit requirement in IAS 34 for disclosure of comparative information in the explanatory notes; this is a requirement of IAS 1.

MATERIALITY

Materiality of the elements of financial statements is important in the context of recognition, measurement, classification, and disclosure. For the purpose of the interim financial report, *materiality* of an item is assessed in relation to the interim period financial data and not for the whole-year data. An interim financial report should provide all of the information that is relevant to understanding the financial position and performance of the entity during the interim period. Therefore, while preparing the interim financial report it is inappropriate to base quantitative estimates of materiality on projected annual figures; rather the materiality should be based on interim financial report period data.

ACCOUNTING POLICIES

The interim financial report is prepared either on the basis of the same accounting policies that are followed in the most recent financial statements or changed accounting policies that are to be adopted in the next financial statements. Therefore, an entity shall implement the proposed changes in accounting policies for the next annual financial statements in the interim financial report as well. In case there is a change in accounting policies from those applied in the most recent financial statements, the impact of change is to be disclosed.

Paragraph 28 of IAS 34 does not prohibit an entity from changing accounting policies at any time during the financial year. If an entity prepares an interim financial report on a quarterly basis, it need not adopt changes in accounting policies from the first quarter if it wishes to change accounting policies. It can change accounting policy in any quarter, but the quarterly interim financial report of the appropriate quarter should reflect that change.

Paragraph 28 of IAS 34 requires an entity to adopt a stand-alone approach to measurement for the purpose of the interim financial report. This implies that various elements of financial statements as on the interim financial report date are measured independently. Of course, IAS 34 requires a less detailed approach in accounting estimation. The stand-alone approach of measurement may create difficulties in some write-downs of intangibles (for example, goodwill write-downs) that cannot be written back. When reversal of impairment is not allowed, the interim financial report measurement might (most likely will) create complexity. However, principles to be followed for recognizing assets, liabilities, income, and expenses for interim periods are the same as in annual financial statements.

Example 3

Paragraph 29 of IAS 34 sets out that the principles to be followed for recognizing assets, liabilities, income, and expenses for interim periods are the same as in annual financial statements.

While there is concern about inventory valuation and asset impairment at the end of the interim reporting period, the entity evaluates that there will be no write-down of inventory or impairment by the year-end as the economic environment will improve. How should an entity account for inventory write-downs or impairments? Should the entity consider possible year-end effects as well as events in the interim period?

Solution

The entity should adopt a stand-alone approach. It has to measure the inventory as on the interim financial report date. So it should write down the inventory and charge an impairment loss.

As per IAS 2 and IAS 36, reversal of this write-down is possible. But there are exceptions to the reversal principle in the case of impairment of goodwill, which can create additional complexity.

The principles for recognizing and measuring losses from inventory write-downs, restructurings, or impairments in an interim period are the same as those that an entity would follow if it prepared only annual financial statements. Therefore, if such items are recognized and measured in one interim period and the estimate changes in a subsequent interim period of that financial year, the original estimate is changed in the subsequent interim period either by accrual of an additional amount of loss or by reversal of the previously recognized amount [paragraph 30(a), IAS 34].

Example 4

Entity E publishes a quarterly interim financial report. It has measured the following data relating to inventory valuation:

	Quarter 1 March 31, 2008	Quarter 2 June 30, 2008	Quarter 3 September 30, 2008	Annual financial statement date December 31, 2008
Cost (€ thousand)	100	110	95	110
Net realisable value	95	90	110	112

How should the entity account for the inventory?

Solution

Quarter 1 €95 thousand at net realizable value
Quarter 2 €90 thousand at net realizable value
Quarter 3 €95 thousand at cost
Quarter 4 €110 thousand at cost

Example 5

Paragraph 30(b) of IAS 34 sets out that "a cost that does not meet the definition of an asset at the end of an interim period is not deferred in the statement of financial position either to await future information as to whether it has met the definition of an asset or to smooth earnings over interim periods within a financial year." An entity has incurred development expenses for internally generated intangibles that do not satisfy the recognition criteria of paragraph 57 of IAS 38. However, IAS 38 does not allow writing back of previously expensed cost items once the conditions of paragraph 57 are satisfied. The entity is sure that it will be able to demonstrate compliance with the condition of paragraph 57 of IAS 38 by the year-end.

The entity is in a dilemma—if it expenses development expense under paragraph 30(b) of IAS 34, can it write back the same?

Solution

There is no conflict. IAS 38 provides that asset recognition (cost capitalization) begins at the point in time at which the recognition criteria are met, not at the start of the financial reporting period in which those criteria are met.

Paragraph 31 of IAS 34 re-emphasizes that "the definitions of assets, liabilities, income, and expenses are fundamental to recognition, at the end of both annual and interim financial reporting periods." Paragraph 32 of IAS 34 explains that recognition of an asset on the interim financial report date should follow the same principle of "probable future economic benefit." On the interim financial report date it is to be demonstrated that from the cost incurred, which is to be recognized as an asset, a flow of future economic benefit is probable. Therefore, the entity should expense those development expenses when the recognition condition of paragraph 57 of IAS 38 are not met.

Example 6

An entity publishes a quarterly interim financial report. Is it required to measure income tax expense applying the actual rate prevailing on the interim financial report date?

Solution

Paragraph 30(b) of IAS 34 explains that "income tax expense is recognized in each interim period based on the best estimate of the weighted-average annual income tax rate expected for the full financial year. Amounts accrued for income tax expense in one interim period may have to be adjusted in a subsequent interim period of that financial year if the estimate of the annual income tax rate changes."

Therefore, an entity uses the weighted-average rate. It avoids using a jurisdiction-specific actual rate for the measurement of income tax expense on the interim financial report date.

MEASUREMENT OF INTERIM FINANCIAL REPORT INCOME TAX EXPENSE

The interim period income tax expense is accrued using the tax rate that would be applicable to expected total annual earnings. The *applicable tax rate* is taken as the estimated average annual effective income tax rate applied to the pretax income of the interim period.

Example 7

An entity has estimated its annual pretax profit of €300,000 and annual tax expense of €47,000 taking into account various deductions and exemptions to which it is entitled, as per tax law. It prepares a quarterly interim financial report. As per the quarterly report, its pretax profit is €100,000. How should the entity charge tax expense? Does it need to change the annual estimate?

Solution

The entity has its quarterly estimate of pretax profit. It has estimated uneven pretax profit and that is acceptable as per IAS 34. Its weighted-average tax rate is 15.66%. Accordingly, it can charge €15,667 as tax expense of Quarter 1.

Example 8

An entity has estimated zero annual pretax profit and zero annual tax expense. It prepares a quarterly interim financial report. As per the quarterly report its pretax profit is €50,000. How should the entity charge tax expense? Does it need to change the annual estimate?

Solution

No tax expense should be charged. Paragraph B13 of IAS 34 explains that the same accounting recognition and measurement principles shall be applied in an interim financial report as are applied in annual financial statements. Income taxes are assessed on an annual basis. Interim period income tax expense is calculated by applying to an interim period's pretax income the tax rate that would be applicable to expected total annual earnings; that is, the estimated average annual effective income tax rate would be applied.

Of course, if the financial reporting year and the income tax year differ, income tax expense for an interim period which falls in a different tax year is measured using a separate weighted-average estimated effective tax rate.

EXCERPTS FROM PUBLISHED FINANCIAL STATEMENTS

Serabi Mining PLC

Interim Report 2009

1. Basis of Preparation

These interim accounts are for the six-month period ended June 30, 2009. Comparative information has been provided for the unaudited six-month period ended June 30, 2008, and the audited twelve-month period from January 1 to December 31, 2008.

The accounts for the period have been prepared in accordance with IAS 34, *Interim Financial Reporting* and with the policies that the group will adopt for its annual accounts, notably

- The financial statements are presented in US dollars. They are prepared on the historical cost basis or the fair value basis where the fair valuing of relevant assets and liabilities has been applied.
- The financial statements have been prepared in accordance with the measurement and presentation principles of IFRS in force at the reporting date and their interpretations issued by the IASB and adopted for use within the European Union (IFRS), and those parts of the Companies Act 2006 applicable to companies reporting under IFRS.
- The adoption of new accounting standards that are in effect for the calendar year ended December 31, 2009, notably IAS 1 (revised), *Presentation of Financial Statements*, IFRS 8, *Operating Segments,* and IAS 23, *Borrowing Costs.*

8. Impairment

Consistent with the review process performed as at December 31, 2008, the Directors have undertaken an impairment review of the group's exploration, development, and production assets. The Directors note that as a result of changing exchange rates between December 31, 2008, and June 30, 2009, the value of these assets in the accounts of the group has increased. The majority of the assets are held by and recorded in the accounts of the Serabi Mineracao Limitada, the group's 100% owned Brazilian subsidiary, the financial statements of which are denominated in Brazilian Real. Following this review and making estimates of the value in use, the Directors have concluded that as a result of the variation in exchange rates the carrying value of the Palito mine property and its associated infrastructure has increased to a level in excess of the valuation supported by the value in use calculation. As a result and in accordance with the provisions of IAS 36, *Impairment of Assets*, the Directors have agreed to make an impairment charge of US $2,422,737 against the carrying value of the assets of the group relating to the Palito mine. No impairment charge has been made in respect of any of the remainder of the group's exploration and development projects.

In deriving an estimate of the value in use in respect of the Palito mine the Directors have calculated a net present value of the projected cash flow to be derived from the exploitation of the known reserves of 187,538 gold equivalent ounces as estimated at the end of March 2008. The key assumptions underlying the net present value are unchanged from those detailed in the Annual Report 2008 save that commencement of operations has been set as July 1, 2011 (six months later than previously), the exchange rate BrR$ to US$ has been set at 1.9516 (previously 2.356) and the long-term gold price set at US $800 (previously $750). The value in use taking into account these parameters of Palito has been estimated at US $34.4 million (previously US $34.8 million).

Roche Capital Market Ltd, Interim Report 2009

Notes to the Roche Capital Market Ltd, Interim Financial Statements

Reference numbers indicate corresponding Notes to the Interim Financial Statements. The Interim Financial Statements are unaudited. The Interim Financial Statements have been reviewed by the Roche Capital Market Ltd's auditors and their review report is presented on page 7.

1. Accounting Policies

Basis of Preparation of Financial Statements

These financial statements are the unaudited interim financial statements (hereafter 'the Interim Financial Statements') of Roche Capital Market Ltd, (Roche Kapitalmarkt AG), a company registered in Switzerland (hereafter 'the Company') for the six-month period ended June 30, 2009 (hereafter 'the interim period'). The Company is 100% owned by Roche Holding Ltd (Roche Holding AG), a public company registered in Switzerland. Roche Holding Ltd, is the parent company of the Roche Group, and therefore the Company is a member of the Roche Group.

The main activity of the Company is the provision of financing to other affiliates of the Roche Group. Refinancing takes place on the bond or loan markets. During the first half of 2009, the Company resumed its financing activities on behalf of the Roche Group and issued bonds, which are guaranteed by Roche Holding Ltd, the parent company of the Roche Group (see Note 4). The Company subsequently entered into new financing arrangements with other members of the Roche Group (see Note 3).

The Interim Financial Statements have been prepared in accordance with International Accounting Standard 34 (IAS 34), *Interim Financial Reporting*. These Interim Financial Statements should be read in conjunction with the Financial Statements for the year ended December 31, 2008 (hereafter 'the Annual Financial Statements'), as they provide an update of previously reported information. They were approved for issue by the Board of Directors on July 20, 2009.

The Interim Financial Statements have been prepared in accordance with the accounting policies and methods of computation set out in the Annual Financial Statements, except for accounting policy changes made after the date of the Annual Financial Statements. The presentation of the Interim Financial Statements is consistent with the Annual Financial Statements, except where noted.

The preparation of the Interim Financial Statements requires management to make estimates and assumptions that affect the reported amounts of revenues, expenses, assets, and liabilities, and the disclosure of contingent liabilities at the date of the financial statements. If in the future such estimates and assumptions, which are based on management's best judgements at the date of the Interim Financial Statements, deviate from the actual circumstances, the original estimates and assumptions will be modified as appropriate in the year in which the circumstances change.

The Company has only one operating segment and undertakes its operation in Switzerland. Therefore no segment reporting is included in these financial statements.

Income tax expense is recognized based upon the best estimate of the income tax rate expected for the full financial year.

Changes in Accounting Policies Adopted by the Roche Group and, Consequently, by the Company

In 2007, the Roche Group early adopted IFRS 8, *Operating Segments,* and IAS 23 (revised), *Borrowing Costs,* which were required to be implemented from January 1, 2009, at the latest. In 2008, the Roche Group early adopted the revised versions of IFRS 3, *Business Combinations,* and IAS 27, *Consolidated and Separate Financial Statements*, which are required to be implemented from January 1, 2010, at the latest. While these changes were also adopted by the Company, none of them had any impact on these Interim Financial Statements.

5. Equity

Share Capital

The authorized and issued share capital of the Company consists of 1,000 shares with a nominal value of 1,000 Swiss francs each and has not changed during the interim period. All the shares are owned by Roche Holding Ltd, a public company registered in Switzerland.

Dividends

There were no dividend payments in the interim period (2008: none).

6. Contingent Liabilities

No changes in the Company's contingent liabilities have occurred since the approval of the Annual Financial Statements by the Board of Directors.

26 IMPAIRMENT OF ASSETS (IAS 36)

INTRODUCTION

The objective of IAS 36 is to ensure that assets are carried at an amount not in excess of their recoverable amount, and to provide guidelines on calculation of recoverable amount.

SCOPE

The standard applies to

- Land
- Buildings
- Machinery and equipment
- Investment property carried at cost
- Intangible assets
- Goodwill
- Investments in subsidiaries, associates, and joint ventures

EXCLUSIONS

The following assets are not covered:

- Inventories (see IAS 2)
- Assets arising from construction contracts (see IAS 11)
- Deferred tax assets (see IAS 12)
- Assets arising from employee benefits (see IAS 19)
- Financial assets (see IAS 39)
- Investment property carried at fair value (see IAS 40)
- Biological agricultural assets carried at fair value (see IAS 41)
- Insurance contract assets (see IFRS 4)
- Assets held for sale (see IFRS 5)

KEY TERMS

Impairment. An asset is impaired when its carrying amount exceeds its recoverable amount.

Carrying amount. The amount at which an asset is recognized in the statement of financial position after deducting accumulated depreciation and accumulated impairment losses.

Recoverable amount. The higher of an asset's fair value less costs to sell (net selling price) and its value in use.

Fair value. The amount obtainable from the sale of an asset in a bargained transaction between knowledgeable, willing parties.

Value in use. The present value of estimated future cash flows expected to arise from

- The continuing use of an asset; and
- Its disposal at the end of its useful life.

Cash-generating unit. The smallest identifiable group of assets that generates cash inflows that are largely independent of the cash inflows from other assets or groups of assets.

IDENTIFICATION OF ASSETS THAT MAY BE IMPAIRED

At each reporting date, an entity should review all assets covered by the standard to identify whether there are indicators that an asset may be impaired (i.e., its carrying amount may be in excess of the recoverable amount). The standard provides a list of external and internal indicators of impairment.

External Sources

- Market value declines
- Negative changes in technology, markets, economy, or laws
- Increases in market interest rates
- Company stock price is below book value

Internal Sources

- Obsolescence or physical damage
- Asset is part of a restructuring or held for disposal
- Worse economic performance than expected

These lists are not exhaustive. Further, an indication that an asset may be impaired may indicate that the asset's useful life, depreciation method, or residual value may need to be reviewed and adjusted.

If there is an indication that an asset may be impaired, then calculate the asset's recoverable amount. The recoverable amounts of the following intangible assets should be measured annually whether there is any indication that it may be impaired:

- An intangible asset with an indefinite useful life
- An intangible asset not yet available for use
- Goodwill acquired in a business combination

CALCULATION OF RECOVERABLE AMOUNT

- If either fair value less costs to sell or value in use is more than carrying amount, it is not necessary to calculate the other amount. The asset is not impaired.
- If fair value less costs to sell cannot be determined, then recoverable amount is value in use.
- For assets to be disposed of, recoverable amount is fair value less costs to sell.

CALCULATION OF FAIR VALUE LESS COSTS TO SELL

- If there is a binding sale agreement, use the price under that agreement less costs of disposal.
- If there is an active market for that type of asset, use market price less costs of disposal (only direct costs). Market price means current bid price if available; otherwise, the price is the most recent transaction.
- If there is no active market, use the best estimate of the asset's selling price less costs of disposal.

CALCULATION OF VALUE IN USE

The calculation of value in use should reflect the following elements:

- An estimate of the future cash flows the entity expects to derive from the asset in an arm's length transaction;
- Expectations about possible variations in the amount or timing of those future cash flows;
- The time value of money, represented by the current market risk-free rate of interest; and
- Other factors, such as illiquidity, that market participants would reflect in pricing the future cash flows the entity expects to derive from the asset.

Cash flow projections should be based on reasonable and supportable assumptions, the most recent budgets and forecasts, and extrapolation for periods beyond budgeted projections.

Cash flow projections should relate to the asset in its current condition—future restructurings to which the entity is not committed and expenditures to improve or enhance the asset's performance should not be anticipated.

Estimates of future cash flows should not include cash inflows or outflows from financing activities, or income tax receipts or payments.

SELECTION OF DISCOUNT RATE

In measuring value in use, the discount rate used should be the pretax rate that reflects current market assessments of the time value of money and the risks specific to the asset.

The discount rate should not reflect risks for which future cash flows have been adjusted and should equal the rate of return that investors would require if they were to choose an investment that would generate cash flows equivalent to those expected from the asset.

If a market-determined asset-specific rate is not available, then the rate used must reflect the time value of money over the asset's life as well as country risk, currency risk, price risk, and cash flow risk. The following would normally be considered:

- The enterprise's own weighted-average cost of capital;
- The enterprise's incremental borrowing rate; and
- Other market borrowing rates.

Example 1

Anthony Inc. has an item of plant with a carrying amount of $200 million on March 31, 2003. Its remaining useful life is five years and residual value at the end of five years is $10 million. Estimated future cash flows from using the plant in the next five years are

For the year ended on	Estimated cash flow ($ million)
March 31, 2004	100
March 31, 2005	60
March 31, 2006	60
March 31, 2007	40
March 31, 2008	40

Calculate *value in use* for the plant if the discount rate is 25% and also calculate the recoverable amount if fair value less cost to sell is $140 million on March 31, 2003?

Solution

1. **Value in use**

Year	Cash Inflows	@ 25%	Present Value of Cash Inflows
March 31, 2004	100	0.80	80.0
March 31, 2005	60	0.64	38.4
March 31, 2006	60	0.512	30.72
March 31, 2007	40	0.410	16.40
March 31, 2008	50 (40 + 10)	0.328	16.40
			181.92

2. **Recoverable amount** = Value in use $181.92 million *or* fair value less cost to sell $140 million, whichever is more, that is, $181.92 million.

   Since the carrying amount is greater than the recoverable amount, the asset is impaired.

3. **Impairment loss**
   = Carrying amount – Recoverable amount
   = $200 million – $181.92 million
   = $18.08 million

RECOGNITION OF AN IMPAIRMENT LOSS

- An impairment loss should be recognized whenever the recoverable amount is below the carrying amount.
- The impairment loss should be charged as an expense in the income statement (unless it relates to a revalued asset where the value changes are recognized directly in equity).
- Adjustment to depreciation for future periods is required.

Example 2

Marsh Inc. provides the following estimates of expected cash flows relating to a fixed asset on December 31, 2007. The discount rate is 15%.

Year	Cash flow ($)
2008	4,000
2009	6,000
2010	6,000
2011	8,000
2012	4,000
Residual value at the end of 2012	1,000

Fixed asset purchased on January 1, 2005 for $40,000
Useful life: 8 years.
Residual value is estimated at $1,000 at the end of eight years. Net selling price is estimated of $20,000

Compute

1. Impairment loss to be recognized for the year ended December 31, 2007.
2. Depreciation charge for 2008.

Solution

1. **Value in use**

Year	Cash inflows	DF @ 15%	Present value of cash inflows
2008	4,000	0.870	3,480
2009	6,000	0.756	4,536
2010	6,000	0.658	3,948
2011	8,000	0.572	4,576
2012	5,000	0.497	2,485
			19,025

2. **Recoverable amount** = Value in use $19,025 *or* Fair value less costs to sell $20,000, whichever is more, that is, $20,000.
3. **Calculation of carrying amount and impairment loss** (in US dollars)

Cost on January 1, 2005	$40,000
(–) Depreciation for 3 years to December 31, 2007	(14,625)

$$\left(\frac{40,000 - 1,000}{8} \right) \times 3$$

Carrying amount as on December 31, 2007	25,375
(–) Recoverable amount	20,000
Impairment loss	$5,375
Carrying amount on December 31, 2007 (before Impairment loss)	$25,375
(–) Impairment loss	(5,375)
Revised carrying amount as on December 31, 2007 after impairment loss	$20,000

Depreciation charged for 2008

$$= \frac{20,000 - 1,000}{5} = 3,800$$

CASH-GENERATING UNITS

Recoverable amount should be determined for the individual asset, if possible. At times, it is not possible to determine the recoverable amount (fair value less cost to sell and value in use) for the individual asset. In these cases, the entity should determine recoverable amount for the asset's cash-generating unit (CGU). The CGU is the smallest identifiable group of assets. They generate cash inflows that are largely independent of the cash inflows from other assets or groups of assets.

IMPAIRMENT OF GOODWILL

Goodwill should be tested for impairment annually. To test for impairment, goodwill must be allocated to each of the acquirer's cash-generating units, or groups of cash-generating units, that are expected to benefit from the synergies of the combination, irrespective of whether other assets or liabilities of the acquiree are assigned to those units or groups of units. Each unit or group of units to which the goodwill is so allocated shall

- Represent the lowest level within the entity at which the goodwill is monitored for internal management purposes; and
- Not be larger than a segment based in accordance with IFRS 8, *Operating Segments.*

A CGU to which goodwill has been allocated shall be tested for impairment at least annually by comparing the carrying amount of the unit, including the goodwill, with the recoverable amount of the unit

- If the recoverable amount of the unit exceeds the carrying amount of the unit, the unit and the goodwill allocated to that unit is not impaired.
- If the carrying amount of the unit exceeds the recoverable amount of the unit, the entity must recognize an impairment loss.

The impairment loss is allocated to reduce the carrying amount of the assets of the unit or group of units in the following order:

- First, reduce the carrying amount of any goodwill allocated to the CGU (group of units); and

- then, reduce the carrying amounts of the other assets of the unit (group of units) pro rata on the basis of the carrying amount of each asset in the unit (group of units).

The carrying amount of an asset should not be reduced below the highest of

- Its fair value less costs to sell (if determinable);
- Its value in use (if determinable); and
- Zero.

REVERSAL OF AN IMPAIRMENT LOSS

- Assess at each reporting date whether there is an indication that an impairment loss may have decreased. If so, calculate recoverable amount.
- No reversal for unwinding of discount.
- The increased carrying amount due to reversal should not be more than what the depreciated historical cost would have been if the impairment had not been recognized.
- Reversal of an impairment loss is recognized as income in the income statement.
- Adjustment in depreciation for future periods is required.
- Reversal of an impairment loss for goodwill is not allowed.

DISCLOSURES

- Impairment losses recognized in the income statement and the line items of the statement of comprehensive income in which the impairment losses are included.
- Impairment losses reversed in the income statement and the line items of the statement of comprehensive income in which the impairment losses are reversed.

Other Disclosures

If an individual impairment loss (reversal) is material disclose

- Events and circumstances resulting in the impairment loss
- Amount of the loss
- Individual asset: nature and segment to which it relates
- CGU: description, amount of impairment loss (reversal) by class of assets and segment
- If recoverable amount is fair value less costs to sell, disclose the basis for determining fair value
- If recoverable amount is value in use, disclose the discount rate
- If fair value less costs to sell is determined by discounted cash flow projections, disclosures about the period over which the management has projected the cash flows, the growth rate used to extrapolate the cash flow projection and the discount rate applied to the cash flow projections are required

Disclose detailed information about the estimates used to measure recoverable amounts of CGU containing goodwill or intangible assets with indefinite useful lives.

Example 3

Venus Inc. has an asset that is carried in the balance sheet on March 31, 2005, at $500 million. As of that date, the value in use is $400 million and the net selling price is $375 million.
Using this data:

1. Calculate impairment loss.
2. Prepare journal entries for adjustment of impairment loss.
3. Illustrate how the impairment loss will be shown in the balance sheet.

Solution

1. *Impairment loss* is the amount by which the carrying amount of an asset exceeds its recoverable amount. Thus,

$$\text{Impairment loss} = \text{Carrying amount} - \text{Recoverable amount}^{**}$$
$$= \$500 \text{ million} - \$400 \text{ million}$$
$$= \$100 \text{ million}$$

**Recoverable amount is higher of asset's net selling price $375 million and its value in use $400 million.*

Therefore, recoverable amount is $400 million.

2. Journal Entries ($ million)

Particulars		Dr. Amount	Cr. Amount
1. Impairment loss account Dr.		100	
To asset account			100
Being the entry for accounting impairment loss			
2. Profit and loss account Dr.		100	
To impairment loss account			100
Being the entry to transfer impairment loss to profit and loss account			

3. Balance Sheet of Venus Inc. as on March 31, 2005

	$ million
Asset less depreciation	$500
Less: Impairment loss	100
	$400

EXCERPTS FROM PUBLISHED FINANCIAL STATEMENTS

Holcim, Annual Report 2006

Notes to the Financial Statements

Accounting Policies

Impairment of Nonfinancial Assets

At each balance sheet date, the group assesses whether there is any indication that a nonfinancial asset may be impaired. If any such indication exists, the recoverable amount of the nonfinancial asset is estimated in order to determine the extent of the impairment loss, if any. Where it is not possible to estimate the recoverable amount of an individual nonfinancial asset, the group estimates the recoverable amount of the smallest cash-generating unit to which the nonfinancial asset belongs.

If the recoverable amount of a nonfinancial asset or cash-generating unit is estimated to be less than its carrying amount, the carrying amount of the nonfinancial asset or cash-generating unit is reduced to its recoverable amount. Impairment losses are recognized immediately in the income statement.

Where an impairment loss subsequently reverses, the carrying amount of the nonfinancial asset or cash-generating unit is increased to the revised estimate of its recoverable amount. However, this increased amount cannot exceed the carrying amount that would have been determined had no impairment loss been recognized for that nonfinancial asset or cash-generating unit in prior periods. A reversal of an impairment loss is recognized immediately in the income statement.

Impairment of Financial Assets

At each balance sheet date, the group assesses whether there is any indication that a financial asset may be impaired. An impairment loss in respect of a financial asset measured at amortized cost is calculated as the difference between its carrying amount and the present value of the future estimated cash flows discounted at the original effective interest rate. The carrying amount of the asset is reduced through the use of an allowance account. The amount of the loss is recognized in profit or loss.

If, in a subsequent period, the amount of the impairment loss decreases and the decrease can be related objectively to an event occurring after the impairment was recognized, the previously recognized impairment loss is reversed, to the extent that the carrying value of the asset does not exceed its amortized cost at the reversal date. Any reversal of an impairment loss is recognized in profit or loss.

An impairment loss in respect of an available-for-sale financial asset is recognized in the income statement and is calculated by reference to its fair value. Individually significant financial assets are tested for impairment on an individual basis. Reversals of impairment losses on equity instruments classified as available-for-sale are recognized directly in equity and not in the income statement while reversals of impairment losses on debt instruments are recognized in profit or loss if the increase in fair value of the instrument can be objectively related to an event occurring after the impairment loss was recognized in the income statement.

In relation to accounts receivables, a provision for impairment is made when there is objective evidence (such as the probability of insolvency or significant financial difficulties of the debtor) that the group will not be able to collect all of the amounts due under the original terms of the invoice. The carrying amount of the receivable is reduced through use of an allowance account. Impaired receivables are derecognized when they are assessed as uncollectible.

LECTRA, Annual Report 2008

Notes to Consolidated Financial Statements

Accounting Policies

Fixed Asset Impairment—Impairment Tests

When events or changes in the market environment, or internal factors, indicate an impairment of value of goodwill, other intangible assets or property, plant, and equipment, these are subjected to detailed scrutiny. In the case of goodwill, impairment tests are carried out systematically at least once a year.

Goodwill is tested for impairment by comparing its carrying value with its recoverable amount or value in use, which is defined as the present value of future cash flows attached to them, excluding interest and tax. The results utilized are derived from the group's three-year plan. Beyond the timeframe of the three-year plan, cash flows are projected to infinity, the assumed growth rate being dependent on the growth potential of the markets and/or products concerned by the impairment test. The discount rate is computed under the weighted-average cost of capital (WACC) method, the cost of capital being determined by applying the capital asset pricing model (CAPM). If the impairment test reveals an impairment of value relative to the carrying value, an irreversible impairment loss is recognized to reduce the carrying value of the goodwill to its recoverable amount. This charge, if any, is recognized under "Goodwill impairment" in the income statement.

Other intangible assets and property, plant, and equipment are tested by comparing the carrying value of each relevant group of assets (which may be an isolated asset or a cash-generating unit) with its recoverable amount. If the latter is less than the carrying value, an impairment charge equal to the difference between these two amounts is recognized. In the case of LECTRA's new information system, impairment testing consists in periodically verifying that the initial assumptions regarding the useful life and functions of the system remain valid. The base and the schedule of amortization/depreciation of the assets concerned are reduced if a loss is recognized, the resulting charge being recorded as an amortization/depreciation charge under *Cost of goods sold*, *Research and development expenses*, or *Selling, general and administrative expenses* in the income statement depending on the nature and use of the assets concerned.

27 PROVISIONS, CONTINGENT LIABILITIES, AND CONTINGENT ASSETS (IAS 37)

INTRODUCTION

The objective of IAS 37 is to ensure that appropriate recognition criteria and measurement bases are applied to provisions, contingent liabilities, and contingent assets and that sufficient information is disclosed in the notes to the financial statements so that users can understand their nature, timing, and amount. The standard aims to ensure that only present obligations arising from past obligating events (if they meet all criteria of recognition as required by the standard) are recognized within the financial statements. Thus, for example, a planned future expenditure, even though authorized by the board of directors (or an equivalent governing body of the board), is excluded from recognition.

SCOPE

IAS 37 excludes obligations and contingencies arising from

- Financial instruments within the scope of IAS 39
- Nononerous executory contracts
- Insurance contracts (but IAS 37 does apply to nonpolicy–related liabilities of an insurance company)
- Items covered by another standard (IAS 11, *Construction Contracts*, applies to obligations arising under such contracts; IAS 12, *Income Taxes*, applies to obligations for current or deferred income taxes; IAS 17, *Leases*, applies to lease obligations; and IAS 19, *Employee Benefits*, applies to pension and other employee benefit obligations)

KEY TERMS

Provision. A liability of uncertain timing or amount.

Liability. Present obligation as a result of past events. Settlement is expected to result in an outflow of resources (payment).

Contingent liability. A possible obligation arising from past events—its existence depends on whether some uncertain future event occurs, or a present obligation that arises from past events but payment is not probable or the amount cannot be measured reliably

Contingent asset. A possible asset that arises from past events—its existence will be confirmed only by the occurrence or nonoccurrence of one or more uncertain future events not entirely within the control of the enterprise.

RECOGNITION OF A PROVISION

An entity must recognize a provision if, and only if

- A *present obligation* (legal or constructive) has arisen as a result of a *past event* (that should an *obligating event)*,
- Outflow of resources is *probable* (i.e., more likely than not), and
- The amount to be recognized can be *estimated reliably.*

An *obligating event* is an event that creates a legal or constructive obligation and, therefore, results in an entity having no realistic alternative but to settle the obligation.

A *constructive obligation* arises if past practice creates a valid expectation on the part of a third party.

For example, a retail store that has a long-standing policy of allowing customers to return merchandise within, say, a 30-day period establishes a constructive obligation.

Similarly, in case an entity has signed an onerous contract, an obligation is established when it is terminated. An *onerous contract* is an agreement that an entity cannot get out of legally without incurring costs. An example of an onerous contract is when an entity has signed an agreement to market the products of a principal for a period of five years and the terms of the agreement provide for payment of compensation in the case of its early termination. The obligation under this agreement is the amount of penalty that is to be paid.

A possible (less than more likely than not) obligation (a contingent liability) is to be disclosed and not accrued or recognized. However, disclosure is not required if the probability is remote.

MEASUREMENT OF PROVISIONS

The amount recognized as a provision should be the best estimate of the expenditure required to settle the present obligation at the reporting date; that is, the amount that an enterprise would rationally pay to settle the obligation at the reporting date or to transfer it to a third party. This means

- Provisions for one-off events (restructuring, environmental cleanup, settlement of a lawsuit) are measured at the most likely amount.
- Provisions for large populations of events (warranties, customer refunds) are measured at a probability-weighted expected value.
- Both measurements are at discounted present value using a pretax discount rate that reflects the current market assessments of the time value of money and the risks specific to the liability.

In reaching its best estimate, the enterprise should take into account the risks and uncertainties that surround the underlying events. Expected cash outflows should be discounted to their present values, where the effect of the time value of money is material.

If some or all of the expenditure required to settle a provision is expected to be reimbursed by another party, the reimbursement should be recognized as a reduction of the required provision when, and only when, it is virtually certain that reimbursement will be received if the enterprise settles the obligation. The amount recognized should not exceed the amount of the provision.

REMEASUREMENT OF PROVISIONS

Review and adjust provisions at each balance sheet date. If outflow is no longer probable, reverse the provision to income. The following are examples of commonly encountered provisions.

Situation	*Recognition of Provision*
Restructuring by sale of an operation	Accrue a provision only after a binding sale agreement
Restructuring by closure or reorganization	Accrue a provision only after a detailed formal plan is adopted and announced publicly. A Board decision is not enough
Warranty	Accrue a provision (past event was the sale of defective goods)
Customer refunds	Accrue if the established policy is to give refunds
Offshore oil rig must be removed and sea bed restored	Accrue a provision when installed, and add to the cost of the asset
Entity should carry out staff training for recent changes in tax law	No provision (there is no obligation to provide the training)
Onerous (loss-making) contract	Accrue a provision

RESTRUCTURINGS

A *restructuring* may result from

- Sale or termination of a line of business
- Closure of business locations
- Changes in management structure
- Fundamental reorganization of the company

Restructuring provisions should be accrued as follows:

- *Sale of operation:* Accrue provision only after a binding sale agreement. If the binding sale agreement is after the reporting date, disclosure is required but no accrual is needed.
- *Closure or reorganization:* Accrue only after a detailed formal plan is adopted and announced publicly. A board decision alone is not enough to warrant a provision.
- *Future operating losses:* Provisions should not be recognized for future operating losses, even in the case of a restructuring.

Restructuring provisions should include only direct expenditures as a result of the restructuring and should not be costs that are associated with the ongoing activities of the entity.

CONTINGENT LIABILITIES

Since there is common ground in terms of liabilities that are uncertain, the standard also deals with contingencies. It requires that contingent liabilities should not be recognized; instead, the entity should disclose them, unless the probability of an outflow of economic resources is remote.

CONTINGENT ASSETS

Contingent assets should not be recognized. However, they should be disclosed where an inflow of economic benefits is probable. When the realization of income is virtually certain, then the related asset is not a contingent asset and its recognition is appropriate.

DISCLOSURES

Reconciliation for each class of provision is shown as

- Opening balance
- Additions
- Amounts used (i.e., amounts charged against the provision)
- Amounts released (reversed)

- Unwinding of the discount
- Closing balance

For each class of provision, provide a brief description of

- Nature
- Timing
- Uncertainties
- Assumptions
- Reimbursement

In case the disclosure of any or all the information regarding the reimbursement will be prejudicial to the entity in a dispute with other parties on the subject matter of the provision, an entity need not disclose the information but should disclose the general nature of the dispute, together with the fact that, and reason why, the information has not been disclosed.

Example 1

John Academy has 50 students studying for their MBA. As part of its admission process, it offers a guarantee to return fees ($10,000) if a student does not succeed in the examination. A realistic assessment of probability of success for MBA students is 60%. Should John Academy make a provision or disclose a contingent liability?

Solution

Since the probability of failure is 40% and there are 50 MBA students that have, in total, paid $500,000 in fees, a provision is required for $200,000.

Example 2

Mark Inc. took a factory premises on lease on January 1, 2008, for $2 million per month. The lease is an operating lease. During March 2008, Mark Inc. relocates its operation to a new factory building. The lease on the old factory premises continues to be effective up to December 3, 2010. As per the terms of the lease, the lease cannot be cancelled and Mark Inc. cannot sublease it to another lessee. The company is consulting IFRS experts as to whether the lease rentals for the remaining 33 months up to December 31, 2010, should be provided in the financial statements for the year ending December 31, 2008.

Solution

In accordance with IAS 37, *Provisions, Contingent Liabilities, and Contingent Assets*, if an entity has entered into a contract that is onerous, the present obligation under the contract should be recognized and measured as a provision. In the given circumstances, the operating lease contract has become onerous as the economic benefits from the lease contract for the next 33 months up to December 31, 2010, are zero; however, the lessee, Mark Inc., has an obligation to pay lease rentals of $66 million ($2 million per month for the next 33 months). Therefore, a provision of $66 million is to be made (at its present value) in the financial statements for the year ended December 31, 2008.

EXCERPTS FROM PUBLISHED FINANCIAL STATEMENTS

Holcim, Annual Report 2006

Notes to the Financial Statements

Accounting Policies

Site Restoration and Other Environmental Provisions

The group provides for the costs of restoring a site where a legal or constructive obligation exists. The cost of raising a provision before exploitation of the raw materials has commenced is included in property, plant, and equipment and depreciated over the life of the site. The effect of any adjustments to the provision due to further environmental damage is recorded through operating costs over the life of the site to reflect the best estimate of the expenditure required to settle the obligation at balance sheet date. Changes in the measurement of a provision that result from changes in the estimated timing or amount of cash outflows, or a change in the discount rate, are added to, or deducted from, the cost of the related asset as appropriate in the current period. All provisions are discounted to their present value based on a long-term borrowing rate.

Emission Rights

The initial allocation of emission rights granted is recognized at nominal amount (nil value). Where a group company has emissions in excess of the emission rights granted, it will recognize a provision for the shortfall based on the market price at that date. The emission rights are held for compliance purposes only and therefore the group does not intend to speculate with these in the open market.

Other Provisions

A provision is recognized when there exists a legal or constructive obligation arising from past events. It is probable that an outflow of resources embodying economic benefits will be required to settle the obligation and a reliable estimate can be made of this amount.

Contingent Liabilities

Contingent liabilities arise from conditions or situations where the outcome depends on future events. They are disclosed in the notes to the financial statements.

31. Provisions

CHF million	Site restoration and other environmental liabilities	Specific business	Other provisions	Total 2008	Total 2007
January 1	**518**	**365**	**605**	**1,488**	**1,503**
Change in structure	8	4	(33)	(21)	11
Provisions recognized	75	129	139	343	266
Provisions used during the year	(35)	(20)	(91)	(146)	(150)
Provisions reversed during the year	(13)	(26)	(27)	(66)	(140)
Currency translation effects	(75)	(71)	(77)	(223)	(2)
Of which short-term provisions	29	29	143	201	192
Of which long-term provisions	449	352	373	1,174	1,296

Site restoration and other environmental liabilities represent the group's legal or constructive obligations of restoring a site. The timing of cash outflows of this provision is dependent on the completion of raw material extraction and the commencement of site restoration.

Specific business risks comprise litigation and restructuring costs that arise during the normal course of business. Provisions for litigations mainly relate to antitrust investigations, product liability, as well as tax claims and are set up to cover legal and administrative proceedings. It includes CHF 120 million related to the German antitrust investigation set up in 2002. The total provisions for litigations amounted to CHF 309 million (2007: 294) at December 31. The timing of cash outflows of provisions for litigations is uncertain since it will largely depend on the outcome of administrative and legal proceedings. Provisions for restructuring costs relate to various restructuring programs and amounted to CHF 72 million (2007: 71) at December 31. These provisions are expected to result in future cash outflows mainly within the next one to three years.

Other provisions relate mainly to provisions that have been set up to cover other contractual liabilities. The composition of this item is extremely manifold and comprises as at December 31, among other things: various severance payments to employees of CHF 71 million (2007: 72), provisions for sales and other taxes of CHF 70 million (2007: 73), and provisions for health insurance and pension scheme, which do not qualify as benefit obligations, of CHF 68 million (2007: 85). The expected timing of the future cash outflows is uncertain.

36. Contingencies, Guarantees and Commitments

Contingencies

In the ordinary course of business, the group is involved in lawsuits, claims, investigations and proceedings, including product liability, commercial, environmental, health and safety matters, and so on. There are no single matters pending that the group expects to be material in relation to the group's business, financial position, or results of operations.

At December 31, 2008, the group's contingencies amounted to CHF 347 million (2007: 239). It is possible, but not probable, that the respective legal cases will result in future liabilities.

The group operates in countries where political, economic, social, and legal developments could have an impact on the group's operations. The effects of such risks that arise in the normal course of business are not foreseeable and are therefore not included in the accompanying consolidated financial statements.

Guarantees

At December 31, 2008, guarantees issued to third parties in the ordinary course of business amounted to CHF 330 million (2007: 276).

Barloworld, Annual Report 2008

Notes to the Consolidated Annual Financial Statements for the Year Ended September 30

16. Provisions

	2008 Rm	2007 Rm	2006 Rm
Noncurrent	325	344	468
Current	731	600	536
	1,056	944	1,004
Per business segment:			
Continuing operations			
Equipment	446	422	318
Automotive	390	253	309
Handling	67	31	44
Logistics	9	15	4
Corporate and other	155	190	161
Total continuing operations	1,067	911	836
Discontinued operations			
Car rental Scandinavia	1	2	
Cement			116
Coatings		31	32
Scientific		11	20
Steel tube		—	20
Total discontinued operations	1	44	188
Total group	1,068	955	1,024
Amounts classified as held for sale	(12)	(11)	(20)
Total per balance sheet	1,056	944	1,004

Movement of provisions	Total 2008 Rm	Insurance claims Rm	Warranty claims Rm	Credit life and warranty products Rm	Maintenance contracts Rm	Postretirement benefits Rm	Restructuring Rm	Other Rm
Balance at beginning of year	944	81	153	35	335	162	36	142
Amounts added	1 447	36	680	42	485	28	16	160
Amounts used	(1,300)	(48)	(640)	(31)	(397)	(31)	(20)	(133)
Amounts reversed unused	(64)		(2)		(8)	2	3	(59)
Unwinding of discount on present valued amounts	15		(5)	7		(33)	(13)	59
Disposal of subsidiaries	(37)	(1)	(14)	(1)	(14)	(2)	(4)	(1)
Translation adjustments	51	4	14	6	5	13	2	7
Balance at end of year	1,056	72	186	58	406	139	20	175
To be incurred								
Within one year	731	72	185	40	243	25	11	155
Between two to five years	220		1	18	163	12	9	17
More than five years	105					102		3
	1,056	72	186	58	406	139	20	175

Warranty Claims

The provisions relate principally to warranty claims on capital equipment, spare parts, and service. The estimate is based on claims notified and past experience.

Maintenance Contracts

This relates to deferred revenue on maintenance and repair contracts on equipment, forklift trucks, and motor vehicles. Assumptions include the estimation of maintenance and repair costs over the life cycle of the assets concerned.

Restructuring

The provision includes obligations related to the closure of operations.

28 INTANGIBLE ASSETS (IAS 38)

INTRODUCTION

IAS 38 prescribes the accounting treatment for intangible assets that are not dealt with specifically by any other standard. IAS 38 requires an entity to recognize an intangible asset when specified criteria are met. The standard also outlines ways to measure the carrying amount of intangible assets and requires disclosures relating to intangible assets.

SCOPE

The standard applies to all intangible assets *other than*

- *Financial assets* as defined in IAS 32, *Financial Instruments: Presentation*;
- *Mineral rights and exploration and development costs* incurred by mining and oil and gas companies (see IFRS 6); and
- *Intangible assets covered by another standard* such as assets held for sale in the ordinary course of business (IAS 2 and IAS 11), noncurrent intangible, classified as held for sale (IFRS 5), deferred tax assets (IAS 12), leases (IAS 17), assets arising from employee benefits (IAS 19), goodwill acquired in a business combination (covered by IFRS 3), and deferred acquisition costs and intangible assets, arising from an insurer's contractual rights under insurance contracts within the scope of IFRS 4.

KEY TERMS

Asset. A resource that is controlled by the entity as a result of past events (e.g., purchase or self-creation) and from which future economic benefits (inflows of cash or other assets) are expected.

Intangible asset. An identifiable nonmonetary asset without physical substance.

Research. Original and planned investigation undertaken with the prospect of gaining new scientific or technical knowledge and understanding.

Development. The application of the research findings or other knowledge to a plan or design for the production of new or substantially improved materials, devices, products, processes, systems, or services before the commencement of commercial production or use.

INTANGIBLE ASSETS

The three critical attributes of an *intangible asset* are

- Identifiability
- Control
- Future economic benefits

Identifiability

An intangible asset is *identifiable* when it

- Is separable (capable of being separated and sold, transferred, licensed, rented, or exchanged, either individually or as part of a package); or

- Arises from contractual or other legal rights, regardless of whether those rights are transferable or separable from the entity or from other rights and obligations.

Control

An entity controls an asset when it has the power to obtain future economic benefits flowing from the underlying resources and to restrict the access of others to those benefits. Generally, the capacity to control would arise from legally enforceable rights, such as copyrights, restraint of trade agreements (*only in those jurisdictions where it is permissible to enter into such an agreements*). However, legal enforceability of a right is not a necessary condition for control because an entity may be able to control the future economic benefits in some other way.

Future economic benefits. Future economic benefits flowing to the entity from an intangible asset may include

- Revenue from the sale of products or services;
- Cost savings; or
- Other benefits resulting from the use of the assets by the entity.

Examples of *possible* intangible assets.

- Computer software
- Patents
- Copyrights
- Motion picture films
- Customer lists
- Mortgage servicing rights
- Licenses
- Import quotas
- Franchises
- Customer and supplier relationships
- Marketing rights

RECOGNITION

IAS 38 requires an entity to recognize an intangible asset, whether purchased or self-created (at cost), if

- It is probable that the future economic benefits that are attributable to the asset will flow to the entity; and
- The cost of the asset can be measured reliably.

(The probability of expected future economic benefits is assessed using reasonable and supportable assumptions that represent the management's best estimate of the conditions that will exist over the useful life of the asset.)

The recognition requirements apply whether an intangible asset is acquired externally or generated internally. The standard specifies *additional recognition* criteria for internally generated intangible assets. If an intangible item does not meet both the definition of and the criteria for recognition as an intangible asset, then the expenditure on the item is to be recognized as an expense when it is incurred.

Goodwill, brands, mastheads, publishing titles, customer lists, and items similar in substance that are *internally generated* should *not be recognized* as intangible assets under this standard.

The following items must be *charged to expense* when incurred:

- Start-up, preopening, and preoperative costs
- Training costs
- Advertising and promotional costs (including expenditure on mail-order catalogues)
- Relocation costs and costs of reorganizing part or all of an entity

There is a rebuttable presumption that the fair value (and therefore the cost) of an intangible asset acquired in a business combination can be measured reliably. An expenditure (included in the cost of acquisition) on an intangible item that does not meet both the definition of, and recognition criteria for, an intangible asset should form part of the amount attributed to the goodwill recognized at the acquisition date.

In-process research and development acquired in a business combination is recognized as an asset at cost, even if a component is research. Subsequent expenditure on that project is accounted for as any other research and development cost (expensed except to the extent that the expenditure satisfies the criteria laid in the standard for recognizing such expenditure as an intangible asset).

INITIAL RECOGNITION FOR RESEARCH AND DEVELOPMENT COSTS

All research costs should be expensed. Development costs are capitalized *only after* technical and commercial feasibility of the asset for sale or use have been established. This means that the entity must intend and be able to complete the intangible asset and either use it or sell it and be able to demonstrate how the asset will generate future economic benefits. The entity must also have adequate technical, financial and other resources to complete the development and to use or sell the intangible asset and be able to measure reliably the expenditure attributable to the intangible asset during its development.

If an entity cannot distinguish the research phase of an internal project to create an intangible asset from the development phase, the entity treats the expenditure for that project as if it were incurred in the research phase only.

IAS 38 also prohibits an entity from reinstating an intangible asset at a later date, if it was originally charged to expense.

Example 1

XYZ Pharmaceutical Inc. incurred $100 million during the accounting year ended December 31, 2008, on a research project to develop a drug to treat AIDS. Experts are of the view that it may take four years to establish whether the drug will be effective and even if found effective, it may take two to three more years to produce the medicine that can be marketed. The company wants to treat the expenditure as an intangible asset (instead of expensing the amount spent).

Solution

As per IAS 38 no intangible asset arising from research (or from the research phase of an internal project) should be recognized. Expenditure on research (or on the research phase of an internal project) should be recognized as an expense when it is incurred. Therefore, the company cannot treat the expenditure on research as an intangible asset. The entire amount of $100 million spent on the research project should be charged as an expense in the year ended December 31, 2008.

Example 2

Alpha Inc. is developing a new distribution system of its material. The following are the costs it incurred at different stages of research and development of the system.

Year	Phase/Expenses	Amount ($ million)
2001	Research	16
2002	Research	20
2003	Development	60
2004	Development	72
2005	Development	80

On December 31, 2005, Alpha Inc. identified the level of cost savings at $32 million per annum expected to be achieved by the new system over a period of five years. In addition to this, the system developed can be marketed by way of consultancy, which will earn cash flow of $20 million per annum. Alpha Inc. demonstrated that the new system met the criteria for asset recognition on January 1, 2003.

What amount or cost should be capitalized as an intangible asset? Presume that no active market exists to determine the selling price of the product, that is, the system developed. The system shall be available for use from 2005.

Solution

Amortization will commence once the asset is ready for use; that is, when the development phase is over.

As per IAS 38, research cost is to be expensed in the year in which it is incurred. So, $16 million will be expensed in 2001 and $20 million will be expensed in 2002.

The development costs can be capitalized if the internally generated asset meets the recognition criteria. Alpha Inc. has demonstrated that the new distribution system meets the recognition criteria on January 1, 2003. Development costs incurred during the years 2003, 2004, and 2005 amount in total to ($60 + $72 + $80) = $212 million. The amount should be capitalized as an intangible asset.

INITIAL MEASUREMENT

Intangible assets are initially measured *at cost.*

Measurement Subsequent to Acquisition

An entity must choose either the cost model or the revaluation model for each class of intangible asset.

- *Cost model.* After initial recognition, intangible assets should be carried at cost less any amortization and impairment losses.
- *Revaluation model.* Intangible assets may be carried at a revalued amount (fair value) less any subsequent amortization and impairment losses, only if fair value can be determined by reference to an active market. Such active markets are expected to be uncommon for intangible assets.

Revaluations shall be made with such regularity that at the end of the reporting period the carrying amount of the asset does not differ materially from its fair value. Under the revaluation model, revaluation increases are credited directly to revaluation surplus within equity except to the extent that the increase reverses a revaluation decrease previously recognized in the statement of comprehensive income.

Intangible assets are classified as

- *Finite life.* A limited period of benefit to the entity.
- *Indefinite life.* No foreseeable limit to the period over which the asset is expected to generate net cash inflows for the entity.

INTANGIBLE ASSETS WITH FINITE LIVES

The cost less residual value of an intangible asset with a finite useful life should be amortized on a systematic basis over that life.

- The amortization method should reflect the pattern of benefits.
- If the pattern cannot be determined reliably, the asset shall be amortized using the straight-line method.
- The amortization charge is recognized in the statement of comprehensive income, unless another IFRS requires that it be included in the cost of another asset.
- The amortization period should be reviewed at least annually.

The asset should also be assessed for impairment in accordance with IAS 36, *Impairment of Assets.*

If a revalued intangible has a finite life and is, therefore, being amortized, the revalued amount is amortized.

INTANGIBLE ASSETS WITH INDEFINITE LIVES

An intangible asset with an indefinite useful life should not be amortized.

Its useful life should be reviewed each reporting period to determine whether events and circumstances continue to support an indefinite useful life assessment for that asset. If they do not, the change in the useful life assessment from indefinite to finite should be accounted for as a change in an accounting estimate.

The asset should also be assessed for impairment in accordance with IAS 36, *Impairment of Assets.*

Example 3

Swift Inc. acquired a patent at a cost of $8 million for a period of five years, and the product life cycle is also five years. The company capitalized the cost and started amortizing the asset at $1 million per annum. After two years, it was found that the product life cycle may continue for another five years from that point forward. The net cash flows from the product during the next five years are expected to be: $3.6 million, $4.6 million, $4.4 million, $4 million, and $3.4 million. What is the amortizable cost of the patent for each of the next five years?

Solution

Swift Inc. amortized $1 million per annum for the first two years; that is, $2 million. The remaining carrying cost can be amortized during the next five years on the basis of net cash flows arising from the sale of the product. The amortization may be determined as follows:

Year	Net cash flows ($ million)	Amortization ratio	Amortization amount ($ million)
1	—	0.125	1.00
2	—	0.125	1.00
3	3.6	0.180	1.08
4	4.6	0.230	1.38
5	4.4	0.220	1.32
6	4.0	0.200	1.20
7	3.4	0.170	1.02
Total	20.0	1.000	8.00

Based on this information, after the third year, the balance of the carrying amount ($6 million) has been amortized in the ratio of net cash flows arising from the product of Swift Inc.

NOTE: The above conclusion is based on the assumption that the patent is renewable and Swift Inc. is successful in renewing it after the expiry of the first five years.

SUBSEQUENT EXPENDITURE

Subsequent expenditure on an intangible asset after its purchase or completion should be recognized as an expense when it is incurred, unless it is probable that this expenditure will enable the asset to generate future economic benefits in excess of its originally assessed standard of performance and the expenditure can be measured and attributed to the asset reliably.

DISCLOSURES

For each class of intangible asset, distinguishing between internally generated intangible assets and other intangible assets, disclose

- Useful life or amortization rate, if finite
- Amortization method
- Gross carrying amount
- Accumulated amortization and impairment losses
- Line items in the income statement in which amortization is included
- Reconciliation of the carrying amount at the beginning and the end of the period showing
  - Additions (business combinations separately)
  - Assets held for sale
  - Retirements and other disposals
  - Revaluations
  - Impairments
  - Reversals of impairments
  - Amortization
  - Foreign exchange differences
- Basis for determining that an intangible has an indefinite life
- Description and carrying amount of individually material intangible assets
- Disclosures about intangible assets acquired by way of government grants
- Information about intangible assets whose title is restricted
- Commitments to acquire intangible assets

EXCERPTS FROM PUBLISHED FINANCIAL STATEMENTS

BASF, Annual Report 2006

Notes to the Financial Statements

Accounting Policies

Internally generated intangible assets. Internally generated intangible assets are primarily comprised of internally developed software. Such software as well as other internally generated assets for internal use are valued at cost and amortized over their useful lives. Impairments are recorded if the carrying amount of an asset exceeds the recoverable amount.

Development costs also include, in addition to those costs directly attributable to the development of the asset, an appropriate allocation of overhead cost. Borrowing costs are capitalized to the extent that they are material and related to the period over which the asset is generated.

The average amortization period for intangible assets with definite useful lives is ten years for 2006 and nine years for 2005 based on the following expected useful lives:

Amortization Periods in Years

Distribution and similar rights	2–20
Product rights, licenses, and trademarks	2–30
Know-how, patents, and production technologies	3–25
Internally generated intangible assets	3–5
Other rights and values	2–20

Nokia, December 31, 2006

Notes to the Consolidated Financial Statements

13. Intangible Assets

EUR m	*2006*	*2005*
Capitalized development costs		
Acquisition cost January 1	1,445	1,322
Additions during the period	127	153
Disposals during the period	(39)	(30)
Accumulated acquisition cost December 31	1,533	1,445
Accumulated amortization January 1	(1,185)	(1044)
Disposals during the period	39	30
Amortization for the period	(136)	(171)
Accumulated amortization December 31	(1,282)	(1,185)
Net book value January 1	260	278
Net book value December 31	251	260
Goodwill	—	—
Acquisition cost January 1	90	1,298
Transfer of accumulated amortization on adoption of IFRS 3	—	(1,208)
Translation differences	(26)	—
Additions during the period (Note 9)	488	—
Other changes	(20)	—
Accumulated acquisition cost December 31	532	90
Net book value January 1	90	90
Net book value December 31	532	90
Other intangible assets		
Acquisition cost January 1	676	631
Translation differences	(26)	—
Additions during the period (Note 9)	488	—
Other changes	(20)	—
Accumulated acquisition cost December 31	532	90
Net book value January 1	90	90
Net book value December 31	532	90
Other intangible assets		
Acquisition cost January 1	676	631
Translation differences	(21)	3
Additions during the period	99	59
Acquisition of subsidiary (Note 9)	122	—
Impairment losses	(33)	—
Disposals during the period	(71)	(17)
Accumulated acquisition cost December 31	772	676
Accumulated amortization January 1	(465)	(422)
Translation differences	10	7
Disposals during the period	66	14
Amortization for the period	(85)	(64)
Accumulated acquisition cost December 31	(474)	(465)
Net book value January 1	211	209
Net book value December	298	211

Adidas Group, Annual Report 2006

Notes to the Financial Statements

13. Trademarks and Other Intangible Assets

Trademarks and other intangible assets consist of the following:

Trademarks and Other Intangible Assets (€ in millions)

	December 31, 2006	December 31, 2005
Trademarks, gross	1,454	15
Less: accumulated amortization	0	0
Trademarks, net	1,454	15
Software, patents and concessions, gross	447	242
Less: accumulated amortization	224	166
Other intangible assets, net	223	76
Trademarks and other intangible assets, net	1,677	91

Intangible asset amortization expenses (continuing operations) were €69 million and €4 million for the years ending December 31, 2006 and 2005, respectively (see also Note 25).

Trademarks with indefinite useful lives amount to €1.436 billion. They were estimated to be indefinite due to the high degree of brand recognition as well as their foundation a long time ago. The trademarks are allocated to the cash-generating unit Reebok.

The group determines whether trademarks with indefinite useful lives are impaired at least on an annual basis. This requires an estimation of the fair value less costs to sell of the cash-generating units to which the trademark is allocated. Estimating the fair value less costs to sell requires the group to make an estimate of the expected future brand-specific sales and appropriate arm's-length royalty rates from the cash-generating unit and also to choose a suitable discount rate in order to calculate the present value of those cash flows.

There was no impairment expense for the year ending December 31, 2006.

Future changes in expected cash flows and discount rates may lead to impairment of the accounted trademarks in the future.

29 FINANCIAL INSTRUMENTS: RECOGNITION AND MEASUREMENT (IAS 39)

INTRODUCTION

IAS 39 establishes the basis for recognizing and measuring financial assets, financial liabilities and some contracts to buy or sell nonfinancial items. The key issues covered in this standard are

- Definition of derivatives;
- Classification of financial instruments into four categories, namely, held for trading, held to maturity, loans and receivables, and available for sale;
- Principles to be followed for recognition and derecognition of various categories of financial instruments;
- Embedded derivatives;
- Reclassification of financial assets and financial liabilities;
- Impairment and uncollectibility of financial assets; and
- Hedge accounting.

Key terms like *financial instrument*, *financial asset*, *financial liability,* and *equity instrument* are defined in IAS 32, *Financial Instruments: Presentation.* Disclosure requirements are covered in IFRS 7, *Financial Instruments: Disclosures.*

CLASSIFICATION OF FINANCIAL ASSETS

Financial assets are classified into four categories (see Exhibit 29.1):

- Financial assets at fair value through profit or loss
- Held-to-maturity investments
- Loans and receivables
- Available-for-sale financial assets

Exhibit 29.1: Financial Assets

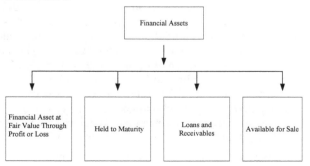

Financial liabilities are classified into two categories:

*   Financial liabilities at fair value through profit or loss
*   Other financial liabilities

Amendment to Classifications as Per IFRS 9

Classification of financial assets and liabilities has been changed by the new standard IFRS 9, *Financial Instruments*. As per IFRS 9, there are two primary measurement categories for financial instruments. A financial asset or financial liability would be measured at amortized cost if two conditions are met:

*   The instrument has basic loan features; and
*   The instrument is managed on a contractual yield basis.

A financial asset or financial liability that does not meet both conditions would be measured at fair value.

The financial assets that are measured at fair value can be further classified into fair value through profit or loss or fair value through other comprehensive income.

In effect, held-to-maturity investments and loans and receivables categories (presently both are measured at amortized cost in subsequent recognition) are merged together with relaxation of presently applicable tainting rule for premature selling of held-to-maturity financial assets. Moreover, an instrument having basic loan features managed on a contractual yield basis cannot be classified as fair value through other comprehensive income.

IFRS 9 will become effective for the accounting periods beginning on or after January 1, 2013. Early application is permitted.

FINANCIAL ASSET OR FINANCIAL LIABILITY AT FAIR VALUE THROUGH PROFIT OR LOSS

Held for trading financial assets required to be classified as at fair value through profit and loss if

*   The financial asset or financial liability is acquired or incurred principally for the purpose of selling or repurchasing in the near term;
*   It is part of a portfolio of identified financial instruments that are managed together, and there is evidence of recent short-term and actual profit taking; or
*   It is a derivative, other than a financial guarantee contract, that is not designated as an effective hedging instrument.

An entity classifies these types of financial instruments as at *fair value through profit or loss* (FVTPL) upon initial recognition.

The term *trading* indicates active and frequent buying and selling. Financial instruments that are used for trading for generating short-term profit are described as *held for trading*.

The term *portfolio* is not explicitly defined in IAS 39. But the standard implicitly indicates that a portfolio means a set of identified financial assets or financial liabilities that are managed as a group. When there is recent evidence of short-term profit taking for the portfolio as a whole, then the entire portfolio can be classified as held for trading. If a part of the portfolio is for short-term profit taking, then that particular part should be classified as held for trading. Other components may be classified differently. A part of the portfolio that is classified as held for trading may have a constituent element which is held for a longer term.

The following financial liabilities are classified as held for trading:

*   Liabilities for derivatives that are not hedging instruments;

- Obligations to deliver financial assets by a short seller;
- Financial liabilities that are incurred with an intention to repurchase them in near term; and
- Financial liabilities that are managed together for short-term profit taking.

Held-to-Maturity Investments

Held-to-maturity investments are nonderivative financial assets with fixed or determinable payments and fixed maturity, for which the entity has the positive intent and ability to hold them to maturity. Excluded from these are instruments that are designated upon initial recognition as at FVTPL or available for sale, or which meet the definition of loans and receivables.

An equity instrument cannot be classified by the holder as held to maturity (HTM) as it has no fixed maturity. However, an investment in redeemable preference shares, loans, debentures, and so on may be classified as a HTM financial asset if other conditions are satisfied.

An entity may classify a financial asset as HTM if it has the positive intention and ability to hold the asset to maturity. The intention should be supported by financial resources demonstrating the ability to continue to hold the investment to maturity. Also existing legal and other constraints might affect the entity's intention. The intention to hold the asset to maturity should be evaluated at the time of initial recognition, as well as at each reporting date.

Tainting rule. An entity is not permitted to classify a financial instrument as a HTM financial asset for a period of two years, if there is past evidence of selling or reclassification of a significant portion of HTM assets. The past evidence is evaluated based on the data of the current year and immediately preceding two financial years. Three exceptions are granted to the entity:

- The entity sold HTM assets close to their maturity or call date such that no substantial price change was expected;
- The entity sold HTM assets after it collected all substantial payment and prepayments; or
- Such selling or reclassification is attributable to an isolated and nonrecurring event that is beyond the control of the entity.

This stringent *tainting rule* relating to HTM financial assets is under review in the proposed replacement of IAS 39.

Selling of a HTM financial asset in the following circumstances does not prohibit an entity from classifying a new financial asset as HTM:

- HTM assets were sold because of significant deterioration of creditworthiness of the issuer;
- Change in tax law that eliminates or reduces the tax exempt status of HTM assets;
- Sale arising out of a major business combination;
- Change in statutory requirements;
- Change in capital requirement for HTM assets; or
- Significant increase in risk weights.

A disaster scenario, such as a bank run or insolvency, does not frustrate the positive intention to hold to maturity.

Amortized cost method. HTM financial assets are measured at fair value at initial recognition. All directly attributable transaction costs incurred to acquire or issue this type financial asset are added to the fair value. In subsequent measurement, these HTM financial assets are measured at *amortized cost* applying the *effective interest rate method*. The same principle is applied for initial and subsequent measurement of financial assets classified as loans and receivables. The amortized cost method is also applied for the measurement of a number of financial liabilities.

The effective interest rate is the internal rate of return (IRR) of the cash flow of the financial instrument. Transaction costs (which are directly attributable to acquisition or issuance of the financial instrument) are included in the cash flow. Similarly, premium/discount on issue or redemption is included in the cash flow. The effect of other contractual terms of the instrument such as prepayments, or embedded options, is adjusted. However, normally no adjustment is carried out for possible credit losses. A deep discount bond is often issued at a price that takes care of interest as well as credit risk factors. For this type of instrument, cash flow is not adjusted for credit risk factors while computing the effective interest rate.

Example 1

A Ltd. purchased 10% debentures of face value €100 issued by MN Ltd. for €99.5 on January 1, 2004. The debentures will pay an annual coupon every December 31 and be repaid after five years at 100.10. A Ltd. incurred transaction costs of €0.2 per debenture.

The computation of the effective interest rate and amortized cost follows.

Solution

Computation of Effective Interest Rate

Year	Cash flow (€)	Remaining principal balance (RPB) (€)*	Interest (€)	Principal repayment (€)
0	–99.7	99.70		
1	10	99.77	10.07	–0.07
2	10	99.84	10.07	–0.07
3	10	99.92	10.08	–0.08
4	10	100.01	10.09	–0.09
5	110.1	100.10	10.09	–0.09
IRR	10.10%			

RPB signifies amortized cost.

Notes:

1. Find out cash flow of the debentures. Initial investment = 99.5 + 0.2 = 99.7.

   Subsequent cash flow

   Year 1 through Year 4 = coupon amount €10. In Year 5, cash flow comprises both the coupon payment of € 10 and principal repayment €100.1. Thus, the redemption premium as well as transaction cost, is included in computing the effective interest rate.

2. Effective interest rate is the IRR of cash flow shown in Column 2.
3. Interest in Column 4 is computed applying the effective rate on the remaining principal balance at the beginning of the year.

   For Year 1: 99.7 × 10.1% = 10.07

4. Principal repayment in Column 5 = Coupon – Interest. If interest is higher than coupon, there is a negative principal repayment meaning that Remaining Principal Balance of Column 3 will increase.
5. Remaining Principal Balance (Column 3) RPB = Opening balance – Principal repayment. In case principal repayment in Column 5 is negative, RPB will rise. *RPB signifies amortized cost as at a particular date.*

Loans and Receivables Originated by the Enterprise

Loans and receivables originated by the enterprise are nonderivative financial assets with fixed or determinable payments and that are not quoted in an active market. These items do not include loans and receivables, which are originated with an intent to be sold immediately or in the short run; they should be classified as held for trading. Similarly, financial assets that are initially recognized as available for sale are excluded from the definition of loans and receivables. Also, if the holder of the financial asset may not be able to recover all of its initial investment (other than because of credit deterioration), it is classified as available for sale.

Example 2

ABC Ltd. grants a loan of €110 million to XYZ Ltd. that the latter will pay after two years with 10% interest. Analyze the following situations and determine the classification possibilities.

Different Situations	*Classification*
1. ABC Ltd. intends to sell the loan in the near term to P Ltd. at a 9% yield. The loan clause permits the initiator to sell the loan to a third party.	Held for trading
2. ABC Ltd. intends to classify this loan at inception as available for sale.	Available for sale
3. ABC Ltd. intends to classify this loan at inception as at fair value through profit and loss.	Held for trading
4. A situation other than three cases stated above.	Loans and receivables

Example 3: Are Unquoted Redeemable Preference Shares Loans and Receivables to the Holder?

X Ltd. purchases 10,000 7% €100 preference shares of ABC Ltd. for €99.5 redeemable at €101 after five years. These preference shares are not quoted.

1. Can the holder classify the financial asset (investment in redeemable preference shares) as loans and receivables?
2. Will the answer be different if the preference shares are quoted?
3. What should be the accounting method if they are classified as loans and receivables?
4. Can they be classified as a held-to-maturity asset?

Solution

1. By definition, loans and receivables are nonderivative financial assets with fixed or determinable maturity and that are not quoted in an active market. When the holder does not wish to sell these preference shares in the near term, it can classify them as loans and receivables. These preference shares satisfy the conditions stated in the definition of loans and receivables as per IAS 39; therefore, they can be classified as a debt instrument in the hands of the issuer.
2. If they are quoted in an active market, they cannot be classified as loans and receivables. In that case, they are classified as available for sale (or FVTPL if the specified conditions are satisfied).
3. Loans and receivables are measured at fair value at initial recognition. Any transaction cost (directly attributable for purchase of preference shares) is added to the fair value. In subsequent measurement, the amortized cost method (applying the effective interest rate) is followed.
4. They can be classified as held to maturity if the intention to hold these preference shares to maturity is satisfied. When these unquoted preference shares are held for an undefined period, they should be classified as loans and receivables.

Example 4

ABC bank has a deposit with another bank that is negotiable, but the depositor has not negotiated these deposit documents. What should be the appropriate classification of the deposit?

Solution

It should be classified as loans and receivables. When the entity has the intention to sell the instrument in the near term, it should be classified as held for trading.

Available-for-Sale Financial Assets

Available-for-sale financial assets are nonderivative financial assets other than those classified under the already mentioned three categories; that is, those that are not financial assets at FVTPL, held to maturity, or loans and receivables.

RECOGNITION PRINCIPLES

The general principle is to recognize a financial asset or a financial liability by an entity on its statement of financial position *when and only when it becomes a party to the contractual provisions of the instrument.*

Timing of Initial Recognition of Financial Assets and Liabilities

Financial Assets/ Financial Liabilities	Initial Recognition
Receivables	At the time of revenue recognition under IAS 18.
Payables	At the time delivery of purchase.
Purchase of equity instrument or debentures	When contract to purchase the financial instruments are entered into.
	In an initial public offering (IPO), when the application money is paid, the contract to purchase shares/debentures is not entered into. Issuance of the allotment letter by the issuer signifies the formal contract. So a share/debenture application advance is just like a receivable. This receivable is derecognized and investment in shares/debentures is recognized on receipt of the allotment letter.
	In a purchase of shares or debentures from the secondary market, the purchase contract may be recognized on trade date or settlement date.
Commitment to grant a loan	A firm commitment to grant a loan is not recognized as a financial asset by the prospective lender (similarly, not recognized as a financial liability by the prospective borrower) unless one of the parties performs as per the firm commitment.
	However, the firm commitment can be recognized as a financial asset or financial liability under IAS 39 when it is: (1) a loan commitment for trading, (2) a loan commitment in the nature of a derivative, or (3) a below-market-rate loan commitment. In that case, a financial asset/ financial liability is recognized at fair value on the commitment date.
Granting loans	When the parties entered into the loan agreement.
Firm commitment to buy/sell nonfinancial item	It may be recognized as a financial asset/financial liability under IAS 39. If the firm commitment fulfills the conditions stated in IAS 39, a financial asset/financial liability is recognized at fair value when funds are advanced/received.

MEASUREMENT PRINCIPLES

Measurement principles to be followed in respect of financial assets at initial recognition and subsequent measurement are presented in the following table.

Accounting and Measurement of Financial Assets

Category of Financial Assets	Measurement at Initial Recognition	Measurement at Subsequent Reporting Date	Gain or Loss on Sale or Transfer
1. Fair value through profit and loss All stand-alone derivatives are classified under this category	Measured at fair value on the date of acquisition, which is the acquisition price Directly attributable transaction cost is charged to statement of comprehensive income separately	At fair value Change in fair value between reporting dates is charged/credited to statement of comprehensive income directly	Computed with reference to last valuation Gain or loss is credited/charged to statement of comprehensive income
2. Held to maturity	Measured at fair value on the date of acquisition, which is the acquisition price plus transaction costs that are directly attributable to the acquisition or issue of the financial asset	At amortized cost applying effective interest rate	Computed with reference to last valuation at amortized cost Gain or loss is credited/charged to statement of comprehensive income
3. Loans and receivables	Short-term receivables and payables with no stated interest rate should be measured at original invoice amount if the effect of discounting is immaterial Other items are measured at fair value on the date of acquisition, which is the acquisition price plus transaction costs that are directly attributable to the acquisition or issue of the financial asset	At amortized cost applying effective interest rate	Computed with reference to last valuation at amortized cost Gain or loss is credited/charged to statement of comprehensive income
4. Available for sale	Measured at fair value on the date of acquisition, which is the acquisition price plus transaction costs that are directly attributable to the acquisition or issue of the financial asset	At fair value Change in fair value between reporting dates is charged/credited to a separate component of equity, say, investment valuation reserve	Computed with reference to last valuation at amortized cost Gain or loss is credited/charged to statement of comprehensive income Balance of investment valuation reserve is transferred to statement of comprehensive income
5. Financial assets fair value of which cannot be reliably measured	At cost	At cost	Sale/transfer price minus cost is gain or loss, which should be credited/charged to statement of comprehensive income
6. Financial assets designated as hedged item or hedging instrument		As per hedge accounting principles	

REGULAR-WAY PURCHASE OR SALE CONTRACT

A regular-way purchase or sale contract is defined as a contract to purchase or sell a financial asset whose terms require delivery of the asset within the time frame established generally by regulation or convention in the marketplace. The contract is not limited to transactions in formal stock or derivative exchanges or over-the-counter exchanges. This definition refers to a broad market wherein the financial assets are customarily exchanged. So delivery should be within the time frame that is reasonable and customarily required for the parties to prepare and execute closing documents. Sometimes an entity may deal in financial assets in different exchanges wherein there are different delivery rules. The entity should follow the delivery rule of the market in which the purchase or sale contract has been entered.

A regular-way purchase or sale contract is recognized using either *trade date accounting* or *settlement date accounting*. On the *trade date*, the entity commits to purchase or sell the financial instrument, whereas on the *settlement date* the financial instrument is delivered to or by the entity.

Under trade-date accounting, a financial asset purchased is recognized on the trade date along with simultaneous recognition of the related liability to pay for it. Similarly, a financial asset sold is derecognized on the trade date with recognition of gain/loss on sale of that asset and related receivables. If the financial asset is an interest-bearing instrument like debt or a bond, interest does not accrue on and from the trade date.

Under settlement date accounting, a financial asset purchased is recognized on the settlement date along with simultaneous recognition of the related liability to pay for it. Similarly, a financial asset sold is derecognized on the settlement date, with recognition of gain/loss on sale of that asset and related receivables.

ACCOUNTING FOR FINANCIAL LIABILITIES

Measurement bases of four types of financial liabilities are presented here.

Measurement Bases of Financial Liabilities

Nature of Financial Assets	Initial Recognition	Subsequent Measurement
Financial liabilities at fair value through profit and loss Includes derivative liability	At fair value Directly attributable transaction cost is charged to statement of comprehensive income	At fair value Derivatives that are linked to unquoted equity instruments or to be settled by unquoted equity instruments, whose fair value cannot be measured, are measured at cost
Financial liability arising out of continuing involvement in financial asset*	Measured in accordance with paragraphs AG48-AG 51, which are separately discussed	Measured in accordance with paragraphs AG48-AG 51, which are separately discussed
Financial guarantee contract	At fair value	Higher of 1. Amount initially recognized, less cumulative amortization recognized 2. Valuation as per IAS 37
Other financial liabilities including debentures, bonds, preference shares classified as financial liabilities, loans, advances, payables	At fair value Directly attributable transaction costs are included in the fair value	At amortized cost

*Certain financial liabilities arise out of continuing involvement in financial assets after transfer. When such financial assets are not derecognized, the consideration received is accounted for as a financial liability. Measurement techniques of such financial liabilities are not discussed.

LOAN COMMITMENTS

Loan commitments are contingent obligations. Normally, IAS 37 applies to loan commitments. However, as per IAS 39, paragraph 4, the following loan commitments fall within the ambit of IAS 39:

- *Loan commitments for trading.* Loan commitments that the entity designates as financial liabilities at FVTPL.

  An entity that has a past practice of selling the assets resulting from its loan commitments shortly after origination shall apply this standard to all its loan commitments in the same class.
- *Loan commitments in the nature of a derivative.* Loan commitments that can be settled net in cash or by delivering or issuing another financial instrument.
- *Below market interest rate loan commitments.* Accounted for in accordance with IAS 39, paragraph 47(d).

FINANCIAL GUARANTEE

A *financial guarantee* is a contract that requires the issuer to make specified payments to reimburse the holder for a loss that it incurs because a specified debtor fails to make a payment when due in accordance with the original or modified terms of a debt instrument. The issuer of such a financial guarantee would account for it initially at fair value under IAS 39, and subsequently at the higher of (1) the amount initially recognized less cumulative amortization recognized in accordance with IAS 18 and (2) the amount determined in accordance with IAS 37. Guarantees based on an underlying price or index are derivatives within the scope of IAS 39.

A financial guarantee contract may have various legal forms, and includes some types of letter of credit, a credit default contract, or an insurance contract. Often a financial guarantee contract meets the definition of an insurance contract in IFRS 4 . But it is necessary to check if the risk transferred is significant. When the risk transferred is significant, the issuer is required to apply IAS 39. However, IAS 39 grants the issuer the option to elect to apply IFRS 4 when the issuer has previously asserted explicitly that it regards such contracts as insurance contracts and has used accounting applicable to insurance contracts.

If the financial guarantee contract was issued to an unrelated party in a stand-alone arm's-length transaction, its fair value at inception is likely to equal the premium received, unless there is evidence to the contrary. The issuer may elect to classify it as FVTPL and subsequently remeasure at fair value. Otherwise, in subsequent remeasurement the issuer measures it at the higher of

- The amount determined in accordance with IAS 37; and
- The amount initially recognized less, when appropriate, cumulative amortization recognized in accordance with IAS 18.

Some credit-related guarantees are not linked to failure of a specific debtor. Rather, the holder is required to pay if there is a change in a specified credit rating or credit index. This type of contract is classified as a derivative and accounted for accordingly.

If a financial guarantee contract was issued in connection with the sale of goods, the issuer applies IAS 18 in determining when it recognizes the revenue from the guarantee and from the sale of goods.

DERIVATIVES

A derivative contract is characterized by all the following three features:

1. Its value changes in response to the change in a specific interest rate, financial instrument price, commodity price, foreign exchange rate, index of prices or rates, credit rating or credit index or other variables; however, in the case of a nonfinancial variable, the variable is not specific to a party to the contract;
2. It requires no initial investment, or an initial net investment that is smaller as compared to other contracts that have similar responses to changes in market factors; and
3. It is settled at a future date.

Common examples of derivatives are an interest rate swap, currency swap, commodity swap, equity swap, credit swap, total return swap, purchased or written treasury bond option, purchased or written currency option, purchased or written commodity option, purchased or written stock option, interest rate futures linked to a government bond, currency futures, commodity futures, stock futures, currency forward, commodity forward, and equity forward.

One important defining characteristic of a derivative is that either there is no initial investment or a initial investment that is smaller than what is otherwise required for any other contract which would give a similar response to changes in market factors. In a purchased option, premium is paid up front. If the initial investment in an option premium is higher than taking a spot position, then no rational person would take the option position. Similarly, in a pay-fixed receive-variable interest rate swap contract if the interest payment for the fixed leg is paid up front, normally it will remain as a derivative because the present value of the fixed leg interest (normally) cannot be higher than the notional principal amount of the swap. Also the variable leg reflects the value change characteristics of a derivative. On the other hand, if the variable leg is prepaid, it does not remain a derivative (not on the basis of initial investment issue) as there will be no value change in response to market factors.

Common Underlying of Derivative Contracts

The following list provides examples of derivative contracts and underlying:

Derivative Contract	Underlying
Stock index futures/option	Benchmark index, for example Nifty 50 of National Stock Exchange in India
Stock futures/options	Particular equity share
Interest rate swap	Interest rate
Currency swap/currency futures/currency option/currency forward	Exchange rate of the currencies involved
Commodity swap/commodity futures/commodity option/commodity forward	Commodity price
Equity swap/forward	Equity price
Credit swap	Credit rating/credit index
Total return swap	Fair value of the reference asset
Interest rate futures/options/future rate agreement	Interest rate

A derivative usually has a notional amount. In stock index futures and options, as well as stock futures and options, it is characterized by the number of shares. In commodity futures and options, it is characterized by weights. In currency forwards, futures and options, and interest rate futures, options and swaps, it is characterized by currency units. In an interest rate swap, it may also require fixed payment against a change in a benchmark interest. The floating-rate payments will be in accordance with a benchmark interest rate, such as LIBOR, whereas the fixed-rate payer will make payment of fixed amount.

Derivative contracts are either net settled or gross settled. For example, in a fixed to floating swap, the fixed leg payer pays a fixed amount whereas the variable leg payer pays as per the benchmark interest rate. However, this may either be settled net in cash or be delivery based. For example, in a commodity derivative, it is possible to settle gross by taking or giving delivery of the underlying asset. Even if the transaction is gross settled involving a nonfinancial item, the contract is classified as a financial instrument, depending on whether the underlying nonfinancial item can be readily converted into cash or whether the entity has the practice of selling the underlying immediately after taking delivery.

Contracts to buy or sell nonfinancial items normally do not meet the definition of a financial instrument. Accordingly, delivery-based derivatives contracts to buy or sell nonfinancial items are not financial instruments.

Derivative financial instruments are classified as a *financial asset or financial liability at fair value through profit or loss*. Derivatives having a positive value are classified as financial assets and derivatives having a negative value are classified as financial liabilities. This is on a stand-alone basis. When derivatives are used as hedging instruments or are a hedged item, they are accounted for applying special hedge accounting requirements.

Example 5

On June 12, 2009, ABC Ltd. purchased a month stock future (which is a derivative contract) at €112. As per the specification of the futures contract, 1 lot = 200 shares. As on the reporting date of June 30, 2009, the future price is €108. What is the value of the derivative contract at the date of entering into the contract and on the reporting date? Is it a financial asset/liability on the reporting date?

Solution

There is no value of the derivative on the date of entering into the contract. The purchase price and the market price are the same.

On the reporting date, the market price is €108 as against a purchase price of €112—so there is a loss of €4, that is, €800 per lot. The derivative is recognized as a financial liability, with a loss in profit and loss.

The following issues relating to definition of derivatives are discussed in the Guidance on Implementing—IAS 39, *Financial Instruments, Recognition and Measurement*:

Derivatives: Issues and Analyses

1. An interest rate swap contract requires gross settlement of interest. Can it be classified as a derivative contract under IAS 39?

   Analysis: Yes. Net settlement is not a precondition of a derivative.

2. If the fixed leg of an interest rate swap is prepaid, does it remain a derivative contract despite a high initial investment?

   Analysis: Yes. The initial investment for the prepaid fixed leg should be compared with the spot investment required to get a similar floating leg position.

   The present value of a prepaid fixed leg shall be lower than the spot investment to get a similar floating rate exposure. So it will satisfy the initial investment test set out in paragraph 9, IAS 39. It is a derivative contract.

3. If the fixed leg of an interest rate swap is prepaid subsequently, does it remain a derivative contract despite a high initial investment?

   Analysis: It is to be treated as a termination of the old swap and origination of a new instrument. Payment made for the balance life of the contract is equivalent to taking a floating rate position in the underlying.

   If the present value of the prepaid fixed leg is lower than the spot investment to get similar floating rate exposure, then it will be classified as derivative contract.

4. If the floating leg of an interest rate swap is prepaid subsequently, does it remain a derivative contract despite a high initial investment?

   Analysis: The first characteristic of a derivative contract, that the value of the instrument changes in response to an underlying, is missing if the floating leg is prepaid (identification of the underlying and response to value change is must). It no longer remains a derivative contract.

5. Can two nonderivative contracts be aggregated to make it a derivative contract? For example, can a fixed-rate loan payable and a floating-rate loan receivable offset each other?

Analysis: Yes.

6. Is an out-of-the-money option a derivative contract?

Analysis: This question arises out of the settlement issue. A feature of a derivative contract is that it is settled on a future date. Settlement includes expiry without exercise. If an out-of-the-money contract expires worthless, that signifies a settlement.

7. Can a foreign currency contract based on purchase/sales volume be treated as a derivative contract?

Analysis: A volume-based foreign currency contract has two variables, it has no initial investment and it is settled on a future date(s). So it is a derivative.

Similarly, a basis swap contract has two variables.

8. Is a prepaid forward a derivative?

Analysis: Here, the issue is the initial investment. The prepaid amount should be compared with alternative investments to get the same degree of exposures.

9. Should the initial margin in futures/option contracts be considered when evaluating the initial investment in a derivative contract?

Analysis: No. Margin is just a collateral not an investment.

Example 6

X Ltd. has entered a five-year, pay-fixed, receive-variable swap contract with a swap dealer for a notional amount of €10 million (Exhibit 29.2). The swap rate is 6.5% per annum but the contract requires that X would pay gross at fixed rate every January 1 and July 1 and receive gross at floating rate.

Exhibit 29.2   Sample Swap Contract

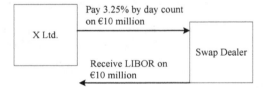

Does this swap contract satisfy the definition of a derivatives?

Solution

Yes. The value of the instrument changes in response to an underlying (identification of the underlying and response to value change is required), no initial investment or smaller initial investment if similar value changes to be achieved through the underlying, and settlement at a future date. In view of these three criteria the interest rate swap contract (IRS) is a derivative. IAS 39, paragraph 9, does not put gross settlement under a derivative as a disqualification.

Example 7

Prepaid fixed leg at the inception of the contract: In an interest rate swap there are two legs: a fixed leg and a floating leg. One party pays a fixed rate. In exchange, the counterparty pays a variable rate, say six-month LIBOR. X Ltd. enters into a pay 8% fixed, receive floating swap for four years on notional principal of €100 million. Settlement date is every January 2 and July 2. If X Ltd. pays the present value of the fixed leg discounted at the current market yield of 8%, the fixed leg of the swap is prepaid at the inception. Should the contract still be considered as a derivative?

Solution

The appropriate test is based on no initial investment or comparatively smaller initial investment in view of the large amount of initial investment. It requires no initial net investment or an initial net investment that is smaller than would be required for other types of contracts that would be expected to have a similar response to changes in market factors.

As an alternative, X Ltd. could invest Euros 100 million in a LIBOR-denominated bond, which would pay it 6-month LIBOR.

$$\text{Prepaid fixed leg} = €4 \text{ million} \times \text{half–yearly annuity factor for 4 years}$$

$$= €4 \text{ million} \times 6.7327 = €26.93 \text{ million}$$

X Ltd. could get the same amount based on six-month LIBOR by investing €26.93 million rather than €100 million. So the transaction satisfies the requirement of a comparatively smaller initial investment. It is a derivative contract under IAS 39, paragraph 9.

Example 8

This is a cancellation of the old contract. Suppose X Ltd. prepays the fixed leg after the third six months. Then it pays for five fixed installments. If the current market yield is 8.5%, then the prepaid fixed leg is

$$€4 \text{ million} \times \text{half-yearly annuity factor for 2.5 years}$$

$$= €4 \text{ million} \times 4.4833 = €17.93 \text{ million}$$

This is a one-time payment (representing a financial asset) to get a PV of five installments of expected six-month LIBOR on €100 million.

The new contract will remain as a derivative because that satisfies the lower initial investment condition. Refer to IAS 39.IG B.4, which states that the new contract should be evaluated afresh.

Example 9

X Ltd. enters into a pay six-month LIBOR and receives 8% fixed swap for four years on a notional principal of €100 million. Settlement date is every January 2 and July 2. If X Ltd. pays the present value of the floating leg, discounted at the current market yield of 8%, the floating leg of the swap is prepaid at the inception. Should the contract still be considered as a derivative?

The amount to be paid at the inception is evaluated applying the forward interest rate:

1	2	3	4	5	6
		Forward	*Floating*		
Year	*Spot rate (%)*	*rate (%)*	*rate interest*	*PVFactor*	*DCF*
0.5	6.50	6.50	3.25	0.9685	3.15
1.0	6.55	6.60	3.30	0.9378	3.09
1.5	6.60	6.70	3.35	0.9079	3.04
2.0	6.65	6.80	3.40	0.8786	2.99
2.5	6.75	7.15	3.58	0.8500	3.04
3.0	6.85	7.35	3.68	0.8218	3.02
3.5	6.85	6.85	3.43	0.7946	2.72
4.0	6.85	6.85	3.42	0.7683	2.63
					23.68

Notes: Column 2—Spot rates that are normally derived from a zero coupon bond.

Column 3—Calculation of forward rate: Year 0.5 same as spot rate

$$\text{Year 1 forward rate} = \frac{[(1 + 6.55\%/2)^1]^2 - 1}{(1 + 6.50\%/2)^{0.5}}$$

$$\text{Year 1.5 forward rate} = \frac{[(1 + 6.6\%/2)^{1.5}]^2 - 1}{(1 + 6.55\%/2)^1} \text{ and so on}$$

Column 4—€100 million × (forward rate/2)
Column 5—PV factor at spot rate.
Column 6—Column 4 × Column 5.

In this case, an initial investment of €23.68 million has been made to receive 8% on €100 million on a half-yearly basis. It fails to satisfy the following criteria set out in IAS 39, paragraph 9:

[I]ts value changes in response to the change in a specified interest rate, financial instrument price, commodity price, foreign exchange rate, index of prices or rates, credit rating or credit index, or other variable, provided in the case of a non-financial variable that the variable is not specific to a party to the contract (sometimes called the "underlying").

There will be no value change. So the transaction does not meet the definition of a derivative. However, the initial payment made is a financial asset. If it is accounted for as at FVTPL, then it can be evaluated as the PV of eight installments of €4 million at the current market yield, or incremental borrowing rate, of the entity.

Example 10

ABC Ltd. issued five-year, 8 percent debentures of €100 million to XYZ Ltd. In turn, XYZ Ltd. issued three-month LIBOR-based debentures of €100 million for a maturity of five years. Should these offsetting loans be treated as derivatives?

Solution

Nonderivative contracts are aggregated based on the following criteria:

1. They are contracted at the same time and in contemplation of one another;
2. They have the same counterparty;
3. They relate to the same type of risk—in this case interest rate risk;
4. There is no economic need or substantive business purpose for structuring these transactions.

Example 11

ABC Ltd. has purchased an out-of-the-money call option to buy equity shares of X Ltd.— current market price €120, strike price €160, call premium €100 for a lot size of 100. Since this call is expected not to be exercised, should be it be treated as a derivative?

Solution

An option is settled on maturity. Even if the option expires worthless at maturity, that is a kind of settlement. This instrument is a derivative.

Example 12

ABC purchases goods in U.S. dollars. It enters into a contract with a U.S. bank to convert its U.S. dollars purchases for the year 2008 into Indian Rupees at a fixed exchange rate of US $1 = Rupees 44.80. Is this contract a derivative?

Solution

Yes. It is derivative contract having two underlying variables, purchase volume and exchange rate. It has no initial investment and is to be settled at a future date.

Example 13

X Ltd. has a US $140 million LIBOR-based loan. It enters into a €100 million LIBOR swap [spot exchange rate €1 = US $1.40]. Swap: US $ LIBOR + 50 basis point = € LIBOR. So X Ltd. will pay € LIBOR and receive US $ LIBOR + 50 basis point. Is it a derivative contract?

Solution

Yes. The basis swap has two variable interest rates, no initial investments, and it is settled on a future date.

Example 14

X Ltd. enters into a contract to buy 1,000 equity shares of A Ltd. from one of its existing shareholders, Mr. S, at €100 per share. Delivery is to be given after three months. The current market price of such shares is €125. Mr. X pays the forward price up front. X Ltd. could buy one lot of call option with €100 strike price at a call premium of Euros 55. Is the transaction a derivative?

Solution

Yes. The value of the forward contract changes in response to the change in price of the underlying. Moreover, X Ltd. made an initial net investment that is smaller than would be required for other types of contracts that would be expected to have a similar response to changes in market factors to make an outright purchase, X Ltd. would have invested at €125. X Ltd. could have resorted to buying a call option, but then the cost per share would have been €155.

FAIR VALUE MEASUREMENT

The best measure of fair value is the price in an active market. However, fair value can be measured applying valuation techniques when there is no active market quotation. For example, interest bearing financial assets can be valued at the present value of future cash flows, with current market yield as the discount factor. However, in the case of equity instruments, future cash flows are uncertain. Various valuation techniques are available for equity instruments—an important technique is present value of free cash flow. Other techniques are forward price-to-earnings (P/E) ratio, revenue price multiple, and so on.

IAS 39 AG 69-82 provides guidance on fair value measurement. (The IASB has issued an Exposure Draft of the proposed Fair Value Measurement standard which will be the single source reference for fair value measurement principles.)

Guidance on Fair Value Measurement

Issues	Details
Basic principle	Fair value measurement is based on the going concern presumption. Fair value is not based on realization in a forced or distressed sale.
Active market quoted price	Active market does not necessarily mean a stock exchange. Availability of regular and ready quotations for a financial asset from an exchange, industry group, pricing service or regulatory agency means an active market quoted price.
Use of bid or ask price Mid-market price Price of recently observed transaction	The appropriate quoted market price for an asset held or liability to be issued should be the current bid price. The appropriate quoted market price for an asset to be acquired or liability held should be the current ask price. If the entity has financial assets and liabilities with offsetting market risk, it can use the mid-market price. In the absence of current bid or ask prices, the entity may use the price of the most recent transaction.
Adjustment to last observed price	If the entity demonstrates that the last observed price was not a fair market quotation, for example it was a distressed sale, it can make an adjustment to the last observed price. Also, if there is a change in conditions since the last transaction has taken place, there is a need to adjust the fair value.
Adjustment for credit risk	This is of course adjusted by the entity for counterparty risk, country risk, and so forth. When the entity uses a market yield for determining fair value of a debt instrument, it is necessary to consider whether such a rate includes a credit risk factor. If not, there is a need to adjust for credit risk.
Meaning of fair value	Price agreed by a willing buyer and willing seller in an arm's-length transaction.
No active market valuation technique	1. Valuation technique includes (a) recent price of a comparable transaction, (b) discounted cash flow, (c) application of option price model. 2. A valuation technique would be expected to arrive at a realistic estimate of the fair value if (a) it reasonably reflects how the market could be expected to price the instrument, and (b) the inputs to the valuation technique reasonably represent market expectations and measures of the risk-return factors inherent in the financial instrument. 3. A valuation technique should therefore (a) incorporate all factors that market participants would consider in arriving at a price, and (b) be consistent with accepted economic methodologies for pricing financial instruments. 4. An entity should periodically calibrate the valuation by reference to recently observed prices of comparable transactions.

	5. The transaction price is the best evidence of the fair value at initial recognition.
	6. In subsequent measurement, a change in fair value should arise from the factors that market participants would consider in setting a price.
	7. If the financial instrument is a debt instrument (such as a loan), its fair value can be determined by reference to the market conditions that existed at its acquisition or origination date and current market conditions or interest rates currently charged by the entity or by others for similar debt instruments (i.e., similar remaining maturity, cash flow pattern, currency, credit risk, collateral and interest basis).
	8. The entity may not have the same information at all measurement dates.
	9. While applying discounted cash flow analysis, an entity uses one or more discount rates equal to the prevailing rates of return for financial instruments having substantially the same terms and characteristics, including the credit quality of the instrument, the remaining term over which the contractual interest rate is fixed, the remaining term to repayment of the principal and the currency in which payments are to be made.
	10. Short-term receivables and payables with no stated interest rate are measured at the original invoice amount if the effect of discounting is immaterial.
If there is no active market for equity instruments	Fair value of equity instruments, and derivatives linked to an equity instrument for which there is no active market, can be reliably measured if: (1) the variability in the range of reasonable fair value estimates is not significant for that instrument, or (2) the probabilities of the various estimates within the range can be reasonably assessed and used in estimating fair value.
	If the range of reasonable fair value estimates is significant and the probabilities of the various estimates cannot be reasonably assessed, an entity is precluded from measuring the instrument at fair value. It is measured at cost.
Inputs to valuation techniques	Important inputs to fair value measurement are
	1. *Time value of money:* Can be derived from observable government bond prices and are often quoted in financial publications. For example, yield curve published by central bank or other investment banking companies in various countries.
	2. *Credit risk:* Can be derived from observable market price traded instruments of different credit quality. In India, the debt market is not deep enough to provide such information.
	3. *Foreign exchange risk:* Currency prices are available in financial publications for all major currencies.
	4. *Commodity price risk:* Spot prices are normally quoted in financial publications for different markets. Futures prices can be obtained from commodity exchanges.
	5. *Equity prices:* Stock exchanges.
	6. *Volatility:* Can be computed using the standard deviation of historical prices.
	7. *Prepayment risk:* Pattern can be observed from historical data.

Fair Value on Initial Recognition

The transaction price is normally the fair value of a financial instrument on initial recognition. It is the consideration given or received. Premium or discount on a debt instrument is part of the fair value of the instrument.

Transaction costs are *incremental costs* that are directly attributable to the acquisition, issue, or disposal of financial assets or financial liability. The term *incremental costs* signifies costs that would not have been incurred other than for the acquisition or disposal of financial instruments. Transactions costs comprise

- Fees and commissions paid to agents (including fees and commissions to employees acting as agents), advisers, brokers and dealers;
- Levies by regulatory agencies and securities exchanges; and
- Transfer taxes and duties.

Transaction costs do not include debt premium or discount, financing costs or internal management expenses.

RECLASSIFICATION

Normally, an entity should not reclassify a financial instrument into or out of the FVTPL category except in rare circumstances set out in paragraphs 50B and 50C of IAS 39. Derivatives financial instruments that are designated as at FVTPL at initial recognition are not reclassified. When a financial asset that was classified as at FVTPL initially is no longer held for sale in the near term it can be reclassified in accordance with paragraphs 50B and 50C of IAS 39.

A change in classification in the following three circumstances are not considered as reclassification of financial assets designated as at FVTPL:

1. When a derivative financial asset is designated as an effective hedging instrument in a cash flow hedge or hedge of net investments in foreign operations;
2. A derivative that was previously designated hedging instrument but the hedge no longer qualifies for hedge accounting; or
3. Financial assets arising out of changes in insurance accounting policies (like a financial guarantee which was previously accounted for as insurance asset/liability, but classified as financial asset through change in insurance accounting policies).

A financial asset that has been designated as at FVTPL can be reclassified either as loans and receivables or AFS investments in rare circumstances. A financial asset that would have met the definition of loans and receivables if not required to be classified as at FVTPL at initial recognition can be reclassified into the loans and receivables category. The fair value of the asset as on the date of reclassification becomes the cost or amortized cost of the loans and receivables. Previously recognized profit/loss on the reclassified FVTPL is not reversed.

Similarly, a financial asset that has been designated as at FVTPL can be reclassified into the AFS financial asset category in rare circumstances. The fair value of the asset as on the date of reclassification becomes the fair value of AFS investments.

AFS investments can be reclassified into loans and receivables category as well. A financial asset that would have met the definition of loans and receivables at initial recognition if not classified as AFS investments fall into this type of reclassification. The fair value of the asset as on the date of reclassification becomes the cost or amortized cost the loans and receivables. Previously recognized accumulated fair value gains/losses (that have been accounted through other comprehensive income and appearing as investment valuation reserve) is amortized over the remaining maturity of the newly classified loans and receivables. In case the newly classified loans and receivables do not have fixed maturity, the accumulated fair value gain/loss shall be recognized at the time of derecognition.

For held-to-maturity financial assets, reclassification is required when the intention to hold till maturity is no longer there. Then, such an asset is reclassified as available for sale and fair value measurement of such an asset is necessary. The difference is charged to other comprehensive income (fair value reserve).

For an unquoted equity instrument or derivative linked to unquoted equity (to be settled by delivery of an unquoted equity) if at the initial recognition fair value could not be measured, once the circumstances changed and the fair value can be measured reliably the difference between the cost and the fair value shall be accounted for in accordance with the classification of the financial asset. If it is classified as held for trading, the profit/loss arising out of fair value changes is charged to profit or loss. On the other hand, if the financial asset is classified as available for sale, then the profit/loss arising out of fair value changes is charged to other comprehensive income.

IMPAIRMENT AND UNCOLLECTIBILITY OF FINANCIAL ASSETS

Financial assets are subject to impairment testing under IAS 39. Paragraphs 58–65, AG 84–93 and IG E4.1–E4.10 of IAS 39 cover impairment measurement and accounting techniques.

Impairment of financial assets is caused by any of the following reasons, individually or in combination. Keep in mind that this is not an exhaustive list.

- Significant financial difficulty of the issuer;
- Breach of contract by the issuer, including default in payment of interest and or principal;
- Lender granted concession to the issuer, which is not granted under normal business situations;
- Higher probability of bankruptcy of the issuer;
- Active market for financial asset has vanished; or
- Observable data reflects default of the borrower belonging to the same line of business.

There may not be a single or discrete event signifying objective evidence of impairment. Many factors may collectively signify existence of impairment.

If an equity, or other financial, instrument is delisted—this event alone cannot be treated as a vanishing active market triggering impairment testing. It should be supported by other evidence to demonstrate that impairment has been caused.

Similarly, downgrading of a debt instrument in itself does not demonstrate impairment. Also, a decrease in value of a debt instrument arising out of an increase in market interest rate is not a symptom of impairment.

As per IAS 39, paragraph 58, an entity is required to evaluate at each reporting date if there exists any objective evidence of impairment of any of the financial assets or groups of financial assets. When there exists evidence of an impairment loss, it is measured in accordance with the following paragraphs:

Financial assets carried at amortized cost	IAS 39.63
Financial assets carried at cost	IAS 39.66
Available-for-sale financial assets	IAS 39.67

The following general guidance is provided by the Application Guidance of IAS 39:

1. Credit quality assessment

   An entity should reassess the credit quality of financial assets across the credit grades. It should not be restricted only to lower or vulnerable grades.

2. Collective evaluation of impairment

   Financial assets that are subject to credit risk are individually assessed for impairment. As well, they are grouped together based on common characteristics for collective evaluation of impairment. For example, debtors may be grouped by industry, geographical location, and so on. At the group level, average loss possibility is assessed, which is expected to be different from the loss possibility of an individual asset included in the group. However, the entity computes loss possibility at the aggregate level.

Impairment losses recognized on a group basis represent an interim step, pending the identification of impairment losses on individual assets in the group. As soon as information is available that specifically identifies losses on individually impaired assets in a group, those assets are removed from the group and impairment loss is assessed individually for that asset.

Pending specific evidence of individual losses, a bank or other financial institution may very well adopt the collective evaluation procedure explained earlier.

An entity should not recognize an impairment loss on a financial asset at the initial recognition. At the initial recognition it is measured at its fair value.

EMBEDDED DERIVATIVES

An *embedded derivative* is a component of a hybrid (combined) instrument that also includes a nonderivative host contract—with the effect that some of the cash flows of the combined instrument vary in a way similar to a stand-alone derivative (IAS 39, paragraph 10). The holder of a compound financial instrument, like convertible debentures, treats it as an embedded derivative.

The host contract might be a debt or equity instrument, a lease, an insurance contract, or a sale or purchase contract. An embedded derivative causes some or all of the cash flows of the host contract to be modified, based on a specified interest rate, financial instrument price, commodity price, foreign exchange rate, index of prices or rates, credit rating or credit index or other variable.

Example 15

A bank has granted a twenty-year subordinated loan of €100 million to a start-up company at 7%, which is below the market yield. As per the loan agreement, the borrower company shall issue 1% of its equity shares outstanding on the date of listing at 70% of the listing price apart from annual payment of interest and repayment of principal. Is the equity kicker an embedded derivative?

It is an embedded derivative, because the host contract is a debt instrument and it is an option-based derivative to exercise for 1% of equity shares of the borrower company at a strike price. The option can be valued based on current valuation of equity (which may be on the basis of cash flow or any other model). It should be segregated from the host contract.

Preconditions for segregation of embedded derivatives are as follows:

- The economic characteristics and risks of the embedded derivative are not closely related to the economic characteristics and risks of the host contract.
- A separate instrument having the same term as the embedded derivative would be characterized as an independent derivative.
- The hybrid instrument is not accounted for as at FVTPL.

When the embedded derivative is separated, the host contract is classified as a financial instrument, analyzing its independent features. The embedded derivative is classified as at FVTPL. The host contract may be a financial instrument or a nonfinancial item. If the host contract is a financial instrument, then IAS 39 applies for recognition and measurement; otherwise the appropriate IFRS is applied to account for the host contract.

If the holder cannot determine the fair value of an embedded derivative, the whole contract should be classified as at *fair value through profit or loss*. This may be the case for a debenture containing a conversion option for shares of a non-listed entity.

Reassessment of Embedded Derivative

Whether an embedded derivative is required to be separated is assessed when the entity first enters into the contract. Subsequent reassessment is prohibited, unless there is a change in the terms of the contract that *significantly modifies the cash flows* that otherwise would be required under the contract, in which case reassessment is required. IFRS 9, *Financial Instruments* does not require separation of an embedded derivative if the host contract is a financial instrument within the scope of it (Paragraph 4.7 of IFRS 9).

HEDGE ACCOUNTING

Principles of hedging and hedge accounting are set out in paragraphs 71–102 of IAS 39 along with guidance in paragraphs AG 101–AG 132 and Section F of the Implementation Guidance to IAS 39.

In a financial sense, *hedge* stands for defense against financial risk using derivative or nonderivative instruments. However, a nonderivative financial asset/-financial liability may be used for hedging foreign currency risk only.

IAS 39 prescribes special hedge accounting techniques for accounting for gains or losses arising out of a hedged instrument, if a designated hedging relationship exists. There are three types of hedging relationships:

1. *Fair value hedge:* hedges the exposure arising out of changes in fair value of the hedged item
2. *Cash flow hedge:* hedges the exposure arising out cash flow volatility of the hedged item
3. *Hedge of net investment in foreign operation:* hedges the foreign currency risk of the net investment

Definitions Relating to Hedge Accounting

- *Hedged item:* It is an asset, liability, firm commitment, highly probable forecast transaction or net investment in a foreign operation that (1) exposes the entity to risk of changes in fair value or future cash flows and (2) is designated as being hedged.
- *Hedging instrument:* It is (1) a designated derivative or (2) for a hedge of the risk of changes in foreign currency exchange rates only, a designated nonderivative financial asset or nonderivative financial liability, that has a fair value or cash flows that is expected to offset changes in the fair value or cash flows of a designated hedged item.
- *Hedge effectiveness:* It signifies the degree of offsetting of the changes in the fair value or cash flows of the hedged item that are attributable to a hedged risk by the changes in the fair value or cash flows of the hedging instrument.

A *hedged item* can be

- A recognized asset or liability—a single asset/liability or a group of assets/liabilities;
- An unrecognized firm commitment—a single unrecognized firm commitment or a group of unrecognized firm commitments;
- A single, highly probable forecast transaction or group of highly probable forecast transactions;
- A net investment in a foreign operation or group of foreign operations that carry similar risk;
- In a portfolio hedge of interest rate risk only, a portion of financial assets or financial liabilities that share the risk being hedged.

It is clear from the above definition that hedged items can be nonfinancial assets and nonfinancial liabilities as well as financial assets and financial liabilities. Normally, nonfinancial assets or nonfinancial liabilities are designated as hedged items only for foreign currency risk. However, they can be considered as hedged items in their entirety for all risk if it is not possible to isolate and measure the change in fair value or cash flow for specific risks other than foreign currency risk.

Issues relating to the selection of *hedging instruments* are as follows:

- A nonderivative financial asset/financial liability can be designated only to hedge foreign currency risk.
- A held-to-maturity instrument carried at amortized cost can be designated as a hedging instrument in foreign currency hedge.
- A derivative is normally designated as a hedging instrument, except for written options. However, a written option can be designated as a hedging instrument if it is used to hedge a purchased option.
- Investments in an unquoted equity instrument, or a purchased option on an unquoted instrument, are not designated as a hedging instrument because the fair value of an unquoted equity instrument cannot be reliably measured.
- An entity's own equity instrument cannot be designated as a hedging instrument because it is not a financial asset/financial liability.
- As in the case of designating a hedged item, an instrument designated as a hedging instrument should involve two external parties.
- Normally, there is a single fair value measure for the hedging instrument in its entirety.

Two exceptions are permitted:

- Separating time value and intrinsic value of an option; and
- Separating interest element and spot price of a forward contract.

A proportion of a derivative or nonderivative financial instrument can be designated as a hedging instrument.

The same hedging instrument can be used for hedging different types of risk provided (1) risks that are hedged are clearly identified, (2) hedging effectiveness can be demonstrated, and (3) it is possible to establish specific designation of the hedging instrument and specific risks.

Two or more derivatives (or proportions of them) can be designated for a hedging instrument if none of them is a written option or a net written option. A collar or similar derivative instrument that combines a written option and purchased option with the net effect of a written option cannot be designated as a hedging instrument.

Two or more nonderivative financial instruments (or proportions of them) can be designated as a hedging instrument for hedging foreign currency risk.

Hedge accounting is applied only if the hedging relationship qualifies. Five qualifying conditions are:

- *Designation of hedging relationship and documentation:* At the inception of the hedge there should be formal designation and documentation of the hedging relationship and the entity's risk management objective and strategy for undertaking the hedge. That documentation should include
  - Identification of the hedging instrument;
  - The hedged item or transaction;
  - The nature of the risk being hedged; and
  - How the entity will assess the hedging instrument's effectiveness in offsetting the exposure to changes in the hedged item's fair value or cash flows attributable to the hedged risk.

- *Hedging effectiveness:* The hedge is expected to be highly effective in achieving offsetting changes in fair value or cash flows attributable to the hedged risk, consistently with the originally documented risk management strategy for that particular hedging relationship.

- *Highly probable forecast transaction and presence of cash flow volatility:* For cash flow hedges (1) a forecast transaction that is the subject of the hedge must be highly probable, and (2) there should be an exposure to variations in cash flows that could ultimately affect profit or loss.
- *Reliable measurement of hedging effectiveness:* The effectiveness of the hedge should be reliably measurable, that is, the fair value or cash flows of the hedged item that are attributable to the hedged risk and the fair value of the hedging instrument can be reliably measured.
- *Ongoing assessment of hedging effectiveness:* The hedge is assessed on an ongoing basis and determined actually to have been highly effective throughout the financial reporting periods for which the hedge was designated.

As per IAS 39, paragraph 88, at the inception of the hedge and in subsequent periods, the hedge is expected to be highly effective in achieving offsetting changes in fair value or cash flows attributable to the hedged risk during the period for which the hedge is designated. This can be demonstrated in various ways, which include (1) comparison of past changes in the fair value or cash flows of the hedged item that are attributable to the hedged risk with past changes in the fair value or cash flows of the hedging instrument, or (2) demonstrating a high statistical correlation between the fair value or cash flows of the hedged item and those of the hedging instrument.

The actual results of the hedge should fall within a range of 80–125%.

Accounting for a Fair Value Hedge

- If the hedging instrument is a derivative, charge the change in fair value to profit and loss. There should be a corresponding offset to the statement of comprehensive income as a result of the change in the fair value of the hedged item that is attributable to the hedged risk.

    If the hedged item is carried at cost, its carrying amount should be adjusted.

    If the hedged item is an available-for-sale financial asset, its fair value is adjusted, but the gain or loss that is attributable to the hedged risk is charged/credited to profit and loss.
- In case of a fair value hedge of interest rate risk of a portion of the portfolio of financial assets/financial liabilities, the change in fair value should be added/deducted in a separate line within the financial asset/financial liability for the relevant financial periods for which these are designated as hedged item.
- Changes in fair value of the hedged item that relates to an element of the risk that is not designated as a hedged risk should be accounted for in accordance with the requirements of IAS 39, paragraph 55.

Hedge accounting is discontinued prospectively when:

- It does not meet five qualifying criteria stated in paragraph 88 of IAS 39 (refer to the earlier discussion);
- The hedging instrument expires or is sold, terminated, or exercised.

    However, when a hedging instrument is rolled over, it is not termed as an expiration. For example, if exchange-traded futures and options are designated as a hedging instrument, they have a specific expiry date that is required to be rolled over. In such a case, the life of the hedging instrument is apparently shorter than the hedged item, which is contrary to the principle of designating a hedging instrument. However, the entity may document a strategy by which such instruments will be rolled over such that they will have an uninterrupted life equal to longer than the hedged item.
- If the entity revokes the designation.

Example 16

Entity E has €100 million investments in equity shares of other entities that are classified as AFS financial assets. It has designated stock index futures as fair value hedge that is a qualified hedge in accordance with paragraph 88 of IAS 39. At the end of the reporting period, fair value of the AFS financial assets was €95 million and fair value of the stock index futures was €4.5 million (i.e., 90% of the fair value change in the hedged item). How should the entity account for this fair value hedge?

Solution

In this case, hedging effectiveness lies within the 80–125% range. So, it remains as qualified hedging relationship and fair value hedge accounting can be followed. At the end of the reporting period, the fair value of the investments in equity shares has declined by €5 million, but the fair value of the stock index futures has increased by €4.5 million. The entity shall debit fair value loss of €4.5 million to the statement of income and balance loss of €0.5 million is accounted for in other comprehensive income. Change in fair value of the stock index future (that is, €4.5 million) is credited to the statement of income. The journal entries to be passed are (figures in € million)

Fair Value Loss on AFS Financial Assets	Dr. 5.0	
AFS Financial Assets		Cr. 5.0
Recognition of fair value loss on the reporting date		

Derivative Financial Assets (Stock Index Futures)	Dr. 4.5	
Fair Value Gain on Derivative Financial Asset		Cr. 4.5
Recognition of fair value gain on hedging instrument and corresponding recognition derivative asset on the reporting date		

Statement of Income	Dr. 4.5	
Statement of Other Comprehensive Income	Dr. 0.5	
Fair Value Loss on AFS Financial Assets		Cr. 5.0

Fair Value Gain on Derivative Financial Assets	Dr. 4.5	
Statement of Income		Cr. 4.5

Accounting for a Cash Flow Hedge

The portion of the gain or loss on the hedging instrument that is determined to be an effective hedge (as per IAS 39, paragraph 98) is recognized directly in an appropriate equity account, say, Cash Flow Hedge Reserve; and the portion of the gain or loss on the hedging instrument that is determined to be an ineffective hedge is recognized in the statement of profit and loss.

The cash flow hedge reserve is adjusted for the lower of the cumulative gain or loss on the hedged item or the hedging instrument from inception of the hedge. The remaining amount of gain or loss on the hedging instrument is recognized in profit and loss.

A forecast transaction under a cash flow hedge may subsequently result in

- Recognized financial assets or financial liabilities;
- Recognized nonfinancial assets or nonfinancial liabilities; or
- Revenue or expense item to be recognized in profit and loss.

Accounting policies for these three situations are covered in IAS 39.97, IAS 39.98, and IAS 39.102, respectively, and are explained as follows.

If a hedge of a forecast transaction subsequently results in the recognition of a financial asset or a financial liability, the associated gains or losses that were recognized directly in the appropriate equity (cash flow hedge reserve) account are reclassified into (i.e., recognized in) the statement of profit and loss in the same period or periods during which the asset acquired or liability assumed affects profit or loss (such as in the periods that interest income or interest expense is recognized). However, if an entity expects that all or a portion of a loss recognized directly in the equity account will not be recovered in one or more future periods, it should reclassify into the statement of profit and loss the amount that is not expected to be recovered.

If a hedge of a forecast transaction subsequently results in the recognition of a nonfinancial asset or a financial liability, the associated gains or losses that were recognized directly in the appropriate equity (cash flow hedge reserve) account are reclassified into the statement of profit and loss in the same period or periods during which the asset acquired or liability assumed affects profit or loss (such as in the periods that depreciation expense or cost of sales is recognized). Alternatively, the cash flow hedge reserve may be removed from equity and adjusted in the initial cost or other carrying amount of the asset or liability. However, if an entity expects that all or a portion of a loss recognized directly in the equity account will not be recovered in one or more future periods, it should reclassify into the statement of profit and loss the amount that is not expected to be recovered.

Example 17

Entity E, an Indian entity with functional currency INR, has €10 million forecast transaction (expected payment obligation for purchase of goods to materialize after three months) as on March 1, 2009. On that date, it bought a three-month currency forward for €10 million at €1= Rs. 67.8590 and designated it as a cash flow hedge against the budgeted € denominated payables. As on the reporting date March 31, 2009, rate of two-month € forward was €1= Rs. 68.9590. E purchased goods on May 31, 2009 which is also the transaction date for the highly probable cash flow transaction. As on that date the spot €1 = Rs. 67.4933. On that date, the currency forward matured and E settled its € denominated payables. How should E account for the transaction? Assume domestic interest rate in India for 1 month maturity borrowing is considered to be 6 percent.

Solution

Date	Transaction	Accounting
March 1, 2009	Three-month currency forward for €10 million at €1= Rs. 67.8590 was purchased.	No entry required. Currency forward did not have any value on the date of purchase.
March 31, 2009	Fair value of currency forward is determined as it is a derivative financial asset that shall be classified as at FVTPL on stand-alone basis.	Fair value: €10 million $\times \dfrac{\text{Rs.68.9590–Rs.67.8590}}{1.06^{1/12}}$ = + Rs. 10.947 million Fair value gain of Rs. 10.947 million on the currency forward is accounted for in the other comprehensive income as Cash Flow Hedge Reserve. This will appear as a separate element of equity. On the other hand, currency forward will appear as an item of current asset for the same amount.
May 31, 2009	Purchase of goods Maturity of currency forward Entity E may opt for adjusting the profit/loss arising out of cash flow hedge into the purchase price of the nonfinancial item that was reference item of the highly probable cash flow transaction.	This transaction shall be measured at the spot exchange rate : Purchases Dr. Rs. 674.933 million Payables Cr. Rs. 674.933 million On maturity, the difference between the spot rate and last referred forward rate (i.e., two-month forward rate is profit/loss). (Rs. 67.4933 – Rs. 67.859) $\times$ €10 million = (Rs. 3.657 million) Fair value loss of Rs. 14.604 million Loss net of adjustments Rs. 3.657 million, which is the fair value of the currency forward.

	Reclassification adjustment for cash flow hedge reserve of Rs. 10.947 million.	Net fair loss is adjusted against purchases. Purchases (net of adjustment will stand at Rs. 768.59 which is €10 million at forward rate.)		
	Adjustment against purchase.	Rs. in Million		
		Payables	Dr.	674.933
		Currency Forward Liability	Dr.	3.657
	Settling the currency forward liability that stands at Rs. 3.657 million. Extra payment was required to settle the currency forward liability.	Bank	Cr.	678.590

Accounting for a Hedge of a Net Investment in a Foreign Operations

A *foreign* operation is an entity that is a subsidiary, associate, joint venture or branch of a reporting entity, the activities of which are based or conducted in a country or currency other than those of the reporting entity.

An entity often has amounts due from its foreign operation in the form loans or receivables. An important identification criterion is an item for which settlement is neither planned nor likely to occur in the foreseeable future. It is, in substance, a part of the entity's net investment in that foreign operation. It includes long-term loans granted by another subsidiary of the entity to the foreign operation. But it excludes trade receivables or trade payables.

It is accounted for similarly to a cash flow hedge. The gain or loss of the hedging instrument that is determined as an effective hedge is recognized in equity. The gain or loss of the ineffective portion of the hedging instrument is recognized in profit and loss. On disposal of the foreign operation, the cumulative gain or loss of the hedging instrument so recognized in equity is transferred to profit and loss.

EXCERPTS FROM PUBLISHED FINANCIAL STATEMENTS

Volvo Group, Annual Report 2008

Note 1. Accounting Principles

Reporting of Financial Assets and Liabilities

Financial assets treated within the framework of IAS 39 are classified either as

- Financial assets at fair value through profit and loss
- Investments held to maturity
- Loans and receivables
- Available-for-sale financial assets

Financial Liabilities Are Reported at Amortized Cost

Purchases and sales of financial assets and liabilities are recognized on the transaction date. A financial asset is derecognized (extinguished) in the balance sheet when all significant risks and benefits linked to the asset have been transferred to a third party. The same principles are applied for financial assets in the segment reporting of Volvo Group.

The fair value of assets is determined based on the market prices in such cases they exist. If market prices are unavailable, the fair value is determined for each asset using various valuation techniques. Transaction expenses are included in the asset's fair value except in cases in which the change in value is recognized in the income statement. The transaction costs arising in conjunction with assuming financial liabilities are amortized over the term of the loan as a financial cost.

Embedded derivatives are detached from the related main contract, if applicable. Contracts containing embedded derivatives are valued at fair value in the income statement if the contracts' inherent risk and other characteristics indicate a close relation to the embedded derivative.

Financial Assets at Fair Value Through Profit and Loss

All of Volvo's financial assets that are recognized at fair value in the income statement are classified as held for trading. Included are derivatives that are not part of an evidently effective hedge accounting. Gains and losses on these assets are recognized in the income statement. Short-term investments that are reported at fair value through profit and loss mainly consist of interest-bearing financial instruments and are reported in Note 21.

Derivatives used for hedging interest-rate exposure in the customer financing portfolio are included in this category as it is not practically possible to apply hedge accounting in accordance with IAS 39 due to the large number of contracts that the customer finance portfolio consist of. Volvo intends to keep these derivatives to maturity, why, over time, the market valuation will be offset as a consequence of the interest-rate fixing on borrowing and lending for the customer finance operations, and accordingly not affect result or cash flow.

Financial Assets Held to Maturity

Held-to-maturity investments are nonderivative assets with fixed payments and term and that Volvo intends and is able to hold to maturity. After initial recognition, these assets are measured in accordance with the effective interest method, with adjustment for any impairment. Gains and losses are recognized in the income statement when assets are divested or impaired as well as in pace with the accrued interested being reported. At year-end 2008, Volvo did not have any financial instruments classified in this category.

Loan Receivables and Other Receivables

Loans and receivables are nonderivative financial assets with fixed or determinable payments, originated or acquired, that are not quoted in an active market. After initial recognition, loans and receivables are measured in accordance with the effective interest method. Gains and losses are recognized in the income statement when the loans or receivables are divested or impaired as well as in pace with the accrued interested being reported.

Accounts receivables are recognized initially at fair value, which normally corresponds to the nominal value. In the event that the payment terms exceed one year, the receivable is recognized at the discounted present value.

Assessment of Impairment—Loan Receivables and Other Receivables

Volvo conducts routine controls to ensure that the carrying value of assets valued at amortized cost, such as loans and receivables, has not decreased, which would result in an impairment loss reported in the income statement. Allowances for doubtful receivables are continuously reported based on an assessment of a possible change in the customer's ability to pay.

Impairments consist of the difference between carrying value and current value of the estimated future payment flow attributable to the specific asset with consideration to the fair value of any collateral.

Discounting of future cash flow is based on the effective rate used initially. Initially, the impairment requirement is evaluated for each respective asset. If, based on objective grounds, it cannot be determined that one or more assets are subject to an impairment loss, the assets are grouped in units based, for example, on similar credit risks to evaluate the impairment loss requirement collectively. Individually written-down assets or assets written-down during previous periods are not included when grouping assets for impairment test. If the conditions for a completed impairment loss later prove to no longer be present, and that can be related to a specific event after the impairment event, the impairment loss is reversed in the income statement as long as the carrying value does not exceed the amortized cost at the time of the reversal.

Volvo discloses loan receivables and accounts receivables in the Notes 16, 17, 19, and 20.

Available-for-Sale Assets

This category includes assets available for sale or those that have not been classified in any of the other three categories. These assets are initially measured at fair value. Fair value changes are recognized directly in shareholders' equity. The cumulative gain or loss that was recognized in equity is recognized in profit or loss when an available-for-sale financial asset is sold. Unrealized value declines are recognized in equity, unless the decline is significant or prolonged. Then the impairment is recognized in the income statement. If the event causing the impairment no longer exists, impairment can be reversed in the income statement if it does not involve an equity instrument.

Earned or paid interest attributable to these assets is recognized in the income statement as part of net financial items in accordance with the effective interest method. Dividends received attributable to these assets are recognized in the income statement as Income from other investments.

Volvo reports shares and participations in listed companies at market value on the balance sheet date, with the exception of investments classified as associated companies and joint ventures. Holdings in unlisted companies for which a market value is unavailable are recognized at acquisition value. Volvo classifies these types of investments as assets available for sale.

Assessment of Impairment—Available-for-Sale Assets

If an asset available for sale is to be impaired, it shall be effected by taking the difference between the asset's acquisition value (adjusted for any accrued interest if it involves that type of asset) and its fair value. If it instead involves equity instruments such as shares, a completed impairment shall not be reversed in the income statement. On the other hand, impairments that have been made on debt instruments (interest-bearing instruments) shall in whole or part be reversed in the income statement, in those instances where an event that is proven to have occurred after the impairment was performed is identified and impacts the valuation of that asset.

Hedge Accounting

In order to apply hedge accounting in accordance with IAS 39, the following criteria must be met: the position being hedged is identified and exposed to market value movements, for instance related to exchange-rate or interest-rate movements, the purpose of the loan/instrument is to serve as a hedge and the hedging effectively protects the underlying position against changes in the fair value. Financial instruments used for the purpose of hedging future currency flows are accounted for as hedges if the currency flows are considered highly probable to occur.

- Volvo applies hedge accounting for hedging against currency rate risk and interest-rate risks pertaining to commercial assets and liabilities. For financial instruments used to hedge forecasted internal commercial cash flows and forecasted electricity consumption, the fair value is debited or credited to a separate component of equity to the extent the requirements for cash-flow hedge accounting are fulfilled. To the extent that the requirements are not met, the unrealized gain or loss will be charged to the income statement. Unrealized and realized gains and losses on hedges are reported in operating income within other operating income and expenses.
- Volvo applies hedge accounting for financial instruments used to hedge interest and currency risks on loans only for cases when hedge accounting requirements are fulfilled. For cases when hedge accounting is not considered to be fulfilled, unrealized gains and losses up until the maturity date of the financial instrument will be charged to the financial net in the income statement.
- Volvo applies hedge accounting for certain net investments in foreign operations. The current result for such hedges is reported in a separate component in shareholders' equity. In the event of a divestment, the accumulated result from the hedge is recognized in the income statement.

Notes to the Consolidated Financial Statements

Amounts in SEK M unless otherwise specified.

Note 16. Long-Term Customer-Financing Receivables

	2007	2008
Installment credits	19,836	23,029
Financial leasing	20,298	26,874
Other receivables	352	529
Total	**40,486**	**50,432**

Effective interest rate for long-term customer-financing receivables was 7.20% as per December 31, 2008.

Long-term customer-financing receivables maturities

2010	20,643
2011	15,653
2012	9,243
2013	3,552
2014 or later	1,341
Total	**50,432**

Note 17. Other Long-Term Receivables

	2007	2008
Other loans to external parties	177	219
Prepaid pensions	2,131	2,442
Other financial receivables	1,088	1,857
Other receivables	1,383	1,641
Total	**4,779**	**6,159**

Note 19. Short-Term Customer-Financing Receivables

	2007	2008
Installment credits	13,620	16,747
Financial leasing	10,494	14,324
Dealer financing	13,191	16,135
Other receivables	1,056	851
Total	**38,361**	**48,057**

Effective interest rate for short-term customer-financing receivables was 6.89% as per December 31, 2008.

Note 20. Other Short-Term Receivables

	2007	2008
Accounts receivable	30,504	30,523
Prepaid expenses and accrued income	2,855	3,032
VAT receivables	2,884	3,348
Loans to external parties	403	121
Other financial receivables	12,903	4,791
Other receivables	4,868	5,697
Total, after deduction of valuation allowances for doubtful accounts receivable	**44,417**	**47,512**

Note 21. Marketable Securities

Marketable securities consist mainly of interest-bearing securities, distributed as shown below:

	2007	2008
Government securities	778	298
Banks and financial institutions	6,293	504
Real estate financial institutions	9,419	5,100
Total	**16,490**	**5,902**

TeliaSonera Annual Report 2008—Consolidated Financial Statements

Notes to Consolidated Financial Statements

Derivatives and hedge accounting—measurement and classification

TeliaSonera uses derivative instruments, such as interest and cross currency interest rate swaps, forward contracts and options, primarily to control exposure to fluctuations in exchange rates and interest rates.

Derivatives and embedded derivatives, when their economic characteristics and risks are not clearly and closely related to other characteristics of the host contract, are recognized at fair value. Derivatives with a positive fair value are recognized as noncurrent or current receivables and derivatives with a negative fair value as noncurrent or current liabilities. Currency swaps, forward exchange contracts and options are classified as noninterest-bearing and interest rate swaps and cross currency interest rate swaps as interest-bearing items. For classification in the income statement, see sections "Other operating income and expenses" and "Finance costs and other financial items" above.

Hedging instruments are designated as either fair value hedges, cash flow hedges, or hedges of net investments in foreign operations. Hedges of foreign exchange risk on firm commitments are accounted for as cash flow hedges. Documentation on hedges includes the relationship between the hedging instrument and the hedged item; risk management objectives and strategy for undertaking various hedge transactions; and whether the hedging instrument used is highly effective in offsetting changes in fair values or cash flows of the hedged item.

For fair value hedges, the effective and ineffective portions of the change in fair value of the derivative, along with the gain or loss on the hedged item attributable to the risk being hedged, are recognized in the income statement.

For cash flow hedges, the effective portion of the change in fair value of the derivative is recognized in the hedging reserve as a component of equity until the underlying transaction is reflected in the income statement, at which time any deferred hedging gains or losses are recognized in the income statement. The ineffective portion of the change in fair value of a derivative used as a cash flow hedge is recognized in the income statement. However, when the hedged forecast transaction results in the recognition of a nonfinancial asset or liability, the gains and losses are transferred from equity and included in the initial measurement of the cost of the asset or liability.

Hedges of net investments in foreign operations are accounted for similarly to cash flow hedges. Any gain or loss on the hedging instrument relating to the effective portion of the hedge is recognized in the foreign currency translation reserve as a component of equity. The gain or loss relating to the ineffective portion is recognized in the income statement. Gains and losses deferred in the foreign currency translation reserve are recognized in the income statement on disposal of the foreign operation.

Changes in the fair value of derivative instruments that do not meet the criteria for hedge accounting are recognized in the income statement. Hedge accounting is not applied to derivative instruments that economically hedge monetary assets and liabilities denominated in foreign currencies (economic hedges) or that are initiated in order to manage, e.g., the overall interest rate duration of the debt portfolio. Changes in the fair value of economic hedges are recognized in the income statement as exchange rate differences, offsetting the exchange rate differences on monetary assets and liabilities. Changes in the fair value of portfolio management derivatives are recognized in the income statement as finance costs.

30 INVESTMENT PROPERTY (IAS 40)

INTRODUCTION

IAS 40 addresses the issue of accounting for real estate properties (building, land, or both) that are held for the purpose of capital appreciation or rental income, or both, and not for the purpose of using them internally in the production of goods or services (commonly called plant assets) or for sale in the ordinary course of business as part of its inventory. Such property should be labeled in the statement of financial position as investment property. The valuation basis of such assets can either be at cost, net of depreciation, or at fair value. The rental-producing property that is subject to this standard can either be owned outright or leased by a lessee as a finance lease.

KEY TERMS

Investment property. Property (land or a building—or part of a building—or both) held (by the owner or by the lessee under a finance lease) to earn rentals or for capital appreciation or both.

Cost. The amount of cash or cash equivalents paid or the fair value of other consideration given to acquire an asset at the time of its acquisition or construction.

Fair value. The amount for which an asset could be exchanged between knowledgeable, willing parties in an arm's-length transaction.

Owner occupied property. Property that is held (by the owner or by the lessee under a finance lease) for use in the production or supply of goods or services or for administrative purposes.

SCOPE

IAS 40 covers properties that are classified as investment properties. Examples of investment properties under IAS 40 are

1. Land held for long-term capital appreciation rather than for short-term sale in the ordinary course of business.
2. Land held for a currently undetermined future use. (If an entity has not determined that it will use the land as owner-occupied property or for short-term sale in the ordinary course of business, the land is regarded as held for capital appreciation.)
3. A building owned by the entity (or held by the entity under a finance lease) and leased out under one or more operating leases.
4. A building that is vacant but is held to be leased out under one or more operating leases.
5. Property that is being constructed or developed for future use as investment property (applicable for reporting periods commencing on or after January 1, 2009).

The following are examples of items that are *not* investment property and are, therefore, outside the scope of this standard:

1. Property intended for sale in the ordinary course of business or in the process of construction or development for such sale (see IAS 2, *Inventories*), for example, prop-

erty acquired exclusively with a view to subsequent disposal in the near future or for development and resale.

2. Property being constructed or developed on behalf of third parties (see IAS 11, *Construction Contracts*).

3. Owner-occupied property (see IAS 16), including (among other things) property held for future use as owner-occupied property, property held for future development and subsequent use as owner-occupied property, property occupied by employees (whether the employees pay rent at market rates), and owner-occupied property awaiting disposal.

4. Property that is leased to another entity under a finance lease.

Example 1

Excellent Inc. and its subsidiaries have provided a list of the properties they own:

1. Land held by Excellent Inc. for undetermined future use
2. A vacant building owned by Excellent Inc. and to be leased out under an operating lease
3. Property held by Hush Hush Inc, a subsidiary of Excellent Inc., a real estate firm, in the ordinary course of its business
4. Property held by Excellent Inc. for the use in production
5. A hotel owned by Taj Mahal Inc., a subsidiary of Excellent Inc., and for which Taj Mahal Inc. provides security services for its guests' belongings

Excellent Inc. and its subsidiaries are inquiring as to which of the aforementioned properties qualify under IAS 40 as investment properties. If they do not qualify thus, how should they be treated under IFRS?

Solution

Properties described under items (1), (2), and (5) would qualify as investment properties under IAS 40. With respect to item (5), it is to be noted that IAS 40 requires that when the ancillary services are provided by the entity and they are considered a relatively insignificant component of the arrangement, then the property is considered an investment property.

These properties qualify as investment properties because they are being held for rental or for capital appreciation as opposed to actively managed properties that are used in the production of goods.

Property described in item (3) is to be treated as inventory under IAS 2. Property described in item (4) is treated as a long-lived asset under IAS 16.

MEASUREMENT OF INVESTMENT PROPERTY

Initial measurement will be at cost that approximates fair value at the time of acquisition. Cost will include the purchase price and any costs needed to prepare the asset for its intended use including, but not limited to, legal fees and real estate taxes.

Subsequent to acquisition, IAS 40 permits entities to value investment properties either at cost less accumulated depreciation and impairment or at fair value. Fair value is the price a knowledgeable third party is willing to pay for the property. The fair value should be measured at each reporting period. The increase or decrease of the fair value should be recorded in the statement of income. The lessee of a property under finance lease is required to use only the fair value approach.

For the reporting periods commencing on or after January 1, 2009, if the fair value of the investment property that is under construction is not reliably determinable but it is expected that the fair value can be reliably determinable when the construction is complete, it shall measure the investment property at cost until either its fair value becomes reliably determinable, or the construction is complete, whichever is earlier.

Example 2

Atrium Properties Ltd. purchased a lot of land in Chicago downtown. The land was fore-closed for a good price at $1.2 million. The management of Atrium Properties Ltd. has not decided whether to hold the land for a couple of years and then sell it or to develop it into a high-rise rental property. The company incurred the following costs, in addition to the purchase price:

Cost of demolishing an old building	$10,000
Erecting a fence around the perimeter of the land	$40,000
Paying overdue real estate tax	$80,000

Required

1. Does this property qualify as investment property under IAS 40?
2. What is the total cost to be recorded for this land?

Solution

1. The purchase of this land does qualify as investment property under IAS 40 since management intends to sell the property or develop it as a rental property.
2. The land will be recorded at its acquisition cost plus all the necessary cost to prepare it for its intended use. The land cost is computed as follows:

Purchase cost	$1,200,000
Demolition cost	10,000
Fence	40,000
Real estate tax	80,000
Total	$1,330,000

TRANSFERS TO AND FROM INVESTMENT PROPERTY

IAS 40 permits transfers of investment property from and to other type of assets, such as inventory or plant assets when and only when there is evidence that there is a change of use of that asset. Transfers may include any one of the following situations:

- From investment property to inventories when the intention changed to sale of the asset.
- From inventories to investment property when the asset is leased under an operating lease arrangement.
- From investment property to owner-occupied property when the company occupies the property.

If the company uses the cost principle in valuing investment property, the transfer will effectively use the carrying value of the asset before the transfer; that is, cost less accumulated depreciation and impairment. If the company uses the fair value method, then a new valuation will be made at the time of the transfer and the loss or gain will be recorded in the profit and loss statement. The new fair value will be the new basis of the asset recorded going forward.

Example 3

Refer to Example 2. A year after purchasing the land, Atrium Properties Ltd. decided not to sell the land but rather to build its own office building since the location is excellent. However, because of the decline in property price in Chicago, the appraised value of this land now is $1.1 million. What action does Atrium Properties Ltd. have to take in relation to this decision?

Solution

Atrium Properties Ltd. has to reclassify the land from investment property to property, plant, and equipment. Since the appraised value of the land is lower than its historical cost, Atrium Properties Ltd. has to record an impairment loss of $200,000. Thus, the land should be recorded at $1.1 million.

DISPOSALS

Investment property may be disposed of (sold or leased) or derecognized (retired). When that happens, companies are required to book the gain or loss on disposal or retirement in the profit and loss statement. When there is an asset sale, the difference between the selling price and the carrying amount of the property will be a gain or a loss and should be recognized immediately in the statement of income.

DISCLOSURES

IAS 40 requires extensive disclosures in relation to investment property. In brief, the entity should disclose whether it uses the cost or fair value methods. If the company uses the cost method in the statement of financial position, a supplemental disclosure in the notes should be made of the fair value of the asset. (Some interpret this that IASB is pushing toward valuing investment property at fair value.) The entity is also required to provide how it arrived at the fair value including the assumptions used and the qualifications of the party that performed the valuation. In addition, a disclosure is also required of the amount of rental income recorded in the statement of income, direct operating expenses and the cumulative change in fair value. In the following sections, detailed disclosure requirements under IAS 40 are included.

FAIR VALUE AND COST MODEL

An entity shall disclose

- Whether it applies the cost or fair value model;
- If it applies the fair value model, whether and under what circumstances property interests held under operating leases are classified and accounted as investment property;
- When classification is difficult, the criteria used to distinguish investment property, owner-occupied property and property held for disposal in the ordinary course of business;
- The methods used and significant assumptions made in determining fair value including a statement whether the determination of fair value was supported by market evidence or was more heavily based on other factors (which the entity shall disclose) because of the nature of the property and lack of comparable market data;
- The extent to which fair values are based on assessments by an independent and qualified valuer. If there are no such valuations, that fact shall be stated;
- The amounts recognized in the statement of income for

  - Rental income from investment property
  - Direct operating expenses that generated rental income
  - Direct operating expenses that did not generate rental income
  - Cumulative change in fair value recognized in the statement of income on sale of investment property from a pool of assets in which the cost model is used to a pool in which the fair value model is used;

- Existence and amounts of restrictions on the realizability of investment property; or for the remittance of income and proceeds on disposal; or
- Contractual obligations to purchase, construct, or develop investment property or for repairs, maintenance, or enhancements.

Fair Value Model

If an entity applies the fair value model, it shall also disclose a reconciliation of the opening and closing carrying values of investment property, showing

- Additions, showing separately acquisitions, subsequent expenditure, and additions through business combinations
- Assets classified as held for sale under IFRS 5
- Net gains or losses from fair value adjustments
- Net exchange differences arising on translation of financial statements in a different reporting currency
- Transfers to and from inventories and owner-occupied property
- Other changes

When a valuation for an investment property is adjusted to avoid double counting of assets such as equipment that may be recognized separately, a reconciliation of the adjustments shall be disclosed.

When fair value cannot be measured reliably and the asset is stated in accordance with IAS 16, such assets shall be disclosed separately from those at fair value. In addition to the movement disclosures just detailed, disclosures shall be made of the

- Description of properties stated in accordance with IAS 16
- Explanation as to why fair value cannot be reliably measured
- Range of estimates, if possible, within which the fair value is highly likely to fall
- Disposal of investment property not carried at fair value

  - The fact that the entity has disposed of investment property not carried at fair value;
  - The carrying amount of that investment property at the time of sale; and
  - The amount of gain or loss recognized.

Cost Model

For investment properties measured under the cost model, an entity shall disclose

- Depreciation methods used;
- Useful lives or depreciation rates used;
- A reconciliation of the opening and closing gross carrying amounts and the accumulated depreciation and impairment losses showing

  - Additions, showing separately acquisitions, subsequent expenditure, and additions through business combinations;

- Assets classified as held for sale under IFRS 5;
- Depreciation;
- Impairment losses recognized and reversed;
- Net exchange differences;
- Transfers to and from inventories and owner-occupied property;
- Other changes;
- The fair value of investment property and, if fair value cannot be reliably measured, an explanation as to why fair value cannot be reliably measured;

  - Range of estimates, if possible, within which the fair value is highly likely to fall; and
  - Disposals of investment property not carried at fair value.

EXCERPTS FROM UNPUBLISHED FINANCIAL STATEMENTS

Ahold, Annual Report 2008

Notes to the Consolidated Financial Statements

3. Significant Accounting Policies

Investment Property

Investment property consists of land and buildings held by Ahold to earn rental income or for capital appreciation, or both. These properties are not used by Ahold in the ordinary course of business. Ahold often owns (or leases under a finance lease) shopping centers containing both an Ahold store and third-party retail units. In these cases, the third-party retail units generate rental income, but are primarily of strategic importance for operating purposes to Ahold in its retail operations. Ahold recognizes the part of an owned (or leased under a finance lease) shopping center that is leased to third-party retailers as investment property, unless it represents an insignificant portion of the property. Land and buildings leased to franchisees are not considered to be investment property as they contribute directly to Ahold's retail operations. For the measurement of investment property a reference is made to the accounting policies on property, plant, and equipment.

12. Investment Property

In € million	2008	2007
At the beginning of the year		
At cost	658	592
Accumulated depreciation and impairment losses	(195)	(161)
	463	431
Additions	52	8
Depreciation	(18)	(14)
Impairment losses	(2)	(1)
Assets classified as held for sale or sold	(32)	(20)
Transfers from property, plant, and equipment	18	89
Exchange rate differences	14	(30)
Closing carrying amount	495	463
At the end of the year		
At cost	658	658
Accumulated depreciation and impairment losses	(163)	(195)
Carrying amount	495	463

A significant portion of Ahold's investment property is comprised of shopping centers containing both an Ahold store and third-party retail units. The third-party retail units generate rental income, but are primarily of strategic importance to Ahold in its retail operations. Ahold recognizes the part of shopping centers leased to third-party retailers as investment property, unless it represents an insignificant portion of the property.

The carrying amount of investment property includes an amount of EUR 49 million (December 30, 2007: EUR 41 million) and EUR 38 million (December 30, 2007: EUR 37 million) in respect of assets held under finance leases and financings, respectively. Ahold does not have legal title to these assets. Company-owned investment property with a carrying amount of EUR 65 million (December 30, 2007: EUR 67 million) has been pledged as security for liabilities, mainly for loans.

31 AGRICULTURE (IAS 41)

INTRODUCTION

The objective of IAS 41 is to stipulate the accounting treatment and disclosures in the financial statements of operations relating to agricultural activity.

SCOPE

IAS 41 applies to biological assets, agricultural produce at the point of harvest, and government grants received for agricultural activity. This standard does not apply to land related to agricultural activity (covered by IAS 16, *Property, Plant, and Equipment*, and IAS 40, *Investment Property*) or to intangible assets that are related to agricultural activity (covered by IAS 38, *Intangible Assets*). It is applicable only to the agriculture produce, which is the entity's harvested product at the point of harvest and not to the produce after harvest. In this case, the items that are harvested become inventory, and the provisions of IAS 2, *Inventories*, or other related standard, are applicable. Similarly, this standard does not deal with processing of product after harvesting; for example, processing of coffee beans into coffee powder since such activities are only an extension of the agricultural activity and are not included within the definition of agricultural activity in this standard.

Examples

Biological assets	*Agriculture produce*	*Products resulting from processing after harvest*
Plants	Coffee beans	Coffee powder
Cattle	Milk	Cheese
Vines	Grapes	Wine
Sheep	Wool	Yarn

KEY TERMS

Agricultural activity. The process of managing the biological transformation and harvesting of biological assets, either for sale or for converting into agricultural produce or additional biological assets.

Agricultural produce. The product obtained on harvesting the biological assets.

Biological asset. A living plant or animal.

Biological transformation. The processes of growth, degeneration, production, and procreation that cause quantitative or qualitative changes in a biological asset.

Active market. A market where the items traded are homogenous, willing buyers and sellers are normally found at any time, and the prices are available to the public.

Fair value. The amount for which an asset can be exchanged or a liability settled in an arm's-length transaction between knowledgeable and willing parties. The fair value of an asset is based upon the present location and condition of the asset.

Costs to sell. The direct incremental costs, other than finance costs and income tax, to be incurred on the disposal of an asset.

Government grants. As defined in IAS 20, *Accounting for Government Grants and Disclosure of Government Assistance.* They are government assistance in the form of transfers of resources by government to an entity in return for past or future compliance by the entity with certain conditions relating to the operating activities of the entity. They exclude those forms of government assistance that cannot reasonably be valued and transactions with government that cannot be distinguished from other normal trading transactions of the entity. Government grants are sometimes referred to as subsidies, subventions, and premiums.

RECOGNITION AND MEASUREMENT

A biological asset or agriculture produce must be recognized by an entity only when all the following conditions are satisfied:

- The entity controls the assets as a result of past events;
- It is probable that future economic benefits of the asset will flow to the entity; and
- The fair value or cost of the asset can be measured reliably.

All biological assets must be measured initially and at each subsequent reporting date at their fair value less costs to sell, except in cases where the fair value cannot be measured reliably. Agricultural produce that is harvested from the entity's biological asset must be measured at its fair value less costs to sell at the point of harvest. Subsequent to the harvest, the produce is measured applying the principles of IAS 2, *Inventories*, or any another applicable standard.

In determining the fair value for a biological asset or agricultural produce, it may be necessary to group together items in accordance with their significant attributes, like age or quality. When an active market based on its present location and condition exists for the biological asset or agricultural produce, the quoted price in that market is the fair value of the asset. If an entity has access to different active markets, then the entity must choose the quoted price of the market that the entity is most likely to use to sell the asset. When an active market does not exist, the entity can use, depending on its availability, either the most recent market transaction price or the market prices for similar assets, after adjustment to reflect any differences in the asset or any specified sector benchmarks, such as value of cattle expressed as meat per kilogram.

In some cases, an entity may contract to sell its biological assets or produce at a future date, and these contract prices do not necessarily represent the current fair value for the biological asset or produce. If an active market exists for the asset or produce, then the price in that market should be considered as the fair value.

Sometimes market prices or values may not be available for an asset in its present condition. In such cases, the entity can use the present value of the expected net cash flow from the asset discounted at a current market rate, which can either be a post- or pretax rate.

In some circumstances, cost can be considered as the fair value, especially where little biological transformation has taken place after initial costs have been incurred or the impact of biological transformation on the price is not expected to be significant. An example of this is seedlings or trees planted immediately prior to the reporting date.

There are situations where there is no separate active market for the biological assets on their own when they are physically attached to land (for example, rubber trees in a plantation). However, an active market might be available for the combined assets. In such cases, the entity should value the combined assets and then reduce the fair value by deducting the fair value of the land and land improvements to determine the fair value of the biological asset.

Costs to sell include commission to brokers and dealers, levies by regulatory authorities, and commodity exchanges. Fair value of biological assets or produce at a particular location is the price for the assets in the relevant market less the transport and other costs of getting the assets to that market.

GAINS AND LOSSES

The gain that arises on the initial recognition of a biological asset at fair value less costs to sell and any changes in that fair value less costs to sell of the biological assets during the reporting period is included in profit or loss for the period. An example is the gain that arises when a calf is born to a cow. Similarly, any gain or loss that arises on the initial recognition of agricultural produce at fair value less costs to sell should be included in profit or loss for the period to which it relates. An example of this is the gain or loss on initial recognition of agricultural produce, since the crop when harvested can have more value than the crop that has not been harvested. All costs related to the biological assets, other than those that related to its purchase, should be measured at fair value and recognized in profit or loss when incurred.

IAS 41 presumes that the fair value of a biological asset can be measured reliably. However, it is possible that there is no quoted market price in an active market when the biological asset is first recognized and no other valuation methods are appropriate. In such cases, the asset is measured at cost less accumulated depreciation and any impairment losses. When circumstances do change and fair value becomes reliably measurable, then the entity must measure the asset at fair value less costs to sell.

When a noncurrent biological asset meets the criteria to be classified as held for sale in accordance with IFRS 5, *Noncurrent Assets Held for Sale and Discontinued Operations*, then it is presumed that fair value can be measured reliably. To determine cost, depreciation, and impairment losses, the provisions of IAS 2, *Inventories*, IAS 16, *Property, Plant, and Equipment*, and IAS 36, *Impairment of Assets*, are used.

Example 1

An entity has these balances in its financial records

	$m
Value of biological asset at cost on December 31, 2007	600
Fair valuation surplus on initial recognition at fair value December 31, 2007	700
Change in fair value to December 31, 2008, due to growth and price fluctuations	100
Decrease in fair value due to harvest	90

Show how these values would be incorporated into the financial statements at December 31, 2008.

Solution

Balance sheet at December 31, 2008

	$m
Biological assets	600
Fair valuation (included in profit or loss year ended December 31, 2007)	700
Carrying value January 1, 2008	1,300
Change in fair value in 2008	100
Decrease due to harvest in 2008	(90)
Carrying value at December 31, 2008	1,310

Income statement for year ended December 31, 2008

	$m
Biological assets change in fair value	100
Decrease due to harvest	(90)
Net gain	10

GOVERNMENT GRANTS

An unconditional government grant that is related to a biological asset and measured at fair value less costs to sell should be recognized as income when the grant becomes receivable. When conditions are attached to the government grant, income must be recognized only when those conditions are fulfilled. The provisions of IAS 20, *Accounting for Government Grants and Disclosure of Government Assistance*, are applied only to government grants that are related to biological assets that have been measured at cost less accumulated depreciation and impairment losses

Disclosures

The following are disclosures prescribed by IAS 41:

- The aggregate gain or loss that arises on the initial recognition of biological assets and agricultural produce and from the change in value less costs to sell of the biological assets;
- Description of each group of biological assets. If this information is not disclosed in the financial statements, the nature of its activities and nonfinancial measures or estimates of the physical quantity of each group of the entity's biological assets at period end and that of the output for agricultural produce during the period should be disclosed;
- Methods and assumptions applied in determining fair value of each group of agricultural produce at the point of harvest and of each group of biological assets;
- Fair value less costs to sell of agricultural produce harvested during the period shall be disclosed at the point of harvest;
- Existence and carrying amounts of biological assets whose title is restricted and that of any biological assets that are placed as security for liabilities;
- Amount of any commitments for the development or acquisition of biological assets;
- Financial risk management strategies;
- Reconciliation of the changes in the carrying amount of biological assets that discloses

  - Gain or loss arising from changes in fair value less costs to sell;
  - Increase on purchases;
  - Decrease on sales and biological assets classified as held for sale in accordance with IFRS 5;
  - Decrease due to harvest;
  - Increase resulting from business combinations; and
  - Net exchange differences arising on translation of financial statements into different presentation and on translation of a foreign operation into the presentation currency of the reporting entity.

When biological assets that are stated at cost less accumulated depreciation and impairment losses are disposed of, the entity shall disclose any gain or loss on disposal and provide reconciliation as above, and provide the details of impairment losses and depreciation. When the fair value of biological assets cannot be measured, additional disclosure should be made relating to the description of the asset, an explanation of why fair value cannot be measured reliably, the range, if possible, of estimates within which the fair value is likely to fall, the depreciation method used, useful lives or depreciation rates used and gross carrying amount, and accumulated depreciation at the beginning and end of the period. When the fair value of the biological assets that were previously measured at cost less accumulated depreciation and impairment losses is now measurable, additional disclosures regarding description of the biological assets, explanation as to why fair value is now reliably measurable, and the effect of the change must be disclosed.

Regarding government grants, disclosures should be made as to the nature and extent of the grants, any conditions that have not been fulfilled, and any significant decreases in the expected level of the grants.

EXCERPTS FROM PUBLISHED FINANCIAL STATEMENTS

Rainbow Chicken, Annual Report 2009

Notes to Group Financial Statements

Accounting Policies

Biological Assets

Breeding stock includes the Cobb grandparent breeding and the parent rearing and laying operations. Broiler hatching eggs are included in breeding stock.

Biological assets are measured at fair value less estimated point-of-sale costs at reporting dates. Fair value is determined based on market prices or, where market prices are not available, by reference to sector benchmarks.

Gains and losses arising on the initial recognition of biological assets at fair value less estimated point-of-sale costs and from a change in fair value less estimated point-of-sale costs are charged to the income statement in the year in which they arise.

5. Biological assets

	2009 R'000	2008 R'000
Breeding stock		
At the beginning of the year	212,315	159,822
Gain arising from cost inputs	728,982	575,560
Decrease due to harvest	(700,411)	(526,380)
Fair value adjustment	3,346	3,313
At the end of the year at fair value	**244,232**	**212,315**
Broiler stock		
At the beginning of the year	156,909	156,909
Gain arising from cost inputs	3,577,857	2,810,293
Decrease due to harvest	(3,558,795)	(2,774,593)
Fair value adjustment	9,350	11,753
At the end of the year at fair value	**109,456**	**98,885**
Total at the end of the year at fair value	269,278	242,199

Crookes Brothers Limited, Annual Report 2009

Balance sheets (extracts) at March 31, 2009

Company				Group	
2008 R'000	2009 R'000		Note	2009 R'000	2008 R'000
		Assets			
247,115	180,901	**Noncurrent assets**		202,050	274,002
165,367	104,690	Property, plant, and equipment	10	126,310	186,175
70,652	57,502	**Bearer biological assets**	11.1	65,680	77,526
4,503	3,518	Unlisted investments	3.1	3,518	4,503
5,080	5,767	Investment in associate companies	3.2	5,805	5,115
830	8,687	Investment in subsidiary companies	4		
683	683	Long-term receivable	17	737	683
98,288	281,370	**Current assets**		309,646	127,483
345,403	462,271	**Total assets**		521,696	401,485

Company			Note	Group	
2008 R'000	2009 R'000			2009 R'000	2008 R'000
		Equity and Liabilities			
198,664	238,569	Capital and reserves		342,095	288,354
57,952	67,211	Noncurrent liabilities		82,648	72,234
88,787	156,491	Current liabilities		96,953	40,897
345,403	462,271	Total equity and liabilities		521,696	401,485

Accounting Policies

Biological Assets

Biological assets are measured on initial recognition and at each balance sheet date at their fair values and any change in values is included in the net profit or loss for the period in which it arises, as more fully set out below:

Growing Crops and Orchards

Growing crops and orchards comprise two elements:

1. Bearer biological assets—sugar cane roots, citrus trees, deciduous trees, and banana plants; and
2. Consumable biological assets—standing sugar cane, citrus fruit, deciduous fruit, bananas, wheat, and barley.

Bearer biological assets are valued at fair value based on the current replacement cost of planting and establishment, subsequently reduced in value over the period of their productive lives. Consumable biological assets are measured at their fair value, determined on current estimated market prices less estimated harvesting, transport, packing, and point-of-sale costs.

- Standing cane at estimated sucrose content, age, and market price; and
- Growing fruit at estimated yields, quality standards, age, and market prices.

Livestock

Livestock are measured at their fair value less estimated point-of-sale costs, fair value being determined upon the age and size of the animals and market price. Market price is determined on the basis that the animal is sold to be slaughtered. Livestock held for sale are classified as consumable biological assets.

Consumable Stores

Consumable stores are valued at the lower of cost or net realizable value. Cost is calculated using the weighted-average method. Redundant and slow moving items are written down to their net realizable values.

Merchandise

Merchandise is valued at the lower of cost or net realizable value, cost being determined on the average method basis.

Agricultural Produce

Deciduous fruit and grain stocks are valued at fair value less estimated point-of-sale costs.

Judgments made by management. Preparing financial statements in accordance with IFRS requires estimates and assumptions that affect reported amounts and related disclosures. Certain accounting policies have been identified as involving complex or subjective judgments or assessments. The items for consideration have been identified as biological asset valuations. The accounting policy is detailed on page 33 of this report and the assumptions that have been used to determine the fair value of the consumable biological assets are detailed in Note 11 to the financial statements on pages 44 and 45.

Crookes Brothers Limited, Annual Report 2009

Notes to the Financial Statement for the Year Ended March 31, 2009

1. **Revenue**

Revenue comprises the proceeds from

Company			Group	
2008	2009		2009	2008
R'000	R'000		R'000	R'000
98,858	111,885	Sugar cane	159,592	142,436
44,978	55,421	Bananas	55,421	44,978
20,752	52,196	Deciduous fruit	52,196	20,752
13,464	14,080	Grain	14,080	13,464
4,606	2,646	Sheep	2,646	4,606
14,692	15,155	Citrus fruit	15,155	14,692
3,526	4,457	Crocodile farming/tourism	4,457	3,526
		Cattle	1,618	1,181
1,110	2,049	Rentals on buildings	2,203	1,244
201,986	**257,889**		**307,368**	**246 879**

Other Operating Income

Company			Group	
2008	2009		2009	2008
R'000	R'000		R'000	R'000
		Loss/profit and disposal of property, plant, and		
757	(52)	equipment	(32)	669
129	129	Royalties on sale of sand and stone	675	129
231	231	Sundry revenue	799	245
3,066	3,066	Change in fair value—biological assets—livestock	5,343	4,894
—	(213)	Loss on sale of shares	(213)	—
—	568	Management fees—subsidiaries		
4,183	**5,311**		**6,572**	**5,937**

11. **Biological Assets**

11.1 Growing Crops and Orchards

(At fair value less estimated point-of-sale costs)

Company			Group	
2008	2009		2009	2008
R'000	R'000		R'000	R'000
73,920	52,188	Sugar cane	91,656	101,261
18,167	6,090	Bananas	6,090	18,167
29,884	49,912	Deciduous	49,912	29,884
13,481	15,698	Citrus	15,698	13,481
135,452	**123,888**	**Carrying amount at end of year**	**163,356**	**162,793**
70,652	57,502	Noncurrent assets—bearer biological assets	65,680	77,526
64,800	66,386	Current assets—crops	97,676	85,267
135,452	**123,888**		**163,356**	**162,793**

Reconciliation of carrying amounts of growing crops and orchards

Company			Group	
2008	2009		2009	2008
R'000	R'000		R'000	R'000
119,640	135,452	Net book value at beginning of year	162,793	145,672
3,057	11,030	Increases due to purchases	11,030	3,057
—	(14,494)	Decreases due to disposal of farms	(14,494)	—
80,766	112,593	Gain arising from changes attributable to physical changes and price changes	145,985	101,397
(68,011)	(84,890)	Decreases due to sales/harvest	(106,155)	(87,333)
—	(35,803)	Transfers to assets classified as held for sale	(35,803)	—
135,452	**123,888**	**Net book value at end of year**	**163,356**	**162,793**

The areas under crops are detailed on pages 13 to 14 of this annual report.

11.2 Livestock

Reconciliation of carrying amounts of livestock—cattle, sheep and crocodiles

Company			Group	
2008	2009		2009	2008
R'000	R'000		R'000	R'000
7,685	7,381	Carrying amount at beginning of year	11,271	10,721
169	697	Increases due to purchases	782	2
3,066	3,066	Gain arising from changes attributable to physical changes and price changes	5,343	4,894
(3,539)	(3,539)	Decreases due to sales	(3,894)	(4,576)
7,381	**9,207**	Carrying amount at end of year	**13,502**	**11,271**
142,833	**133,095**	**Total biological assets**	**176,858**	**174,064**

The following key assumptions have been used in determining the fair value of biological assets:

Company			Group	
2008	2009		2009	2008
R'000	R'000		R'000	R'000
		Sugar cane		
		(1) Standing sugar cane		
		Expected area to harvest (ha)		
6,351	5,885	–South Africa	6,413	6,351
		–Swaziland	1,548	1,604
		Estimated yields (tons cane/ha)		
77.9	78.0	–South Africa	78.4	77.9
		–Swaziland	106.5	107.0
		Average maturity of cane at March 31		
61%	61%	–South Africa	61%	61%
		–Swaziland	64%	64%
R1,795	R2,194	Estimated RV price—South Africa	R2,194	R1,795
		Estimated sucrose price—Swaziland	R2,100	R1,747
		(2) Cane roots		
6 to 8	6 to 8	Estimated productive rations	6 to 8	6 to 8
R3,628	R4,268	Average indexed current replacement cost of establishment (per ha)—reduced according to age	R4,268	R3,738

11. The following key assumptions have been used in determining the fair value of biological assets (Continued):

Company			Group	
2008	*2009*		*2009*	*2008*
R'000	*R'000*		*R'000*	*R'000*
		Bananas		
		(1) Crop		
320	320	Expected area to harvest (ha)	320	320
53.1	56.9	Estimated yields (tons/ha)	56.9	53.1
50%	50%	Average maturity of crop at March 31	50%	50%
R 57.27	R 59.78	Estimated price per carton	R 59.78	R 57.27
		(1) Banana plants		
9	9	Estimated productive life (years)	9	9
R29,806	R35,990	Average indexed current replacement cost of establishment (per ha)—reduced according to age	R35,990	R29,806
		Deciduous fruit		
		(1) Crop		
85	52	Expected area to harvest (ha) after March 31	152	85
46.6	51.0	Estimated yields (tons /ha)	51.0	46.6
87%	86%	Average maturity of crop at March 31	86%	87%
R 2.13	R 2.19	Estimated net price per kg—apples	R 2.19	R 2.13
		(2) Deciduous trees		
30	30	Estimated productive life (years)	30	30
R101,799	R106,389	Average indexed current replacement cost of establishment (per ha)—reduced according to age	R106,389	R101,799
		Citrus fruit		
		(1) Crop		
148	167	Expected area to harvest (ha)	167	148
52.2	48.6	Estimated yields (tons /ha)	48.62	52.2
66%	66%	Average maturity of crop at March 31—grapefruit	66%	66%
50%	50%	Average maturity of crop at March 31—oranges	50%	50%
R 53.00	R 62.00	Estimated net price per carton—grapefruit	R 62.00	R 53.00
R 42.59	R 50.00	Estimated net price per carton—oranges	R 50.00	R 42.59
		(2) Citrus trees		
15	15	Estimated productive life (years)—grapefruit	15	15
30	30	Estimated productive life (years)—oranges	30	30
R45,153	R51,359	Average indexed current replacement cost of establishment (per ha)——reduced according to age	R51,359	R45,153

12. Assets Classified as Held for Sale

Company			Group	
2008	*2009*		*2009*	*2008*
R'000	*R'000*		*R'000*	*R'000*
		Noncurrent assets		
—	93,421	Property, plant, and equipment	93,421	—
—	29,197	Bearer biological assets	29,197	—
—	122,618		122,618	—
		Current assets		
—	6,606	Biological assets—crops	6,606	—
—	**129,224**	**Total Assets**	**129,224**	—
—	(10,000)	Total Liabilities	(10,000)	—
—	**119,224**	**Net carrying value at end of the year**	**119,224**	—

Company			Group	
2008	2009		2009	2008
R'000	R'000		R'000	R'000
—	10,000	The company has concluded an agreement of sale with Two-A-Day Group Ltd. for the disposal of 10 hectares ex the Farm Vygeboom No. 86 for R10m. The sale is inclusive of land, packhouse buildings, cold stores, bulk bins, and packhouse equipment	10,000	—
—	13,990	The company has concluded the sale of its Cedars farm to the National Department of Land Affairs for R26,2m. Transfer of the properties was effected on April 3, 2009	13,990	—
—	105,234	The company concluded an agreement of sale with the National Department of Land Affairs for the disposal of its Komatipoort Estate for the sum of R200m. The agreement was dated April 2, 2009, and the sale includes property, plant, and bearer biological assets, but excludes biological assets (crops) and movable assets	105,234	—
—	**129,224**	**Total assets**	**129,224**	—
—	(10,000)	Amount due to Two-A-Day Group Ltd. until registration of transfer of the abovementioned property is effected	(10,000)	—
—	**(10,000)**	**Total liabilities**	**10,000**	—

13. Inventories

Company			Group	
2008	2009		2009	2008
R'000	R'000		R'000	R'000
7,396	10,366	Consumable stores	11,880	8,733
6,945	14,007	Agricultural produce	14,007	6,945
274	314	Merchandise	314	274
14,615	**24,687**		**14,615**	**24,687**
6,945	14,007	The value of inventories included above at fair value.	26,201	15,952
		The increase in agricultural produce is related to the additional inventory ex the Vygeboom deciduous fruit farm purchased during the year		

25. Financial Risk Management

25.5 Commodity Price Risk

In order to hedge prices for the group's local market grain sales, the company has entered into forward agreements with Bester Feeds to sell them certain commodities using fixed and minimum price sales contracts. The fair value of this transaction as at March 31, 2009, was R1 721,000 (2008: Nil).

32 FIRST-TIME ADOPTION OF INTERNATIONAL FINANCIAL REPORTING STANDARDS (IFRS 1)

INTRODUCTION

The International Accounting Standards Board (IASB) standards make it incumbent upon a new convert to IFRS to meet certain conditions set out in IFRS 1, *First-Time Adoption of IFRS,* and follow procedures outlined in this standard for conversion before a new adherent to IFRS can describe its financial statements as IFRS compliant. All first-time adopters of IFRS have to necessarily pass the IFRS 1 test before their financial statements can carry the label "prepared in accordance with IFRS." These conversion provisions and requirements are contained in IFRS 1. This standard is therefore regarded as the gateway to IFRS compliance. In other words, it is a very important first step that any entity (that chooses to convert to IFRS) has to take before it can categorically announce that it has adopted IFRS and complies with IFRS.

With more than 100 countries already having adopted these standards and many more countries (including global players such as China, India, and the United States) expected to convert to IFRS in the coming years, this standard assumes a very important role. In fact, this IASB standard received considerable attention in Europe during 2005 when more than 8,000 listed entities in all countries within the European Union adopted and applied IFRS for the first time in their consolidated financial statements. Many global players outside Europe have also adopted IFRS as their national standards since then. For instance, Australia, Hong Kong, New Zealand, Philippines, and Singapore have adopted national standards that mirror IFRS. In all cases, when entities are preparing to adopt IFRS for the first time, they need to understand and apply the requirements of IFRS 1.

SCOPE

A first-time adopter of IFRS is an entity that makes an explicit and unreserved statement that its financial statements are prepared in accordance with IFRS. IFRS 1 applies to all such entities that present for the first time their financial statements under IFRS. In other words, according to IFRS 1, an entity's first IFRS financial statements are those that are the *first annual financial statements* in which the entity adopts IFRS by an *explicit and unreserved statement* (in those financial statements) *of compliance with IFRS.*

In the past, some companies did not fully comply with all requirements of IFRS and their accounting policies, as outlined in the notes to the financial statements, even referred to such departures from IFRS. On the grounds that they were complying with most aspects of IFRS, that is, they were materially in compliance with IFRS (except to the extent of the departure from IFRS referred to the notes), such entities believed that they did not have to refrain from describing their financial statements as presented in accordance with IFRS. The IASB did not approve of such a practice—for the IASB, in order to describe a set of financial statements as prepared in accordance with IFRS, an entity has to be in full compliance with

IFRS. With the mandatory adoption of IFRS by several countries as their national generally accepted accounting practices (GAAP), entities operating in those jurisdictions have to adopt IFRS fully. If such companies then comply fully with IFRS, according to IFRS 1, the year they switch fully to IFRS is the year in which the companies present the first IFRS financial statements.

According to IFRS 1, the financial statements that an entity presents in the year it first adopts IFRS would qualify as its first IFRS financial statements, if, for instance, the entity presented its most recent previous financial statements

- With a statement of compliance with some, but not all IFRS; or
- Under national GAAP, by including a reconciliation of certain items to IFRS; or
- In conformity with IFRS in all respects; however, these financial statements did not contain an explicit and unreserved statement that they complied with IFRS; or
- Under national GAAP by using some individual IFRS to account for items that are not addressed by its national GAAP; or
- Under national GAAP that are not consistent with IFRS in all respects.

IFRS 1 provides other examples of situations in which an entity's current year's financial statements would qualify as first IFRS financial statements if

- The entity prepared financial statements in the previous period under IFRSs but the financial statements were meant for internal use only and were not made available to the entity's owners or any other external users; or
- The entity prepared a reporting package in the previous period under IFRSs for consolidation purposes without preparing a complete set of financial statements as mandated by IAS 1; or
- The entity did not present financial statements for the previous periods.

KEY TERMS

Date of transition to IFRS. This refers to the beginning of the earliest period for which an entity presents full comparative information under IFRS in its first IFRS financial statements.

Deemed cost. An amount substituted for cost or depreciated cost at a given date. In the subsequent period, depreciation or amortization is based on such deemed cost on the premise that the entity had initially recognized the asset or liability at the given date and that its cost was equal to the deemed cost.

Fair value. The amount for which an asset could be exchanged, or a liability settled, between knowledgeable, willing parties in an arm's length transaction.

First IFRS financial statements. The first annual financial statements in which an entity adopts IFRS by an *explicit and unreserved* statement of compliance with IFRS.

First-time adopter (of IFRS). An entity that presents its first IFRS financial statements in the period in which it does so.

International financial reporting standards (IFRS). Collective name for the standards issued by the IASB and the interpretations issued by the International Financial Reporting Interpretations Committee (IFRIC). They also include all previous standards (IAS) issued by the International Accounting Standards Committee (IASC), the IASB's predecessor standard-setting body, and the interpretations issued by the erstwhile Standards Interpretations Committee (SIC) and adopted by the IASB.

Opening IFRS statement of financial position. The statement of financial position prepared in accordance with the requirements of IFRS 1 as of the date of transition to IFRS.

Previous GAAP. The basis of accounting (say, national standards) that a first-time adopter used immediately prior to IFRS adoption.

Reporting date. The end of the latest period covered by financial statements or by an interim financial report.

EXCEPTIONS TO THE FIRST-TIME ADOPTION RULE

In a case where an entity's financial statements in the previous year contained an explicit and unreserved statement of compliance with IFRS but in fact did not fully comply with all aspects of IFRS, such an entity would *not* be considered a first-time adopter for the purposes of IFRS 1. In other words, disclosed or undisclosed departures from IFRS in previous year's financial statements of an entity that has made an explicit and unreserved statement of IFRS compliance would be treated by IFRS 1 as errors that warrant correction under IAS 8.

IFRS 1 identifies three instances, as examples, under which this standard does not apply. These deemed *exceptions* are

- When an entity presented its financial statements in the previous year that contained an explicit and unreserved statement of compliance with IFRS and auditors qualified their report on those financial statements.
- When an entity in the previous year presented its financial statements under national GAAP along with another set of financial statements that contained an explicit or un-reserved statement of compliance with IFRS and in the current year it discontinues this practice of presenting under its national GAAP and presents only under IFRS.
- When an entity in the previous year presented its financial statements under national GAAP and those financial statements contained an explicit and unreserved statement of IFRS compliance.

Therefore, as mentioned above, even though an explicit and unreserved statement of compliance with IFRS is made in the entity's previous year financial statements, when it did not fully comply with all its aspects, the entity will not be considered a first-time adopter for the purpose of IFRS.

OPENING IFRS STATEMENT OF FINANCIAL POSITION

A first-time adopter of IFRS is required, under this standard, to prepare an opening statement of financial position on the date of transition to IFRS. This opening IFRS statement of financial position serves as the starting point for the entity's accounting under IFRS.

The *date of transition to IFRS* refers to the beginning of the earliest period for which an entity presents full comparative information under IFRS in its first IFRS financial statements. Therefore, the date of transition to IFRS depends on two factors:

- The date of adoption of IFRS; and
- The number of years of comparative information that the entity decides to present along with the financial information of the year of adoption.

Example 1

Excellent Inc. presented its financial statements under its previous GAAP annually as at December 31 each year. The most recent financial statements it presented under its previous GAAP were as of December 31, 2007. Excellent Inc. decided to adopt IFRS as of December 31, 2008, and to present one-year comparative information for the year 2007.

When should Excellent Inc. prepare its opening IFRS balance sheet?

Solution

The beginning of the earliest period for which Excellent Inc. should present full comparative information would be January 1, 2007. In this case, the opening IFRS balance sheet that the entity would need to prepare under IFRS 1 would be as of January 1, 2007.

Alternatively, if Excellent Inc. decided to present two years of comparative information (that is, for 2007 and 2006), then the beginning of the earliest period for which the entity should present full comparative information would be January 1, 2006. In this case, the opening IFRS balance sheet that Excellent Inc. would need to prepare under IFRS 1 would be as of January 1, 2006.

ADJUSTMENTS REQUIRED IN PREPARING THE OPENING IFRS STATEMENT OF FINANCIAL POSITION

In preparing the opening IFRS statement of financial position, an entity should apply these four principles, except in cases where IFRS 1 grants targeted exemptions and prohibits retrospective application:

- *Recognize* **all assets and liabilities whose recognition is required under IFRS but were not recognized under previous GAAP.** Derivative financial instruments are required to be recognized under IAS 39; however, the previous GAAP that the first-time adopter followed may not have recognized them. Therefore, on conversion to IFRS a first-time adopter would need to recognize all such previously unrecognized assets and liabilities.
- *Derecognize* **items as assets or liabilities if IFRS do not permit such recognition.** The previous GAAP (that a first-time adopter followed hitherto) may have allowed a provision for contingencies to be accrued based on the principle of conservatism; however, IFRS would not permit such a provision since it does not meet the requirements of IAS 37 and, therefore, a first-time adopter of IFRS has to derecognize such liabilities on conversion to IFRS.
- *Reclassify* **items that it recognized under previous GAAP as one type of asset, liability, or component of equity, but are a different type of asset, liability, or component of equity under IFRS.** Under the previous GAAP the first-time adopter of IFRS followed before adopting IFRS, mandatorily redeemable preference shares may have been classified as equity; however, under IFRS they should be recognized as liabilities, creating a need to reclassify them according to IAS 39.
- *Measure* **all recognized assets and liabilities according to IFRS.** The previous GAAP followed by a first-time adopter of IFRS might have allowed the entity to measure long-term or noncurrent financial assets (receivables) at undiscounted amounts; however, IAS 39 would measure such assets at discounted amounts to arrive at their fair values, and therefore on conversion to IFRS such assets would need to be measured in accordance with IFRS by discounting them using an appropriate discount rate.

Example 2

Sister Corporation presented its financial statements under the national GAAP of Motherland (country) until 2007. It adopted IFRS from 2008 and is required to prepare an opening IFRS statement of financial position as at January 1, 2007. In preparing the IFRS opening statement of financial position Sister Corporation noted

- Under its previous GAAP, it had deferred advertising costs of $10 million and had classified proposed dividends of $5 million as a current liability.
- It had not made a provision for warranty of $2 million in the financial statements presented under previous GAAP since the concept of constructive obligation was not recognized under its previous GAAP.

- In arriving at the amount to be capitalized as part of costs necessary to bring an asset to its working condition, Sister Corporation had not included professional fees of $3 million paid to architects at the time when the building it currently occupies as its head office was being constructed.

How should Sister Corporation treat these items under IFRS 1?

Solution

In order to prepare the opening IFRS statement of financial position at January 1, 2007, Sister Corporation would need to make these adjustments to its statement of financial position at December 31, 2006, presented under its previous national GAAP:

1. IAS 38 does not allow advertising costs to be deferred whereas Sister Corporations's previous national GAAP allowed this treatment. Thus, $10 million of such deferred costs should be derecognized (expensed) under IFRS.
2. IAS 37 requires recognition of a provision for warranty but Sister Corporations's previous national GAAP did not allow a similar treatment. Thus, a provision for warranty of $2 million should be recognized under IFRS.
3. IAS 10 does not allow proposed dividends to be recognized as a liability; instead, under the latest revision to IAS 10, they should be disclosed in footnotes. Sister Corporations's previous national GAAP allowed proposed dividends to be treated as a current liability. Therefore, proposed dividends of $5 million should be disclosed in footnotes.
4. IAS 16 requires all directly attributable costs of bringing an asset to its working condition for its intended use to be capitalized as part of the carrying cost of property, plant, and equipment. Thus $3 million of the architects' fees should be capitalized as part of (that is, used in the measurement of) property, plant, and equipment under IFRS.

ACCOUNTING POLICIES

IFRS 1 requires that in preparing an opening IFRS statement of financial position, the first-time adopter shall use the same accounting policies as it has used throughout all periods presented in its first IFRS financial statements. Furthermore, the standard stipulates that those accounting policies shall comply with each IFRS effective at the reporting date (explained later) for its first IFRS financial statements, except under certain circumstances wherein the entity claims exemptions from retrospective application of IFRS or is prohibited by IFRS to apply IFRS retrospectively (both concepts discussed later). In other words, a first-time adopter should consistently apply the same accounting policies throughout the periods presented in its first IFRS financial statements, and these accounting policies should be based on the latest version of the IFRS effective at the reporting date. When a new IFRS has been issued on the reporting date but it is not yet effective, but entities are encouraged to apply it before the effective date, then the first-time adopter is permitted, but not required, to apply it.

REPORTING PERIOD

Reporting date for an entity's first IFRS financial statements refers to the end of the latest period covered by

- Either the annual financial statements; or
- Interim financial statements, if any, that the entity presents under IAS 34 for the period covered by its first IFRS financial statements.

Example 3

Brilliant Corporation presents its first annual financial statements under IFRS for the calendar year 2008. The statements include an explicit and unreserved statement of compliance with IFRS in the footnotes. Brilliant Corporation also presents full comparative financial information for the calendar year 2007. In this case, the latest period covered by these annual financial statements would end on December 31, 2008, and the reporting date for the purposes of IFRS 1 is December 31, 2008 (presuming the entity does not present interim financial statements under IAS 34 for the calendar year 2008).

Example 4

Alternatively, if Brilliant Corporation decides to present its first IFRS interim financial statements for the six months ended June 30, 2008, in addition to the first IFRS annual financial statements for the year ended December 31, 2008, there might be an additional reporting date of June 30, 2008; it is dependent on how the interim financial statements are prepared. If the interim financial statements for the six months ended June 30, 2008, were prepared in accordance with IAS 34, then the reporting period for those interim financial statements would be June 30, 2008. If, however, the interim financial statements for the six months ended June 30, 2008, were not prepared in accordance with IAS 34, then the only reporting date would be December 31, 2008.

OPTIONAL EXEMPTIONS FROM OTHER IFRS

Under IFRS 1, paragraph 13, a first-time adopter of IFRS may elect to use exemptions from the general measurement and restatement principles in one or more of these instances:

1. Business combinations (that occurred before the date of transition to IFRS)
2. Fair value or revaluation as deemed cost (e.g., property, plant, and equipment; intangible assets; and investment property measured at fair value or revalued under previous GAAP)
3. Employee benefits
4. Cumulative translation differences
5. Compound financial instruments
6. Investments in subsidiaries, jointly controlled entities, and associates
7. Assets and liabilities of subsidiaries, associates, and joint ventures
8. Designation of previously recognized financial instruments
9. Share-based payment transactions
10. Insurance contracts
11. Decommissioning liabilities included in the cost of property, plant, and equipment
12. Leases
13. Fair value measurement of financial assets or financial liabilities at initial recognition
14. Financial asset or an intangible asset accounted for in accordance with IFRIC 12, *Service Concession Arrangements*
15. Borrowing costs

We'll explain some of these optional exemptions here.

Business Combinations

IFRS 1 allows an exemption to the first-time adopter from retrospective application in the case of business combinations that occurred before the date of transition to IFRS. In other words, under IFRS 1 an entity may elect to use previous GAAP accounting relating to such business combinations. If a first-time adopter restates any business combination, it should restate all business combinations that took place thereafter.

Fair Value or Revaluation as Deemed Cost

An entity may elect to measure an item of property, plant, and equipment at fair value at the date of its transition to IFRS and use the fair value as its deemed cost at that date. A first-time adopter may elect to use a previous GAAP revaluation of an item of property, plant, and equipment at or before the date of transition to IFRS as deemed cost at the date of revaluation if the revaluation amount, at the date of revaluation, was broadly comparable to either its fair value or cost (or depreciated cost under IFRS adjusted for changes in general or specific price index).

These elections are equally available in other circumstances such as for investment property measured under the cost model and intangible assets that meet the recognition criteria and the criteria for revaluation (including existence of an active market).

If a first-time adopter has established a deemed cost under the previous GAAP for any of its assets or liabilities by measuring them at their fair values at a particular date because of an event such as privatization or an initial public offering (IPO), it is allowed to use such an event-driven fair value as deemed cost for IFRS at the date of that measurement.

Employee Benefits

Under IAS 19, an entity may have unrecognized actuarial gains or losses when it has used the corridor approach. Retrospective application of this approach would necessitate splitting the cumulative gains and losses, from inception of the plan until the date of transition to IFRS, into a recognized and an unrecognized portion.

IFRS 1 allows a first-time adopter to elect to recognize all cumulative actuarial gains and losses at the date of transition to IFRS, even if it uses the corridor approach for subsequent actuarial gains or losses. IFRS 1 does, however, mandate that if an election is made for one employee benefit plan, it should apply to all other employee plans.

Cumulative Translation Differences

IAS 21 requires an entity to classify certain translation differences as a separate component of equity and upon disposal of the foreign operation to transfer the cumulative translation difference (CTA) relating to the foreign operation to the statement of comprehensive income as part of the gain or loss on disposal.

A first-time adopter is exempted from this transfer of the CTA that existed on the date of transition to IFRS. If it uses this exemption, the CTA for all foreign operations would be deemed to be zero at the date of transition to IFRS, and the gain or loss on subsequent disposal of any foreign operation should exclude translation differences that arose before the date of transition to IFRS but should include all subsequent translation adjustments.

Compound Financial Instruments

If an entity has issued a compound financial instrument, say, a convertible debenture, IAS 32 requires that at inception, it should split and separate the liability component of the compound financial instrument from equity. If the liability portion is no longer outstanding, retrospective application of IAS 32 would produce this result with respect to the equity portion still outstanding: The part representing cumulative interest accreted to the liability component is in retained earnings and the other portion represents the original equity component.

IFRS 1 exempts a first-time adopter from this split accounting if the liability component is no longer outstanding at the date of transition to IFRS.

Assets and Liabilities of Subsidiaries, Associates, and Joint Ventures

IFRS 1 discusses exemptions under two circumstances.

- If a subsidiary becomes a first-time adopter later than its parent, the subsidiary shall, in its separate (stand-alone) financial statements, measure its assets and liabilities at either (1) the carrying amounts that would be included in its parent's consolidated financial statements, based on its parent's date of transition to IFRS (if no adjustments were made for consolidation procedures and for the effect of the business combination in which the parent acquired the subsidiary), or (2) the carrying amounts required by the rest of this IFRS, based on the subsidiary's date of transition to IFRS.

- If an entity becomes a first-time adopter later than its subsidiary (or associate or joint venture), the entity shall, in its consolidated financial statements, measure the assets and liabilities of the subsidiary (or associate or joint venture) at the same carrying amounts as in the separate (stand-alone) financial statements of the subsidiary (or associate or joint venture), after adjusting for consolidation and equity accounting adjustments and for effects of the business combination in which an entity acquired the subsidiary. In a similar manner, if a parent becomes a first-time adopter for its separate financial statements earlier or later than for its consolidated financial statements, it shall measure its assets and liabilities at the same amounts in both financial statements, except for consolidation adjustments.

MANDATORY EXCEPTIONS
TO RETROSPECTIVE APPLICATION OF OTHER IFRS

IFRS 1, paragraph 26, *prohibits* retrospective application of some aspects of other IFRS relating to:

- *Derecognition of financial assets and financial liabilities.* If a first-time adopter derecognized financial assets or financial liabilities under its previous GAAP in a financial year prior to January 1, 2004, it should not recognize those assets and liabilities under IFRS.

  However, a first-time adopter should recognize all derivatives and other interests retained after derecognition and still existing and consolidate all special-purpose entities (SPEs) that it controls at the date of transition to IFRS (even if SPEs existed before the date of transition to IFRS or hold financial assets or financial liabilities that were derecognized under previous GAAP).

- *Hedge accounting.* A first-time adopter is required, at the date of transition to IFRS, to measure all derivatives at fair value and eliminate all deferred losses and gains on derivatives that were reported under its previous GAAP.

  However, a first-time adopter shall not reflect a hedging relationship in its opening IFRS statement of financial position if it does not qualify for hedge accounting under IAS 39. But if an entity designated a net position as a hedged item under its previous GAAP, it may designate an individual item within that net position as a hedged item under IFRS, provided it does so prior to the date of transition to IFRS. Transitional provisions of IAS 39 apply to hedging relationships of a first-time adopter at the date of transition to IFRS.

- *Estimates.* An entity's estimates under IFRS at the date of transition to IFRS should be consistent with estimates made for the same date under its previous GAAP, unless there is objective evidence that those estimates were in error.

  Any information an entity receives after the date of transition to IFRS about estimates it made under previous GAAP should be treated by it as a nonadjusting event after the reporting date and accorded the treatment prescribed by IAS 10 (i.e., disclosure in footnotes as opposed to adjustment of items in the financial statements).

- *Assets classified as held for sale and discontinued operations.* The exemption in IFRS 1 is not available to first-time adopters with transition dates to IFRS on or after January 1, 2005; they are required to apply IFRS 5 retrospectively. (This exemption thus has no practical implications for entities adopting IFRS now for the first time.)

- *Some aspects of accounting for noncontrolling interests.* The entity is allowed to apply certain requirements of IAS 27 prospectively from the date of transition to IFRS unless the entity elects to apply IFRS 3 and IAS 21 retrospectively, in which case IAS 27 must also be applied retrospectively.

PRESENTATION AND DISCLOSURE

A first-time adopter should present at least one year's worth of comparative information. If an entity also presents historical summaries of selected data for periods prior to the first period it presents full comparative information under IFRS, and IFRS does not require them to be in compliance with IFRS, such data should be labeled prominently as not being in compliance with IFRS and also disclose the nature of the adjustment that would make it IFRS compliant.

A first-time adopter should explain how the transition to IFRS affected its reported financial position, financial performance, and cash flows. In order to comply with the requirement, reconciliation of equity and profit and loss as reported under previous GAAP to IFRS should be included in the entity's first IFRS financial statements.

If an entity uses fair values in its opening IFRS statement of financial position as deemed cost for an item of property, plant, and equipment, an investment property, or an intangible asset, disclosure is required for each line item in the opening IFRS statement of financial position of the aggregate of those fair values and of the aggregate adjustments to the carrying amounts reported under previous GAAP.

If an entity presents an interim financial report under IAS 34 for a part of the period covered by its first IFRS financial statements, in addition to disclosures made under IAS 34, the first-time adopter should also present a reconciliation of the equity and profit and loss under previous GAAP for the comparable interim period to its equity and profit and loss under IFRS.

EXCERPTS FROM PUBLISHED FINANCIAL STATEMENTS

Marks and Spencer Group PLC, Annual Report 2006

Notes to the Financial Statements

1. Accounting Policies

First-Time Adoption of International Financial Reporting Standards

IFRS 1—*First-Time Adoption of International Financial Reporting Standards*, sets out the requirements for the first-time adoption of IFRS. The group is required to establish its IFRS accounting policies for the year to April 1, 2006, and in general apply these retrospectively to determine the IFRS opening balance sheet at its date of transition, April 4, 2004.

The standard permits a number of optional exemptions to this general principle. The group has adopted the following approach to the key exemptions:

- *Business combinations:* The group has chosen not to restate business combinations prior to the transition date;
- *Fair value or revaluation as deemed cost:* The group has adopted a valuation as deemed cost on transition for freehold land and buildings;
- *Employee benefits:* All cumulative actuarial gains and losses, having been recognized in equity under IFRS 17 for U.K. GAAP purposes, have continued to be recognized in equity at the transition date;
- *Financial instruments*: The group has taken the exemption not to restate comparatives for IAS 32, *Financial Instruments: Presentation*, and IAS 39, *Financial Instruments: Recognition and Measurement*. Comparative information for 2005 in the 2006 financial statements in respect of these items is presented on a U.K. GAAP basis as previously reported;
- *Share-based payments:* The group has not adopted the exemption to apply IFRS 2, *Share-Based Payments,* only to awards made after November 7, 2002. Instead, a full retrospec-

tive approach has been followed on all awards granted but not fully vested at the date of transition to maintain consistency across reporting periods; and

* *Cumulative translation differences:* The cumulative translation differences for all foreign operations are deemed to be zero at the date of transition to IFRS.

Marks and Spencer Group PLC

Notes to the Financial Statements

33. Adoption of International Financial Reporting Standards

	Notes**	As at April 2, 2005 £m	As at April 3, 2004 £m
Net assets and equity under U.K. GAAP		521.4	2,454.0
Adjustments (after taxation)			
IFRS 1—*Property Revaluation*	a	376.2	378.5
IFRS 2—*Share Schemes*	b	9.8	6.2
IAS 10—*Dividend Recognition*	c	124.3	160.7
IAS 17—*Leases*			
Treatment of leasehold land	d	(72.4)	(102.4)
Finance leases	e	(1.8)	(1.7)
Lease incentives	f	(21.0)	(17.2)
Fixed rental uplifts	g	(13.5)	(10.3)
IAS 19—*Employee Benefits*	h	(27.2)	(30.7)
IAS 38—*Intangible Assets*			
Software assets	i	13.0	22.7
Goodwill and brands	j	1.3	—
Other		(0.9)	(0.7)
Net assets and equity under IFRS		909.2	2,859.1

	Notes**	Year ended April 2, 2005 £m
Net income under U.K. GAAP		587.0
Adjustments (before taxation)		
IFRS 1—*Property Revaluation*	a	1.1
IFRS 2—*Share Schemes*	b	(23.0)
IAS 17—*Leases*		
Treatment of leasehold land	d	29.9
Finance leases	e	(0.2)
Lease incentives	f	(5.1)
Fixed rental uplifts	g	(4.5)
IAS 19—*Employee Benefits*	h	5.3
IAS 38—*Intangible Assets*		
Software assets	i	1.4
Goodwill and brands	j	0.5
Other		(0.1)
		5.3
Taxation		4.6
Discontinued operations—software assets		(10.7)
Net income under IFRS		586.2

** *Authors' editorial clarification of "Notes" a, b, c, d, e, f, g, h, i, and j are set out below.*

    a. *IFRS 1—Property Revaluation*

       Under U.K. GAAP, property was stated at historical cost, subject to certain properties having been revalued as at March 31, 1988. A property revaluation was prepared on an existing use basis by external valuers DTZ Debenham Tie Leung as at April 2, 2004. The group has elected under IFRS 1 to reflect this valuation, in so far as it relates to freehold land and buildings, as deemed cost on transition at April 4, 2004.

b. *IFRS 2—Share Schemes*

   The group operates a range of share-based incentive schemes. Under U.K. GAAP, where shares (or rights to shares) were awarded to employees, UITF 17 required that the charge to the profit and loss account should be based on the difference between the market value of shares at the date of grant and the exercise price (i.e., an intrinsic value basis) spread over the performance period. Save as You Earn (SAYE) schemes were exempt from this requirement and no charge was made. IFRS 2 requires that all shares or options (including SAYE) awarded to employees as remuneration should be measured at fair value at grant date, using an option pricing model, and charged against profits over the period between grant date and vesting date, being the vesting period. This treatment has been applied to all awards granted but not fully vested at the date of transition.

c. *IAS 10—Events after the Balance Sheet Date*

   Under U.K. GAAP, dividends are recognized in the period to which they relate. IAS 10 requires that dividends declared after the balance sheet date should not be recognized as a liability at that balance sheet date as the liability does not represent a present obligation as defined by IAS 37, **Provisions, Contingent Liabilities, and Contingent Assets.** Accordingly the final dividends for 2003/04 (£160.7m) and 2004/05 (£124.3m) are derecognized in the balance sheets for April 2004 and April 2005 respectively.

d. *IAS 17—Leases—Treatment of Leasehold Land*

   The group previously recognized finance leases under the recognition criteria set out in SSAP 21. IAS 17 requires the land and building elements of property leases to be considered separately, with leasehold land normally being treated as an operating lease. As a consequence, payments made to acquire leasehold land, previously treated as fixed assets, have been recategorized as prepaid leases and amortized over the life of the lease. In addition, the revaluation previously attributed to the land element had been derecognized.

e. *IAS 17—Leases—Finance Leases*

   Also under the provisions of IAS 17, the building elements of certain property leases, classified as operating leases under U.K. GAAP have been reclassified as finance leases. The adjustments are to include the fair value of these leased buildings within fixed assets and to set up the related obligation, net of finance charges, in respect of future periods, within creditors.

f. *IAS 17—Leases—Lease Incentives*

   Under U.K. GAAP, leasehold incentives received on entering into property leases were recognized as deferred income on the balance sheet and amortized to the profit and loss account over the period to the first rent review. Under IAS 17, these incentives have to be amortized over the term of the lease. Consequently, as the term of the lease is longer than the period to the first rent review, amounts previously amortized to the profit and loss account are reinstated on the balance sheet as deferred income and released over the term of the lease.

g. *IAS 17—Leases—Fixed Rental Uplifts*

   The group has a number of leases that contain predetermined, fixed rental uplifts. Under IAS 17, it is necessary to account for these leases such that the predetermined, fixed rental payments are recognized on a straight-line basis over the life of the lease. Under U.K. GAAP, the group accounted for these property lease rentals such that the increases were charged in the year that they arose.

h. *IAS 19—Employee Benefits*

   Previously no provision was made for holiday pay. Under IAS 19, Employee Benefits, the expected cost of compensated short-term absences (for example, holidays) should be recognized when employees render the service that increases their entitlement. As a result, an accrual has been made for holidays earned but not taken.

i. *IAS 38—Software Assets*

   The cost of developing software used to be written off as incurred. Under IAS 38, Intangible Assets, there is a requirement to capitalize internally generated intangible assets provided certain recognition criteria are met. Results have been adjusted to reflect the capitalization and subsequent amortization of costs that meet the criteria. As a result expenses previously charged to the profit and loss account have been brought onto the balance sheet as intangible software assets and amortized over their estimated useful lives.

j.   IAS 38—Goodwill

Goodwill used to be capitalized and amortized over its useful economic life. Under IAS 38, Intangible Assets, there is a requirement to separately identify brands and other intangibles acquired rather than include these as part of goodwill. Intangible assets, other than goodwill, are amortized over their useful lives. Goodwill, which is considered to have an indefinite life, is subject to an annual impairment review. As a result, the goodwill recognized under U.K. GAAP on the acquisition of per una of £125.5m has been split between brand (£80m) and goodwill (£45.5m). The goodwill amortization under U.K. GAAP has been reversed but the brand has been amortized as required under IFRS.

Cash Flow Statement

The cash flows reported under IFRS relate to movements in cash and cash equivalents (defined as short-term highly liquid investments that are readily convertible into known amounts of cash and subject to insignificant risk of changes in value). Under U.K. GAAP, only the movement in cash (defined as cash in hand and deposits repayable on demand, less overdrafts) were reported in the cash flow statement. As a result of adopting IFRS, a £55.7m movement in cash equivalents in the year to April 2, 2005, is now reported as a cash flow movement rather than as movement in financial investment.

34. First-Time Adoption of IAS 32 and IAS 39

The adoption of IAS 32, *Financial Instruments: Presentation*, and IAS 39, *Financial Instruments: Recognition and Measurement*, with effect from April 3, 2005, results in a change in the group's accounting policy for financial instruments. The impact of these standards on the group's opening balance sheet is shown below.

The principal impacts of IAS 32 and IAS 39 on the group's financial statements relate to the recognition of derivative financial instruments at fair value and the reclassification of nonequity B shares as debt. Any derivatives that do not qualify for hedge accounting are held on the balance sheet at fair value with the changes in value reflected through the income statement. The accounting treatment of derivatives that qualify for hedge accounting depends on how they are designated, as follows:

Fair Value Hedges

The group uses interest rate swaps to hedge the exposure to interest rates of its issued debt. Under U.K. GAAP, derivative financial instruments were not recognized at fair value in the balance sheet.

Under IAS 39, derivative financial instruments that meet the fair value hedging requirements are recognized in the balance sheet at fair value with corresponding fair value movements recognized in the income statement. For an effective fair value hedge, the hedged item is adjusted for changes in fair value attributable to the risk being hedged with the corresponding entry in the income statement. To the extent that the designated hedge relationship is fully effective, the amounts in the income statement offset each other. As a result, only the ineffective element of any designated hedging relationship impacts the financing line in the income statement.

Cash Flow Hedges

Under IAS 39, derivative financial instruments that qualify for cash flow hedging are recognized on the balance sheet at fair value with corresponding fair value changes deferred in equity. In addition, the Group hedges the foreign currency exposure on inventory purchases. Under U.K. GAAP, foreign currency derivatives were held off-balance-sheet and these are now treated as cash flow hedges.

The adjustments to the opening balance sheet as at April 3, 2005, are as follows:

	Opening balance sheet under IFRS £m	Effect of IAS 32 and IAS 39 £m	Restated opening position as at April 3, 2005 £m
Noncurrent assets			
Derivative financial instruments	—	71.1	71.1
Deferred tax asset	26.4	1.3	25.9
Current assets			
Derivative financial instruments	—	2.8	2.8
Inventories	338.9	0.4	339.3
Current liabilities			
Derivative financial instruments	—	(1.9)	(1.9)
Borrowings	(478.8)	(66.2)	(545.0)
Trade and other payables	(717.9)	24.7	(693.2)
Noncurrent liabilities			
Derivative financial instruments	—	(12.0)	(12.0)
Borrowings	(1,948.5)	(87.8)	(2,036.3)
Impact on net assets		(67.6)	
Nonequity B shares		(65.7)	
Hedging reserve		(1.6)	
Retained earnings		(0.3)	
Impact on shareholders' funds		(67.6)	

Company Income Statement

	Notes***	52 Weeks ended April 1, 2006 £m	52 Weeks ended April 2, 2005 £m
Operating profit	C2, C3		
Income from shares in group undertakings		205.2	946.7
Interest receivable	C4	—	1.7
Interest payable and similar charges	C4	(2.5)	—
Profit on ordinary activities before taxation		202.7	948.4
Income tax expense		—	(0.5)
Profit for the year attributable to shareholders		202.7	947.9

Company Balance Sheet

	Notes***	2006 £m	2005 £m
Assets			
Noncurrent assets			
Investments in group undertakings	C6	9,046.1	9,046.0
Current assets			
Trade and other receivables		0.4	0.1
Total assets		9,046.5	9,046.1
Liabilities			
Current liabilities			
Amounts owed to group undertakings		2,051.7	2,100.1
Current tax liabilities		—	0.5
Trade and other payables		0.3	0.4
Nonequity B shares		54.7	—
Total liabilities		2,106.7	2,101.0
Net assets		6,939.8	6,945.1
Equity			
Called up share capital—equity		420.6	414.5
Called up share capital—nonequity		—	65.7

	Notes***	2006 £m	2005 £m
Share premium account	C7	162.3	106.6
Capital redemption reserve	C7	2,113.8	2,102.8
Merger reserve	C7	1,397.3	1,397.3
Retained earnings	C7	2,845.8	2,858.2
Total equity		6,939.8	6,945.1

*** *Authors' editorial clarification—Notes C1, C2, C3, C4, C5, C6, C7, C8, and C9 are set out below.*

Company Statement of Changes in Shareholders' Equity

	52 Weeks ended April 1, 2006 £m	52 Weeks ended April 2, 2005 £m
Profit attributable to shareholders	202.7	947.9
Dividends	(204.1)	(239.7)
	(1.4)	708.2
Shares issued on the exercise of share options	61.8	68.4
Purchase of own shares	—	(2,300)
Tender offer expenses	—	(14.9)
Redemption of B shares	—	(19.2)
Change in shareholders' equity	60.4	(1,557.5)
Opening shareholders' equity	6,945.1	8,502.6
First-time adoption of IAS 32 and 39	(65.7)	--
Closing shareholders' equity	6,939.8	6,945.1

Company Cash Flow Statement

	52 Weeks ended April 1, 2006 £m	52 Weeks ended April 2, 2005 £m
Cash flows from operating activities		
Cash generated from operations	(0.4)	0.7
Tax paid	(0.5)	—
Net cash (outflow)/inflow from operating activities	(0.9)	0.7
Cash flows from investing activities		
Dividends received	205.2	946.7
Preacquisition dividend received	—	1,626.7
Investment in subsidiary	(0.1)	(5.5)
Interest received	—	1.7
Net cash inflow from investing activities	205.1	2,569.6
Cash flows from financing activities		
Interest paid	(2.5)	—
Nonequity dividends paid	----	(2.8)
Purchase of own shares	—	(2,300.0)
Redemption of nonequity B shares	(11.0)	(19.2)
Shares issued under employee share schemes	61.8	68.4
Repayment of intercompany loan	(48.4)	(64.9)
Tender offer expenses	—	(14.9)
Equity dividends paid	(204.1)	(236.9)
Net cash outflow from financing activities	(204.2)	(2,570.3)
Net cash inflow from activities		
Cash and cash equivalents at beginning and end of period		

NOTES:

C1 **Accounting Policies** *The company's accounting policies are given in Note 1 of the group financial statements.*

C2 **Employees** *The company had no employees during the current or prior period. Directors received emoluments in respect of their services to the company during the period of £502,000 (last year £401,000). The company did not operate any pension schemes during the current or preceding financial year.*

C3 Auditors' Remuneration *Auditors' remuneration of £0.3m (last year £0.2m) in respect of the company's annual audit has been borne by its subsidiary Marks and Spencer plc.*

C4 Interest

	2006 £m	2005 £m
Bank and other interest receivable		1.7
Dividends on nonequity B shares[1]	(2.5)	
Net interest (payable)/receivable	(2.5)	1.7

[1] *Under IAS 32*—Financial Instruments *dividends on nonequity shares, previously shown as dividends, are now treated as interest payable.*

C5 Dividends

	2006 Per share	2005 Per share	2006 £m	2005 £m
Dividends on equity ordinary shares				
Paid final dividend	7.5p	7.1p	124.3	161.3
Paid interim dividend	4.8p	4.6p	79.8	75.6
	12.3p	11.7p	204.1	236.9
Dividends on nonequity B shares[1]				
Interim dividend		3.36%		1.4
Final dividend		3.78%		1.4
			204.1	239.7

[1] *Under IAS 32*—**Financial Instruments**—*dividends on nonequity shares, previously shown as dividends, are now treated as interest payable.*

In addition, the directors have proposed a final dividend in respect of the financial year ended April 1, 2006, of 9.2p per share mounting to a dividend of £154.8m. It will be paid on July 14, 2006 to shareholders who are on the Register of Member on June 2, 2006. In line with the requirements of IAS 10, **Events after the Reporting Period**, the dividend has not been recognized in these results.

C6 Preacquisition Profits

a. *Investments in Group undertakings*

	2006 £m	2005 £m
Beginning of the year	9,046.0	10,667.2
Additional investment in subsidiary	0.1	5.5
Dividends paid out of preacquisition profits	0	(1,626.7)
End of year	9,046.1	9,046

Shares in group undertakings represent the company's investment in Marks and Spencer plc.

b. *Principal subsidiary undertakings*

The company's principal subsidiary undertakings are set out below. A schedule of interests in all undertakings is filed with the annual return.

	Principal activity	Country of incorporation and operation	Proportions of voting rights and shares held by Company	A subsidiary
Marks and Spencer plc	Retailing	Great Britain	100%	—
Marks and Spencer International Holdings Limited	Holding Company	Great Britain	—	100%
Marks and Spencer (Nederland) BV	Holding Company	The Netherlands	—	100%
Marks and Spencer Finance Inc.	Holding Company	United States	—	100%
Marks and Spencer (Ireland) Limited	Retailing	Republic of Ireland	—	100%
Kings Super Markets Inc	Retailing	United States	—	100%
Marks and Spencer (Asia Pacific) Limited	Retailing	Hong Kong	—	100%

	Principal activity	Country of incorporation and operation	Proportions of voting rights and shares held by	
			Company	A subsidiary
Marks and Spencer Simply Foods Limited	Retailing	Great Britain	—	100%
M.S. Insurance L.P.	Financial Services	Guernsey	—	100%
Marks and Spencer Investments Limited	Finance	Great Britain	—	100%
St. Michael Finance plc	Finance	Great Britain	—	100%
Marks and Spencer Finance plc	Finance	Great Britain	—	100%
Amethyst Leasing (Properties) Limited	Finance	Great Britain	—	100%
Amethyst Finance plc	Finance	Great Britain	—	100%
Marks and Spencer Chester Limited	Property Investment	Great Britain	—	100%
Marks and Spencer SCM Limited	Procurement	Great Britain	—	100%
Per Una Group Limited	Procurement	Great Britain	—	100%
The Zip Project Limited	Procurement	Great Britain	—	100%

The company has taken advantage of the exemption under Section 231(5) of the Companies Act 1985 by providing information only in relation to subsidiary undertakings whose results or financial position, in the opinion of the directors, principally affected the financial statements.

C7   **Statement of Changes in Shareholders' Equity**

Share Capital

	Ordinary shares £m	Nonequity B shares £m	Share premium account £m	Capital Redemption Reserve £m	Merger reserve £m	Profit and loss account £m	Total £m
At April 4, 2004	566.3	84.9	45.2	1,924.8	3,024.0	2,857.4	8,502.6
Profit for the year attributable to shareholders	—	—	—	—	—	947.9	947.9
Dividends	—	—	—	—	—	(239.7)	(239.7)
Shares issued on exercise of share options	7.0	—	61.4	—	—	—	68.4
Redemption of B shares	—	(19.2)	—	19.2	—	(19.2)	(19.2)
Purchase of own shares	(158.8)	—	—	158.8	—	(2,300.0)	(2,300.0)
Tender offer expenses	—	—	—	—	—	(14.9)	(14.9)
Realization of merger reserve for dividends paid out of preacquisition profits	—	—	—	—	(1,626.7)	1,626.7	—
At April 2, 2005	414.5	65.7	106.6	2,102.8	1,397.3	2,858.2	6,945.1
At April 3, 2005	414.5	65.7	106.6	2,102.8	1,397.3	2,858.2	6,945.1
First time adoption of IAS 32 and IAS 39	—	(66.7)	—	—	—	—	(65.7)
	414.5	—	106.6	2,102.8	1,397.3	2,858.2	6,879.4
Profit for the year attributable to shareholders	—	—	—	—	—	202.7	202.7
Dividends	—	—	—	—	—	(204.1)	(204.1)
Shares issued on exercise of share options	6.1	—	55.7	—	—	—	61.8
Redemption of B shares	—	—	—	11.0	—	(11.0)	—
At April 1, 2006	420.6	—	162.3	2,113.8	1,397.3	2,845.8	6,939.8

C8 Related-Party Transactions

During the year, the company has received dividends from Marks and Spencer plc of £205.2m (last year £2,573.4m) and has made loan repayments of £48.4m (last year £64.9m). There were no other related-party transactions.

C9 Adoption of International Financial Reporting Standards

	Notes*	As at April 2, 2005 £m	As at April 3, 2004 £m
Net assets and equity under U.K. GAAP		5,628.5	5,580.0
Adjustments (after taxation)			
IAS 10—**Dividend Recognition**	a	(81.0)	(101.4)
IAS 27—**Consolidated and Separate Financial Statements**	b	1,397.3	3,024.0
Net assets and equity under IFRS		6,945.8	8,502.6

	Notes*	As at April 2, 2006 £m
Net income under U.K. GAAP		2,516.6
Adjustments (after taxation)		
IAS 10—**Dividend Recognition**	a	58.0
IAS 27—**Consolidated and Separate Financial Statements**	b	(1,626.7)
Net income under IFRS		947.9

* Authors' editorial clarification—"Note" a and "Note" b are set out below.

a. **IAS 10, Events after the Reporting Period.** Under U.K. GAAP, dividends are recognized in the period to which they relate. IAS 10 requires that dividends declared after the balance sheet date should not be recognized as a liability at that balance sheet date as the liability does not represent a present obligation as defined by IAS 37, **Provisions, Contingent Liabilities, and Contingent Assets**.

b. **IAS 27, Consolidated and Separate Financial Statements.** Under U.K. GAAP, the Company's investment in Marks and Spencer plc was measured at the nominal value of the shares issued. In accordance with IAS 27, **Consolidated and Separate Financial Statements**, the Company's investment was restated to the fair value of shares issued with a corresponding entry being made to a merger reserve. During the year ended April 2, 2005, dividends of 1,626.7m were paid out of preacquisition profits. Under IAS 27, this payment is treated as a reduction in the cost of investment and a transfer was made between the profit and loss account and merger reserve.

33 SHARE-BASED PAYMENTS (IFRS 2)

INTRODUCTION

Companies may grant shares or share options to its employees, especially to its directors and senior executives, as a form of compensation that is tied to future performance. IFRS 2 deals with the issue of measuring and disclosing share-based compensation and requires that such amounts be recorded as expense over the employees' service years. IFRS 2 covers issues such as share appreciation rights, employee share purchase plans, employee ownership plans or share option plans, among others. The scope of IFRS 2, however, goes beyond shares or options issued to employees in exchange for services, to include all exchanges of shares or options for goods or services received from nonemployees. Goods include inventories; consumables; property, plant, and equipment; intangible assets; and other nonfinancial assets. An example of an exchange of options for services would be to issue share options in exchange for specialized consulting services received by the company.

SCOPE

IFRS 2 addresses both equity-settled share-based payment transactions and cash-settled share-based payment transactions. Equity-settled share-based payment transactions are transactions in which the entity receives goods and services in exchange for equity instruments it has issued. Cash-settled share-based payments are transactions in which the entity acquires goods or services by incurring liabilities to the suppliers of these goods and services for amounts that are based on the value of the entity's shares.

IFRS 2 does not cover share-based payments as part of a business combination. Also, it does not cover acquisition of treasury shares or the issuance of shares in exchange for financial instruments, which are addressed by IAS 32 or IAS 39.

KEY TERMS

Share-based payment transaction. A transaction in which the entity acquires goods or services by incurring a liability to transfer cash or other assets to the provider of those goods or services for amounts that are tied to the value of the entity's own shares

Vesting. One's right to receive cash, other assets, or equity instrument when preexistence conditions are met, such as length of employment or reaching income or share price targets.

ACCOUNTING FOR EQUITY-SETTLED SHARE-BASED PAYMENTS

IFRS 2 adopts the fair-value method in accounting for shares or options granted to its employees. Under this approach, companies measure the value of the share options on the date of the grant, instead of the date of the exercise. Measuring the value of an option on the date of the grant is a complicated process that requires a specialized option-pricing model. One such widely used model is the Black-Scholes model, although other models may be used. Once the value of the share option is determined, IFRS 2 requires that the option value be expensed over the service period the employees are expected to work.

Vesting

Often granting share options is conditional upon certain vesting conditions. For example, the employee is expected to stay in employment a certain number of years and/or achieve specific growth in profit or the entity's share price. Such conditions will require the company to anticipate the likelihood that employees will meet the vesting conditions and, thus, the amount of expenses recorded in the books should reflect the vesting conditions. Initial estimated compensation expenses should be adjusted periodically and by the end of the vesting period the final expense recorded should equal the value of the share options that are ultimately vested.

Example 1

AUS, Inc. granted 100 share options to each of its 300 employees in year 1. Employees need to work at least three years to fully vest (entitle) in receiving these options. AUS, Inc. used the Black-Scholes model to price its options on the date of the grant. The value of each of the options granted using the pricing model is $10. From past experience, AUS, Inc., on average, retains 75% of its employees for three years. What is the total option-compensation expense for each of the three years?

Using these assumptions the fair value of the share options granted will be calculated as follows:

$$100 \text{ options} \times 300 \text{ employees} \times 75\% \times \$10 = \$225,000$$

In addition, we should take into consideration the number of employees who will leave the company over the next three years. AUS Inc. estimates that 25 percent of its employees will leave evenly over the three-year period. Thus, the number of service years to be provided by the vested employees by the end of the third year is computed as follows:

Total service years: 300 employees × 3 years =	900
Less: Average years for leaving employees 25% × 300 × 3/2 =	(113)
Number of estimated service years =	787

Thus the average estimated fair value of each service year is $225,000/787 = $285.90

Let us assume that AUS Inc. receives 310 service years in year 1, 280 in year 2, and 197 in year 3. Thus, the amount of expense to be recorded will be as follows:

Year	Service years	Value per option ($)	Option expense
Year 1	310	$285.90	$88,620
Year 2	280	285.90	80,051
Year 3	197	285.90	56,321
Total	787		$225,000

ACCOUNTING FOR CASH-SETTLED TRANSACTIONS

IFRS 2 also addresses transactions that include settlement of liabilities for cash, but the amount of these liabilities are tied to the company's stock prices. The best example is when the company grants its employees share appreciation rights (SAR) as part of their compensation package, whereby the employees will become entitled to a future cash payment (rather than an equity instrument), based on the increase in the entity's share price from a specified level over a specified period of time. The entity is required by IFRS 2 to record the services received and a liability to pay for these services as the employee provides these services.

The liability shall be measured initially and at the end of each reporting period until settled at the fair value of the SAR by applying an option pricing model taking into account the terms and conditions on which the SAR were granted, and the extent the employees have rendered service to date. In many ways, cash-settled transactions are very similar to share-based compensation. The key difference is that one is settled by payment of cash while the other by issuing shares.

Example 2

AUS, Inc. on January 1, 2009, granted stock appreciation rights (SAR) valued at $100,000 on that date using an option pricing model. The SAR will vest in three years. By the end of 2009, the value of the SAR went up to $120,000. In addition, assume that the fair value of the SAR went down to $115,000 in 2010 and to $110,000 in 2011.

Required

Compute the annual SAR compensation expense for each of the three years cited in Example 1.

Here are the computations of the compensation expense for each of the three years.

Date	*SAR fair value ($)*	*Percentage accrued (%)*	*Cumulative compensation accrued ($)*	*Annual expense ($)*
2009	$120,000	33.34	$40,000	$40,000
2010	115,000	66.67	76,670	36,670
2011	110,000	100	110,000	33,330
Total				$110,000

As shown in these calculations, the compensation expenses and liabilities related to SAR will be continuously remeasured each year until employees choose to exercise their options and the cash liability is paid.

ACCOUNTING FOR TRANSACTIONS THAT CAN BE SETTLED THROUGH CASH OR ISSUANCE OF SHARES

In some situations, the entity may issue SAR that can be settled by either payment of cash or by issuing shares. The party that decides on the format of the settlement may be the company or the holder of the SAR. If the holder of the SAR has the option to choose, then the company has effectively issued a compound financial instrument and the two components need to be separated.

DISCLOSURE

IFRS 2 requires extensive disclosure of share-based payments. Three main categories of disclosures are required:

1. Disclosure about the nature and extent of share-based payment arrangements that existed during the reporting period. This disclosure should at least include

    a. A description of types of share-based payment plans including the general terms and conditions of the plans, vesting conditions, and method of settlement (e.g., cash or equity).
    b. The number of options outstanding at the beginning and end of the year, and the number of options that are granted, forfeited, exercised, and expired during the year.
    c. The weighted-average share price at the date of exercise.
    d. For share options outstanding at the end of the period, the range of exercise prices and weighted-average remaining contractual life.

2. Information about how the value of the goods or services received or the value of the option price is determined. Such disclosure should include description of the option-pricing model used.
3. Sufficient disclosure about the effect of share-based payment transactions on the entity's net profit or loss for the period.

EXCERPTS FROM PUBLISHED FINANCIAL STATEMENTS

Ahold, Annual Report 2008

Notes to the Consolidated Financial Statements

3.   Significant Accounting Policies

Share-Based Compensation

The grant date fair value of share-based compensation plans is expensed, with a corresponding increase in equity, on a straight-line basis over the vesting periods of the grants. The cumulative expense recognized at each balance sheet date reflects the extent to which the vesting period has expired and the company's best estimate of the number of options or shares that will eventually vest. No expense is recognized for awards that do not ultimately vest, except for awards where vesting is conditional upon a market condition (e.g., total shareholder return). Those are treated as vested irrespective of whether the market condition is ultimately satisfied, provided that all nonmarket conditions (e.g., continued employment) are satisfied.

31.   Share-Based Compensation

In 2008, Ahold's share-based compensation program consisted of a conditional share grant program (Global Reward Opportunity "GRO"). This program, introduced in 2006, replaced the company's share option plans. In addition, conditional shares are incidentally granted to employees outside the GRO program as part of their remuneration. In principle, plan rules will not be altered during the term of the plans.

Total share-based compensation expenses were as follows:

in € million	2008	2007
GRO program	24	17
Other conditional shares	7	6
Share option plans	1	7
Total share-based compensation expenses	**32**	30

Ahold's share-based compensation programs are equity settled. At December 28, 2008, the company held 15,202,890 of its own shares for delivery under share-based compensation programs (December 30, 2007: 19,965,205). The grant date fair value of the shares granted under the GRO program in 2008 was EUR 45 million, of which EUR 4 million related to Corporate Executive Board members. This fair value is expensed over the vesting period of the grants. For the share-based compensation expenses allocable to the individual Corporate Executive Board members, see Note 30.

GRO Program

Main Characteristics

Under the GRO program, Ahold shares are granted through a mid-term (three-year) and a long-term (five-year) program. The number of conditional shares to be granted depends on the at-target value, the annual incentive multiplier of the preceding year and the average share price for six months preceding the date of the grant. The shares are granted on the day after the Annual General Meeting of Shareholders and vest on the day after the publication of Ahold's full-year results in the third year (mid-term component) or fifth year (long-term component) after the grant, provided the participant is still employed by Ahold. Shares granted to Corporate Executive Board members vest after three years (mid-term component) or five years (long-term component), subject to continued employment. Corporate Executive Board members are not allowed to sell their shares within a period of five years from the grant date, except to finance tax due at the date of vesting. For participants other than the Corporate Executive Board members, the midterm component of the program contains a matching feature. For every five shares a participant holds for an additional two years after the vesting date, the participant will receive one additional share.

The conditional shares granted through the long-term component are subject to a performance condition. The number of shares that will ultimately vest depends on Ahold's performance compared to 11 other retail companies (refer to Remuneration section of this Annual Report for the composition of the peer group), measured over a five-year period using the Total Shareholder Return (TSR, share price growth and dividends). The table that follow indicates the percentage of conditional shares that could vest based on the ranking of Ahold within the peer group:

Rank	*1*	*2*	*3*	*4*	*5*	*6*	*7*	*8*	*9*	*10*	*11*	*12*
Corporate Executive Board	150%	130%	110%	90%	70%	50%	25%	0%	0%	0%	0%	0%
Other participants	150%	135%	120%	105%	90%	75%	60%	45%	30%	15%	7.5%	0%

As of the end of 2008, Ahold held the third position with respect to the 2006 share grant, the fourth position for the 2007 share grant and the fifth position for the 2008 share grant. These positions are not an indication of Ahold's final ranking at the end of the performance periods, nor do they provide any information related to vesting of shares. Upon termination of employment due to retirement, disability or death, the same vesting conditions apply.

Upon termination of employment without cause (e.g., restructuring or divestment), a pro rata part of the granted shares will vest on the date of termination of employment

The following table summarizes the status of the GRO program during 2008 for the individual Corporate Executive Board members and for all other employees in the aggregate (with each year's grant consisting of an equal number of shares granted under the three-year and five-year program).

Description of Grants	*Outstanding at beginning of 2008*[1]	*Granted*[1]	*Settled*[2]	*Forfeited*	*Outstanding at the end of 2008*[1]
J.F. Rishton					
2006 grant	69,848	—	—	—	69,848
2007 grant	70,536	—	—	—	70,536
2008 grant	—	159,284	—	—	159,284
K.A. Ross					
2006 grant	12,386	—	—	—	12,386
2007 grant	22,398	—	—	—	22,398
2008 grant	—	84,278	—	—	84,278
P.N. Wakkie					
2006 grant	59,974	—	—	—	59,974
2007 grant	48,852	—	—	—	48,852
2008 grant	—	101,134	—	—	101,134
A.D. Boer					
2006 grant	57,926	—	—	—	57,926
2007 grant	79,558	—	—	—	79,558
2008 grant	—	105,348	—	—	105,348
Other employees					
2006 grant	5,079,536	—	142,294	242,238	4,695,004
2007 grant	3,722,980	—	47,392	261,354	3,414,234
2008 grant	—	4,589,770	11,821	194,231	4,383,718
Total number of shares	9,223,594	5,039,814	201,507	697,823	13,364,078

[1] *Represents number of shares originally granted.*

[2] *Includes increases/(decreases) based on TSR performance.*

Valuation Model and Input Variables

The weighted-average fair value of the conditional shares granted in 2008 amounted to EUR 9.00 and EUR 8.93 per share for the three-year and five-year component, respectively (2007: EUR 9.28 and EUR 9.05, respectively). The fair value of the three-year component is based on the share price on the grant date, reduced by the present value of dividends expected to be paid during the vesting period. The fair value of the five-year component is determined using a Monte Carlo simulation model. The most important assumptions used in the valuation were as follows:

	2008		*2007*	
Weighted-average assumptions				
Risk-free interest rate (percent)	**4.1**		4.2	
Volatility		**30.7**		32.4
Assumed annual forfeitures		**6.0**		6.0
Assumed dividend yield		**2.1**		1.3

Expected volatility has been determined as the average of the implied volatility and the historical volatility, whereby the extraordinarily volatile month after February 24, 2003 has been excluded.

Other Conditional Shares

In addition to the shares granted under the GRO program, Ahold granted an at-target number of 950,000 conditional shares in 2007. The fair value per share, determined in the same manner as the three-year GRO shares, was EUR 9.44. The shares vested at the end of 2008, after two years of continued employment. Half of these shares were subject to a performance condition. The final number of performance shares will be determined in 2009, based on the average annual incentive multiplier for 2007 and 2008.

Share Option Plans

In 2005, Ahold had one global share option plan with a uniform set of rules and conditions (the "2005 Plan") for all participants, except members of the Corporate Executive Board. The term of the 2005 share options is eight years and the exercise of these options is conditional upon continued employment during a three-year vesting period. Upon termination of employment, share options that have vested can be exercised during four weeks after termination and are forfeited thereafter, while share options that have not vested will be forfeited immediately. In 2005, share options were granted on the first Monday in April and the exercise price of each share option equaled the closing market price of Ahold's common shares on the last trading day prior to the grant date. A separate plan applies to members of the Corporate Executive Board. The share option grant made in 2005 to members of the Corporate Executive Board had a five- and ten-year term and was subject to a performance criterion at vesting, being the average economic value added improvement versus targeted improvement over the three financial years prior to vesting. The number of options that could vest was 80% to 120% of the targeted number of options depending on performance against the vesting criteria (with zero options vesting if performance against the vesting criteria would have been below 80% of target). In 2008, the final vesting percentage was determined at 96%. Other characteristics of the plan are the same for the year 2005.

Plan Described Above

Until January 2, 2005, Ahold had three share option plans (the Dutch, U.S., and International Share Option Plans—collectively the "Plans"). Under these Plans, participants were granted share options with either a five- or ten-year term, generally exercisable after three years. Share options were granted on the first business day of each year and the exercise price of each share option equaled the closing market price of Ahold's common shares on the last trading day prior to the grant date. Upon termination of employment, all share options granted under the Dutch Plan can be exercised within four weeks after termination and are forfeited thereafter. Share options granted under the U.S. and International Plans can, upon termination of employment, be exercised within four weeks after termination provided they have vested and are forfeited thereafter, while share options that have not vested will be forfeited immediately. Under all option plans, upon termination of employment due to retirement, disability or death, all share options are exercisable during their relevant exercise periods.

The following table summarizes the status of the share option plans during 2008 for the individual Corporate Executive Board members and for all other employees in the aggregate. After the introduction of GRO, options were discontinued as a remuneration component:

Description of grants	Outstanding at beginning of 2008	Granted	Exercised	Forfeited	Expired	Outstanding at the end of 2008	Exercise price	Expiration date
J.F. Rishton	—	—	—	—	—	—	—	—
K.A. Ross								
5-year 2004 grant	9,000	—	9,000	—	—	—	5.83	12/28/2008
8-year 2005 grant	33,150	—	—	—	—	33,150	6.36	04/03/2013
10-year 2002 grant	833	—	—	—	—	833	32.68	12/30/2011
10-year 2003 grant	9,000	—	—	—	—	9,000	11.65	12/29/2012
10-year 2004 grant	9,000	—	—	—	—	9,000	5.83	12/28/2013
P.N. Wakkie								
5-year 2005 grant[1]	45,000	—	—	9,000	—	36,000	6.36	04/03/2010
10-year 2005 grant[1]	45,000	—	—	9,000	—	36,000	6.36	04/03/2015
A.D. Boer								
5-year 2004 grant	21,000	—	21,000	—	—	—	5.83	12/28/2008
8-year 2005 grant	70,200	—	—		—	70,200	6.36	04/03/2013
10-year 2001 grant	12,000	—	—		—	12,000	34.36	12/31/2010
10-year 2002 grant	12,000	—	—	—	—	12,000	32.68	12/31/2011
10-year 2003 grant	21,000	—	—	—	—	21,000	11.65	12/29/2012
10-year 2004 grant	21,000	—	—	—	—	21,000	5.83	12/28/2013
Subtotal Corporate Executive Board members	308,183	—	30,000	18,000	—	260,183	—	
Weighted-average-exercise price	8.96	—	5.83	6.36	—	9.50	—	
Other employees								
5-year	2,202,714	—	1,891,119	50,268	73,227	188,100	6.40	
8-year	5,116,888	—	1,499,270	126,734	—	3,490,884	6.36	
10-year	6,833,707	—	295,291	207,680	4,619	6,326,117	19.18	
Subtotal other employees	14,153,309	—	3,685,680	384,682	77,846	10,005,101	14.47	
Total options	14,461,492	—	3,715,680	402,682	77,846	10,265,284	14.34	
Weighted-average exercise price	12.14	—	5.96	11.87	6.99	14.34	—	
Weighted-average share price at date	—	—	9.06	—	—	—	—	

[1] *The options granted to members of the Corporate Executive Board in 2005 were subject to a performance criterion at vesting, as described under the Share option plans in this note 31. The number of options outstanding at the beginning of 2008 represented the maximum (120% -level), whereas the number outstanding at the end of 2008 represents the number that ultimately vested in 2008.*

The following table summarizes information about the total number of outstanding share options at December 28, 2008:

	Number outstanding at December 28, 2008	*Weighted-average exercise price*	*Weighted-average remaining contractual years*	*Number exercisable at December 28, 2008*	*Weighted-average exercise price*	*Weighted-average remaining contractual years*
Exercise price (range)						
5.20–6.57	5,554,119	6.16	4.39	5,419,119	6.15	4.38
11.65	1,902,997	11.35	4.00	1,902,997	11.65	4.00
25.38–34.36	2,808,168	32.35	1.91	2,808,168	32.35	1.91
Total	**10,265,284**			**10,130,284**		

Holcim, Annual Report 2008

Consolidated Financial Statements

Accounting Policies

Adoption of Revised and New International Financial Reporting Standards and New Interpretations

In 2009, Group Holcim will adopt the following new and revised standards and interpretations relevant to the group:

IAS 1 (revised), *Presentation of Financial Statements*
IAS 23 (amended), *Borrowing Costs*
IFRS 2 (amended), *Share-Based Payments*
IFRS 8, *Operating Segments*
IFRIC 16, *Hedges of a Net Investment in a Foreign Operation*

Improvements to IFRSs Clarifications of existing IFRSs

The revised IAS 1 and the new IFRS 8 are presentation and disclosure related only. The amendment to IAS 23 will have no impact on the consolidated financial statements as the accounting policy already specify capitalization of attributable interest costs. The amendment to IFRS 2 clarifies that vesting conditions are either service conditions or performance conditions. IFRIC 16 provides guidance in respect of hedges of foreign currency risks on net investments in foreign operations. The amendments will have no material impact on the group. The improvements to IFRS relate largely to clarification issues only. Therefore, the effect of applying these amendments will have no material impact on the group's financial statements.

33. Share Compensation Plans

Employee Share Purchase Plan

Holcim has an employee share ownership plan for all employees of Swiss subsidiaries and some executives from group companies. This plan entitles employees to acquire a limited amount of discounted Holcim shares generally at 70% of the market value based on the prior-month average share price. The shares cannot be sold for a period of two years from the date of purchase. The total expense arising from this plan amounted to CHF 2.4 million in 2008 (2007: 1.5).

Senior Management Share Plans

Part of the variable, performance-related compensation of senior management is paid in Holcim shares, which are granted based on the market price of the share in the following year. The shares cannot be sold by the employee for the next five years. The total expense arising from these share plans amounted to CHF 2.7 million in 2008 (2007: 6.5). No dilution of Holcim shares occurs as all shares granted under these plans are purchased from the market.

Share Option Plans

Two types of share options are granted to senior management of the Holcim Group. In both cases, each option represents the right to acquire one registered share of Holcim Ltd at the market price of the shares at the date of grant (see explanations on pages __ and __).

The contractual term of the first type of option plan is eight years. The options cannot be exercised for the first three years and vest immediately as there are no vesting conditions attached to them.

The contractual term of the second type of option plan is twelve years and the options have a vesting period (service related only) of nine years from the date of grant.

The group has no legal or constructive obligation to repurchase or settle the options in cash.

Movements in the number of share options outstanding and their related weighted-average exercise prices are as follows:

	Weighted-Average Exercise Price[1]	Number[1] 2008	Number[1] 2007
January 1	CHF 75.61	**537,944**	**544,462**
Granted and vested (individual component of variable compensation)	CHF 106.10	71,083	49,674
Granted and vested (single allotment)	CHF 68.91	67,100	0
Forfeited		0	0
Exercised		0	(56,192)
Lapsed		**0**	**0**
December 31	**CHF 78.15**	**676,127**	**537,944**
Of which exercisable at the end of the year		161,297	89,874

[1] *Adjusted to reflect former share splits and/or capital increases.*

Share options outstanding at the end of the year have the following expiry dates and give the right to acquire one registered share of Holcim Ltd. at the exercise prices listed.

Option Grant Date	Expiry Date	Exercise Price[1]	Number[1] 2008	Number[1] 2007
2002	2014	CHF 68.91	201,300	201,300
2003	2012	CHF 35.61	48,775	48,775
2003	**2015**	CHF 68.91[2]	33,550	33,550
2004	2013	CHF 65.11	41,099	41,099
2004	2016	CHF 68.91[2]	**33.550**	**33.550**
2005	2014	CHF 76.30	71,423	71,423
2006	2014	CHF 102.45	58,573	58,573
2007	2015	CHF 127.10	49,674	49,674
2008	2016	CHF 106.10	71,083	—
2008	2020	CHF 68.91[2]	67,100	—
Total			**676,127**	**537,944**

[1] *Adjusted to reflect former share splits and/or capital increases.*
[2] *Valued according to the single allocation in 2002.*

In 2008, no options have been exercised.

Options exercised in 2007 resulted in 56,192 shares being issued at a weighted average exercise price of CHF 66.55. The weighted-average share price related to the options exercised during the year 2007 was CHF 125.95.

The fair value of options granted for the year 2008 using the Black-Scholes valuation model is CHF 5.20 (2007: 24.76). The significant inputs into the model are the share price and an exercise price at the date of grant, an expected volatility of 26% (2007: 25), an expected option life of six years, a dividend yield of 5% (2007: 1.9), and an annual risk-free interest rate of 1.2% (2007: 2.6). Expected volatility was determined by calculating the historical volatility of the group's share price over the respective vesting period.

All shares granted under these plans are either purchased from the market or derive from treasury shares. The total personnel expense arising from the grant of options based on the individual component of variable compensation amounted to CHF 2 million in 2008 (2007: 1.8). In

2008, options have been allocated to two new Executive Committee members. In 2007, there was no allocation of options upon appointment of members of the Executive Committee.

Due to trade restrictions in 2008, the expiry date of the annual options granted for the years 2003 to 2005 has been extended by one year.

35. Details of Shares

Number of Registered Shares December 31	*2008*	*2007*
Total outstanding shares	**258,454,029**	**262,917,241**
Treasury shares		
Shares reserved for convertible bonds	4,441,733	**0**
Shares reserved for call options	676,127	537,944
Unreserved treasury shares	14,201	130,905
Total treasury shares	**5,132,061**	**668,849**
Total issued shares	**263,586,090**	**263,586,090**
Shares out of conditional share capital		
Reserved for convertible bonds	1,422,350	1,422,350
Unreserved	0	0
Total shares out of conditional share capital	**1,422,350**	**1,422,350**
Total shares	**265,008,440**	**265,008,440**

The par value per share is CHF 2. The share capital amounts to nominal CHF 527 million (2007: 527) and the acquisition price of treasury shares amounts to CHF 401 million (2007: 67).

During the year 2007, USD convertible bonds (0%, 2002–2017) with a nominal value of USD 130 million and CHF convertible bonds (1%, 2002–2012) with a nominal value of CHF 600 million were converted into 8,237,465 newly issued, fully paid-in registered shares of Holcim Ltd. with a par value per share of CHF 2 (through the use of conditional share capital). As a result, the share capital increased by CHF 16,474,930 to CHF 527,172,180. The related increase in capital surplus amounted to CHF 792 million.

As most of both USD convertible bonds and CHF convertible bonds have been converted, Holcim exercised its right to redeem the remaining outstanding bonds.

34 BUSINESS COMBINATIONS (IFRS 3)

INTRODUCTION

Mergers and acquisitions (M&A) are common examples of business combinations. During times when markets are booming and good economic conditions prevail, M&A activity thrives and a great deal of cross-border M&A activity is also witnessed in the corporate world. In order to ensure that business combinations are accounted for and reported in a consistent manner, it is essential that comprehensive guidance be provided on this important subject.

The objective of IFRS 3 is to improve the relevance, reliability, and comparability of the information that a reporting entity provides in its financial statements about a business combination and its effects. To that end, IFRS 3 lays down principles and requirements for how the acquirer

1. Recognizes and measures in its financial statements the identifiable assets acquired, the liabilities assumed and any noncontrolling interest in the acquiree;
2. Recognizes and measures the goodwill acquired in the business combination or a gain from a bargain purchase; and
3. Determines what information to disclose to enable users of the financial statements to evaluate the nature and financial effects of the business combination.

SCOPE

The standard applies to a transaction or other event that meets the definition of a *business combination*. It is essential to determine whether a transaction is a business combination or a transaction to acquire a group of assets.

A *business* is defined in IFRS 3, Appendix A, as "an integrated set of activities and assets that is capable of being conducted and managed for the purpose of providing a return in the form of dividends, lower costs or other economic benefits directly to investors or other owners, members or participants." Therefore, by implication, if a transaction represents an acquisition of a group of assets, as opposed to acquisition of a business, it is not a business combination and is therefore not within the scope of IFRS 3.

The application guidance to IFRS 3 is contained in Appendix B which, amongst other things, explains that there are three key elements of a business, namely, (1) inputs, and (2) processes applied to inputs, that together can be used to create (3) outputs. It further explains these elements and clarifies that *inputs* are economic resources including employees, materials and noncurrent assets; *processes* are systems, standards, protocols, conventions or rules that when applied to inputs create outputs; and *outputs* provide a return in the form of dividend, lower costs, or other economic benefits to stakeholders. Appendix B clarifies that "to be capable of being conducted and managed for the purposes defined, an integrated set of activities and assets requires two essential elements, namely, 'inputs' and 'processes.'" In other words, according to Appendix B, while a business usually has outputs, they are not required for an integrated set to qualify as a business. For example, a development stage enterprise (i.e., an entity that is in a very early stage of development, wherein principal business activities have not commenced yet), which does not have outputs, would qualify as a business.

The following transactions are *scoped out* of IFRS 3:

1. The formation of a joint venture.
2. The acquisition of an asset or a group of assets that does not constitute a business.
3. A combination of entities or businesses under common control.

Example 1

> X Ltd and Y Corp. are subsidiaries of Excellent Inc.
>
> Excellent Inc. transfers the shares held by it in X Ltd to Y Corp.
>
> Y Corp. issues additional equity shares to Excellent Inc. in exchange for the shares of X Ltd originally held by Excellent Inc. and now transferred to Y Corp. by Excellent Inc.
>
> This is a *common control transaction* since both X Ltd and Y Corp. are under the common control of Excellent Inc. Therefore, this transaction is outside the scope of IFRS 3.

KEY TERMS

Acquiree. The business or businesses that the acquirer obtains control of in a business combination.

Acquirer. The entity that obtains control of the *acquiree*.

Acquisition date. The date on which the *acquirer* obtains control of the *acquiree*.

Business. An integrated set of activities and assets that is capable of being conducted and managed for the purpose of providing a return in the form of dividends, lower costs or other economic benefits directly to investors or other owners, members, or participants.

Business combination. A transaction or other events in which an *acquirer* obtains control of one or more *businesses*. Transactions sometimes referred to as *true mergers* or *mergers of equals* are also *business combinations* as that term is used in this IFRS.

Contingent consideration. Usually, an obligation of the acquirer to transfer additional assets or equity interests to the former owner of an acquire as part of the exchange for control of the acquire if specified future events occur or conditions are met. However, contingent consideration also may give the acquirer the right to the return of previously transferred consideration if specified conditions are met.

Control. The power to govern the financial and operating policies of an entity so as to obtain benefit from its investor.

Equity interests. For the purposes of this IFRS, *equity interests* is used broadly to mean ownership interest of the investor-owned entities and owner, member or participants interests of *mutual entities*.

Fair value. The amount for which an asset could be exchanged, or a liability settled between knowledgeable, willing parties in an arm's-length transaction.

Goodwill. An asset representing the future economic benefits arising from other assets acquired in a business combination that are not individually identified and separately recognized.

Identifiable. An asset is *identifiable* if it either

1. Is separable, that is, capable of being separated or divided from the entity and sold, transferred, licensed, rented, or exchanged, either individually or together with a related contract, identifiable asset or liability, regardless of whether the entity intends to do so; or
2. Arises from contractual or other legal rights, regardless of whether those rights are transferable or separable from the entity or from other rights and obligations.

Intangible asset. An identifiable nonmonetary asset without physical substance.

Mutual entity. An entity, other than an investor-owned entity, that provides dividends, lower costs, or other economic benefits directly to its *owner*, members, or participants. For example, a mutual insurance company, a credit union and a cooperative entity are all mutual entities.

Noncontrolling interest. The equity in a subsidiary not attributable, directly or indirectly, to a parent.

INDENTIFYING A BUSINESS COMBINATION

An acquirer may obtain control of an acquiree in a variety of ways. The following are examples of the ways in which an acquirer may obtain control of an acquiree:

- By transferring cash, cash equivalents or other assets
- By incurring liabilities
- By issuing equity interests
- By providing more than one type of consideration
- Without transferring consideration (e.g., by contract alone)

Business combinations can be structured in different ways, which include

- One or more businesses become subsidiaries of an acquirer
- Net assets of one or more businesses are legally merged into the acquirer
- One combining entity transfers its net assets to another combining entity
- Owner of the combining entity transfers their equity interests to another combining entity
- Roll-up transaction in which all of the combining entities transfer their net assets
- Owners of those entities transfer their equity interests to a newly formed entity
- A group of former owners of one of the combining entities obtains control of the combined entity

Application of acquisition accounting requires

- Identifying the acquirer;
- Determining the acquisition date;
- Recognizing and measuring the identifiable assets acquired and liabilities assumed and any noncontrolling interest in the acquirer; and
- Recognizing and measuring goodwill, including any gain from bargain purchase.

Indentifying the Acquirer

The *acquirer* is the entity that obtains control over the business of the acquiree. *Control* should be tested by applying IAS 27, *Consolidated and Separate Financial Statements*. Control is the power to govern financial and operating activities so as to obtain benefits from activities.

The following characteristics signify control:

- Owning more than half of the voting power directly or indirectly through subsidiaries
- Power over more than half of the voting rights by virtue of an agreement with other investors
- Power to govern the financial and operating policies of the entity under a statute or an agreement
- Power to appoint or remove the majority of the members of the board, or governing body, of the entity
- Power to cast majority votes in a meeting of the board or governing body of the entity

While evaluating control, the existence of potential voting rights arising out of share warrants, share call options, debt or preferred stock that are convertible into ordinary shares or other similar instruments, should be considered.

If it is not possible to identify the acquirer applying the principle of control as stated in IAS 27, then the following criteria are applied.

- Identify the entity that transferred cash in a cash-transferred acquisition.
- Identify which entity has issued equity in an equity-based acquisition.
- If the acquirer is the combining entity, determine which group of owners receives or retains the largest portion of the voting rights.
- When there is no group of shareholders holding majority voting rights, determine which group holds the largest minority voting rights.
- If the acquirer is the combining entity, determine which group has the ability to elect or remove the majority members of the board of directors.
- If the acquirer is a combining entity, assess which group dominates the senior management of the combined entity. The acquirer is usually the combining entity whose relative size is larger, or is the combining entity that has initiated the combination.

Date of Acquisition

This is the date on which the acquirer effectively obtains control of the acquiree. It may be signified by the date on which:

- The acquirer transfers the consideration of acquisition.
- The acquirer acquires the assets and assumes the liabilities of the acquire.
- The business combination transaction closes.
- An agreement gives the acquirer control before, or after, the transaction closing date.

Acquisition Method of Accounting

IFRS 3 requires use of the acquisition method of accounting. In this method of accounting, the acquirer recognizes and measures on the date of acquisition:

- All assets acquired and liabilities assumed at fair value
- Goodwill based on the excess of

  - Consideration transferred by the acquirer and noncontrolling interests
  - Fair value of assets acquired and liabilities assumed

- Gain on a bargain purchase

Recognizing Assets and Liabilities

The recognition principle states that "as of the acquisition date, the acquirer shall recognize, separately from goodwill, the identifiable assets acquired, the liabilities assumed and any noncontrolling interest in the acquiree."

Within this broad principle, recognition of assets and liabilities in a business combination transaction is as follows:

- Identify assets and liabilities within the *Framework for Presentation of Financial Statements* and check the liabilities that do not arise out of the business combination.
- Recognize assets that were not recognized by the acquiree, since these were internally generated intangibles.
- The acquirer may not recognize some assets and liabilities. For example, the following items are not liabilities on the acquisition date:

- Costs estimated to be incurred to exit an activity but which do not comprise an obligation; or
- Costs to be incurred to terminate or relocate employees of the acquiree.

Intangible Assets

- The acquiree does not recognize internally generated intangibles like brand names, customer lists and patents, when the acquiree expensed the costs incurred for developing these assets.
- The acquirer, on a business combination, may recognize these assets.
- IFRS 3 requires that intangibles should be segregated from acquisition goodwill.
- Intangibles are separated from goodwill on the basis of separability and contractual-legal criteria.
- It should be established whether intangible assets are separable from the business.

Contingent Liabilities

A *contingent liability* is defined in IAS 37, *Provisions, Contingent Liabilities and Contingent Assets,* as

- A possible obligation that arises from past events and whose existence will be confirmed only by the occurrence or nonoccurrence of one or more uncertain future events not wholly within the control of the entity; or
- A present obligation that arises from past events but is not recognized because:

  - It is not probable that an outflow of resources embodying economic benefits will be required to settle the obligation; or
  - The amount of the obligation cannot be measured with sufficient reliability. In the context of a business combination, the acquirer is required to recognize a contingent liability assumed in a business combination as of the acquisition date if it is a present obligation that arises from past events and its fair value can be measured reliably.

Under IAS 37, a *present obligation* is not recognized as a liability because an outflow of economic resources is not probable, or the amount of the obligation could not be reliably measured. A contingent liability recognized in a business combination is measured subsequent to initial recognition at the higher of

- The amount that would be recognized in accordance with IAS 37; and
- The amount initially recognized less cumulative amortization recognized in accordance with IAS 18, *Revenue.*

The principle is followed until the contingent liability is settled, cancelled, or expires.

In terms of IFRS 3, contingent liabilities that arise from possible obligations are not recognized by the acquirer. Only contingent liabilities that represent present obligations are recognized.

Income Tax

- The acquirer has to measure a deferred tax asset or liability based on the assets acquired and liabilities assumed on the date of acquisition, applying IAS 12.
- The acquirer has to recognize such a deferred tax asset/liability.

Employee Benefits

- The acquirer has also to measure employee benefits of the business acquired on the date of acquisition, in accordance with IAS19, *Employee Benefits.*

Indemnification of Assets

Indemnification assets are amounts receivable from the acquiree or other third parties for a particular liability that the acquiree is, or may be exposed to. For example, acquiree gives guarantee that uncollectible amount will not exceed 10%.

If the acquirer recognizes the liability of the acquiree, then it should also recognize the indemnification asset. The indemnification asset measurement is equal to the value of the underlying liability unless the asset is impaired due to noncollectability of funds.

Operating Leases (Lessee)

- The acquirer evaluates the terms and conditions of an operating lease, where the acquiree is a lessee.
- On acquisition date, if the terms are favorable as compared to market terms, the acquirer recognizes an intangible asset. Otherwise, the acquirer recognizes a liability, provided market participants are willing to pay a price for this.
- IFRS 3 explains that recognition of an intangible asset arising from favorable market terms should be substantiated by *contractual-legal* criteria other than *separability*.
- If the acquiree is a lessee, the terms of the favorable or unfavorable lease will normally be captured in the fair valuation of the underlying asset.

Reaquired Rights

- In the process of a business combination, the acquirer may reacquire rights granted earlier to the acquiree, such as franchisee rights, patent rights or licenses, trade names, and so forth.
- These are separable intangible assets that the acquirer should separate from goodwill. They are revalued based on market conditions on the date of acquisition.
- These are recognized and amortized over the remaining contractual terms of the right.

Share-Based Awards

- If, in a business combination, the acquiree has share-based awards that the acquirer has to replace by its own share-based awards, the new award should be measured applying IFRS 2.

Assets Held for Sale

- Sometimes the acquirer may take over noncurrent assets held for sale under a business combination. These acquired noncurrent assets held for sale are valued applying IFRS 5.

Classification of Assets and Liabilities

- After identification of the assets acquired and liabilities assumed, the assets and liabilities are classified, in order to apply other IFRS subsequently.
- For example, the acquirer has to classify financial assets as
  - Fair value through equity
  - Available for sale
  - Held to maturity depending on the intention of the management

- Other examples include

  - Derivatives as hedging instruments, as per IAS 39
  - Whether an embedded derivative should be separated from the host contract

- There is no need to classify

  - Lease contracts as operating or finance leases; and
  - Insurance contracts under IFRS 4 as on the acquisition date.

Measurement Principles

The next step is to apply the *fair value* measurement principle to identified assets and liabilities.

- *No separate valuation allowance is allowed for uncertain cash flows.* While measuring the fair value of assets/liabilities, the uncertain element of the cash flow should be adjusted for within the valuation. The entity should not recognize a separate valuation allowance.
- *Valuation of assets under an operating lease in which the acquiree was lessor.* Assets are valued after taking into account the lease term and related market value. Therefore, no separate intangible is recognized based on lease terms that are favorable as compared to market condition.
- *Valuation of acquired assets that the acquirer does not wish to use in the traditional manner that other market participants would normally use the asset for.* These assets should be valued at fair value in accordance with their use by other market participants.

Valuation of Goodwill

- *Goodwill* is defined as an asset representing the future economic benefits arising from other assets acquired in a business combination that are not individually identified and separately recognized.
- IFRS 3 requires the acquirer to recognize goodwill at the acquisition date, measured as the difference between (1) and (2):

  1. The aggregate of

     a. The acquisition date fair value of the consideration transferred;
     b. The amount of any noncontrolling interest in the entity acquired; and
     c. In a business combination achieved in stages, the acquisition date fair value of the acquirer's previously held equity interest in the entity acquired.

  2. The net of the acquisition-date amounts of the identifiable assets acquired and the liabilities assumed, both measured in accordance with IFRS 3.

FAIR VALUE OF CONSIDERATION

For the computation of goodwill on acquisition, the acquirer should measure

- Fair value of assets transferred or equity issued; and
- Fair value of liabilities incurred toward former owners of the acquiree.

When the assets transferred as consideration have a different fair value from book value, the acquirer has to remeasure the fair value of such assets and recognize gain or loss in its profit or loss.

Full Goodwill and Partial Goodwill

- Full goodwill means that goodwill is recognized in a business combination for the noncontrolling interest in a subsidiary as well as the controlling interest.
- A partial goodwill acquirer may either recognize noncontrolling interest in the subsidiary at fair value or the acquirer can recognize noncontrolling interest in net assets excluding goodwill.
- Recognizing full goodwill will increase reported net assets on the statement of financial position.

Accounting for Expenses of the Business Combination

Expenses on a business combination include the following:

- Finder's fees
- Fees for advisory, legal, accounting, valuation and other professional or consulting services
- General administrative expenses, including the expenses of maintaining an internal acquisitions department
- Costs of registering and issuing debt and equity securities

These expenses are accounted for in the periods in which these are incurred and the services are received. These costs can no longer be included as part of the costs of the business combination. Under the previous IFRS 3, these costs could be included as part of the business combination. The cost to issue debt or equity securities should be recognized in accordance with IAS 32 and IAS 39.

Bargain Purchases

- Bargain purchases create a gain on acquisition.
- If the fair value of the consideration transferred is lower than the fair value of the net assets acquired and noncontrolling interest, then this gain is recognized in the profit and loss of the acquirer.
- Before recognizing this gain, the acquirer should review

  - Whether all assets acquired and liabilities assumed are recognized;
  - Whether noncontrolling interest is properly accounted for;
  - Whether previously held interest is included with the consideration (in the case of a stage-by-stage acquisition); and
  - Whether consideration transferred is properly measured.

MEASUREMENT PERIOD

- The measurement period shall not exceed one year from the acquisition date.
- During this period, the acquirer may finalize the accounts based on information that is provisional and new information collected.
- The measurement period ends when the new information becomes available, and may not exceed a year.
- If a measurement is finalized after a year, then it is treated in accordance with IAS 8.

Accounting for a Reverse Acquisition

- In a reverse acquisition, a smaller-size entity acquirers the larger entity.
- In the postacquisition period, the larger entity maintains control.
- Through this technique a private company can go public.
- The acquirer is the legal subsidiary.

- The value of the purchase consideration is the fair value of the additional shares that the legal subsidiary would have had to issue to the legal parent's preacquisition shareholders for their ongoing interest in the combined entity.

DISCLOSURES

General description

1. The name and description of acquiree.
2. The acquisition date.
3. The percentage of voting equity interests acquired.
4. The primary reasons for the business combination and a description of how the acquirer obtained control of the acquired.
5. A qualitative description of the factors that make up the goodwill recognized.

Fair value of consideration transferred

6. The acquisition date fair value of the total consideration transferred and the acquisition date fair value of each major class of consideration such as

   a. Cash;
   b. Other tangible or intangible assets, including a business or subsidiary of the acquirer;
   c. Liabilities incurred, for example, a liability for contingent consideration; and
   d. Equity interest of the acquirer, including the number of instruments or interests issued or issuable and the method of determining the fair value of instruments or interests.

Contingent consideration

7. For contingent consideration arrangements and indemnification assets:

   a. The amount recognised as of the acquisition date;
   b. A description of the arrangement and the basis for determining the amount of payment;
   c. An estimate of the range of the outcomes or, if a range cannot be estimated, that fact and the reasons why a range cannot be estimated. If the maximum amount of the payment is unlimited, the acquirer shall disclose that fact.

Major classes of assets acquired and liabilities assumed

8. The amount recognized as of the acquisition date for each major class of assets acquired and liabilities assumed.

Assets that are separately recognized

9. For transactions that are recognized separately from the acquisition of assets and assumption of liabilities in the business combination

   a. A description of each transaction;
   b. How the acquirer accounted for each transaction;
   c. The line item of the statement of financial position in which the item is recognized; and
   d. If it is related to settling a preexisting relationship, the method used to determine the settlement amount.

Acquisition-related cost

10. The disclosure of separately recognized transactions required by (9) shall include the amount of acquisition-related costs.

    Disclose the amount of those costs recognized as an expense and the line item or items in the statement of comprehensive income in which those expenses are recognized.

    Disclose the amount of any issue costs not recognized as an expense and explain how they were recognized.

Bargain purchase

11. Disclose the amount of any gain recognized and a description of the reasons why the transaction resulted in a gain.

Noncontrolling interest

12. For each business combination in which the acquirer holds less than 100% of equity interests in the acquiree at the acquisition date: Disclose the amount of the noncontrolling interest in the acquiree recognized at the acquisition date and the measurement basis for that amount; Disclose the valuation techniques and key model inputs used for determining that value.

| Business acquisition after the reporting date | 13. | If the acquisition date of a business combination is after the end of the reporting period, but before the financial statements are authorized for issue, the acquirer shall disclose additional information required by paragraph B64 of IFRS 3 such as name and description of acquire, the acquisition date, and percentage of voting equity interests acquired. |

If the business combination is incomplete, the acquirer shall describe which disclosures could not be made and the reasons why they cannot be made.

| Provisional accounting during the measurement period | 14. | The acquirer shall disclose the following information for each material business combination, or in the aggregate for individually immaterial business combinations that are material collectively: Provisional amount recognized for particular assets, liabilities, noncontrolling interests or items of consideration. Also indicate |

   a. The reason why the initial accounting for the business combination is incomplete;
   b. The assets, liabilities, equity interests or items of consideration for which the initial accounting is incomplete; and
   c. The nature and amount of any measurement period adjustments recognized during the reporting period.

| Contingent consideration | 15. | For each reporting period after the acquisition date until the entity collects, sells or otherwise loses the right to a contingent consideration asset, or until the entity settles a contingent consideration liability or the liability is cancelled or expires, disclose |

   a. Any changes in the recognized amounts, including any differences arising upon settlement;
   b. Any changes in the range of outcomes (undiscounted) and the reasons for those changes; and
   c. The valuation techniques and key model inputs used to measure contingent consideration.

Example 2

A Ltd. plans to acquire B Ltd. The following information is available:

1. B Ltd. has property, plant, and equipment (book value $100 million, fair value $250 million).
2. B Ltd. has operating lease assets for which it has to pay lease rental of $40 million p.a. for the next five years, as compared to current market rental of $45 million p.a. Discount rate: 10%. PV of five-year annuity at 10% is 3.7908.
3. B Ltd. has inventories (book value $80 million; net realizable value $95 million).
4. B Ltd. has debtors of $102 million; it has been assessed that $80 million will be collectable. However B Ltd. guarantees that collection from debtors will not be less than $90 million.
5. B Ltd. is one of the suppliers of A Ltd. with which it has a five-year supply contract at a fixed rate that is now unfavorable. A Ltd. has assessed that its losses are $3 million per annum under the existing contract. Under the existing clause of this agreement A Ltd. would pay $6 million compensation for premature termination of the agreement before two years of remaining maturity. The contract has four years of validity. Discount rate: 10%. PV of four-year annuity at 10% is 3.1699.
6. A Ltd. offers employment to the Managing Director of B Ltd. at 25% above the comparable term, which works out to $2 million.
7. B Ltd. has not recognized value of a brand name, which is worth $3 million.
8. The customer list of B Ltd. is valued by A Ltd. at $2 million.
9. B Ltd. has a pending order that would earn a profit of $20 million. A Ltd. has valued that a competitor would have spent at least $3 million for obtaining this contract.
10. Sundry creditors and other liabilities taken over are $50 million.
11. A Ltd. replaces the existing share-based award of B Ltd. The market-based value of the acquirer's award is $12 million, as compared to the market-based value of the acquiree's award of $10 million. Under the acquiree's award the employees are required to complete

two years vesting period out of an original vesting period of five years. Under the acquirer's award the employees are not required to complete any further service.

12. A Ltd. issued 1 million equity shares to the erstwhile shareholder of B Ltd. Market value of shares of A Ltd. is $410 each.

What would be *goodwill,* if any, in this business combination?

Solution

In $ million

Fair Value of Assets Acquired

Property, plant, and equipment	250.0
Inventories	95.0
Debtors	80.0
Indemnification assets—for guarantees given by the acquiree about collectability of debtors.	10.0
Intangible assets—arising from favorable operating lease contract. (5 × 3.7908)	18.95
Customer-related intangibles: brand name	3.0
Customer-related intangibles: customer list	2.0
Customer-related intangibles: value of pending customer	3.0
Total	**467.95**

Liabilities assumed

Sundry creditors and other liabilities		50.0
Contingent consideration: payment to Managing Director		2.0
Obligation under replacement share-based award	(10 × 3/5)	6.0
Total		**58.0**

Net assets acquired		**409.95**
Consideration transferred	(410 × 1,000,000)	**410.0**
Less: Adjustment for preexisting relationship	(3 × 3.1699 = 9.51) which is higher than $6 million	6.0
Adjusted consideration		404.0
Goodwill		**5.95**

EXTRACTS FROM PUBLISHED FINANCIAL STATEMENTS

Ahold, Annual Report 2008

Notes to the Consolidated Financial Statements

4. Acquisitions

2008 Acquisitions

In December 2008, Stop & Shop completed the acquisition of three stores from Grand Union Markets. The total purchase consideration amounted to EUR 16 million. Intangible assets were recognized for EUR 11 million relating to lease rights. No goodwill was recognized on this acquisition.

Ahold completed several other acquisitions that were insignificant both individually and in the aggregate. All acquisitions have been accounted for by the purchase method of accounting. Under the Purchase and Sale Agreement between Ahold, Schuitema and CVC Capital Partners ("CVC"), as described in Note 5, Ahold retained 56 Schuitema stores and transferred these to the Albert Heijn segment. This transaction was not accounted for as an acquisition; the assets and liabilities related to these stores have been retained in Ahold's consolidated balance sheet at their carrying amounts.

2007 Acquisitions

In 2007, Ahold completed several acquisitions that were insignificant both individually and in the aggregate. All acquisitions have been accounted for by the purchase method of accounting.

Nokia Seimens, Annual Report 2008

Notes to the Consolidated Financial Statements[*]

2.   Summary of Significant Accounting Policies

Business combinations—All business combinations are accounted for under the purchase method. The cost of an acquisition is measured at the fair value of the assets given and liabilities incurred or assumed at the date of exchange plus costs directly attributable to the acquisition. Identifiable assets acquired and liabilities assumed in a business combination (including contingent liabilities) are measured initially at their fair values at the acquisition date, irrespective of the extent of any minority interest. The excess of the cost of acquisition over the fair value of the company's share of the identifiable net assets acquired is recorded as goodwill.

4.   Acquisitions, Dispositions and Discontinued Operations

a.   Acquisitions

During the years ended September 30, 2008 and 2007, the company completed a number of acquisitions. These acquisitions have been accounted for under the purchase method and have been included in the company's Consolidated Financial Statements since the date of acquisition.

Acquisitions in Fiscal 2008

At the beginning of November 2007, Siemens completed the acquisition of Dade Behring Holdings, Inc. (Dade Behring), USA, a leading manufacturer and distributor of diagnostic products and services to clinical laboratories. Dade Behring, which was consolidated as of November 2007, will be integrated into Sector Healthcare's Diagnostics division and complements the acquisitions of Diagnostic Products Corporation and Bayer Diagnostics.

The aggregate consideration, including the assumption of debt, amounts to approximately €4.9 billion (including €69 cash acquired). The company has not yet finalized the purchase price allocation. Based on the preliminary purchase price allocation, approximately €1,171 was allocated to intangible assets subject to amortization and approximately €3,349 was recorded as goodwill. Of the €1,171 intangible assets, €955 was allocated to customer relationships, €116 to trademarks and €74 to patented and unpatented technology.

In fiscal 2008, Siemens completed the acquisitions of a number of entities that are not significant individually including BJC, Spain, a supplier of switches and socket-outlets at Sector Industry, Building Technologies Division; Innotec, a leading software provider for life cycle management solutions at Sector Industry's Industry Automation division; and the rolling mill technology specialist Morgan Construction Co., USA, at Sector Industry,

Industry Solutions Division. The combined preliminary purchase price of these acquisitions amounts to €302.

Acquisitions in Fiscal 2007

On January 2, 2007, Siemens completed the acquisition of the diagnostic division of Bayer Aktiengesellschaft (Bayer). The acquisition, which was consolidated as of January 2007, was integrated into Sector Healthcare's Diagnostics division. The purchase price, payable in cash, amounts to €4.4 billion (including €185 cash acquired). Based on the final purchase price allocation, €753 was allocated to intangible assets subject to amortization and €2,735 to goodwill. Of the €753 intangible assets, €573 relate to customer relationships with a weighted-average useful life of 14 years and €139 to trademarks and tradenames with a weighted-average useful life of 10 years.

On May 4, 2007, Siemens completed the acquisition of U.S.-based UGS Corp. (UGS), one of the leading providers of product lifecycle management (PLM) software and services for manufacturers. UGS was integrated into Sector Industry's division Industry Automation and consolidated as of May 2007. The acquisition enables Siemens to provide an end-to-end software and hardware portfolio for manufacturers encompassing the complete lifecycle of products and production facilities. The acquisition costs including the assumption of debt, amount to €2.752 billion

---

[*] *Amounts in € millions except where otherwise stated and per share amounts.*

(including €75 cash acquired). Based on the final purchase price allocation, €1,094 was allocated to intangible assets subject to amortization and approximately €1,983 was recorded as goodwill. Of the €1,094 intangible assets, €294 relate to customer relationships with a weighted average useful life of 12 years and €718 to technology with a weighted-average useful life of 7 years.

The company made certain other acquisitions during the years ended September 30, 2008 and 2007, which did not have a significant effect on the Consolidated Financial Statements.

16. Goodwill

Goodwill has changed as follows:

	Year ended September 30	
	2008	*2007*
Cost		
Balance at beginning of year	13,589	10,818
Translation differences and other	(135)	(726)
Acquisitions and purchase accounting adjustments	3,737	5,096
Adjustments from the subsequent recognition of deferred tax assets	(3)	(34)
Dispositions and reclassifications to assets held for disposal	(630)	(1,565)
Balance at year-end	16,558	13,589
Accumulated impairment losses and other changes		
Balance at beginning of year	1,088	1,129
Translation differences and other	(16)	(92)
Impairment losses recognized during the period	78	60
Dispositions and reclassifications to assets held for disposal	(596)	(9)
Balance at year-end	554	1,088
Net book value		
Balance at beginning of year		
Balance at year-end	16,004	12,501

	Net book value as of 10/1/2007	*Translation differences and other*	*Acquisitions and purchase accounting adjustments**	*Disposition and reclassifications to assets held for disposal*	*Impairments*	*Net book value as of 9/30/2008*
Sectors						
Industry	4,739	(48)	233	(17)	—	4,907
Energy	2,210	(55)	85	—	—	2,240
Healthcare	5,197	7	3,413	—	—	8,617
Cross-sector businesses						
Siemens IT Solutions and Services	129	(9)	3	—	—	123
Siemens Financial Services (SFS)	126	(15)	—	—	—	111
Other operations	100	1	—	(17)	(78)	6
Siemens	12,501	(119)	3,734	(34)	(78)	16,004

* *Includes adjustments from the subsequent recognition of deferred tax assets.*

	Net book value as of 10/1/2006	*Translation differences and other*	*Acquisitions and purchase accounting adjustments**	*Disposition and reclassifications to assets held for disposal*	*Impairments*	*Net book value as of 9/30/2007*
Sectors						
Industry	2,869	(169)	2,050	(11)	—	4,739
Energy	2,081	(64)	203	(10)	—	2,210
Healthcare	2,793	(396)	2,800	—	—	5,197

	Net book value as of 10/1/2006	Translation differences and other	Acquisitions and purchase accounting adjustments*	Disposition and reclassifications to assets held for disposal	Impairments	Net book value as of 9/30/2007
Cross-sector businesses						
Siemens IT Solutions and Services	127	(1)	3	—	—	129
Siemens Financial Services (SFS	130	(4)	—	—	—	126
Other operations	159	1	—	—	(60)	100
Siemens VDO automotive (SV)	1,530	(1)	6	(1,535)	—	—
Siemens	9,689	(634)	5,062	(1,556)	(60)	12,501

* *Includes adjustments from the subsequent recognition of deferred tax assets.*

Commencing with the third quarter of fiscal 2008, the company adjusted its reporting format to its rearranged organization. The previous twelve segments were consolidated and newly structured into six remaining reportable segments (for further information see Note 37). New cash-generating units have been identified. The goodwill impairment test is primarily performed at the division level. Goodwill has been allocated based on expected synergies derived from the business combination in which the goodwill arose.

In fiscal 2008, acquisitions and purchase accounting adjustments relate primarily to Healthcare's acquisition of Dade Behring (see Note 4). The purchase accounting adjustments in the Industry Sector amounting to €103 relate to the UGS transaction (see Note 4). Impairment of goodwill of €(70) relates to the buildings and infrastructure activities of VA Technologie AG, which was presented in *Other Operations*.

In fiscal 2007, SV goodwill of €(1,518) was reclassified to *Assets classified as held for disposal* (see Note 4). Acquisitions and purchase accounting adjustments related primarily to Healthcare's acquisition of the diagnostics division of Bayer and Industry's acquisition of UGS, as well as to an Energy Sector acquisition. For further information on acquisitions, dispositions and discontinued operations see Note 4. Impairment of goodwill in fiscal 2007 includes €(52) related to a cash-generating unit made up principally of regional payphone activities, which is part of *Other Operations*.

Siemens tests at least annually whether goodwill suffered any impairment, in accordance with the accounting policy stated in Note 2. Key assumptions on which management has based its determinations of the recoverable amount for the divisions' carrying goodwill include growth rates up to 3% and 3.5% in fiscal 2008 and 2007, respectively and after-tax discount rates of 7.5% to 9% in fiscal 2008 and 7.5% to 10% in fiscal 2007. Where possible, reference to market prices is made.

The following divisions are allocated a significant amount of goodwill: a) Diagnostics within Sector Healthcare €6,131 (2007: €3,331) and b) Imaging & IT in Sector Healthcare €2,418 (2007: €1,856), as well as Industry Automation within Sector Industry €2,259 (2007: €2,169).

Holcim, Annual Report 2008

Consolidated Financial Statements

Accounting Policies

Adoption of Revised and New International Financial Reporting Standards and New Interpretations

In 2010, HOLCIM will adopt the following revised standards relevant to the group:

IAS 27 (revised), *Consolidated and Separate Financial Statements*
IFRS 3 (revised), *Business Combinations*

According to IAS 27 (revised), changes in the ownership interest of a subsidiary that do not result in a loss of control will be accounted for as an equity transaction. The amendment to IFRS 3 (revised) introduces several changes, such as the choice to measure a noncontrolling interest in the acquiree either at fair value or at its proportionate interest in the acquiree's identifiable net assets, the accounting for step acquisitions requiring the remeasurement of a previously held interest to fair value through profit or loss, as well as the expensing of acquisition costs directly to the income statement.

Foreign Currency Translation

Income statements of foreign entities are translated into the group's reporting currency at average exchange rates for the year, and balance sheets are translated at exchange rates ruling on December 31.

Goodwill arising on the acquisition of a foreign entity is expressed in the functional currency of the foreign operation and is translated at the closing rate.

Foreign currency transactions are accounted for at the exchange rates prevailing at the date of the transactions; gains and losses resulting from the settlement of such transactions and from the translation of monetary assets and liabilities denominated in foreign currencies are recognized in the income statement, except when deferred in equity as qualifying cash flow hedges.

Exchange differences arising on monetary items that form part of an entity's net investment in a foreign operation are reclassified to equity (currency translation adjustment) in the consolidated financial statements and are only released to the income statement on the disposal of the foreign operation. The individual financial statements of each of the group's entities are measured using the currency of the primary economic environment in which the entity operates ("the functional currency").

Goodwill

Goodwill represents the excess of the cost of an acquisition over the group's interest in the fair value of the identifiable assets, liabilities, and contingent liabilities of a subsidiary, associate or joint venture at the date of acquisition. Goodwill on acquisitions of subsidiaries and interests in joint ventures is included in intangible assets. Goodwill on acquisitions of associates is included in investments in associates. Goodwill that is recognized as an intangible asset is tested annually for impairment and carried at cost less accumulated impairment losses.

On disposal of a subsidiary, associate or joint venture, the related goodwill is included in the determination of profit or loss on disposal.

Goodwill on acquisitions of subsidiaries and interests in joint ventures is allocated to cash-generating units for the purpose of impairment testing (Note 24). Impairment losses relating to goodwill cannot be reversed in future periods.

In the event that Holcim acquires a minority interest in a subsidiary, goodwill is measured at cost, which represents the excess of the purchase consideration given over Holcim's additional interest in the book value of the net assets acquired.

If the cost of acquisition is less than the fair value of the net assets of the subsidiary acquired, the difference is recognized directly in the income statement.

35 INSURANCE CONTRACTS (IFRS 4)

INTRODUCTION

The major issues covered under IFRS 4 are

1. *Treatment of embedded derivative that meets the definition of an insurance contract.* IFRS 4 clarifies that a derivative embedded in an insurance contract need not be accounted for separately at fair value if the embedded derivative itself is an insurance contract.
2. *Unbundling deposit components.* It requires an insurer to unbundle (i.e., account separately for) deposit components of some insurance contracts, to avoid the omission of assets and liabilities from its statement of financial position.
3. *Liability adequacy test (LAT).* It requires an entity to carry out a LAT to check whether its recognized insurance liability is adequate.
4. *Temporary exemptions from IAS 8.* Subject to certain restrictions, IFRS 4 exempts an entity from applying criteria specified in paragraphs 10–12 of IAS 8 in selecting accounting policies.
5. *Change in accounting policies.* IFRS 4 sets out principles of changes in accounting policies by an insurer, including principles for pursuing shadow accounting.
6. *Discretionary participation features (DPF).* IFRS 4 sets out principles for separating the guarantee element from DPF.

However, the International Accounting Standards Board (IASB) intends to develop a standard in the second phase of its insurance accounting project that will replace the interim standard (existing IFRS 4) and will provide a basis for consistent accounting for insurance contracts. It aims to publish an Exposure Draft in late 2009 and a final standard in 2011.

SCOPE

This standard is applicable to

1. Insurance contracts (including *reinsurance contracts*) that an entity issues and reinsurance contracts that it holds; and
2. Financial instruments with a *discretionary participation feature.* IFRS 7, *Financial Instruments: Disclosures,* is applicable to such instruments as well.

This Standard is not applicable to:

1. Product warranties issued directly by a manufacturer, dealer or retailer (see IAS 18, *Revenue* and IAS 37, *Provisions, Contingent Liabilities and Contingent Assets*);
2. Employers' assets and liabilities under employee benefit plans (see IAS 19, *Employee Benefits,* and IFRS 2, *Share-Based Payment*) and retirement benefit obligations reported by defined benefit retirement plans (see IAS 26, *Accounting and Reporting by Retirement Benefit Plans*);
3. Contractual rights or contractual obligations that are contingent on the future use of, or right to use, a nonfinancial item (e.g., some license fees, royalties, contingent lease payments and similar items), as well as a lessee's residual value guarantee embedded

in a finance lease (see IAS 17, *Leases,* IAS 18, *Revenue,* and IAS 38, *Intangible Assets*);
4. Financial guarantee contracts. However, if the issuer has previously asserted explicitly that it regards such contracts as insurance contracts and has used IFRS 4 accounting applicable to insurance contracts, in such a case the issuer may elect to apply either IAS 39, IAS 32, and IFRS 7 or this standard to such financial guarantee contracts. The issuer may make that election contract by contract, but the election for each contract is irrevocable;
5. Contingent consideration payable or receivable in a business combination (see IFRS 3, *Business Combinations*); and
6. *Direct insurance contracts* that the entity holds (i.e., direct insurance contracts in which the entity is the *policyholder*).

However, a *cedant (the policyholder under a reinsurance contract)* shall apply this IFRS to reinsurance contracts that it holds.

IFRS 4 is applicable to reinsurance contracts. This standard has used the term *insurer* loosely to describe any entity that issues an insurance contract as an insurer. It may or may not be regarded as an insurer for legal or supervisory purposes.

INSURANCE CONTRACT

An *insurance contract* is signified by acceptance of significant insurance risk from another party (the policyholder) by agreeing to compensate the policyholder if a specified uncertain future event (the insured event) adversely affects the policyholder. Insurance risk is distinguished from financial risk.

Financial risk is the risk of a possible future change in one or more of a specified interest rate, financial instrument price, commodity price, foreign exchange rate, index of prices or rates, credit rating or credit index or other variable, provided in the case of a nonfinancial variable that the variable is not specific to a party to the contract.

- Examples of nonfinancial variables that are not specific to a party to the contract are an index of earthquake losses in a particular region or an index of temperatures in a particular city.
- An example of nonfinancial variable that is specific to a party to the contract is the occurrence or nonoccurrence of a fire that damages or destroys an asset of that party.

Example 1

Does a fixed-fee service contract in which the level of service depends on an uncertain future event meet the definition of an insurance contract? Is it possible to classify this contract as a service contract under IAS 18?

The answer to the first question is *yes*. This contract falls within the scope of IFRS 4 but is not regulated as an insurance contract in many countries.

The answer to the second question is *no*. Paragraph 6(c) of IAS 18 states that insurance contracts within the scope of IFRS 4 are outside the scope of IAS 18.

EXAMPLES OF INSURANCE CONTRACTS

The following are examples of insurance contracts, if the transfer of insurance risk is significant:

1. Insurance against theft or damage to property.
2. Insurance against product liability, professional liability, civil liability, or legal expenses.

3. Life insurance and prepaid funeral plans (although death is certain, it is uncertain when death will occur or, for some types of life insurance, whether death will occur within the period covered by the insurance).
4. Life-contingent annuities and pensions (i.e., contracts that provide compensation for the uncertain future event—the survival of the annuitant or pensioner—to assist the annuitant or pensioner in maintaining a given standard of living, which would otherwise be adversely affected by his or her survival).
5. Disability and medical cover.
6. Surety bonds, fidelity bonds, performance bonds, and bid bonds (i.e., contracts that provide compensation if another party fails to perform a contractual obligation, for example an obligation to construct a building).
7. Credit insurance that provides for specified payments to be made to reimburse the holder for a loss it incurs because a specified debtor fails to make payment when due under the original or modified terms of a debt instrument.
8. Product warranties. Product warranties issued by another party for goods sold by a manufacturer, dealer, or retailer are within the scope of this IFRS. However, product warranties issued directly by a manufacturer, dealer or retailer are outside its scope, because they are within the scope of IAS 18 and IAS 37.
9. Title insurance (i.e., insurance against the discovery of defects in title to land that were not apparent when the insurance contract was written). In this case, the insured event is the discovery of a defect in the title, not the defect itself.
10. Travel assistance (i.e., compensation in cash or in kind to policyholders for losses suffered while they are traveling). Paragraphs B6 and B7 discuss some contracts of this kind.
11. Catastrophe bonds that provide for reduced payments of principal, interest, or both, if a specified event adversely affects the issuer of the bond (unless the specified event does not create significant insurance risk, for example if the event is a change in an interest rate or foreign exchange rate).
12. Insurance swaps and other contracts that require a payment based on changes in climatic, geological or other physical variables that are specific to a party to the contract.
13. Reinsurance contracts.

CONTRACTS THAT ARE NOT CLASSIFIED AS INSURANCE CONTRACTS

- Investment contracts that have the legal form of an insurance contract but do not expose the insurer to significant insurance risk (e.g., life insurance contracts in which the insurer bears no significant mortality risk).
- A credit-related guarantee (or letter of credit, credit derivative default contract or credit insurance contract) that requires payments even if the holder has not incurred a loss on the failure of the debtor to make payments when due (see IAS 39).
- Contracts that require a payment based on a climatic, geological or other physical variable that is not specific to a party to the contract (commonly described as weather derivatives).
- Catastrophe bonds that provide for reduced payments of principal, interest or both, based on a climatic, geological or other physical variable that is not specific to a party to the contract.

EMBEDDED DERIVATIVES

A derivative embedded in an insurance contract is required to be separated in accordance with IAS 39. The embedded derivative is to be separated from its host contract, measured at *fair value* and changes in their fair value included in profit or loss. IAS 39 applies to derivatives embedded in an insurance contract unless the embedded derivative is itself an insurance contract.

However, a policyholder's option to surrender an insurance contract for a fixed amount (or for an amount based on a fixed amount and an interest rate) is not separated as an embedded derivative. This is so even if the exercise price differs from the carrying amount of the host *insurance liability*. But, the requirement in IAS 39 applies to a put option or cash surrender option embedded in an insurance contract if the surrender value varies in response to the change in a financial variable (such as an equity or commodity price or index), or a nonfinancial variable that is not specific to a party to the contract. Furthermore, that requirement also applies if the holder's ability to exercise a put option or cash surrender option is triggered by a change in such a variable (e.g., a put option that can be exercised if a stock market index reaches a specified level).

UNBUNDLING OF DEPOSITS

Insurance contracts may contain insurance and deposit components. An insurer is required or permitted to unbundle those components.

1. Unbundling is required if (a) the insurer can measure the deposit component (including any embedded surrender options) separately (i.e., without considering the insurance component), and (b) the insurer's accounting policies do not otherwise require it to recognize all obligations and rights arising from the deposit component.
2. Unbundling is permitted, but not required, if the insurer can measure the deposit component separately as in 1.(a) but its accounting policies require it to recognize all obligations and rights arising from the deposit component, regardless of the basis used to measure those rights and obligations.
3. Unbundling is prohibited if an insurer cannot measure the deposit component separately as in 1.(a).

TEMPORARY EXEMPTION FROM APPLICATION OF IAS 8

An entity applies paragraphs 10–12 of IAS 8, *Accounting Policies, Changes in Accounting Estimates and Errors* for the purpose of developing accounting policies. Accounting policies are selected applying IFRS relevant for similar issues, IFRS framework or pronouncement of standard-setting bodies that use a similar conceptual framework to develop accounting standards.

The requirements of IFRS 8 are not applicable to an insurer for selection of accounting policies for (1) insurance contracts that it issues (including related acquisition costs and related intangible assets) and (2) reinsurance contracts that it holds.

However, an insurer is not permitted to recognize as a liability any provisions for possible future claims, if those claims arise under insurance contracts that are not in existence at the end of the reporting period. Catastrophe provisions and equalization provisions are examples of such type of provisions.

BUSINESS ACQUISITIONS

As per IFRS 4.31, when an insurer acquires assets and liabilities of another insurance contract(s), such assets and liabilities are measured in terms of fair value. However, the insurer may apply expanded presentation that is also termed as *split accounting*. Under this approach, an insurer may measure insurance liabilities in accordance with its existing accounting policies, but measure insurance assets at fair value. Similarly, split accounting can be applied for acquisition of a portfolio of insurance contracts.

An intangible asset is recognized under acquisition of insurance contracts including acquisition of a portfolio of insurance. This is measured at the difference between insurance assets acquired and insurance liabilities assumed.

DEFERRED ACQUISITION COSTS

Deferrable acquisition costs comprise direct and indirect variable costs relating to the acquisition of new and renewal insurance contracts. They include especially

- Acquisition costs and first commissions (excluding recurring commissions other than those related to renewal insurance contracts), incentives and bonuses associated with new business and other remuneration of sales staff in relation to new business
- Administrative costs associated with the issuing of contracts, and costs associated with policy selection and acquisition such as inspection and medical fees

Conversely, the following costs are usually not deferred: (1) general advertising costs, (2) general recruitment of sales staff and agents, (3) classroom training and conferences, (4) product design costs, or (5) recurring commissions other than those related to renewal insurance contracts.

Acquisition costs may only be capitalized and deferred if they will be offset by future revenues including future investment margins. The insurer shall carry out a recoverability test annually.

Generally, deferred acquisition cost is amortized on the following basis:

- Estimated gross profits emerging over the life of the contracts
- Projections of fees collected over the life of the contracts
- Gross premiums
- Expense immediately

LIABILITY ADEQUACY TEST

As per IFRS 4.15 an insurer is required to carry out a liability adequacy test (LAT) at each reporting date. This test evaluates whether the insurance obligation less any deferred acquisition cost and related intangibles is inadequate in the light of the estimated future cash flows. The entire deficiency is charged to profit or loss.

Minimum requirements for this test are

- The test considers current estimates of all contractual cash flows, and of related cash flows such as claims handling costs, as well as cash flows resulting from embedded options and guarantees.
- If the test shows that the liability is inadequate, the entire deficiency is recognized in profit or loss.

Once the insurer's accounting policy meets the minimum requirements, it is applied at a portfolio level aggregating insurance contracts having similar risks.

CHANGE IN ACCOUNTING POLICIES

For a change in accounting policy related to insurance contracts normally *relevance* and *reliability* is evaluated applying the criteria set out in IAS 8. However, it is sufficient if the insurer evaluates whether the changes bring the financial statements closer to meet the criteria set in IAS 8—there is no need to achieve full compliance. However, an insurer should not change its accounting policies to eliminate excessive prudence nor should it change accounting policies to introduce additional prudence when its accounting policies already reflect sufficient prudence.

The insurer is permitted, but not required, to change its accounting policy to reflect current market rates of interest while measuring an insurance liability under IFRS 4.24. If an insurer opts to change the accounting policy and measure designated insurance liabilities reflecting current market rates of interest, then it is necessary to apply other current estimates and assumptions to the designated liability. However, this policy need not be applied to all similar liabilities.

This insurer is allowed under IFRS 4.25 to continue existing policies relating to: (1) measurement of insurance liabilities, at undiscounted value, (2) measuring contractual rights to future investment management fees at an amount that exceeds their fair value as implied by a comparison with current fees charged by other market participants for similar services, and (3) using nonuniform accounting policies for the insurance contracts (and related deferred acquisition costs and related intangible assets, if any) of subsidiaries, except as permitted by IFRS 4.24. But introduction of these policies is not consistent with the requirements of IFRS 4.22. In other words, an insurer may continue with inconsistent accounting policies but should not introduce a new one.

DISCRETIONARY PARTICIPATION FEATURES

Some insurance contracts contain a discretionary participation feature (DPF) as well as a *guaranteed element*. A DPF is a contractual right to receive certain supplemental benefits that are in addition to a guaranteed benefit. These supplemental benefits typically represent a significant portion of the overall benefits under a contract.

However, the timing of their payment is subject to the discretion of the issuer.

1. IFRS 4.34(a): An insurer may (but need not) account for the guaranteed amount separately from the DPF wherein the guaranteed amount is recognized a liability. When it is not recognized separately, the entire contract is treated as a liability.
2. IFRS 4.34(b): If an insurer recognizes the DPF as a separate element (from the guaranteed element), it is classified either as a liability or a separate component of equity. The issuer may split that feature into liability and equity components and shall use a consistent accounting policy for that split.

   However, IFRS 4 prohibits insurers from characterizing any DPF on the insurer's financial statements as an intermediate statement of financial position entry that is neither equity nor a liability.
3. IFRS 4.34(c): An insurer may recognize all premiums received as revenue without separating any portion that relates to the equity component.

   Any change in the guaranteed element and in the portion of the DPF classified as a liability is recognized in the statement of comprehensive income. If part or all of the DPF is classified in equity, a portion of profit or loss may be attributable to that feature (in the same way that a portion may be attributable to noncontrolling interests).

DISCLOSURES

An insurer shall disclose information that identifies and explains the amounts in its financial statements arising from insurance contracts.

1. IFRS 4.38–39: Disclosure of Nature and extent of risk arising from insurance contract

Disclosures will cover objectives, policies, and processes for managing risks arising from insurance contracts and the methods used to manage those risks. Disclosure of information about insurance risk would include

a. Sensitivity to insurance risk
b. Concentrations of insurance risk, including a description of how management determines concentrations
c. Actual claims compared with previous estimates (i.e., claims development)

   The disclosure about claims development shall go back to the period when the earliest material claim arose for which there is still uncertainty about the amount and timing of the claims payments, but need not go back more than 10 years.

2. Disclosures of information about credit risk, liquidity risk and market risk

   Disclosures are made in accordance with paragraphs 31–42 of IFRS 7 if the insurance contracts were within the scope of IFRS 7. But the insurer is not required to provide the maturity analyses if an alternative method to manage sensitivity to market conditions is disclosed.

3. Information about exposures to market risk arising from embedded derivatives contained in a host insurance contract when it is not measured at fair value.

Example 2

Facts

Reliable Insurance Inc. has a reinsurance contract with the following components:

A policyholder under a reinsurance contract pays premiums of $300 every year for 10 years. The entity sets up an experience account equal to 70% of the cumulative premiums less 80% of the cumulative claims under the policy. If the balance in the experience account ever becomes negative, the policyholder has to pay an additional premium based on the balance on the experience account divided by the number of years the policy has left to run. At the end of the contract, if the balance on the experience account is positive, it is refunded to the policyholder. If the balance is negative, the policyholder has to pay the amount as an additional premium. The policy is not able to be canceled before the end of the contract, and the maximum loss that the policyholder is required to pay in any year is $400.

Required

Discuss how the reinsurance contract should be accounted for in the financial statements of the insurer.

Solution

The contract is an insurance contract because it transfers a significant insurance risk to the reinsurer. Where there are no claims on the contract, the policyholder will receive $2,100 at the end of year 10, which is 70% of the cumulative premiums of $3,000. IFRS 4 basically says that the policyholder has made a loan that the reinsurer will repay in one installment in year 10. If current policies of the reinsurer are that it should recognize a liability under the contract, then unbundling is permitted but not required. However, if the reinsurer does not have such policies, then IFRS 4 would require the reinsurer to unbundle the contract. If the contract is unbundled, each payment by the policyholder has two components: a loan advance payment and a payment for insurance cover. IAS 39 will be used to value the deposit element—the loan—and it will be measured initially at fair value. The fair value of the deposit element would be calculated by discounting back the future loan repayment in year 10 using an annuity method. If the policyholder makes a claim, then this in itself will be unbundled into a claim of $X and a loan of $Y, which will be repaid in installments over the life of the policy.

Example 3

Facts

United Insurance Inc. writes a single policy for a $1,000 premium and expects claims to be made of $600 in year 4. At the time of writing the policy there are commission costs paid of $200. Assume a discount rate of 3% risk-free. The entity says that if a provision for risk and uncertainty were to be made, it would amount to $250, and that this risk would expire evenly over years 2, 3, and 4. Under existing policies, the entity would spread the net premiums, the claims expense, and the commissioning costs over the first two years of the policy. Investment returns in years 1 and 2 are $20 and $40, respectively.

Required

Show the treatment of this policy using a deferral and matching approach in years 1 and 2 that would be acceptable under IFRS 4. How would the treatment differ if a fair value approach were used?

Solution

Deferral and Matching (IFRS 4):

	Year 1	Year 2
Premium earned	$500	$500
Claims expense	(300)	(300)
Commission costs	(100)	(100)
Underwriting profit	100	100
Investment return	20	40
Profit	$120	$140

If a fair value approach were used, the whole of the premium earned would be credited in year 1. The expected claims would be provided for on a discounted basis and then unwound over the period to year 4. The provision for risk and uncertainty would be made in year 1 and unwound over the following three years. Commission costs would all be charged in year 1 also. The investment returns would be treated in the same way as in the deferral approach.

EXTRACTS FROM PUBLISHED FINANCIAL STATEMENTS

Barloworld, Annual Report 2008

Notes to the Consolidated Annual Financial Statements for the Year Ended September 30

32. Insurance Contracts

Certain transactions are entered into by the group as insurer that fall within the definition of insurance contracts per IFRS 4, *Insurance Contracts*.

Significant items included are the following:

- Credit life and warranty products sold with vehicles in the automotive segment
- Specific portions of maintenance contracts on equipment and vehicles sold in the equipment, handling and automotive segments
- Guaranteed residual values on equipment and vehicles in the equipment, handling and automotive segments.

	2008 Rm	2007 Rm	2006 Rm
Income	**1,315**	1,195	1,156
Expenses	**1,021**	933	970
Cash (outflow)/inflow	**(67)**	(96)	19
Losses recognized on buying reinsurance	**5**	3	3
Deferral of gains and losses on reinsurance:			
Unamortized amount at the beginning of the period	**2**	4	6
Amortization for the period	**(2)**	(2)	(2)
Unamortized amount at the end of the period	**—**	2	4
Liabilities:			
At the beginning of the period	**482**	434	373
Amounts added	**1,261**	737	582
Amounts used	**(1,080)**	(682)	(520)
Amounts reversed unused	**(36)**	—	(1)
Translation difference	**23**	(7)	—
At the end of the period	**650**	482	434
Maturity profile:			
Within one year	**372**	344	219
Two to five years	**267**	137	214
More than five years	**11**	1	1
	650	482	434
Assets:			
At the beginning of the period	**220**	162	135
Amounts added	**616**	309	38
Amounts used	**(614)**	(276)	(11)
Amounts reversed unused	**—**	—	—
Acquisitions	**—**	25	
Translation difference	**—**	—	—
At the end of the period	**222**	220	162
Age analysis of items overdue but not impaired:			
Overdue 30 to 60 days	**10**	—	1
Overdue 60 to 90 days	**1**	—	—
Overdue 90+ days	**3**	5	—
	14	5	1

Significant Assumptions and Risks Arising from Insurance Contracts

Credit Life and Warranty Products

The sale of credit life and extended warranty products in the automotive segment is conducted through cell captive arrangements. The principal risk that the group faces under these insurance contracts is that the actual claims and benefit payments exceed the carrying amount of the insurance liabilities. This could occur because the frequency or severity of claims and benefits are greater than estimated. Insurance events are random and the actual number and amounts of claims and benefits will vary from year to year from the estimate determined using statistical techniques.

The key financial risk is that the proceeds from financial assets are not sufficient to fund the obligations arising from insurance contracts and includes credit risk, interest rate risk, currency risk and liquidity risk. All risks are managed on behalf of the group by an outside insurance company.

The risks are spread over a large variety of clients in the South African market.

The terms and conditions that have a material effect on the amount, timing and uncertainty of future cash flows arising from these contracts are as follows:

Personal accident—Provides compensation arising out of the death, permanent or temporary total disability of the insured, the family of the insured or the employees of a business. Such death or disability is restricted to certain accidents and does not provide the wider cover available from the life insurance industry.

Automotive—Provides indemnity for loss of or damage to the insured motor vehicle. The cover is normally on an all risks basis providing a wide scope of cover following an accident or a theft of the vehicle but the insured can select restricted forms of cover such as cover for fire and theft only.

The critical accounting judgments made in applying the group's accounting policies relate to the estimation of the ultimate liability arising from claims made under insurance contracts. The group's estimates for reported and unreported losses are continually reviewed and updated, and adjustments resulting from this review are reflected in profit or loss. The process relies on the basic assumption that past experience, adjusted for the effect of current developments are likely trends, is an appropriate basis for predicting future events.

Maintenance Contracts

Maintenance contracts are offered to customers in the Equipment, Automotive, and Handling segments. The contracts are managed internally through ongoing contract performance reviews, review of costs, and regular fleet inspections. Risks arising from maintenance contracts include component lives, component failure and cost of labor. The contracts consist of a variety of forms but generally include cover for regular maintenance as well as for repairs due to breakdowns and component failure which is not covered by manufacturer's warranties or other external maintenance plans. The amounts above include the estimated portion of contracts that meet the definition of an insurance contract. Revenue is recognized on the percentage of completion method based on the anticipated cost of repairs over the life cycle of the equipment/vehicles.

Financial risk mainly relates to credit risk but credit quality of customers is generally considered to be good and similar to the rest of the group's operations. Risks are spread over a large diversity of customers, fleets of equipment and vehicles and geographically in southern Africa, Iberia, United Kingdom and the United States.

36 NONCURRENT ASSETS HELD FOR SALE AND DISCONTINUED OPERATIONS (IFRS 5)

INTRODUCTION

IFRS 5 requires that companies reclassify noncurrent assets in the statement of financial position to be either held for sale or disposal group assets when management decides to sell these assets within one year. Disposal groups may be classified as discontinued operations when they meet specified criteria. IFRS 5 requires that all of these assets be recorded at the lower of carrying value or its estimated selling price less costs to sell (net realizable value). Once these assets are reclassified as held for sale or a disposal group, they are no longer subject to depreciation.

KEY TERMS

Asset held for sale. A noncurrent asset that will be recovered through selling the asset rather than usage.

Disposal group. A group of assets, and possibly some liabilities, that an entity intends to dispose of in a single transaction.

Discontinued operation. A component of an entity that is a separate major line of business or geographical area of operations and has either been disposed of, or is classified as held for sale, as part of a single coordinated plan to dispose.

SCOPE

IFRS 5 addresses most noncurrent assets. However, the standard excludes certain assets from its scope. The excluded assets are classified into two main categories:

1. Noncurrent assets that are already at fair value with changes in fair value recorded in profit or loss, such as financial assets.
2. Assets for which there might be difficulties in determining their fair value, such as deferred tax assets, assets arising from employee benefits and contractual rights under insurance contracts.

WHEN TO RECLASSIFY

When the following conditions are met, IFRS requires companies to reclassify assets as held for sale or as a disposal group:

- A noncurrent asset or disposal group must be available for immediate sale and the sale must be highly probable. The market price should be reasonable in comparison to the current fair value of the noncurrent asset or disposal group.
- For the asset to be available for immediate sale, actions required to complete the sale should have been made or are unlikely to be retracted.
- Sale should be within a year from the date it is classified.

- If the sale is not completed within one year, then the asset should continue to be classified as held for sale only if the following are met:

    - The entity is committed to sell a noncurrent asset, but conditions imposed by other parties render the sale incomplete until a firm purchase commitment is made and this commitment is highly probable within a year.
    - A firm purchase commitment is made, but unexpected conditions are imposed by the buyer of the noncurrent asset.
    - The asset is not sold due to unlikely unforeseen circumstances that arise. The noncurrent asset should be marketed at a reasonable price and should fulfill the criteria to continue to be classified as held for sale.

Example 1

Plastics Fabrication Inc. owns a research and development (R&D) facility in California. Due to the rapid change in plastics technology, the company decided to build another facility in Texas where related oil industry infrastructure is readily available. The company decided to put the R&D facility up for sale by engaging a reputable real estate agency to handle the sale on its behalf. The company will vacate the building when a buyer is identified and a sale contract is drawn.

In this case, the company appears to meet the criteria in IFRS 5, and thus, should be reclassified as a noncurrent asset held for sale.

Example 2

Assuming the same facts as in Example 1, except that the company *will not* vacate the building until its new facility in Texas is completed. With this twist of facts, the company may not meet the requirements of IFRS 5, because the company put restrictions on the sale and thus it should not classify this facility as available for sale.

Example 3

Common Seals Inc. committed to sell its facility in California and hired an agent to promote its sale. The company reclassified this facility from noncurrent plant asset to held-for-sale asset. During the year, the economic conditions in the United States deteriorated significantly, whereby prices dropped and credit dried up for the new facility. A year has gone by and the facility has not sold. Management is still eager to sell the asset and is actively promoting it including multiple reductions in the selling price.

Should Common Seals Inc. revert the classification of the R&D facility into a plant asset or continue to keep it on the books as held for sale?

The fourth criteria in IFRS 5 allows Common Seals Inc. to keep the asset held for sale because management is doing all it can to sell it despite the unusual circumstances facing the company in consummating the sale.

ASSETS HELD FOR SALE

When a company decides to sell a noncurrent asset within a year or less, IFRS 5 requires that the company reclassify that asset as held for sale. The key event that triggers the reclassification is when the company decides to sell the asset instead of continuing to use it.

Example 4

ABC Company is relocating its manufacturing facility in the United States to China. The factory building and the land will not be needed any more and management decides to put it up for sale. It has been two years and management has been unable to sell the building due to the economic downturn in the United States.

In this case, the asset must continue to be reclassified as held for sale even though IFRS 5 requires the sale to take place in one year. Due to circumstances beyond management's control, the company still treats this as a held-for-sale asset instead of a noncurrent asset intended for use. That means the asset should be classified as held for sale and recorded at the lower of cost or net realizable value.

DISPOSAL GROUP ASSETS

IFRS 5 defines a *disposal group* as assets to be disposed (sold) of together as a group in a single transaction. A disposal group normally is a component of an entity. Examples of a component of an entity can be a business segment (geographical location or product line), a cash-generating unit, or a subsidiary.

Example 5

XYZ Company decided to eliminate its operations in the U.S. Midwest that were selling health-care products but will continue operating in other parts of the country.

In this case, the assets that are located in the Midwest will have to be treated as a disposal group because the company's operations in the Midwest are considered by the company's management as a cash-generating unit or a geographical segment.

DISCONTINUED OPERATIONS

Some of the disposal groups may have to be classified as *discontinued operations* if they meet certain criteria and the company's operations are experiencing recurring losses and the company is intending to exit altogether from a line of business or a major geographic location.

Example 6

XYZ Company has decided to sell all its assets related to health-care products and concentrate on its other line of business. Because the company is exiting the health-care business due to accumulated losses, the losses in the statement of comprehensive income should be classified as discontinued operations.

MEASUREMENT OF NONCURRENT ASSETS
HELD FOR SALE OR DISPOSAL GROUP

- An asset should be measured in accordance with the applicable IFRS before classification as held for sale.
- Noncurrent assets classified as a disposal group or held for sale are measured at the lower of the carrying amount and fair value less cost to sell. *Fair value* is the amount a willing party is interested in paying to buy the asset in an arm's-length transaction. *Cost to sell* is the estimated necessary cost to dispose of the asset such as advertising cost or commission.
- Cost to sell is measured at present value when a sale is expected to occur after one year. Increases in the present value are reflected as a finance cost in profit and loss.
- Impairment losses are reflected as profit or loss on any initial or subsequent write-down of the asset or disposal group to fair value less cost to sell.
- Subsequent increases in fair value less cost to sell of an asset are recognized in profit or loss to the extent that it is not in excess of cumulative impairment losses (IAS 36).
- Noncurrent assets or disposal groups held for sale should not be depreciated.

CHANGES IN CLASSIFICATION OF HELD FOR SALE

Management may decide to change the classification of a held-for-sale asset due to circumstances that may make management change its plans about selling the asset. The change of classification from held for sale to plant asset will require that the asset be recorded at the lower of the carrying amount of the asset before its classification to held for sale and the net realizable amount of the asset at the time when management decided not to sell.

Example 7

On January 1, 2008, Mina Production Inc. classified a production facility from noncurrent plant to assets held for sale. The carrying amount of the asset at the time of the decision to sell was $1.5 million (cost of $2.2 million, less accumulated depreciation of $700,000). A year and a half later, on June 30, 2009, management decided not to sell the asset due to a new strategic consideration. The estimated fair value of the asset, net of cost to sell, is estimated to be $900,000.

What is the amount of the production facility to be recorded on the date of reverting the asset back to a noncurrent asset?

IFRS 5 requires companies to select the lower of the carrying value of the asset before classification as held for sale (i.e., $1.5 million) and the fair value of the asset net of cost to sell, on the date of reverting back to plant asset (i.e., $900,000).

Based on this information, Mina Production Inc. should record the asset at $900,000 with a loss of $600,000 to be recorded on remeasurement of noncurrent assets.

DISCLOSURES

IFRS 5 requires the following disclosure:

- Noncurrent assets and disposal group assets and liabilities must be disclosed separately on the statement of financial position.
- Disclosures should also include a description of the noncurrent assets of a disposal group, a description of the facts and circumstances of the sale, and the expected manner and timing of that disposal.
- Any gain or loss results from remeasurement of an asset held for sale or a disposal group should be reported in the statement of comprehensive income in profit or loss from continuing operations.
- Any gain or loss on discontinued operations should be reported as a single item, net of tax, on the face of the statement of comprehensive income as a separate line item, in addition to note disclosure of the revenues and expenses resulting from the discontinued operations.

EXTRACTS FROM PUBLISHED FINANCIAL STATEMENTS

Holcim, Annual Report 2008

Consolidated Financial Statements

Accounting Policies

Noncurrent Assets (or Disposal Groups) Classified as Held for Sale

Noncurrent assets (or disposal groups) are classified as held for sale and stated at the lower of carrying amount and fair value less costs to sell if their carrying amount is to be recovered principally through a sale transaction rather than through continuing use.

19. Assets and Related Liabilities Classified as Held for Sale

The major classes of assets and liabilities classified as held for sale are as follows:

in CHF million	2008	2007
Cash and cash equivalents	6	0
Other current assets	19	0
Property, plant, and equipment	95	44[1]
Investments in associates	237	0
Other assets	44	0
Assets classified as held for sale	**401**	**44**

in CHF million	2008	2007
Short-term liabilities	22	0
Long-term provisions	3	0
Other long-term liabilities	27	0
Liabilities directly associated with assets classified as held for sale	**52**	**0**
Net assets classified as held for sale	**349**	**44**

¹*Reclassified from prepaid expenses and other current assets.*

Investments in associates consist primarily of Holcim Venezuela amounting to CHF 220 million. The remaining assets and liabilities classified as held for sale consist of individually immaterial assets and disposal groups.

In April 2008, the Venezuelan government announced that it would nationalize at least 60% of the share capital of the three foreign cement producers operating in the country. On June 18, the respective decree was published. Holcim and the government have engaged in consultations regarding the compensation Holcim is due under the applicable Bilateral Investment Treaties. On August 18, 2008, as result of these consultations, a Memorandum of Understanding was signed between the government and Holcim, which provides for the negotiation of a final sales agreement by which 85% of *Holcim Venezuela's* shares would be transferred to the government and Holcim would keep a stake of 15%. The Memorandum of Understanding also reflects an agreement in principle regarding the compensation to be paid, subject to due diligence. Although the Venezuelan government has in the meantime taken control of Holcim Venezuela, no compensation has yet been paid. While Holcim still hopes for an amicable resolution of its claim for compensation; it is also considering its legal options under the applicable Bilateral Investment Treaties.

Holcim Venezuela was deconsolidated as of December 31, 2008, and recognized as an associate. In accordance with IFRS 5, the investment was classified as held for sale.

In 2008, Holcim Venezuela reported net sales of CHF 280 million (2007: 245), accounting for approximately 1% (2007: 1) of group net sales.

Smiths Group plc, 2007

7. Discontinued Operations

On May 5, 2007, the company sold its Aerospace operations to General Electric Company. The Aerospace operations sold comprised the Aerospace business segment as reported in previous annual reports and accounts plus the microwave company previously reported in Specialty—Other. The revenue and profit before taxation of the microwave company were £32.2 million (2006: £42.9 million) and £7.6 million (2006: £10.2 million), respectively. As the Aerospace operations represented a separate business segment, the disposal group has been treated as a discontinued operation in this annual report and accounts. The posttax result of the Aerospace operations has been disclosed as a discontinued operation in the consolidated income statement. In the cashflow statement, the operating cash-flows of the Aerospace Group have been aggregated with those of the continuing operations, but are shown separately in the note below.

Profit on Disposal of Operation

in £ million	
Total consideration	2,585.4
Foreign exchange recycled to the income statement on disposal	(48.4)
Provisions and disposal costs	(76.0)
Pension curtailment gains	63.3
Provision for settlement loss	(24.3)
	2,500.0
Net assets disposed	(1,030.4)
Pre-tax profit on disposal	1,469.6
Cash received from disposal of Aerospace operations	2,585.4
Disposal costs	(31.9)
Cash and cash equivalents of subsidiaries disposed	(62.5)
Borrowings of subsidiaries disposed	4.0
Net cash inflow on disposal	2,495.0

Assets and Liabilities of Discontinued Operations at the Date of Disposal

in £ million

Assets

Intangible assets	553.0
Property, plant, and equipment	256.1
Retirement benefit assets	6.8
Inventories	297.0
Trade and other receivables	1,357.1
Intercompany receivables	1,024.5
Cash and cash equivalents	62.5
Financial derivatives	12.1
Total assets	3,569.1

Liabilities
Financial liabilities

– borrowings	(4.0)
– financial derivatives	(2.5)
Provisions for liabilities and charges	(20.6)
Retirement benefit obligations	(0.5)
Deferred tax liabilities	(17.4)
Trade and other payables	(2,493.7)
Total liabilities	(2,538.7)
Net assets	1,030.4

Financial information for the Aerospace operations after Group eliminations is presented here.

Results from Discontinued Operations

in £ million unless otherwise noted	Period ended *July 31, 2007*	Period ended *August 5, 2006*
Revenue	**955.6**	1,342.6
Cost of sales	**(667.9)**	(946.0)
Gross profit	**287.7**	396.6
Sales and distribution costs	**(29.9)**	(37.8)
Administrative expenses	**(116.6)**	(188.7)
Loss on disposal of business	**—**	(1.7)
Operating profit	**141.2**	168.4
Interest payable	**(1.2)**	(1.1)
Other financing gains	**0.7**	—
Other finance income—retirement benefits	**3.1**	2.4
Profit before taxation	**143.8**	169.7
Taxation relating to performance of discontinued operations (Note 6)	**(36.9)**	(42.8)
Profit on disposal	**1,469.6**	—
Attributable tax charge (Note 6)	**(51.3)**	—
Profit for the period	**1,525.2**	126.9
Earnings per share from discontinued operations—pence		
Basic	**277.8p**	22.5p
Diluted	**273.9p**	22.5p

The profit before taxation for the period ended July 31, 2007, represents the results of the operations for the period to the date of disposal.

Analysis by geographical location. The group's revenue from discontinued operations by destination is shown here:

	Period ended July 31, 2007	Period ended August 5, 2006
Revenue		
United Kingdom	**125.7**	186.3
North America	**688.6**	963.0
Europe	**95.0**	112.5
Other overseas	**46.3**	80.8
	955.6	1,342.6

The group operating profit from discontinued operations was after charging:

in £ million	Period ended July 31, 2007	Period ended August 5, 2006
Cost of inventories recognized as an expense	**594.6**	778.7
Employee costs (Note 11)	**342.5**	467.3
Depreciation of property, plant, and equipment	**8.4**	31.2
Amortization of intangible assets	**3.8**	19.4
Impairment losses recognized in the period on receivables	**0.1**	0.3
Research and development costs	**29.4**	53.4
Operating leases		
Land and buildings	**4.1**	7.5
Other	**1.0**	1.4
Fair value movements on derivatives		
Embedded	**(0.1)**	3.5
Held for trading	**0.7**	(0.1)

Cash Flows from Discontinued Operations

in £ million	Period ended July 31, 2007	Period ended August 5, 2006
Profit before taxation (including profit on disposal of Aerospace operations)	**1,613.4**	169.7
Net interest payable	**1.2**	1.1
Financing (gains)/losses		
Charged to financing	**(0.7)**	—
Other finance income—retirement benefits	**(3.1)**	(2.4)
Profit on disposal of discontinued operation	**(1,469.6)**	—
	141.2	168.4
Amortization of intangible assets	**3.8**	19.4
Profit on disposal of property, plant, and equipment	**0.2**	—
Profit on disposal of business	—	1.7
Depreciation of property, plant, and equipment	**8.4**	31.2
Share-based payment expense	**3.5**	5.3
Retirement benefits	**(22.6)**	1.6
Increase in inventories	**(51.0)**	(31.6)
(Increase)/decrease in trade and other receivables	**(17.3)**	16.5
(Decrease)/increase in trade and other payables	**(16.4)**	60.5
(Decrease)/increase in provisions	**(1.1)**	0.5
Cash generated from operations	**48.7**	273.5
Interest	**(1.2)**	(1.1)
Tax paid	**(6.9)**	(22.3)
Net cash inflow from operating activities	**40.6**	250.1
Operating activities	**40.6**	250.1
Investing activities	**2,373.1**	(148.1)
Financing activities	**14.2**	3.0
	2,427.9	105.0

37 EXPLORATION FOR AND EVALUATION OF MINERAL RESOURCES (IFRS 6)

INTRODUCTION

The objective of IFRS 6 is to specify the financial reporting for the exploration for and evaluation of mineral resources.

IFRS 6 deals with only limited aspects of accounting for extractive activities. These include

1. Assessment of exploration and evaluation assets for impairment (impairment is measured in accordance with IAS 36, *Impairment of Assets*); and
2. Disclosures about exploration for and evaluation of mineral resources.

On the introduction of this standard the recognition and measurement of Exploration and Evaluation Assets (E&E assets) fall outside the scope of IAS 38, *Intangible Assets*, and IAS 16, *Property Plant, and Equipment.*

SELECTION AND APPLICATION OF ACCOUNTING POLICIES

When developing accounting policies for E&E assets, an entity is required to apply fundamental principles of selection and application of policies as stated in IAS 8, *Accounting Policies, Changes in Accounting Estimates and Errors*. These principles are

- Relevance in the context of decision-making needs of users;
- Providing faithful representation;
- Reflecting economic substance;
- Neutrality;
- Prudence; and
- Completeness.

As per IAS 8, paragraphs 11–12, management should normally refer to sources of authoritative requirements and guidance in developing an accounting policy for an item if no IFRS applies specifically to that item. However, these paragraphs of IFRS 8 are not required to be followed for recognition and measurement of E&E assets.

KEY TERMS

Exploration and evaluation expenditures. Expenditures that are incurred by an entity in connection with the exploration for and evaluation of mineral resources before the technical feasibility and commercial viability of extracting a mineral resource are demonstrable.

Exploration and evaluation assets. The capitalized portion of exploration and evaluation expenditures recognized as assets in accordance with the entity's accounting policy. They are measured at cost at the time of initial recognition. Paragraph 11 of IFRS 6 requires an entity to recognize an obligation for removal of the remains of the E&E activities and restoration of the site in accordance with the principle in IAS 37, *Provisions, Contingent Liabilities, and Contingent Assets.*

ACCOUNTING FOR E&E COSTS

Expenditures incurred in exploration activities are expensed unless they meet the definition of an asset (see the IASB *Framework*, paragraphs 53–59). An entity should recognize an asset when it is probable that economic benefits will flow to the entity as a result of the expenditure.

Expenditures on an exploration property are expensed until the capitalization point. The capitalization point is the earlier of either (1) when the fair value less cost to sell of the property can be reliably determined as higher than the total of the expenses incurred; or (2) when an assessment of the property demonstrates that commercially viable reserves are present and therefore, there are probable future economic benefits from the continued development and production of the resource.

If this policy is followed, expenses capitalized under IFRS 6 will meet the definition of an asset as stated in the IASB *Framework* as the capitalization criteria followed would demonstrate probable future economic benefits.

IFRS 6, paragraph 9, gives examples of expenditures incurred for E&E assets (the list is not exhaustive):

- Acquisition of rights to explore;
- Topographical, geological, geochemical and geophysical studies;
- Exploratory drilling;
- Trenching;
- Sampling; and
- Activities in relation to evaluating the technical feasibility and commercial viability of extracting a mineral resource.

Expenditures related to the development of mineral resources do not relate to E&E assets. These are covered under development assets. An entity has to take guidance from the IASB *Framework* and IAS 38 for recognizing and measuring development assets.

While recognizing E&E assets, it becomes necessary to recognize any obligations for removal and restoration that are incurred during a particular period as a consequence of having undertaken the exploration for and evaluation of mineral resources under IAS 37, *Provisions, Contingent Liabilities and Contingent Assets.*

Prior to the adoption of IFRS, a number of companies in the oil and gas industry used the *full cost method of accounting* for E&E expenditure. Under this method all E&E expenditure is capitalized within cost pools. Costs are then considered for impairment or depreciated on commencement of production as cost pools rather than on the basis of an individual field. Applying full cost method, a "dry" well may be capitalized as part of the cost pool, but the lack of associated reserves will be taken into account through an increased depletion charge or through the impairment testing performed on the overall pool.

Successful efforts is an alternative method of accounting for E&E that is favored by many larger companies. Under this method, the E&E expenditure is initially capitalized pending the determination of reserves on the basis of an individual field.

As companies opt to change from a full cost method to a successful efforts method on adoption of IFRS, there will be generally a reduction in opening net assets; however, this will result in lower amounts recognized through the statement of comprehensive income going forward in respect of these assets by way of reduced depletion.

In fact, IFRS 6 does not specify the full cost or successful efforts method. It requires an entity to adopt an appropriate accounting policy within the broad principles stated in IAS 8, paragraph 6. However, only expenses specified in IFRS 6, paragraph 9, can be capitalized and the IASB *Framework* definition of an *asset* may not permit capitalization of some expenses as E&E assets.

Exhibit 37.1. Exploration and Evaluation Activities at a Glance

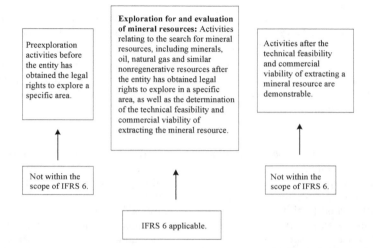

MEASUREMENT AFTER INITIAL RECOGNITION AND PRESENTATION

Subsequent to the initial recognition of E&E at cost, an entity shall apply either the cost model or revaluation model. For the purpose of applying revaluation, the entity should follow the principles set out in IAS 16 or IAS 38.

An entity may change its accounting policies relating to E&E assets. While doing so, it is necessary to judge the principles of reliability and relevance in accordance with IAS 8. A change in accounting policy should make the financial statements more relevant for the users' decision making and should not be less reliable.

It is possible to present E&E assets either as tangible assets or intangibles depending on the nature of the assets. For example, a drilling right is classified as an intangible asset, whereas vehicles and drilling rigs are classified as tangible assets.

E&E assets are no longer classified as such when technical feasibility and commercial viability of extracting minerals is demonstrable.

IMPAIRMENT

E&E assets are tested for impairment when the facts and circumstances suggest that the carrying amount is more than the recoverable amount. In such a case, the entity should apply IAS 36 and measure the impairment loss, if any. Then E&E assets should be presented net of such impairment loss. IFRS 6, paragraph 20, explains those facts and circumstances that should be evaluated for assessing if there is any impairment loss for E&E assets. IAS 36, paragraphs 8–17, are not applied for the identification purpose.

IFRS 6, paragraph 20, illustrates four indicators (this list is not exhaustive):

1. *Expiry of the time with which exploration activities may be carried out.* The time frame within which exploration activity was granted to the entity for a specific area has expired during the accounting period or in the near future, and renewal may not be possible.

2. *Absence of supportive budget.* There is no plan or budget for the substantive expenditure to be incurred for the exploration activities in a specific area.

3. *Nondiscovery of mineral resources.* E&E activities led to nondiscovery of commercially viable quantities of mineral resources and thereby further activities may not be carried out.

4. *Supporting data.* There is sufficient data that proves that although E&E activities continue, the carrying amount of the E&E assets is unlikely to be recovered in full from successful development or by sale.

The entity shall allocate E&E assets to cash-generating units or groups of cash-generating units for the purpose of evaluation of impairment losses. Each such cash-generating unit or group of cash-generating units shall not be larger than an operating segment as defined in IFRS 8.

DISCLOSURES

An entity shall disclose information that identifies and explains the amounts recognized in its financial statements arising from the exploration for and evaluation of mineral resources. This requires: (1) disclosures of accounting policies for exploration and evaluation expenditures including the recognition of exploration and evaluation assets, and (2) the amounts of assets, liabilities, income and expense and operating and investing cash flows arising from the exploration for and evaluation of mineral resources. An entity is required to treat E&E assets as a separate class of assets, either under IAS 16 (classification as tangible assets) or IAS 38 (intangible assets), and make the disclosures required by either IAS 16 or IAS 38, consistent with how the assets are classified.

Recent amendments to IFRS 1 (effective for annual periods beginning on or after January 1, 2010, with early application permitted) allow a first-time adopter using full cost method of accounting under its previous GAAP to elect to measure oil and gas assets at the date of transition to IFRS on the following basis:

• E&E assets at the amount determined under previous GAAP
• Assets in the development or production phases at the amount determined under previous GAAP, allocated to the underlying assets pro rata using reserve volumes or reserve values as of that date

Upon measuring oil and gas assets on this basis, the E&E assets and those assets in the development and production phases are required to be tested for impairment at the date of transition to IFRS in accordance with the provisions of this standard and those of IAS 36, *Impairment of Assets*, to determine that the assets are not stated at more than their recoverable amount. For the purpose of these exemptions, oil and gas assets comprise only those assets used in the exploration, evaluation, development, or production of oil and gas.

If the exemption for oil and gas assets in the development or production phases accounted for using the full cost method under previous GAAP is elected, a first-time adopter is required to disclose that fact and the basis in which carrying amounts determined under previous GAAP were allocated.

EXCERPTS FROM PUBLISHED FINANCIAL STATEMENTS

Royal Dutch Shell plc, Annual Report 2008

2. Accounting Policies

Exploration Costs

Shell follows the successful efforts method of accounting for oil and natural gas exploration costs. Exploration costs are charged to income when incurred, except that exploratory drilling costs are included in property, plant, and equipment, pending determination of proved reserves. Exploration wells that are more than 12 months old are expensed unless (1) proved reserves are booked, or (2) (a) they have found commercially producible quantities of reserves, and (b) they are subject to further exploration or appraisal activity in that either drilling of additional exploratory wells is underway or firmly planned for the near future or other activities are being undertaken to sufficiently progress the assessing of reserves and the economic and operating viability of the project.

3. Key Accounting Estimates and Judgments

Exploration Costs

Capitalized exploration drilling costs more than 12 months old are expensed unless (1) proved reserves are booked, or (2) (a) they have found commercially producible quantities of reserves and (b) they are subject to further exploration or appraisal activity in that either drilling of additional exploratory wells is under way or firmly planned for the near future or other activities are being undertaken to sufficiently progress the assessing of reserves and the economic and operating viability of the project. When making decisions about whether to continue to capitalize exploration drilling costs for a period longer than 12 months, it is necessary to make judgments about the satisfaction of each of these conditions. If there is a change in one of these judgments in a subsequent period, then the related capitalized exploration drilling costs would be expensed in that period, resulting in a charge to income. Information on such costs is given in Note 11.

12. Property, Plant, and Equipment

Exploration and evaluation assets, which mainly comprise unproved properties (rights and concessions) and capitalized exploration drilling costs, included within the amounts shown here for oil and gas properties are as follows:

U.S. dollars (million)	*2008*	*2007*
Cost		
At January 1	**11,480**	8,963
Capital expenditure	**9,293**	2,947
Sales, retirements, currency translation differences, and other movements	**(2,287)**	(430)
At December 31	**18,486**	11,480
Depreciation, depletion, and amortisation		
At January 1	**1,678**	1,633
Charge for the year	**430**	97
Sales, retirements, currency translation differences, and other movements	**(632)**	(52)
At December 31	**1,476**	1,678
Net book amount at December 31	**17,010**	9,802

Capitalized exploration drilling costs are as follows:

Exploration drilling costs capitalized for periods greater than one year and representing 156 wells amounted to $1,499 million at December 31, 2008. Information by year of expenditure is presented here:

U.S. dollars (million)		*Number of wells*
2000	$21	1
2001	20	2
2002	65	6
2003	82	5
2004	81	7
2005	206	15
2006	358	52
2007	666	68
Total	1,499	156

These costs remain capitalized for more than one year because, for the related projects, either (1) firm exploration/exploratory appraisal wells were executed in 2008 and/or are planned in the near future, and/or (2) firm development activities are being progressed with a final investment decision expected in the near future.

38 FINANCIAL INSTRUMENTS: DISCLOSURES (IFRS 7)

INTRODUCTION

IFRS 7, *Financial Instruments: Disclosures,* is a disclosure standard. It requires an entity to provide disclosures in their financial statements that enable users to evaluate

- The significance of financial instruments for the entity's financial position and performance; and
- The nature and extent of risks arising from financial instruments, and how the entity manages those risks.

An entity shall group financial instruments into classes that are appropriate to the nature of the information disclosed and that take into account the characteristics of those financial instruments. An entity shall provide sufficient information to facilitate reconciliation of line items presented in the statement of financial position.

SCOPE

This standard applies to those financial instruments to which IAS 32 applies, with the additional exclusion of equity instruments (including puttable instruments classified as equity).

Definition of Various Kinds of Risk

For purpose of disclosures of financial instruments, the following terms related to risks are defined in Appendix A of this standard.

Credit risk. Risk that arises from failure of one party to a financial instrument to discharge an obligation that will cause a financial loss for the other party.

Currency risk. Risk that the fair value or future cash flows of a financial instrument will fluctuate because of changes in foreign exchange rates.

Interest rate risk. Risk that the fair value or future cash flows of a financial instrument will fluctuate because of changes in market interest rates.

Liquidity risk. Risk that an entity will encounter difficulty in meeting obligations associated with financial liabilities.

Market risk. Risk that the fair value or future cash flows of a financial instrument will fluctuate because of changes in market prices. Market risk comprises three types of risk: currency risk, interest rate risk, and other price risk.

Other price risk. Risk that the fair value or future cash flows of a financial instrument will fluctuate because of changes in market prices (other than those arising from interest rate risk or currency risk), whether those changes are caused by factors specific to the individual financial instrument or its issuer, or factors affecting all similar financial instruments traded in the market.

SIGNIFICANT ACCOUNTING POLICIES
RELATING TO FINANCIAL INSTRUMENTS

IFRS 7 reminds readers that IAS 1 requires that an entity discloses, in the summary of significant accounting policies, the measurement basis (or bases) used in preparing the financial statements and the other accounting policies relevant to an understanding of the financial statements.

Disclosures of Financial Instruments by Categories

The carrying amount of various financial instruments is disclosed by category, either in the statement of financial position or notes, as follows:

- Financial assets at fair value through profit or loss (FVTPL), showing separately (1) those designated as such upon initial recognition and (2) those classified as held for trading in accordance with IAS 39, *Financial Instruments: Recognition and Measurement;*
- Held-to-maturity investments;
- Loans and receivables;
- Available-for-sale financial assets;
- Financial liabilities at FVTPL, showing separately (1) those designated as such upon initial recognition and (2) those classified as held for trading in accordance with IAS 39, *Financial Instruments: Recognition and Measurement;* and
- Financial liabilities measured at amortized cost.

In relation to financial assets or liabilities, which are designated as at fair value through profit or loss, an entity shall disclose

- Maximum credit risk exposure;
- Extent of risk mitigated, if any, using credit derivatives or similar instruments;
- Changes in fair value attributable to credit risk during the year and cumulatively (as distinguished from the market risk which arises out of changes in benchmark interest rate, commodity price, foreign exchange rate, or index of prices or rates). The method applied to determine the credit risk component shall be disclosed;
- Changes in fair value of credit derivatives or similar instruments during the year and cumulatively.

When an entity redesignates a financial asset or liability at FVTPL, it shall segregate the credit risk component from market as a result of change in fair value and disclose the credit risk component arising during the year and cumulatively. It shall also disclose the method applied for the segregation. In addition, it shall disclose differences between the carrying amount of the financial liability and the contractual payment obligation at maturity including the method applied to determine the difference.

If an entity reaches a conclusion that the method applied to separate the credit risk factor of financial asset/liability does not faithfully represent changes attributable to credit risk factors, it shall disclose the reasons thereof.

DISCLOSURES FOR RECLASSIFICATIONS

When an entity reclassifies financial assets from fair value categories (i.e., FVTPL or available for sale [AFS]) to amortized cost-based categories (i.e., held to maturity or loans and receivables), it has to disclose the amount of reclassifications in and out of a category.

An entity shall also disclose the following in regard to any reclassification in or out of AFS category/FVTPL category (allowed only in rare circumstances) to amortized cost-based categories:

- Amount reclassified in and out of each category;
- Fair value of reclassified financial asset for each reporting period till the asset is derecognized;
- Fair value gain/loss of reclassified financial asset recognized in the profit or loss/other comprehensive income in the year of reclassification;
- Amount of fair value gain or loss that would have been recognized in the profit or loss/other comprehensive income in each of the reporting periods after reclassification of a financial asset until derecognition;
- Effective interest rate and estimated cash flows that an entity estimates to recover from the financial asset on the date of reclassification.
- The description of rare circumstances that resulted in reclassification out of FVTPL category to amortized cost-based categories in accordance with IAS 39.50B.

DISCLOSURES FOR DERECOGNITION OF FINANCIAL ASSETS

Certain transfer of financial assets does not meet the conditions of derecognition. In those cases, disclosures cover (1) the nature of the assets, (2) the nature of the risks and rewards of ownership to which the entity remains exposed, (3) the carrying amounts of the assets and of the associated liabilities if the financial asset continued to be recognized in its entirety, and (4) in the case of an entity having continuing involvement in assets transferred, the total carrying amount of the original assets, the amount of the assets that the entity continues to recognize, and the carrying amount of the associated liabilities.

COLLATERAL

Disclosures for collateral issued and collateral held are as follows:

Collateral Issued	Collateral Held

1. Carrying amount of financial assets it has pledged as collateral for liabilities or contingent liabilities.
 	
    It includes amounts that have been reclassified in accordance with paragraph 37(a) of IAS 39.
2. Terms and conditions of the pledge.
	1. Disclosures under IFRS 7.15 are required if an entity holds collateral (of financial or nonfinancial assets) and is permitted to sell or repledge the collateral in the absence of default by the owner of the collateral:
	
	    a. Fair value of the collateral;
	    b. Fair value of any such collateral sold or repledged;
	    c. Obligation of the entity to return the collateral;
	    d. Associated terms and conditions regarding use of the collateral.
	
	2. Disclosures under IFRS 7.38 when financial/nonfinancial assets held as collateral/other credit enhancements (like guarantees):
	
	    a. the nature and carrying amount of the assets obtained; and
	    b. when the assets are not readily convertible into cash, its policies for disposing of such assets or for using them in its operations.

IMPAIRMENT ALLOWANCE

An entity maintains a separate allowance account to recognize individual and/or collective credit loss arising out of impairment of financial assets. Such impairment loss is not directly deducted from the carrying amount of the financial asset. An entity shall disclose a reconciliation showing movements in such allowance account.

Compound Financial Instruments with Multiple Embedded Derivatives

Descriptive disclosure is required to explain the existence of such features in the financial instruments.

Defaults and Breaches

For loans payable, the following disclosures are required:

- Details of any defaults during the period of principal, interest, sinking fund, or redemption terms of those loans payable;
- Carrying amount of the loans payable in default at the end of the reporting period; and
- Description whether the default was remedied, or the terms of the loans payable were renegotiated, before the financial statements were authorized for issue.

DISCLOSURES IN THE STATEMENT OF COMPREHENSIVE INCOME

An entity has to disclose gains or losses, total interest income and expense, fee income and expense covering: (1) net gain or loss classified by categories of financial assets and liabilities, (2) total interest income and expense calculated using effective rate interest method, (3) fees, income and expenses other than those included in determining the effective rate of interest, (4) interest income on impaired financial assets accrued, and (5) impairment losses for each class of financial asset.

HEDGE ACCOUNTING DISCLOSURES

Paragraphs 22–24 of IFRS 7 require the following disclosures:

Hedging in general	For cash flow hedge	For fair value hedge	For hedging net investments in foreign operations
The entity must provide: 1. A description of each type of hedge; 2. A description of the financial instruments designated as hedging instruments and their fair values at the end of the reporting period; and 3. Nature of the risks being hedged.	The entity must provide: 1. The periods when the cash flows are expected to occur and to affect profit or loss; 2. A description of previously applied hedge accounting to a forecast transaction that is no longer expected to occur; 3. The amount that was recognized in other comprehensive income during the period under cash flow hedge reserve;	Disclose gains or losses: 1. On the hedging instrument; or 2. On the hedged item attributable to the hedged risk.	Discloses the ineffectiveness recognized in profit or loss that arises from hedges of net investments in foreign operations.

Hedging in general	For cash flow hedge	For fair value hedge	For hedging net investments in foreign operations
	4. Reclassification adjustment carried out of the cash flow hedge reserve during the period, showing the amount included in each line item in the statement of comprehensive income; 5. Amount of reclassification adjustment that is included in the initial cost or other carrying amount of a nonfinancial asset or nonfinancial liability whose acquisition or incurrence was a hedge; and 6. The ineffectiveness recognized in profit or loss that arises from cash flow hedges.		

FAIR VALUE DISCLOSURES

The fair value of each class of assets and liabilities should be presented in a way that permits it to be compared with its carrying amount. An entity has to classify the fair value measurements of all items of financial assets/liabilities using a fair value hierarchy. The fair value hierarchy reflects the significance of the inputs used in making the measurements. It has three levels.

Level 1: Quoted prices (unadjusted) in active markets for identical assets or liabilities

Level 2: Inputs other than quoted prices included within Level 1 that are observable for the asset or liability, either directly (i.e., as prices) or indirectly (i.e., derived from prices)

Level 3: Inputs for the asset or liability that are not based on observable market data (unobservable inputs)

A tabular presentation may be relevant. Also, fair value of financial assets and liabilities are not offset against each other unless they are offset in accordance with IAS 1, *Presentation of Financial Statements.*

Disclosures when using the valuation model (as it is believed that the best evidence of fair value at initial recognition is the transaction price) include

- Valuation technique and assumptions used including assumptions relating to prepayment rates, rates of estimated credit losses, and interest rates or discount rates wherever applicable;
- Accounting policy for recognizing that difference in profit or loss to reflect a change in factors (including time) that market participants would consider in setting a price; and
- The aggregate difference yet to be recognized in profit or loss at the beginning and end of the period and a reconciliation of changes in the balance of this difference.

Fair value disclosures are *not* required when

- The carrying amount is a reasonable approximation of fair value, for example, for financial instruments such as short-term trade receivables and payables;
- An investment in equity instruments does not have a quoted market price in an active market, or a derivative linked to such equity instruments, that is measured at cost; or
- A contract contains a discretionary participation feature.

DISCLOSURES IN LIEU OF FAIR VALUE DISCLOSURES

In relation to investment in equity instrument discussed earlier and for a contract containing a discretionary participation feature, an entity shall make the following additional disclosures:

- The fact of nondisclosure of fair value information because their fair value cannot be measured reliably;
- A description of the financial instruments, their carrying amount, and an explanation of why fair value cannot be measured reliably;
- Information about the market for the instruments;
- Information about whether and how the entity intends to dispose of the financial instruments; and
- Information explaining that a financial instrument whose fair value previously could not be reliably measured is derecognized, if applicable, its carrying amount at the time of derecognition and the amount of gain or loss recognized.

FAIR VALUE HIERARCHY-BASED DISCLOSURES

For each class of financial instruments, disclosures shall be based on the fair value hierarchy. An entity shall disclose, for each category of financial instruments, the level in the fair value hierarchy into which the fair value measurements are categorized in their entirety.

	Level 1	Level 2	Level 3
1. Classify fair value measurements into appropriate category			
2. Tell significant transfers between Level 1 and Level 2. Show transfer to and transfer from separately; not to be disclosed net. Judge level of significance with reference to profit or loss, and total assets or total liabilities.	$\rightarrow$	$\leftarrow$	
3. Fair value disclosures to be included for Level 3 are Opening balance ± total gains/losses recognized during the period in the statement of comprehensive Income (or separate statement of income, refer to IAS 1) *Describe where they are presented.* ± total gains/losses recognized during the period ± Purchases, sales, issues, and settlements *Disclose each type of movement separately.* ± transfers into and out of Level 3 *Disclose significant transfers in and out separately*			

4. Provide disclosure about inclusion of gains/losses of financial instruments out of Level 3 measurement, which are included in the profit and loss For the items of financial assets/financial liabilities that are held at the end of the reporting period, include a. A description of where those gains or losses are presented in the statement of comprehensive income or the separate income statement (if presented). *Author's comment: It is possible to segregate the total fair value gains/losses into two categories— for financial instruments that are derecognized during the period and for financial instruments that are held at the end of the reporting period.*			
5. Include sensitivity analysis of inputs at Level 3: Significant changes in fair value as a result of changed inputs resulting from alternative assumptions. *Describe the effect of change.* *Significance level is to be arrived at with reference to profit or loss, and total assets or total liabilities.*			

The entity shall disclose the fair value hierarchy based on quantitative information as stated here. An entity shall also disclose the methods and, when a valuation technique is used, the assumptions applied in determining fair values of each class of financial assets or financial liabilities, as well as any changes in valuation techniques and the reasons for making such changes.

RISK DISCLOSURES

There are three types of risks that must be shown in financial instruments: credit risk, market risk, and liquidity risk. Interest rate risk and currency risks are variants of market risk only.

The entity shall make qualitative and quantitative disclosures showing risk, including the following:

Qualitative disclosures

1. Exposure to risks and how such risks came about.
2. Objectives, policies, and processes for managing the risk and the methods used to measure the risk.
3. Any changes of risks and risk management policies from previous period.

Quantitative disclosures

1. Summary of quantitative data about the exposure to that risk at the end of the reporting period. This disclosure shall be based on the information provided internally to key management personnel of the entity.
2. Provide disclosures in accordance with materiality.
3. Further information should be included such as concentrations of risk, if quantitative data provided is not sufficient.

For qualitative risk disclosures, the entity may disclose

- Structure and organization of the entity's risk management function(s), including a discussion of independence and accountability;
- Scope and nature of the entity's risk reporting or measurement systems;
- Entity's policies for hedging or mitigating risk, including its policies and procedures for taking collateral;
- Entity's processes for monitoring the continuing effectiveness of such hedges or mitigating devices; and
- Policies and procedures for avoiding excessive concentrations of risk.

For quantitative disclosures, IFRS 7 requires disclosures of concentration risk. *Concentration risks* can be identified by industry sector, credit qualities, geographical distribution, and limited clients. Similarly, concentration of market risk and liquidity risk may be quantified.

LIQUIDITY RISK DISCLOSURE THROUGH MATURITY ANALYSIS

An entity shall disclose for nonderivative financial liabilities (including issued financial guarantee contracts) a maturity analysis that shows remaining contractual maturities. For derivative financial liabilities, a maturity analysis that includes the remaining contractual maturities for those derivative financial liabilities for which contractual maturities are essential for an understanding of the timing of the cash flows. Examples are an interest rate swap that has three years remaining, loan commitments, and so on. It shall also disclose how the entity will manage liquidity risk.

QUANTITATIVE LIQUIDITY RISK DISCLOSURES

An entity discloses summary quantitative data about its exposure to liquidity risk on the basis of the information provided internally to key management personnel in accordance with IFRS 7.34(a):

	Not later than one month	Later than one month but not later than three months	Later than three months but not later than one year	Later than one year but not later than five years
Nonderivative financial				
Derivatives				

Notes:

1. The entity will decide the appropriate time frame. Embedded derivatives are not segregated from hybrid financial instruments for the purpose of liquidity risk disclosure.
2. The entity is required to explain how those data are determined.
3. The entity shall disclose the fact if the cash flows indicated could arise earlier than indicated in the data or if they could be significantly different than presented.
4. When an entity is committed to make amounts available in installments, each installment is allocated to the earliest period in which the entity can be required to pay.
5. The amounts disclosed in the maturity analysis are the contractual undiscounted cash flows.
6. An entity shall analyze conditions existing at the end of the reporting period for determining the amount payable under a financial instrument that is not fixed For example, when the amount payable varies with changes in an index, the amount disclosed may be based on the level of the index at the end of the reporting period.

Other factors that can be disclosed in the liquidity risk management explanation required under paragraph 39(c) of IFRS 7 and

- Committed borrowing facilities;
- Deposits at central banks to meet liquidity needs; and
- Diverse funding sources.

The entity might consider disclosing

- Significant concentrations of liquidity risk in either its assets or its funding sources;
- Internal control processes and contingency plans for managing liquidity risk;
- Instruments that could require the posting of collateral (e.g., margin calls for derivatives);
- Instruments that allows the entity to choose whether it settles its financial liabilities by delivering cash (or another financial asset) or by delivering its own shares; or
- Instruments that are subject to master netting agreements.

DISCLOSURE OF MARKET RISK SENSITIVITY ANALYSIS

An entity must disclose: (1) sensitivity analysis in regard to changes in risk variables, (2) methods and assumptions adopted for sensitivity analysis, and (3) changes in methods and assumptions from previous period, if any, explaining reasons thereof.

When an entity prepares sensitivity analysis that reflects interdependencies between risk variables such as value-at-risk, it shall disclose (1) an explanation of the method used, parameters and assumptions of the underlying data provided; and (2) an explanation of the objective of the method used and of limitations that may result in the information not fully reflecting the fair value of the assets and liabilities involved.

In case the sensitivity analyses applied are unrepresentative of a risk inherent in a financial instrument (e.g., if the year-end exposure does not reflect the exposure during the year), disclose that fact and the reason thereof.

RISK DISCLOSURES OF INSURANCE CONTRACTS UNDER IFRS 4.39(D)

Information about credit risk, liquidity risk, and market risk that paragraphs 31–42 of IFRS 7 require are to be disclosed for insurance contracts as if the insurance contracts were within the scope of IFRS 7. However, an insurer need not disclose the maturity analysis discussed in this chapter if it discloses information about the estimated timing of the net cash outflows resulting from recognized insurance liabilities instead.

EXCERPTS FROM FINANCIAL STATEMENTS

The Volvo Group, Annual Report 2008

Notes to the Consolidated Financial Statements

Note 36. Goals and Policies in Financial Risk Management

Apart from derivatives, Volvo's financial instruments consist of bank loans, financial leasing contracts, accounts payable, accounts receivable, shares and participations, as well as cash and short-term investments.

The primary risks deriving from the handling of financial instruments are interest-rate risk, currency risk, liquidity risk, and credit risk. All of these risks are handled in accordance with an established financial policy.

Interest-Rate Risk

Interest-rate risk refers to the risk that changed interest-rate levels will affect consolidated earnings and cash flow (cash-flow risks) or the fair value of financial assets and liabilities (price risks). Matching the interest-fixing terms of financial assets and liabilities reduces the exposure. Interest-rate swaps are used to change/influence the interest-fixing term for the Group's financial assets and liabilities. Currency interest rate swaps permit borrowing in foreign currencies from different markets without introducing currency risk. Volvo also has standardized interest-rate forward contracts (futures) and FRAs (forward-rate agreements). Most of these contracts are used to hedge interest-rate levels for short-term borrowing or investment.

Cash-Flow Risks

The effect of changed interest-rate levels on future currency and interest-rate flows refers mainly to the group's customer financing operations and net financial items. Within the customer finance operations, the degree of matching interest-rate fixing on borrowing and lending is measured. The calculation of the matching degree excludes equity, which in the customer finance operations amount to between 8% and 10%. According to the group's policy, the degree of matching for interest-rate fixing on borrowing and lending in the customer financing operations must exceed 80%. At year-end 2008, the degree of such matching was 100% (100). A part of the short-term financing of the customer financing operations can, however, pertain to internal loans from the industrial operations, explaining why the matching ratio in the Volvo group may be slightly lower. At year-end 2008, in addition to the assets in its customer-financing operations, Volvo's interest-bearing assets consisted primarily of cash, cash equivalents, and liquid assets invested in short-term interest-bearing securities. The objective is to achieve an interest-fixing term of six months for the liquid assets in Volvo's industrial operations through the use of derivatives. On December 31, 2008, after taking derivatives into account, the average interest on these assets was 2.9% (4.4). After taking derivatives into account, outstanding loans had interest terms corresponding to an interest-rate fixing term of six months and the average interest at year-end amounted to 4.1% (4.5).

Price Risks

Exposure to price risks as a result of changed interest-rate levels refers to financial assets and liabilities with a longer interest-rate fixing term (fixed interest). A comparison of the reported values and the fair values of all of Volvo's financial assets and liabilities, as well as its derivatives, is provided in Note 37, *Financial Instruments*. After the transition to IFRS in 2005, the market values agree with the book values.

Assuming that the market interest rates for all currencies suddenly rose by one percentage point (100 interest-rate points) over the interest-rate level on December 31, 2008, for the next 12-month period, all other variables remaining unchanged, Volvo's net interest income would be negatively impacted by 88 (negatively 25) considering an interest-rate fixing term of six months. Assuming that the market interest rates for all currencies fell in a similar manner by 1 percentage point (100 interest-rate points), Volvo's net interest income would be positively impacted by a corresponding amount.

The following table shows the effect on income in Volvo's key financing currencies if the interest-rate level were to increase by 1 percentage point, not considering interest-rate fixing terms.

in SEK million	Effect on Income
SEK	62
USD	(17)
EUR	(130)
JPY	(12)
KRW	(125)
	8

The earlier sensitivity analysis is based on assumptions that rarely occur in reality. It is not unreasonable that market interest rates change with 100 interest-rate points over a 12-month period. However, in reality, market interest rates usually do not rise or fall at one point in time. Moreover, the sensitivity analysis also assumes a parallel shift in the yield curve and an identical effect of changed market interest rates on the interest rates of both assets and liabilities. Consequently, the effect of actual interest-rate changes may deviate from the above analysis. Volvo uses derivatives to hedge currency and interest rate risks.

Currency Risks

The content of the reported balance sheet may be affected by changes in different exchange rates. Currency risks in Volvo's operations are related to changes in the value of contracted and expected future payment flows (commercial currency exposure), changes in the value of loans and investments (financial currency exposure), and changes in the value of assets and liabilities in foreign subsidiaries (currency exposure of shareholders' equity). The aim of Volvo's currency-risk management is to minimize, over the short term, negative effects on Volvo's earnings and financial position stemming from exchange-rate changes.

Commercial Currency Exposure

In order to hedge the value of future payment flows in foreign currencies, Volvo uses forward contracts and currency options. For each currency, 75% of the forecast net flows for the coming six months are hedged and 50% for months 7 to 12, while contracted flows after 12 months shall normally be hedged. As a consequence of the financial turmoil, Volvo will gradually and temporarily shift focus from hedging forecast flows to only hedge contracted flows.

The nominal amount of all outstanding forward and option contracts amounted to SEK 73.8 billion (63.1) at December 31, 2008. On the same date, the fair value of these contracts was negative in an amount of SEK 2,936 million (positive 266).

The table that follows presents the effect a change of the value of the Swedish krona in relation to other currencies would have on the fair value of outstanding contracts. In reality, currencies usually do not change in the same direction at any given time, so the actual effect of exchange-rate changes may differ from the below sensitivity analysis.

Change in value of SEK in relation to all foreign currencies (percent)	Fair value of outstanding contracts
(10)	(6,245)
0	(2,936)
10	373

Financial Currency Exposure

Loans and investments in the group's subsidiaries are done mainly through Volvo Treasury in local currencies, which minimizes individual companies' financial currency exposure. Volvo Treasury uses various derivatives in order to facilitate lending and borrowing in different currencies without increasing the company's own risk. The financial net position of the Volvo Group is affected by exchange-rate fluctuations, since financial assets and liabilities are distributed among group companies that conduct their operations in different currencies.

Currency Exposure of Shareholders' Equity

The consolidated value of assets and liabilities in foreign subsidiaries is affected by current exchange rates in conjunction with translation of assets and liabilities to Swedish kronor. To minimize currency exposure of shareholders' capital, the size of shareholders' equity in foreign subsidiaries is continuously optimized with respect to commercial and legal conditions. Currency hedging of shareholders' equity may occur in cases when a foreign subsidiary is considered over capitalized. Net assets in foreign subsidiaries and associated companies amounted at year-end 2008 to SEK 66.0 billion (61.1). Of this amount, SEK 4.3 billion (3.8) was currency-hedged through loans in foreign currencies. Out of the loans used as hedging instruments, SEK 3.3 billion are due in 2010 and the remaining SEK 1.0 billion in 2011. The need to undertake currency hedging relating to investments in associated companies and other companies is assessed on a case-by-case basis.

Credit Risks

Volvo's credit provision is steered by group-wide policies and customer-classification rules. The credit portfolio should contain a sound distribution among different customer categories and industries. The credit risks are managed through active credit monitoring, follow-up routines and, where applicable, product reclamation. Moreover, regular monitoring ensures that the necessary provisions are made for incurred losses on doubtful receivables. In the tables that follow, ageing analyses are presented of accounts receivables overdue and customer finance receivables overdue in relation to the reserves made. It is not unusual that a receivable is settled a couple of days after due date, which affects the extent of the age interval 1–30 days.

The credit portfolio of Volvo's customer-financing operations amounted at December 31, 2008, to approximately SEK 98 billion (79) in the Volvo group and SEK 112 billion (91) in the segment Customer Finance. The difference is due to the reclassification in the segment reporting of Customer Finance as operational leases are reclassified to financial leases in accordance with IAS 14, *Segment Reporting*. The credit risk of this portfolio is distributed over a large number of retail customers and dealers. Collaterals are provided in the form of the financed products. Credit provision aims for a balance between risk exposure and expected yield. The Volvo group's financial assets are largely managed by Volvo Treasury and invested in the money and capital markets. All investments must meet the requirements of low credit risk and high liquidity. According to Volvo's credit policy, counterparties for investments and derivative transactions should have a rating of A or better from one of the well-established credit rating institutions.

The use of derivatives involves a counterparty risk, in that a potential gain will not be realized if the counterparty fails to fulfill its part of the contract. To reduce the exposure, master netting agreements are signed, wherever possible, with the counterparty in question. Counterparty risk exposure for futures contracts is limited through daily or monthly cash transfers corresponding to the value change of open contracts. The estimated gross exposure to counterparty risk relating to futures, interest-rate swaps and interest-rate forward contracts, options and commodities contracts amounted at December 31, 2008, to 3,798 (3,424), 2,763 (2,527), 229 (48), and 38 (113).

Credit Portfolio—Accounts Receivable and Customer Financing Receivables

	2007	*2008*
Accounts receivable		
Accounts receivable gross	31,427	32,272
Valuation allowance for doubtful accounts receivable	(923)	(1.749)
Accounts receivable net	**30,504**	**30,523**

For details regarding the accounts receivable and the valuation for doubtful accounts receivable, refer to Note 20.

	2007	*2008*
Customer financing receivables		
Customer financing receivables gross	80,210	99,931
Valuation allowance for doubtful customer financing receivables	(1.363)	(1.442)
Customer financing receivables net	**78,847**	**98,489**

Change of Valuation Allowances for Doubtful Customer Financing Receivables

	2008
Balance sheet, December 31, preceding year	1,363
New valuation allowance charged to income	483
Reversal of valuation allowance charged to income	(39)
Utilization of valuation allowance related to actual losses	(475)
Translation differences	110
Balance sheet, December 31	**1,442**

For details regarding the long-term customer finance receivables and the short-term customer receivables, refer to Notes 16 and 19.

Age Analysis of Portfolio Value—Accounts Receivable and Customer Financing Receivables

	2007					2008				
	Not due	*1-30*	*31-90*	*≥90*	*Total*	*Not due*	*1-30*	*31-90*	*≥90*	*Total*
Accounts receivable										
Accounts receivable gross	27,520	1,930	704	1,273	31,427	27,045	2,008	1,266	1,953	32,272
Valuation allowance for doubtful accounts receivable	(214)	(39)	(71)	(599)	(923)	(400)	(63)	(79)	(1,207)	(1,749)
Accounts receivable not recognized as impairment losses	27,306	1,891	633	674	30,504	26,645	1,945	1,187	746	30,523
Customer financing receivables										
Overdue amount	—	597	173	126	896	—	955	497	387	1,839
Valuation allowance for doubtful customer financing receivables	(159)	(46)	(70)	(115)	(390)	(82)	(65)	(149)	(146)	(442)
Customer financing receivable not recognized as impairment losses	(159)	551	103	11	506	(82)	890	348	241	1,397

This table presents overdue payments within the customer financing operations in relation to specific reserves. The total contractual amount of overdue payments is presented in the next table. In order to provide for occurred but not yet identified customer financing receivables overdue, there are additional reserves of 1,000 (973). The remaining exposure is secured by liens on the purchased equipment, and, in certain circumstances, other credit enhancements such as personal guarantees, credit insurance, liens on other property owned by the borrower, and so forth. Collaterals taken in possession that meet the recognition criteria amounted to 748 (130) at December 31, 2008.

Customer Financing Receivables: Total Exposure

	2007					2008				
	Not due	*1-30*	*31-90*	*≥90*	*Total*	*Not due*	*1-30*	*31-90*	*≥90*	*Total*
Customer financing receivables	66,812	10,527	2,162	709	**80,210**	83,618	9,237	4,129	2,947	**99,931**

Renegotiated Financial Assets

Financial assets that would otherwise have been overdue whose terms have been renegotiated amount to 2,826 (937) and are mainly related to renegotiated customer contracts within the customer finance operations.

Concentration of Credit Risk

Customer Concentration

The ten largest customers in Customer Finance account for 4.7% (4.7) of the total asset portfolio. The rest of the portfolio is distributed among a large number of customers. This way, the credit risk is spread across both many markets and among many customers.

Concentration by Geographical Market

The table below shows the concentration of the customer financing portfolio divided into geographical markets.

Geographical Market	Percentage of customer financing portfolio
Europe	56.9
North America	29.7
Asia	6.1
Other markets	7.3

Liquidity Risks

Volvo assures itself of sound financial preparedness by always keeping a certain percentage of its sales in liquid assets. A sound balance between short- and long-term borrowing, as well as borrowing preparedness in the form of overdraft facilities, is intended to meet long-term financing needs.

The following table shows expected future cash flows including derivatives related to financial liabilities. *Capital flow* refers to expected payments of loans and derivatives. *Interest flow* refers to the future interest payments on loans and derivatives based on interest rates expected by the market. The interest flow is reported within cash flow from operating activities.

See also Note 26 for long-term loans maturity analysis and for credit facilities granted but not utilized as well as Note 31 for contractual duration analysis of future rental payments of noncancelable finance lease agreements and operating lease agreements.

Future Cash Flow Including Derivatives Related to Financial Liabilities

	Capital flow	*Interest flow*
2009	(60,475)	(4,735)
2010	(23,946)	(2,533)
2011	(19,318)	(1,827)
2012	(6,691)	(1,325)
2013	(9,804)	(1,094)
2014	(4,922)	(832)
2015	(19,335)	(1,768)

Note 37. Financial Instruments

The financial assets treated within the framework of IAS 39 are classified either as financial assets at fair value through profit and loss, as loans and receivables, as investments held to maturity or as available for sale. Financial liabilities are classified as financial liabilities at fair value through profit and loss or as financial liabilities valued at amortized cost.

Information Regarding Reported and Fair Values

In the table that follows, carrying values are compared with fair values of financial instruments.

	December 31, 2007		December 31, 2008	
	Carrying value	Fair value	Carrying value	Fair value
Assets				
Financial assets at fair value through profit and loss				
The Volvo Group's outstanding currency risk contracts—commercial exposure	1,192	1,192	2,280	2,280
The Volvo Group's outstanding raw materials contracts	113	113	38	38
The Volvo Group's outstanding interest risk contracts—financial exposure	2,685	2,685	4,510	4,510
Marketable securities	16,490	16,490	5,902	5,902
	20,480	20,480	12,730	12,730
Loans receivable and other receivables				
Accounts receivable	30,504	—	30,523	—
Customer financing receivables[3]	78,847	—	98,489	—
Loans to external parties and other interest-bearing receivables	525	—	384	—
Conduit loans and other interest-bearing loans	106	102	10	6
	109,982	102	129,406	6

Financial assets available for sale
Shares and participations for which:

A market value can be calculated[1]	1,030	1,030	661	661
A market value cannot be calculated[2]	1,189	—	1,292	—
	2,219	1,030	1,953	661
Cash and cash equivalents	14,544	14,544	17,712	17,712

Liabilities
Financial liabilities at fair value through profit and loss

The Volvo Group's outstanding currency risk contracts—commercial exposure	924	924	5,216	5,216
The Volvo Group's outstanding raw materials contract	20	20	93	93
The Volvo Group's outstanding interest risk contracts—financial exposure	876	876	2,978	2,978
	1,820	1,820	8,287	8,287

Financial liabilities valued at amortized cost

Long-term bond loans and other loans	63,470	66,338	82,948	84,712
Short-term bank loans and other loans	44,630	44,161	62,027	62,148
	108,100	110,499	144,975	146,860
Trade payables	52,663	—	51,025	—

[1] *Refers to Volvo's ownership in Deutz AG valued at market value and Nissan Diesel's holdings in listed shares.*

[2] *Unlisted, for which a reliable fair value cannot be determined, are reported at acquisition value. No single block of shares represent a significant amount.*

[3] *In the current environment of illiquid and highly volatile markets, it is not possible to provide accurate estimates of the price at which an orderly transaction would take place between willing participants. As such, fair value estimates have not been provided for the customer finance portfolio.*

Derecognition of Financial Assets

Financial assets that have been transferred in such a way that part or all of the financial assets do not qualify for derecognition, are included in reported assets of the Volvo Group. In accordance with IAS 39, *Financial Instruments: Recognition and Measurement*, an evaluation is made whether substantially all the risks and rewards have been transferred to an external part. When Volvo has concluded that it is not the case, the part of the financial assets that reflect Volvo's continuous involvement are being recognized. On December 31, 2008, Volvo recognizes SEK 3.9 (3.4) billion corresponding to Volvo's continuous involvement, mostly within the customer financing operations. Of this balance, SEK 3.8 (3.0) billion derives from credit guarantees for customer finance receivables that Nissan Diesel has entered into. A corresponding amount is reported as a financial liability.

Gains, Losses, Interest Income and Expenses Related to Financial Instruments

The table that follows shows how gains and losses as well as interest income and expense have affected income after financial items in the Volvo Group divided on the different categories of financial instruments.

| | 2007 | | | 2008 | | |
	Gains/ Losses	*Interest income*	*Interest expense*	*Gains/ losses*	*Interest income*	*Interest expense*
Financial assets and liabilities at fair value through profit and loss						
Marketable securities	898	0	0	864	0	0
Derivatives for financial exposure	(403)	0	0	(924)	0	0
Loans receivable and other receivables	0	37	0	0	11	0
Financial assets available for sale						
Shares and participations for which a market value can be calculated	8	—	—	42	—	—
Shares and participations for which a market value cannot be calculated	98	—	—	60	—	—
Cash and cash equivalents	—	249	0	0	362	0
Financial liabilities valued at amortized costs	3	0	(4,048)	(1)	0	(5,083)
Effect on income	604	286	(4,048)	41	373	(5,083)

Net Effect of Foreign Exchange Gains and Losses

Foreign exchange gains and losses pertaining to financial instruments have affected income after financial items in the Volvo Group according to the following table:

	2007	2008
Derivative instruments	1,364	(812)
Cash and cash equivalents	(191)	(421)
Loans originated by the company and financial liabilities value at amortized cost—Volvo internal	(133)	12,373
Loans originated by the company and financial liabilities value at amortized cost--External	(965)	(11,041)
Effect on income	75	99

Various categories of financial instruments are treated separately in specific notes. See Note 15 for shares and participations, Notes 16 and 19 for customer-financing receivables, Note 20 for other short-term receivables, Note 21 for marketable securities, Note 22 for cash and cash equivalents, Note 26 for noncurrent liabilities, and Note 27 for current liabilities.

Derivative instruments and options are presented here.

Outstanding Derivative Instruments for Dealing with Currency and Interest-Rate Risks Related to Financial Assets and Liabilities

| | *December 31, 2007* | | *December 31, 2008* | |
	Notional amount	*Carrying value*	*Notional amount*	*Carrying value*
Interest-rate swaps				
Receivable position	103,738	2,519	47,441	2,752
Payable position	47,415	(512)	85,980	(2,038)
Forwards and futures				
Receivable position	21,776	8	19,443	11
Payable position	24,164	(6)	17,740	(32)
Foreign exchange derivative contracts				
Receivable position	18,521	359	32,671	1,608
Payable position	19,636	(595)	30,022	(766)

| | December 31, 2007 | | December 31, 2008 | |
	Notional amount	Carrying value	Notional amount	Carrying value
Options purchased				
Receivable position	503	11	1,675	139
Payable position	503	(11)	428	(26)
Options written				
Receivable position	647	2	42	0
Payable position	155	0	1,147	(116)
Total		**1,775**		**1,532**

Outstanding Forward Contracts and Options Contracts for Hedging of Currency Risk and Interest Risk of Commercial Receivables and Liabilities

| | December 31, 2007 | | December 31, 2008 | |
	Notional amount	Carrying value	Notional amount	Carrying value
Foreign exchange derivative contracts				
Receivable position	28,826	3,065	25,712	2,190
Payable position	31,146	(2,819)	41,773	(4,710)
Options purchased				
Receivable position	1,726	35	3,142	90
Payable position	—	—	—	—
Options written				
Receivable position	—	—	—	—
Payable position	1,382	(15)	3,214	(506)
Subtotal		**266**		**(2,936)**
Raw materials derivative contracts				
Receivable position	208	113	85	38
Payable position	530	(19)	443	(93)
Total		**360**		**(2,991)**

Hedge Accounting

Cash-Flow Hedging

Derivative financial instruments used for hedging of forecasted commercial cash flows and electricity consumption have, in accordance with IAS 39, been reported at fair value, which is debited or credited to a separate component of equity to the extent the requirements for cash-flow hedge accounting are fulfilled.

Accumulated changes in the value of the hedging instruments are booked to the income statement of the same time as the underlying hedged transaction affects the Group results.

The table in note 23, shareholders' equity, shows how the currency risk reserve has changed during the year.

To the extent that the requirements for hedge accounting are not met, any changes in value attributable to derivatives are immediately charged to the income statement.

The hedged amount of projected future flows for all periods are within the framework of Volvo's currency policy.

Volvo tests all cash-flow hedges for effectiveness when they are entered into. Hedging is considered to be effective when the projected future cash flow's currency fluctuation and maturity date coincide with those of the hedging instrument. The hedging relationship is regularly tested until its maturity date. If the identified relationships are no longer deemed effective, the currency fluctuations on the hedging instrument from the last period the instrument was considered effective are reported in the Group's income statement. For 2008, Volvo reported 22 (20) in revenue related to the ineffectiveness of cash-flow hedging. Hedging of forecasted electricity is considered to be effective when predetermined factors that affect electricity prices are in agreement with forecasts of future electricity consumption and designated derivative instruments. The hedging relationship is regularly tested until its maturity date. If the identified relationships are no longer deemed effective, the currency fluctuations on the hedging instrument from the last period the instrument was considered effective are reported in the group's income statement. For 2008, Volvo reported 1 (0) related to the ineffectiveness of the hedging of forecasted electricity consumption.

**The Volvo Group's Outstanding Forward Contracts and Options Contracts
for Hedging of Commercial Currency Risks**

Million		USD	GBP	EUR	JPY	Other currencies Net SEK	Fair value
			Currencies				
Due date 2009	Amount	1,754	185	888	(7,030)	5,944	
Due date 2010	Amount	(12)	(12)	(4)	—	347	
Due date 2011	Amount	(7)	(4)	—	—	0	
Total		1,735	169	884	(7,030)	6,291	
Average contract rate		6.69	11.97	9.48	0.07		
Fair value of outstanding forward contracts		**(1,460)**	**55**	**(1,191)**	**131**	**(471)**	**(2,936)**

Hedging of Currency and Interest-Rate Risks on Loans

Volvo has chosen to apply hedge accounting for a loan of 1 billion euro borrowed in the second quarter 2007. Fair value of the outstanding hedge instrument amounts to 1,088 (159). Volvo has also applied hedge accounting for hedge of a currency risk in future repayment of a loan in foreign currency for which the outgoing fair value of the hedge instrument amounts to 40 (negative 148). This hedge is designated as a cash-flow hedge and changes in fair value have affected the cash flow hedge reserve within equity.

Volvo has not applied hedge accounting for financial instruments used to hedge interest and currency risks on loans before. Changes in market value on the instruments used for hedging of risk in financial assets and liabilities for which hedge accounting has not been applied are reported in net financial income and expense, see Note 11. Going forward, in applicable cases when the requirements for hedge accounting are considered to be fulfilled, Volvo will consider to apply hedge accounting for this kind of instruments.

Hedging of Net Investments in Foreign Operations

Volvo applies hedge accounting for certain net investments in foreign operations. Current earnings from such hedging shall be accounted for in a separate item within shareholders' equity. A total of negative 473 (negative 59) in shareholders' equity relating to hedging of net investments in foreign operations was reported in 2008.

39 OPERATING SEGMENTS (IFRS 8)

INTRODUCTION

As a result of the International Accounting Standards Board's (IASB) joint short-term convergence project with the U.S. Financial Accounting Standards Board (FASB), a project was launched with the primary objective of reducing differences between IFRS and U.S. GAAP and, based on research, was carried on by both standard setters. The IASB adopted the approach of the U.S. standard on segmental reporting; namely, SFAS 131, *Disclosures About Segments of an Enterprise and Related Information*, and revised its standard on segment reporting.

In November 2006, the IASB issued IFRS 8, *Operating Segments,* effective for annual periods beginning on or after January 1, 2009. IFRS 8 replaced IAS 14 and with this new standard on segmental reporting, the emphasis has shifted to disclosing segmental information (for external reporting purposes), based on internal reporting within the entity, to its chief operating decision maker (CODM).

The IASB believes that by requiring entities to report segmental information using the approach prescribed by IFRS 8 (i.e., a management approach) it allows the financial statement user to review segmental information from the "eyes of the management" as opposed to a risks-and-rewards approach that was the cornerstone of the IASB standard on segment reporting (IAS 14). Furthermore, by adopting this new approach under IFRS 8, the cost and time needed to produce segmental information is greatly reduced since most, if not all, of this information is already available within the entity. In the case of public companies that are required to report on a quarterly basis, this is a distinct advantage.

SCOPE

IFRS 8 applies to both the separate or individual financial statements of an entity and to consolidated financial statements of a group within which the entity is the parent:

- Whose debt or equity instruments are publicly listed; or
- That files, or is in the process of filing, its financial statements with a securities commission or other regulatory authority for the purpose of issuing any class of instruments in a public market.

The standard clarifies that when both the parent's separate (stand-alone) financial statements and its consolidated financial statements are presented in the same financial report, segment information, as required by IFRS 8, needs to be presented only for the consolidated financial statements.

Upon first adoption of IFRS 8, *comparatives*, as reported under IAS 14, are required to be restated.

CORE PRINCIPLE

According to the core principle of IFRS 8, an entity should disclose information to enable users of its financial statements to evaluate the *nature and financial effects* of the types of *business activities* in which it engages and the *economic environments* in which it operates.

CHIEF OPERATING DECISION MAKER (CODM)

The chief operating decision maker, or the CODM, as it is sometimes referred to, could be the chief operating officer, or the chief executive officer, or the board of directors, or an executive committee comprising two or three board members, depending on who within the organization is responsible for the allocation of resources and assessing the performance of the entity's operating segments.

In most organizations, the highest ranking individual would qualify as the CODM. However, since the term *CODM* does not always refer to an individual, but to a function, in the case of a complex organizational and reporting setup (where decision-making responsibilities are split amongst the top management personnel), it could make the assessment of who the CODM is difficult. In such a case, where it is difficult to determine the CODM, other factors, such as who decides the management bonuses or who approves the financial information presented to the Board of Directors, may need to be considered as well.

Example 1

Exuberance Inc. is a company listed on a well-known international stock exchange. It has three major lines of business; namely, retail, wholesale, and export. Each major line of business has a chief operating officer (COO) who is the responsible for the business component's profitability. The company has a chief executive officer (CEO) who is overall in charge of the entire business of the entity and reports to the Board of Directors (Board) on the results of operations of Exuberance Inc. The CEO has the authority from the Board to decide on the performance bonus of each COO, for which the CEO has set key performance indications (KPIs) against which they are evaluated each year by the CEO. Discrete financial information for each of the major lines of business of Exuberance Inc. is available. The CEO has been entrusted by the Board to allocate funds for the day-to-day operations of the three lines of business, which he bases on criteria such as their comparative profitability, size of business generated, and cash flows from operations.

Based on the aforementioned details about the functioning of Exuberance Inc. and other relevant information provided, who is the CODM for the purposes of IFRS 8? Is it the Board, the CEO, or each COO for the line of business that he or she is responsible for?

Solution

First, a COO of any line of business of Exuberance Inc. is only responsible for the results of the line of business he or she is responsible for, but is certainly not responsible for the overall business of the entity and thus cannot qualify as the CODM. Second, while the Board is the highest authority in the hierarchy, the CEO has been given the required powers by the Board, that is, the power of allocation of resources and the power to assess the performance of the three major lines of business of the company. In accordance with the requirements of IFRS 8, the CODM is not the Board, but is the CEO.

IDENTIFYING SEGMENTS USING IFRS 8

IFRS 8 prescribes that segments are to be identified on the same basis as the entity's internal reporting to its CODM, with respect to components (of the entity) that are regularly reviewed by its CODM in order to allocate resources to the segments and to assess their performance. The distinct advantages of reporting segmental information under IFRS 8 are that since it is consistent with the manner in which business reports internally to the management (CODM), it *potentially saves costs* by getting rid of the need to produce additional information for external reporting purposes. It also helps in *timely reporting* of segment information both for interim financial reporting and year-end reporting. The disadvantage, however, is that entities in the same sector or business may end up reporting different segments depending on how their respective CODMs review internal segment reporting, thereby making relative comparisons of segmental information between entities difficult. This disadvantage may, to some extent, be mitigated by the requirement of IFRS 8 for additional disclosures of entitywide information about products and services, geographical areas and major customers.

IDENTIFYING OPERATING SEGMENTS

According to IFRS 8 an *operating segment* is a *component* of an entity

- That engages in business activities from which it *may* earn revenues and incur expenses. (In other words, a segment is not required to have external customers and its revenues may therefore be derived from revenues and expenses relating to transactions with *other components* of the same entity.)
- Whose operating results are reviewed regularly by the entity's CODM to make decisions about resources to be allocated to the segment and assess its performance; and
- That has available discrete financial information.

Example 2

Global Inc. is a well-known, publicly listed automobile dealership. Based on the decision of the CEO, the entity is managed and controlled through three divisions, namely, the spare parts division, the workshop division, and the sales division. Both the sales division and the workshop division deal with external customers and handle orders of both walk-in customers as well as long-term customers who have purchased cars through earlier sales through this dealership. The entity's spare parts division, however, only supplies spare parts to its workshop division and does not cater to the demands of any outside customers. In other words, if outside customers desire to purchase spare parts directly from the spare parts division of Global Inc., they cannot do so unless their automobiles are serviced by the workshop division of Global Inc. and the workshop division (of Global Inc.) purchases spare parts from its spare parts division for the purposes of undertaking repairs of vehicles they have been contracted to undertake repair work for.

The CODM, in this case, is the CEO of Global Inc.. He or she is responsible for allocating resources and assessing performance based on the results of the three components; namely, the spare parts division, the workshop division, the sales division, for which Global Inc's financial controller maintains separate and discrete financial information.

For the purposes of IFRS 8, how many operating segments should Global Inc. report segmental disclosures for?

Solution

IFRS 8 clearly specifies that although some operating segments may derive their revenue solely or primarily from other segments of the same entity, these segments cannot be precluded from qualifying as operating segments for the purposes of reporting under this standard on the grounds that they do not derive their revenues from external sources. However, this is subject to the above segments meeting all the other qualifying requirements. In other words, for the purposes of IFRS 8, a segment is not required to have external customers or revenues in order to be classified as an operating segment for financial reporting purposes. Therefore, all three divisions of Global Inc. qualify as operating segments.

REPORTABLE SEGMENTS

As per IFRS 8, an entity should report financial and descriptive information about its reportable segments. Not all operating segments would automatically qualify as reportable segments. The standard prescribes criteria for an operating segment to qualify as a reportable segment called *alternative quantitative thresholds,* which are

1. Its reported revenue, from both external customers and intersegment sales or transfers, is 10% or more of the combined revenue, internal and external, of all operating segments; or
2. The absolute measure of its reported profit or loss is 10% or more of the greater, in absolute amount, of (1) the combined reported profit of all operating segments that did not report a loss and (2) the combined reported loss of all operating segments that reported a loss; or
3. Its assets are 10% or more of the combined assets of all operating segments.

Furthermore, if the total revenue attributable to all operating segments (as identified by applying the alternative quantitative thresholds criteria) constitutes less than 75% of the entity's total revenue as per its financial statements, the entity should look for additional operating segments until it is satisfied that at least 75% of the entity's revenue is captured through such segmental reporting. In identifying the additional operating segments as reportable segments (i.e., for the purposes of meeting the 75% threshold) the standard has relaxed its requirements of meeting the alternative quantitative thresholds criteria. In other words, an entity has to keep identifying more segments even if they do not meet the alternative quantitative thresholds test until at least 75% of the entity's revenue is included in reportable segments.

In addition to quantitative thresholds, based on qualitative considerations, say, the strategic importance of an operating segment, additional segments may be identified for the purposes of segment reporting under IFRS 8.

Furthermore, if management believes that an operating segment reported in the previous financial year is of continuing importance and significance, then, despite this operating segment's not meeting any of the quantitative thresholds in the current year, the management may decide to continue reporting segmental disclosures for this operating segment.

While IFRS 8 does not set an upper limit on the number of operating segments for which information should be disclosed, the standard suggests a practical limit of ten reporting segments, on the basis that beyond this number the level of detail may be construed as too much and may, therefore, defeat the purpose for which disclosure of disaggregated (or segmental) information has been prescribed.

MEASUREMENT OF SEGMENT INFORMATION

The reported information under IFRS 8 does not need to conform with the accounting policies adopted for preparing and presenting the financial statements of the entity. In other words, according to IFRS 8, whatever is the basis on which the segment information is reported to the CODM for the purposes of allocating resources to that segment and assessing its performance will be the measure for reporting segmental information under IFRS 8.

IFRS 8 also does not define segment revenue, segment expense, segment result, segment assets or segment liabilities, but requires that an entity should explain how segment profit or loss, segment assets, and segment liabilities have been measured for the purposes of reporting operating segments. Furthermore, IFRS 8 requires that an entity provides a reconciliation between total amounts disclosed as segmental information (under IFRS 8) and corresponding amounts as reported in the entity's financial statements.

DISCLOSURES

1. IFRS 8 prescribes *extensive* segmental reporting disclosures. These include

    a. General information about how the entity identified its operating segments and the types of products and services from which each operating segment derives its revenues;

    b. Information about the reported segment profit or loss, including certain specified revenues and expenses included in segment profit or loss, segment assets, and segment liabilities and the basis of measurement (An entity shall report a measure of profit or loss for each reportable segment. An entity shall report a measure of total assets and liabilities for each reportable segment if such amounts are regularly provided to the CODM.); and

c. Reconciliations of the totals of segment revenues, reported segment profit or loss, segment assets, segment liabilities and other material items to corresponding items in the entity's financial statements.

2. The standard clarifies that certain entitywide disclosures are required *even when an entity has only one reportable segment.* These disclosures include information about each product and service or groups of products and services.

3. Additional disclosures include

   a. Analyses of revenues and certain noncurrent assets by geographical area, with an expanded requirement to disclose revenues/assets by individual foreign country (if material), irrespective of identification of the operating segments; and

   b. Information about transactions with major customers (i.e., those customers that individually account for revenues of 10% or more of the entity's revenues).

4. IFRS 8 also specifies disclosure requirements pertaining to segment information for interim reporting purposes.

EXCERPTS FROM PUBLISHED FINANCIAL STATEMENTS

Adidas Group, Annual Report 2007

Notes to the Financial Statements

29. Segmental Information

Page 1 of 2

The Group operates predominately in one industry segment—the design, wholesale and marketing of athletic and sports lifestyle products. The Group is currently managed by brands.

Certain Group functions are centralized and an allocation of these functions to specific segments is not considered to be meaningful. This includes functions such as central treasury, worldwide sourcing as well as other headquarter departments. Assets, liabilities, income, and expenses relating to these corporate functions are presented in the HQ/Consolidation column together with other nonallocable items and intersegment eliminations.

The Reebok segment includes the brands Reebok, Reebok-CCM Hockey, and Rockport. The Greg Norman license, which was acquired with the Reebok business and subsequently sold in November 2006, was allocated to the TaylorMade-adidas Golf segment. In 2007, the remaining retail activities were allocated to the Reebok segment. Both the NBA and Liverpool licensed businesses were transferred to brand adidas in the first half of 2006.

Information about the Group's segments in accordance with the management approach is presented on the following page.

There are no intersegment sales between the brands. Net sales to third parties are shown in the geographic market in which the revenues are realized. The global sourcing function is included in the HQ/Consolidation column. Transactions between the segments are based on the dealing-at-arm's-length principle.

Segment assets include all operating assets and comprise mainly accounts receivable, inventory, as well as property, plant, and equipment, and intangible assets. Segment liabilities comprise operating liabilities and consist principally of trade and other payables, as well as accrued liabilities and provisions. Nonallocable items including financial assets or assets and liabilities relating to income taxes and borrowings are included in the HQ/Consolidation column.

Capital expenditure, amortization, and depreciation relate to segment assets; the acquisition of goodwill and the inception of finance leases do not affect capital expenditure.

Primary Segental Information by Brand

€ millions	adidas 2007	adidas 2006	Reebok 2007	Reebok 2006	TaylorMade-adidas Golf 2007	TaylorMade-adidas Golf 2006	HQ/Consolidation 2007	HQ/Consolidation 2006	adidas Group 2007	adidas Group 2006
Net sales to third parties	7,113	6,626	2,333	2,473	804	856	49	129	10,299	10,084
Gross profit	3,370	3,059	902	865	360	376	250	195	4,882	4,495
In % of net sales	47.4%	46.2%	38.7%	35.0%	44.7%	43.9%	—	—	47.4%	44.6%
Operating profit	920	788	109	86	65	73	(145)	(66)	949	881
In % of net sales	12.9%	11.9%	4.7%	3.5%	8.1%	8.5%	—	—	9.2%	8.7%
Assets	3,329	3,211	2,913	3,217	629	656	1,454	1,295	8,325	8,379
Liabilities	900	752	421	477	106	106	3,865	4,208	5,292	5,543
Capital expenditure	150	135	57	72	12	13	70	57	289	277
Amortization and depreciation	104	91	60	53	12	13	25	25	201	182
Impairment	2	11	1	—	—	—	—	—	3	11

Secondary Segmental Information By Region[1]

€ millons	Europe 2007	Europe 2006	North America 2007	North America 2006	Asia 2007	Asia 2006
Net sales to third parties	4,369	4,162	2,929	3,234	2,254	2,020
Assets	1,819	1,808	1,489	1,564	772	719
Capital expenditure	105	84	34	49	49	74

	Latin America 2007	Latin America 2006	HQ/Consolidation 2007	HQ/Consolidation 2006	adidas Group 2007	adidas Group 2006
Net sales to third parties	657	499	89	169	10,299	10,084
Assets	285	217	3,960	4,071	8,325	8,379
Capital expenditure	10	7	91	63	289	277

[1] *Region Europe also includes Middle East and Africa, Region Asia also includes the Pacific region.*

40 FINANCIAL INSTRUMENTS (IFRS 9)

INTRODUCTION

In view of the complexities of IAS 39, *Financial Instruments: Recognition and Measurement*, the International Accounting Standards Board (IASB) had amended this standard many times in the past. Although the IASB was pursuing a long-term objective of improving and simplifying the reporting for financial instruments and issued a discussion paper, "Reducing Complexity in Reporting Financial Instruments," in March 2008, the global financial crisis accelerated the issuance of a completely revamped standard. Following the conclusions of the G20 Summit and the recommendations of various international bodies such as the Financial Stability Board, the IASB announced an accelerated timetable for replacing IAS 39. As a result, in July 2009 the IASB published an Exposure Draft, *Financial Instruments: Classification and Measurement*, followed by issuance of IFRS 9, *Financial Instruments*, on November 12, 2009. The new standard changes classification of financial assets.

The IASB planned improvement of IAS 39 in three main phases. It proposes to delete the relevant portions of IAS 39 and add new chapters in IFRS 9 that replace the requirements in IAS 39. The Board aims to replace IAS 39 in its entirety by the end of 2010.

It has been viewed that accounting difficulties during the financial crisis arose from the classification and measurement of financial assets. Accordingly, the first phase of IFRS 9 covers those issues. The pending issues are

- Classification and measurement of financial liabilities
- Impairment methodology
- Hedge accounting
- Derecognition of financial assets and liabilities

The IASB's overarching intent was to reduce the complexity inherent in IAS 39. To achieve that, IFRS 9 uses a single approach to determine whether a financial asset is measured at amortized cost or fair value, rather than following the many different rules contained in IAS 39.

An entity shall apply this IFRS for annual periods beginning on or after January 1, 2013. Earlier application is permitted. Accordingly, in the case of first-time adoption of IFRSs, an entity may elect to adopt IFRS 9 in place of IAS 39. An entity that has already applied IAS 39 would follow transitional provisions of IFRS 9.

CLASSIFICATION ISSUES

Financial assets are

- Classified on the basis of the entity's business model for managing the financial assets and the contractual cash flow characteristics of the financial asset;
- Initially measured at fair value plus, in the case of a financial asset not at fair value through profit or loss, particular transaction costs; and
- Subsequently measured at amortized cost or fair value.

When financial assets are classified as at fair value through profit or loss (FVTPL) in accordance with IAS 39, transaction costs are directly charged to the statement of comprehensive income. Otherwise transaction costs are added to the fair value of the financial asset at initial recognition.

IFRS 9 requires analysis whether a financial asset can be classified as *financial assets at amortized cost* at the time of initial recognition applying specified conditions described later in the chapter. When the financial asset does not satisfy the specified conditions, it is classified as *financial asset at fair value*. There are exceptions to this general principle, such as when an entity is permitted to designate a financial asset at initial recognition as at FVTPL to avoid accounting mismatch arising out of measuring assets and liabilities or recognizing gains or losses on them using different bases.

Per paragraph 4 in IFRS 9, an entity shall classify financial assets and subsequently measure them at either *amortized cost* or *fair value* on the basis of both

- The entity's business model for managing the financial assets; and
- The contractual cash flow characteristics of the financial asset.

A financial asset is measured at amortized cost if both of the following conditions are met:

- The asset is held within a business model whose objective is to hold assets in order to collect contractual cash flows; and
- The contractual terms of the financial asset give rise on specified dates to cash flows that are solely payments of principal and interest on the principal amount outstanding.

A financial asset may have contractual cash flows that are described as principal and interest but those cash flows do not represent the payment of principal and interest on the principal amount outstanding—such an asset is not classified at amortized cost. The contractual cash flows consist *solely of payments of principal and interest on the principal amount outstanding* (as stated in paragraph 42.2, IFRS 9) if they are to be considered for the time value of money and for the credit risk associated with the principal amount outstanding during a particular period of time. When there are any other cash flows arising out of the asset, or there is a limit on the cash flows in a manner inconsistent with payments representing principal and interest, the financial asset does not meet the condition in paragraph 4.2(b) of IFRS 9.

A financial asset is measured at fair value if it is not at amortized cost.

An entity can classify equity investments as at fair through other comprehensive income at the time of initial recognition by irrevocable election. In that case, any change in fair value of the equity investments will be accounted for in other comprehensive income and accumulated in a separate component of equity. This choice is not available for investment in debt instruments.

Designation of Financial Asset as at Fair Value Through Profit or Loss

By virtue of this designation, an entity can classify a financial asset at amortized cost as at FVTPL. Derivatives are classified as financial assets at FVTPL.

For the purpose of designating a financial asset at FVTPL, an entity follows guidance provided in paragraphs AG 4D–AG 4G of IAS 39. An entity designates a financial asset in this way to avoid accounting mismatch. For example

- An insurer's liability containing a discretionary participation feature that pays benefits based on realized and/or unrealized investment returns of a specified pool of the insurer's assets would be measured at current market prices. If the related financial asset (debt instrument) is measured at amortized cost there will arise an accounting mismatch.

- An entity has financed a specified group of loans by issuing traded bonds whose changes in fair value tend to offset each other. It buys and sells bonds but not the loans. Reporting both the loans and the bonds at FVTPL eliminates the inconsistency in the timing of recognition of gains and losses that would otherwise result from measuring them both at amortized cost and recognizing a gain or loss each time a bond is repurchased.

CLASSIFICATION AT A GLANCE

Financial Assets	*Classification*
Debt instrument	Amortized cost (if meets business model and contractual terms criteria)
	Can be designated at initial recognition as financial assets at FVTPL to avoid accounting mismatch.
Equity instrument	At fair value (through profit or loss)
Equity instrument that is not held for trading	At fair value (through other comprehensive income) by irrevocable election at the time of initial recognition

BUSINESS MODEL

The business model followed by an entity is a critical factor for classification of financial assets. In particular, for classifying a financial asset at amortized cost it is necessary to evaluate *whether the asset is held within a business model whose objective is to hold assets in order to collect contractual cash flows*.

The business model is decided by the key managerial personnel (refer to IAS 24, *Related-Party Disclosures,* for definition of the term). It is not an instrument-specific model and therefore, intention of the management as regards a particular financial asset is not relevant. However, it is possible to have more than one business model. So the *business model* is neither instrument-specific nor a broad concept to cover an entity-wide model. It simply requires a higher level of aggregation than simply evaluating an individual financial asset. For example, it is possible to aggregate all loans to employees together to evaluate the business model.

An entity need not hold a financial asset till maturity to satisfy the criteria that *the asset is held within a business model whose objective is to hold assets in order to collect contractual cash flows*. An entity's business model can be to hold financial assets to collect contractual cash flows even when sales of some of the financial assets occur. For example, the entity may sell a financial asset if

- The financial asset no longer meets the entity's investment policy (e.g., the credit rating of the asset declines below that required by the entity's investment policy);
- An insurer adjusts its investment portfolio to reflect a change in expected duration (i.e., the expected timing of payouts); or
- An entity needs to fund capital expenditures.

When more than an infrequent number of sales occur within the class of financial assets held for collecting contractual cash flows, the entity needs to assess how such sales are consistent with that objective.

The following examples further explain various types of business model and classification of financial assets having contractual cash flows:

Example 1

Entity D purchased 3% debentures of €20 million, which form part of a portfolio of financial assets having contractual cash flows. It has adopted a business model *whose objective is to hold assets in order to collect contractual cash flows*. It evaluates among other information, the financial assets' fair values from a liquidity perspective (i.e., the cash amount that would be realized if the entity needs to sell assets). It also sold during the year certain items of financial assets having contractual cash flows out of the portfolio. Can the entity classify the new purchase as a financial asset at amortized cost?

Solution

Infrequent sale out of the portfolio of financial assets having contractual cash flows does not alter the entity's business objective. An entity may sell some of the financial assets that no longer meet the entity's investment policy, or for adjusting the duration of the portfolio or to meet the fund's capital expenditure. It can classify the new purchase as a financial asset at amortized cost. However, it has to reassess the business model in light of the objective of holding the assets for collecting contractual cash flows when there are a more infrequent number of sales. It may be noted that disclosures are required for these infrequent sales.

Example 2

Entity E purchased floating-rate debentures of €20 million at LIBOR + 40 basis points that form part of a portfolio of financial assets having contractual cash flows. It has adopted a business model *whose objective is to hold assets in order to collect contractual cash flows*. Subsequently, it has entered into an interest-rate-swap transaction that alters the pattern of cash flows. Can the entity classify the floating-rate debentures as a financial asset at amortized cost because it had changed the pattern of contractual cash flows?

Solution

Even if an entity alters or modifies the pattern of contractual cash flows, it can classify the financial asset having contractual cash flows at amortized cost. This principle will also apply when an entity realizes less than the contractual cash flows because of impairment loss (paragraph B4.4, IFRS 9).

Example 3

Entity F invested €200 million in various types of debt instruments that have contractual cash flows. It evaluates performance of that block of financial assets on the basis of fair value. They are not held with an objective of collecting contractual cash flows. It purchased 3% debentures of €20 million, which form part of that portfolio. Can the entity classify the new purchase as a financial asset at amortized cost?

Solution

No. See paragraphs 4.2 and B4.6 of IFRS 9. Similarly, a financial asset having contractual cash flows that is part of an actively managed portfolio whose objective is maximizing return based on change in the maturity spread or credit spread is not classified as a financial asset at amortized cost. It is classified as a financial asset at FVTPL.

Example 4

Entity G issues loans, groups them as a pool and securitizes the pool through a special-purpose vehicle (SPV). It sells the pool of loans to the SPV which securitizes the pool. The SPV is controlled by Entity G within the meaning of IAS 27, *Consolidated and Separate Financial Statements*. It collects the contractual cash flows arising from such loans and services the pass-through security holders. Therefore, for the consolidated group, the contractual cash flows of the loans are collected. Can Entity G classify such loans as a financial asset at amortized cost?

Solution

For the purpose of consolidated financial statements, these loans can be classified as financial assets at amortized cost, but for stand-alone financial statements of G, they are classified as financial assets as at FVTPL.

NATURE OF CONTRACTUAL CASH FLOWS

To be classified as a financial asset at amortized cost, the contractual cash flows inherent in the financial asset shall *consist solely of the payments of principal and interest on the principal amount outstanding* for the currency in which the financial asset is denominated.

Leverages that are part of the contractual cash-flow characteristic of some financial assets can increase the variability of such contractual cash flows. Stand-alone options, futures/forwards, and swaps on fixed-income securities include this leverage feature. They are not regarded as contractual cash flows consisting solely of the payments of principal and interest on the principal amount outstanding in the denominated currency. Therefore, any leveraged financial assets, like interest-rate options, futures, or swaps, are not classified as financial assets at amortized cost. Another example of a leveraged financial asset is a fixed-interest-rate bond in which repayment of the principal is linked to an equity index. However, inflation-adjusted Treasury notes or bonds in which payment of interest is linked to inflation-adjusted principal but repayment of principal is set at the higher of the nominal principal or inflation-adjusted principal (like U.S. TIPS) represent contractual cash flows. Inflation adjustments are simply adjustment for time value of money.

Example 5

Entity E invested in floating-rate debentures at three months LIBOR + 25 basis points. It has the right to opt for one month LIBOR + 40 basis points. Is this debenture having contractual cash flows consisting solely of principal and interest on outstanding principal? Is the answer different if the entity has the additional option to reset interest rate based on one month LIBOR every three months?

Solution

Switching over to one month LIBOR + 40 basis points from three month LIBOR + 25 basis points reflects contractual cash flows consisting solely of principal and interest on outstanding principal. The fact that the LIBOR interest rate is reset during the life of the instrument does not in itself disqualify the instrument.

However, the additional option of resetting one month LIBOR every three months does not reflect contractual cash flows consisting solely of the principal and interest on outstanding principal.

Example 6

Entity E invested in five-year, 4%, €1,000 debentures. The debentures pay interest over eight years and repay principal after five years. Are the debentures having contractual cash flows consisting solely of principal and interest on outstanding principal?

Solution

It is just a readjustment of the timing of the cash flows. If the payment satisfies the condition of time value of money, it can be identified as contractual cash flows consisting solely of the principal and interest on outstanding principal. The entity would satisfy the condition comparing to the benchmark yield of a five-year maturity debt instrument.

Example 7

A constant maturity bond with a five-year term that pays a variable rate, but on which, although the rate is reset periodically, it always reflects a five-year maturity. Is this bond having contractual cash flows consisting solely of the principal and interest on outstanding principal?

Solution

No. The bond does not result in contractual cash flows that are payments of the principal and interest on the principal amount outstanding. That is because the interest payable in each period is disconnected from the term of the instrument (except at origination).

Example 8

Entity E invested in 1,000, five-year floating-rate €1,000 debentures. However, the interest rate cannot be higher than 6.5%. Are the debentures having contractual cash flows consisting solely of the principal and interest on outstanding principal?

Solution

A variable-rate debt instrument in which interest rate is capped satisfies the test of having contractual cash flows consisting solely of the principal and interest on outstanding principal. The contractual cash flows of both (1) an instrument that has a fixed interest rate, and (2) an instrument that has a variable interest rate are payments of principal and interest on the principal amount outstanding as long as the interest reflects consideration for the time value of money and for the credit risk associated with the instrument during the term of the instrument.

Example 9

Entity E invested in five-year, 4% €100,000,000 debentures, which is a full-recourse instrument and is secured by collateral. Is the loan having contractual cash flows consisting solely of the principal and interest on outstanding principal?

Solution

The characteristics of a full-recourse and collaterized loan does not in itself affect the analysis of whether the contractual cash flows are solely payments of the principal and interest on the principal amount outstanding.

Example 10

Entity E invested in a perpetual bond that pays 4%. The issuer has a call option at any point, meaning that the issuer can pay the holder the par amount plus accrued interest due up to the time of redemption. Is the perpetual bond having contractual cash flows consisting solely of the principal and interest on outstanding principal?

Solution

The perpetual instrument has continuous (multiple) extension options. Such options may result in contractual cash flows that are payments of the principal and interest on the principal amount outstanding if interest payments are mandatory and must be paid in perpetuity.

In the case of the following instruments, contractual cash flows do not consist solely of the principal and interest on outstanding principal:

- *Convertible bond/debentures:* The holder would analyze the instrument in its entirety. The instrument includes return from equity instrument as well.
- *Inverse floater:* A bond or other debt security with a variable coupon rate that changes in inverse proportion to some benchmark rate. For example, an inverse floating-rate note may be linked to LIBOR; as the LIBOR decreases, the coupon rate increases and vice versa. An inverse floating-rate note allows a bondholder to benefit from declining interest rates. It is also called an *inverse floater.* In this case, the interest amounts are not consideration for the time value of money on the principal amount outstanding.
- *Perpetual bond in which interest payment can be deferred and no additional interest is payable on deferment:* Consider a case when the issuer pays a market interest rate but payment of interest cannot be made unless the issuer is able to remain solvent immediately afterward. Deferred interest does not accrue additional interest. In this case, the issuer may be required to defer interest payments and additional interest does not accrue on those deferred interest amounts. As a result, interest amounts are not consideration for the time value of money on the principal amount outstanding.

PREPAYMENTS

Some debt instruments carry prepayment options. The contractual provision either permits the issuer to prepay the obligation under the instrument or the holder to put back the instrument to the issuer. The prepayment right of the issuer or put option of the holder is not a prohibitory feature for classifying a debt instrument at amortized cost. Of course, the prepayment options (either by the issuer or the holder) shall not be a contingent provision except for restricted events to protect the holder from (1) credit quality deterioration of the issuer, (2) change in control of the issuer, or (3) change in tax laws. The prepayment amount shall represent the principal outstanding, interest thereon and a reasonable compensation for early termination of the contract (paragraph B4.10, IFRS 9).

EXTENSION OF THE CONTRACTUAL TERM
OF DEBT INSTRUMENTS

Terms of some debt instruments carry provision for extension of the contractual terms. For example, the holder or the issuer has the right to extend the term of five-year maturity debentures by another two years. Still, the debt instrument can be classified as a financial asset at amortized cost. Likewise, the prepayment clause, the provision for term extension (either by the issuer or the holder), shall not be a contingent provision except for restricted events to protect the holder from (1) credit quality deterioration of the issuer, (2) change in control of the issuer, or (3) change in tax laws; and the extension of term would result in payment of contractual cash flows for principal outstanding and interest thereon (paragraph B4.11, IFRS 9).

CHANGE IN TIMING AND AMOUNT OF
THE CONTRACTUAL CASH FLOWS

Amount and timing of cash flows of a debt instrument may change because of swapping fixed to floating rate of interest and *vice versa*, prepayments or extension. Despite these changes, the contractual cash flows consist solely of the payments of principal and interest on the principal amount outstanding for the currency in which the financial asset is denominated if the changes are arising from (1) the variable interest rate that is consideration of time value of money and credit risk on the principal amount outstanding, (2) prepayment that satisfies conditions of paragraph B4.10 of IFRS 9, or (3) extension of terms that satisfies conditions of paragraph B4.11, IFRS 9.

RECOGNITION OF FINANCIAL ASSETS

An entity shall recognize a financial asset in its statement of financial position when, and only when, the entity becomes party to the contractual provisions of the instrument. This implies recognition of all contractual rights and obligations under derivatives in its statement of financial position as assets and liabilities, respectively, except for derivatives that prevent a transfer of financial assets from being accounted for as a sale.

For example, an entity retains a call option on a financial asset that is sold. It cannot derecognize the financial asset because of the call option; and thus recognition of a separate derivative financial asset will cause double counting.

When an entity first recognizes a financial asset, the classification principles as stated in the previous paragraph and measurement principles as stated in the next paragraph will apply. IFRS 9 has retained the same measurement and accounting principles of regular way purchases and sales (covered in IAS 39, *Financial Instruments: Recognition and Measurement*).

MEASUREMENT OF FINANCIAL ASSETS

Financial assets are measured at initial recognition at fair value. Transaction costs (directly attributable to the acquisition of the financial asset) are added to the fair value for financial assets that are not at FVTPL.

The fair value of a financial asset at initial recognition is normally the transaction price (i.e., the fair value of the consideration given). If part of the consideration given is for something other than the financial instrument, the fair value of the financial instrument is estimated using a valuation technique. This may be market price of a similar asset in an arm's-length transaction or discounted cash flow or valuation based on an option pricing model. An entity may adopt a valuation technique that is commonly used by the market participant and that has been demonstrated to provide reliable estimates of prices obtained in actual market transactions.

A valuation technique adopted for the purpose of IFRS 9 is expected to establish what the transaction price would have been on the measurement date in an arm's-length exchange motivated by normal business considerations. It uses market inputs to the maximum, and relies as little as possible on entity-specific inputs. The inputs to the valuation technique shall reasonably represent market expectations and measures of the risk-return factors inherent in the financial instrument.

A valuation technique would incorporate all factors that market participants would consider in setting a price. It shall be consistent with the accepted economic methodologies for pricing financial instruments. A reporting entity shall periodically calibrate the valuation technique and test it for validity using prices from any observable current market transactions in the same instrument (i.e., without modification or repackaging) or based on any available observable market data. An entity obtains market data consistently in the same market where the instrument was originated or purchased.

Example 11

Entity E lends €100 million for five years to one of its group companies at 2% interest when the benchmark yield is 4%. What should be the fair value of the loan for initial recognition?

Solution

The fair value of a long-term loan or receivable that carries no interest can be estimated as the present value of all future cash receipts discounted using the prevailing market rate(s) of interest for a similar instrument (similar as to currency, term, type of interest rate and other factors) with a similar credit rating. Any additional amount lent is an expense or a reduction of income unless it qualifies for recognition as some other type of asset. The difference between the transaction price and fair value is accounted for as a loss/gain at initial recognition.

Example 12

Entity E lends €100 million for five years to one of its group companies at 2% interest when the benchmark yield is 4%. It receives upfront fees of €10 million. Should the fees be adjusted while determining fair value of the loan?

Solution

Fair value the loan on the basis of discounted cash flows using benchmark yield as the discount factor. The cash flows shall include the upfront fees collected.

MEASUREMENT SUBSEQUENT TO INITIAL RECOGNITION

After initial recognition, an entity shall measure the financial asset at either fair value or amortized cost in accordance with the classification followed. When the fair value of a financial asset is negative, an entity shall recognize a financial liability. For example, a derivative may have a positive fair value when it is recognized as an asset, whereas it becomes a liability when its fair value becomes negative.

Example 13

Entity E made investments in equity shares during the year 2009. The transaction price of the shares was €100 million and there was a transaction cost of €0.05 million. It made an irrevocable election to classify the investment as at fair value through other comprehensive income. At the year-end, the fair value of the investment is €102 million. If the investments were sold at the year-end, it would have incurred a transaction cost of €0.06 million. Should the fair value at the year-end be €102 million minus transaction cost of €0.06 million? How should the fair value change be accounted for?

Solution

At subsequent measurement, fair value of the financial asset is not computed net of cost to sell. The fair value is €102 million. Entity E shall recognize the change in fair value (year-end fair value €102 million minus initial fair value €100.05 million = €1.95 million) in the statement of other comprehensive income and accumulate in a separate component of equity.

Example 14

Continue with investments in equity shares discussed in Example 13. Entity E sold the investments in 2010 at €103 million net of transaction cost. How should the entity recognize gain or loss? Should the entity reclassify the accumulated fair value gain/loss in the same way as is required by IAS 39?

Solution

The gain of €1 million (net sale proceeds €103 million minus year-end fair value €102 million) is recognized in the statement of income. Detailed discussion on recognition of gain or loss of financial assets will follow. IFRS 9 does not require a reclassification adjustment. The accumulated fair value gain/loss on the particular financial asset shall be transferred to retained earnings.

EMBEDDED DERIVATIVES

Embedded derivatives are not separated if the host contract is to a financial asset that falls within the scope of IFRS 9. This apparently simplifies the accounting system. An entity will not be required to separate the host and the embedded derivative and account for them separately.

However, the entire hybrid instrument is to be accounted for either at amortized cost or fair value. This will lead to complication.

CASE OF OPTIONALLY CONVERTIBLE DEBENTURE IN THE HANDS OF INVESTOR

The investor has paid for the conversion option. Therefore, it is assumed to be exercised into equity. So there will be a partial contractual cash flow for the interest element (there is no interest cash flow if the convertible debenture is issued in the style of a zero coupon bond) and the principal is settled in equity. The hybrid instrument cannot be measured at amortized cost because a major portion of the cash flows is uncertain. An investor has to classify it as a financial asset at fair value.

CASE OF COMPULSORILY CONVERTIBLE DEBENTURES

If the convertible debentures are interest bearing, there will be contractual cash inflows till conversion. Otherwise, there are no cash inflows in the hands of the holder. The classification of such type convertible instrument will be guided by the level of significance of the contractual cash flows. In case the noncontractual cash flows are material, then the hybrid financial asset shall be classified as financial assets at fair value. It will be a financial asset at fair value, to be measured at the fair value of the equity instrument (on an assumed conversion basis) at the reporting date.

A derivative that is attached to a *financial instrument,* but is contractually transferable independently of that instrument, or has a different counterparty, is not an embedded derivative, but a separate financial instrument. It is recognized and classified applying principles of IFRS 9.

If a hybrid contract contains a host that is not within the scope of IFRS 9, an entity shall separate the embedded derivative applying the principles set out in IAS 39, *Financial Instrument: Recognition and Measurement,* and account for the same as an independent financial asset in accordance with IFRS 9. The host contract is accounted for applying appropriate IFRS. For example, an insurer may elect to separate a derivative embedded in an insurance contract to be accounted for in accordance with IFRS 4. In that case, the derivative shall be accounted for applying IFRS 9, whereas the host insurance contract shall be accounted for applying IFRS 4.

RECLASSIFICATION

An entity reclassifies a financial asset when and only when there is a change in the business model. Reclassification is applied prospectively from the date of reclassification. No restatement is required for previously recognized gains or losses.

Financial assets at amortized cost to financial assets at fair value	The difference between fair value measured at the reclassification date and amortized cost is charged to the statement of income.
Financial assets at fair value to financial assets at amortized cost	The difference between the amortized cost measured at the reclassification date and fair value is charged to the statement of income. The fair value at the date of reclassification becomes the new carrying amount for applying amortized cost method.

Changes in the business model are expected to be very infrequent. Such changes must be determined by the entity's senior management as a result of external or internal changes and must be significant to the entity's operations and demonstrable to external parties. Also the change in the objective of the entity's business model must be effected before the reclassification date.

Examples of changes in the business model:

- The investment objective of a loan portfolio of an entity that has undergone a change consequent to acquisition of another entity whose loan portfolio is managed on the basis of collecting the contractual cash flows. The entity has decided not to manage the loan portfolio with an objective of collecting the contractual cash flows.
- A financial entity was earlier managing its mortgaged loan portfolio of investments with an objective of collecting the contractual cash flows. It has now decided to shut the business and is actively selling the mortgaged loans.

Examples when changes are not considered as change in the business model:

- A change in intention related to particular financial assets (even in circumstances of significant changes in market conditions).
- A temporary disappearance of a particular market for financial assets.
- A transfer of financial assets between parts of the entity with different business models.

GAINS OR LOSSES ON FINANCIAL ASSETS

Presented here is the accounting treatment for gain or loss on financial assets:

When financial assets are not part of a hedging relationship:

1. Financial assets at fair value

a. That are elected at initial recognition to present in other comprehensive income subsequent changes in the fair value of an investment in an equity instrument	Fair value change is accounted for in the statement of other comprehensive income. The accumulated fair value change is retained in a separate fair value reserve. On derecognition of the investment, accumulated fair value gain/loss is reclassified. It is transferred to another component of equity, for example, retained earnings.
b. Other financial assets (1) Equity investments that are held for trading (2) Debt instruments that are designated as FVTPL	Fair value change is accounted for in the statement of income.
2. Financial assets at amortized cost	Recognized in profit or loss when the financial asset is derecognized, impaired or reclassified.

When financial assets are part of a hedging relationship:

> Accounted for in accordance with IAS 39 as specified for fair value hedge, cash flow hedge, and hedging net investments in foreign operations.

Exchange fluctuation gains/losses on monetary assets are recognized in the profit or loss in accordance with IAS 21, *The Effects of Changes in Foreign Exchange Rates.* In the case of an investment in equity shares denominated in a foreign currency (a currency other than the functional currency), a fair value change may arise out of exchange fluctuations. But these kinds of investments are not classified as monetary assets, and therefore, the entire change is recognized as a change in fair value in profit or loss.

Example 15

Entity E invested in listed equity amounting to US \$100 million (equivalent to €64.50 million applying exchange rate on the date of transaction) during 2009. Its functional currency is €. At the reporting date, the market value of the equity was US \$110 million. The closing exchange rate €1 = US \$1,4333. What is the amount of change in fair value? How much of the change shall be accounted for as exchange fluctuation gain/loss in accordance with IAS 21?

Solution

Change in fair value = US \$110/1.4333 – €64.50 million = €76.75 million – €64.50 million = €12.25 million. No part of the fair value gain is accounted for as exchange fluctuation gain/loss in accordance with IAS 21 as the investment in equity is not a monetary asset.

If there is a hedging relationship between a nonderivative monetary asset and a nonderivative monetary liability, changes in the foreign currency component of those financial instruments are presented in profit or loss.

INVESTMENT IN UNQUOTED EQUITY SHARES

Investments in unquoted equity shares are also measured at fair value. Only in limited circumstances is cost taken as the fair value of such instruments. The limited circumstances include

- Cases when insufficient recent information is available to determine fair value, or
- Out of the wide range of possible fair value measurements, cost represents the best estimate of fair value within that range.

Indicators of the situations when cost might not be representative of fair value include

- A significant change in the performance of the investee compared with budgets, plans or milestones
- Changes in expectation of the investee's technical product milestones being achieved
- A significant change in the market for the investee's equity or its products or potential products
- A significant change in the global economy or the economic environment in which the investee operates
- A significant change in the performance of comparable entities, or in the valuations implied by the overall market
- Internal matters of the investee such as fraud, commercial disputes, litigation, or changes in management or strategy
- Evidence from external transactions in the investee's equity, either by the investee (such as a fresh issue of equity), or by transfers of equity instruments between third parties

TRANSITION PROVISIONS

An entity may adopt IFRS 9 from any date between its issue and December 31, 2009, if it is applied before January 1, 2010, or at the beginning of the reporting period if it is applied on or after January 1, 2010. When the date of initial application is not the beginning of the reporting period, an entity shall disclose the reason for using that date for initial application. The following are the transition effects:

- Classifies and measures all financial assets in accordance with IFRS 9 on the date of initial application of IFRS 9 and retrospective effect, irrespective of the business model pursued in the earlier periods.
- An entity shall decide its business model on the date of initial application of IFRS 9. It will decide whether a financial asset should be classified as held for trading in accordance therewith as if that asset is purchased on that date.
- Hybrid financial instruments are measured at fair value on the date of initial application of IFRS 9. Comparatives shall be the sum of the fair value of the components, that is, host and derivative.
- The difference in the fair value of a hybrid instrument at initial application of IFRS 9 and the sum of components of the hybrid instruments are accounted for as follows:
  - Adjust to retained earnings if IFRS 9 is applied from the beginning of a reporting period; or
  - Recognize in the profit/loss if IFRS 9 is applied during the reporting period 2009.
- An entity shall designate a financial asset as at FVTPL, or at fair value through other comprehensive income at the date of initial application of IFRS 9 based on the facts

and circumstances prevailing as on that date. That classification shall be applied retrospectively.

- An entity shall revoke the previous designation of a financial asset as at fair value through profit or loss if conditions set out in paragraph 4.5 of IFRS 9 (condition regarding accounting mismatch) are not satisfied. It may also revoke such a designation even if the conditions set out in paragraph 4.5 of IFRS 9 are satisfied. The entity shall revoke the designation of a financial asset as at FVTPL at the date of initial application of IFRS 9 based on the facts and circumstances prevailing as on that date. That classification shall be applied retrospectively.

- An entity applies IAS 39 to determine when it shall designate a *financial liability* as measured at FVTPL; and when it shall or may revoke its previous designation of a financial liability as measured at FVTPL. The entity shall revoke the designation at the date of initial application of IFRS 9 based on the facts and circumstances prevailing as on that date. That classification shall be applied retrospectively.

- If it is impracticable to apply amortized cost retrospectively, or to carry out impairment testing is impracticable, the entity shall apply fair value at the end of each comparative period as amortized cost. So the fair value at the date of initial application of IFRS 9 shall be the amortized cost of the financial asset.

- An investment in unquoted equity shares, which was earlier measured at cost, shall be measured at fair value at the date of initial application of IFRS 9 with the difference being adjusted to retained earnings.

- *Special transitional exemption for an entity that adopts this IFRS for reporting periods beginning before January 1, 2012:* It is not required to restate prior periods. It shall recognize any difference between the previous carrying amount and the carrying amount at the beginning of the annual reporting period that includes the date of initial application, in the opening retained earnings (or other component of equity, as appropriate) of the reporting period that includes the date of initial application.

- *Special transitional exemption for an entity that prepares interim reports:* Application of IFRS 9 to interim periods prior to the date of initial application is not required if it is impracticable.

An entity shall apply this IFRS retrospectively, in accordance with IAS 8, *Accounting Policies, Changes in Accounting Estimates and Errors*, except in the circumstances covered in this chapter.

41 INTERNATIONAL FINANCIAL REPORTING STANDARDS (IFRS) FOR SMES

INTRODUCTION

In July 2009, The International Accounting Standards Board (IASB) published the International Financial Reporting Standard (IFRS) for small and medium entities (SMEs), which became effective immediately upon its issue.

The IFRS for SMEs has a simplified drafting and contains substantially fewer disclosures compared to the full IFRS. It also provides an accounting framework for entities that do not have the size or resources to adopt full IFRS. In comparison to the full IFRS, the accounting policy choices, recognition, and measurement principles for assets, liabilities, income, and expenses have been simplified in many areas within this standard.

The standard is organized into 35 sections as follows:

- Section 1 describes the characteristics of a SME.
- Section 2 describes the concepts and pervasive principles underlying the preparation of financial statements for a SME.
- Sections 3 to 10 describe the presentation of financial statements (including consolidated and separate financial statements), its components including application of accounting policies, estimates and errors.
- Sections 11 to 34 deal with the recognition, measurement, and related disclosures for assets, liabilities, income, and expenses for a SME.
- Section 35 deals with the transition requirements for a first-time adopter of IFRS for SMEs.

A section-by-section summary of the IFRS for SMEs follows.

SECTION 1, CHARACTERISTICS OF A SME

This standard defines SMEs as entities that

- Do not have public accountability; and
- Publish general purpose financial statements for external users.

An entity is considered to have *public accountability* if it is in the process of issuing any class of instrument in a public market or holds as part of its main activity, assets in a fiduciary capacity for third parties. The latter category includes banks, insurance entities, securities brokers, dealers, and pension funds.

A subsidiary whose parent uses the full IFRSs, or that is part of a consolidated group that uses full IFRSs, is not prohibited from using this IFRS in its own financial statements if that subsidiary by itself does not have public accountability.

Decisions on which entities are required or permitted to use the IASB's standards rest with legislative and regulatory authorities and standard setters in individual jurisdictions. If a publicly accountable entity uses this IFRS, its financial statements shall not be described as conforming to the IFRS for SMEs, even if the law or regulation in its jurisdiction permits or requires this IFRS to be used by publicly accountable entities.

SECTION 2, CONCEPTS AND PRINCIPLES UNDERLYING THE PREPARATION OF FINANCIAL STATEMENTS

As under the full IFRS, the financial statements under the IFRS for SMEs should be prepared on an accruals basis and on the assumption that the entity will continue to be a going concern in the foreseeable future. Also, the financial statements of an entity should show a true and fair view of the financial position, of its performance and changes in financial position. The main characteristics that are applied to achieve this are materiality, reliability, substance over form, relevance, prudence, completeness, and comparability.

The entities that adopt the IFRS for SMEs can depart from it only in the extreme circumstances when the management is of the opinion that compliance with one of its requirements will be misleading. In such cases, the nature, reason, and financial impact of such departure should be disclosed in the financial statements.

SECTIONS 3 THROUGH 8, PRESENTATION OF FINANCIAL STATEMENTS

- The financial statements should contain an explicit statement of compliance with IFRS for SMEs.
- Significant uncertainties regarding an entity's ability to continue as a going concern should be disclosed as in the full IFRS.
- For a change in reporting period, an entity should disclose that fact, the reasons for the change in reporting period and the fact that the figures are not entirely comparable as in the full IFRS.
- Comparative information should be presented similarly to the requirements of full IFRS.
- Financial statements should include

  - Statement of financial position;
  - A single statement of comprehensive income *or* a separate income statement and a separate statement of comprehensive income;
  - Statement of changes in equity;
  - Statement of cash flows; and
  - Notes, including a summary of significant accounting policies and other explanatory information

- A single statement of income and retained earnings can be prepared instead of a statement of comprehensive income and statement of changes in equity, if the only changes to an entity's equity is on account of

  - Profit or loss for the period;
  - Dividend payment;
  - Changes in accounting policies; or
  - Correction of prior period errors.

- Such a statement should include

  - Retained earnings at the beginning of the reporting period;
  - Dividends declared and paid or payable during the period;
  - Restatements of retained earnings for corrections of prior period errors;

- Restatements of retained earnings for changes in accounting policy; and
- Retained earnings at the end of the reporting period.

- If there is no other comprehensive income during the period, an entity may continue to present an income statement or present a statement of comprehensive income and label the bottom line as profit or loss.
- Major categories of assets, liabilities, income, and expenses must be presented in the statement of financial position and statement of comprehensive income as in the full IFRS.
- Disclosures in the notes to the financial statements that are similar to those in the full IFRS relating to the basis of preparation and specific accounting policies adopted must be made besides of the information that is required by the IFRS for SMEs that is not presented elsewhere in the financial statements.

SECTION 9, CONSOLIDATED
AND SEPARATE FINANCIAL STATEMENTS

- A parent need not present consolidated financial statements if both of the following conditions are met:

  - The parent is itself a subsidiary, and
  - Its ultimate parent (or any intermediate parent) produces consolidated general purpose financial statements that comply with full IFRSs or with this IFRS.

  A subsidiary acquired with the intention of disposal within one year also need not be consolidated. Such a subsidiary should either be accounted at FVTPL or cost less impairment

- Principles of SIC 12, *Consolidation for Special Purpose Entities,* have been included in this section.
- Financial statements of an entity that does not have a subsidiary are not considered as separate financial statements.
- An entity that has only investments in associates or joint ventures must present its financial statements in compliance with Sections 14 and 15 relating to investment in associates and investments in joint ventures, respectively. It may also elect to present separate financial statements.

  Investments in subsidiaries, associates, or joint ventures shall be accounted for in the separate financial statements either at cost, less impairment or at fair value with changes in fair value through profit or loss.

- Same accounting shall be applied for all investments in a single class, but different accounting can be applied for different classes.
- The standard introduces the concept of combined financial statements and defines them as a single set of financial statements of two or more entities controlled by a single investor. The combined financial statements shall disclose

  - The fact that the financial statements are combined financial statements;
  - The reason why combined financial statements are prepared;
  - The basis for determining which entities are included in the combined financial statements;
  - The basis of preparation of the combined financial statements; and
  - The related-party disclosures required by Section 33, *Related-Party Disclosures.*

SECTION 10, ACCOUNTING POLICIES, ESTIMATES, AND ERRORS

The principles adopted in this section are similar to those in the full IFRS relating to IAS 8, *Accounting Policies, Changes in Accounting Estimates, and Errors.*

When the IFRS for SMEs does not specifically address a transaction, other event or condition, the management should refer to, and consider the applicability of, the following sources in descending order:

- The requirements and guidance in the IFRS for SMEs dealing with similar and related issues, and
- The definitions, recognition criteria, and measurement concepts for assets, liabilities, income, and expenses and the pervasive principles in Section 2.

Management may also consider the requirements and guidance in full IFRS dealing with similar and related issues.

SECTIONS 11 AND 12, FINANCIAL INSTRUMENTS

Section 11 is applicable to basic financial instruments such as cash, fixed deposits, accounts receivable, accounts payable, shares (nonconvertible and nonputtable). Other (complex) financial instruments such as options, forwards, and hedging are covered in Section 12.

An entity shall choose to apply for all its financial instruments either

- The provisions of both Section 11 and Section 12 in full, or
- The recognition and measurement provisions of IAS 39, *Financial Instruments: Recognition and Measurement,* and the disclosure requirements of Sections 11 and 12.

Under these sections, the segregation of financial instruments into various categories, such as available for sale and held to maturity, no longer exists.

The disclosures under this section have been restricted to carrying value, default/breaches, collateral, gains or losses on financial instruments. The disclosures in IFRS 7, *Financial Instruments: Disclosures*, relating to financial risk management are not required.

Debt instruments (including accounts receivable, payable, etc.) continue to be stated at amortized cost using the effective interest method.

The investments in ordinary shares should be stated at fair value with changes in fair value to be reflected in profit or loss, if the shares are publicly traded or a reliable measurement of fair value exists. Such other investments continue to be carried at cost, less impairment.

An impairment should be recognized for instruments that are carried at cost if objective evidence of impairment exists. Equity instruments should be assessed individually for impairment, irrespective of significance.

Under this section, the hedge accounting categories *cash flow* hedge and *fair value hedge* do not exist, although similar accounting treatments exist.

The hedge accounting criteria in this section are similar to those in IAS 39. Risks qualifying for hedge accounting are limited to the following.

<u>Risk</u>	<u>Treatment</u>
Fixed-interest-rate risk of recognized financial instrument;	Change in the fair value of the hedging instrument and the hedged item in profit or loss.
Commodity price risk of a commodity held.	
Variable interest rate risk of recognized financial instrument;	Recognize in other comprehensive income the effective portion of the hedge.
Foreign exchange risk or commodity price risk in a firm commitment or highly probable forecast transaction; and	Ineffective portion to be reflected in profit or loss. Effective portion to be reflected in profit or loss, when hedging relationship ends.
Foreign exchange risk in net investment in foreign operation.	

SECTION 13, INVENTORIES

The principles adopted in this section are similar to those in the full IFRS relating to IAS 2, *Inventories.* However, the concept of *impairment loss for inventories* has been introduced in the IFRS for SMEs. Allowance for inventories should be termed as *impairment allowance for inventories.*

While all the disclosure requirements under the full IFRS relating to IAS 2 applies to this section, the disclosure of circumstances leading to reversal of impairment provision for inventories is not required to be made under the IFRS for SMEs.

SECTION 14, INVESTMENTS IN ASSOCIATES

As in the case of IAS 28, *Investment in Associates*, investments in associates are accounted for under the following three methods:

- Cost model
- Equity method
- Fair value model

Under the cost model, the investment is recognized at cost, less impairment, if any. The dividend income and other distributions from an associate must be recognized and disclosed in the statement of income. In the case of investments in associates where a published price quotation is available, the fair value method of recognition must be used.

Under the equity method, the share of profits or losses/other comprehensive income after acquisition must be recognized. The dividend and other distributions must be reduced from the carrying value of the investments. Similarly, the disclosure of fair value of the investments in listed associates must be disclosed. All other principles apply as in the full IFRS.

Under the fair value model, the investments are initially recognized at the transaction price. Subsequent to this recognition, the fair valuation guidance of Section 11 should be followed and the fair value changes should be reflected in the statement of comprehensive income. When the fair value is not determinable without undue cost or effort, the cost method of accounting should be followed.

The following significant disclosures mentioned under the full IFRS relating to IAS 28, *Investment in Associates,* have been eliminated in this section:

- Summarized financial information need not be provided;
- Reasons for not following the same year-end as that of an associate need not be mentioned;
- Reasons for concluding an investment to be an associate when holding less than 20%, and vice versa, need not be mentioned.

SECTION 15, INVESTMENTS IN JOINT VENTURES

The principles of Section 14 relating to investment in associates also apply to this section. The main difference as compared to the requirements of IAS 28, *Investment in Associates*, is that proportionate consolidation is not allowed for jointly controlled entities under this section.

SECTION 16, INVESTMENT PROPERTY

As in the case of the full IFRS relating to IAS 40, *Investment Property*, an investment property is initially measured at cost which is its purchase price plus any directly attributable costs, such as professional fees for legal services, property transfer taxes, and other transaction costs.

Subsequent to this, where the fair value of investment property can be measured reliably, without undue cost or effort on a continuing basis, an entity should carry such property at fair value, and the changes in fair value should be recognized in the statement of income.

Where fair value cannot be measured reliably without undue cost or effort on a continuing basis, the property should be measured at cost as property, plant, and equipment in accordance with Section 17, until a reliable measure of fair value is available and can be measured reliably on an ongoing basis at fair value. This option can be applied on a property-by-property basis. In such cases, the disclosure of fair value is not required where the cost basis is followed, since these are accounted for as property, plant, and equipment.

In the case of mixed-use property, segregation between investment property and property, plant, and equipment should be done. However, if the fair value of the investment property component cannot be measured reliably without undue cost or effort, the entire property shall be accounted for as property, plant, and equipment.

When an investment property interest is held under a lease, only the interest in the lease is recognized, not the underlying property.

The transfers to or from investment property will apply when the property meets or ceases to meet the definition of an investment property.

While all the disclosures mentioned in IAS 40, *Investment Property*, have to be made, the reconciliation of the opening and closing carrying values of investment property need not be disclosed for prior years.

SECTION 17, PROPERTY, PLANT, AND EQUIPMENT

Property, plant, and equipment are initially measured at cost. Cost includes purchase price, legal and brokerage fees, import duties and other nonrefundable taxes and any other directly attributable costs that are incurred to bring the asset to the location and condition that is required by the management.

Subsequent to the initial measurement, each class of property, plant, and equipment are carried at cost less accumulated depreciation and any accumulated impairment losses. The gross carrying value of every item of property, plant, and equipment less its estimated residual value should be depreciated on a systematic basis over its useful life.

The major changes of this section as compared to IAS 16, *Property, Plant and Equipment,* are as follows:

- Revaluation model of accounting for property, plant, and equipment is not available.
- Annual review of useful lives, depreciation rates is not required unless there is a change in circumstances.
- Property, plant, and equipment also includes investment property, where fair value cannot be measured without undue cost or effort.

SECTION 18, INTANGIBLE ASSETS OTHER THAN GOODWILL

Under this section, an intangible asset does not result from expenditure incurred internally on an intangible asset. Therefore, expenditure on research and development activities must be recognized as an expense.

In the case of separately acquired intangible assets, they are initially measured at cost. Cost is comprised of purchase price, which includes import duties and nonrefundable purchase taxes, net of trade discounts and rebates and all other costs that are directly attributable to preparing the asset for its intended use.

Subsequent to the initial measurement of intangible assets, they are carried at cost less any accumulated amortization and any accumulated impairment losses.

The amortization of intangible assets has to be carried out on a systematic basis over the useful lives of the intangibles. The *useful life* is determined based on the contractual period of the asset or on other legal rights and cannot be indefinite. When the useful life cannot be determined by the management, the useful life is presumed to be 10 years.

The residual value of the intangible assets is assumed to be zero, unless there is either a commitment by a third party to purchase the asset at a determined value or there is an active market for the asset.

As in the case of Section 17, the revaluation model is not available for intangible assets.

SECTION 19, BUSINESS COMBINATIONS AND GOODWILL

The provisions of this section are similar to that of IFRS 3, *Business Combinations,* before its revision in 2008. Therefore, the cost of combination under this section will include the costs that are directly attributable to the combination.

Similarly, goodwill must be considered for amortization as in the case of other intangible assets. When the useful life cannot be determined by the management, the useful life is presumed to be 10 years.

In any situation that is not addressed in this section, the provisions mentioned in the full IFRS relating to IFRS 3, *Business Combinations,* will apply.

SECTION 20, LEASES

The principles adopted in this section are similar to those in the full IFRS relating to IAS 17, *Leases.* However, for operating leases, an option other than the straight-line method is also given under this section to recognize the lease payments, if the payments to the lessor are structured, to increase in line with expected general inflation.

SECTION 21, PROVISIONS AND CONTINGENCIES

All the principles adopted in this section are similar to those in the full IFRS relating to IAS 37, *Provisions, Contingent Liabilities, and Contingent Assets.*

SECTION 22, LIABILITIES AND EQUITY

This section establishes principles for classifying financial instruments as either liabilities or equity and addresses accounting for equity instruments issued to individuals or other parties acting in their capacity as owners.

If the equity instruments are issued before the entity receives the cash or other resources, the entity should present the amount receivable as an offset to equity in its statement of financial position, not as an asset.

If the entity receives the cash or other resources before the equity instruments are issued, and the entity cannot be required to repay the cash or other resources received, the entity should recognize the corresponding increase in equity to the extent of consideration received.

An entity should measure equity instruments at the fair value of the cash or other resources received or receivable, net of direct costs of issuing the equity instruments. If payment is deferred and the time value of money is material, the initial measurement shall be on a present value basis.

An entity should account for the transaction costs of an equity transaction as a deduction from equity, net of any related income tax benefit.

An entity should treat changes in a parent's controlling interest in a subsidiary that do not result in a loss of control as transactions with equity holders in their capacity as equity holders.

Accordingly, the entity should not recognize any changes in the carrying value of assets (including goodwill) and liabilities as a result of such a transaction.

SECTION 23, REVENUE

The principles adopted in this section are similar to those in the full IFRS relating to IAS 18, *Revenue.*

This section also includes the criterion for recognition and measurement of revenue for construction contracts. When the outcome of the construction contract can be estimated reliably, the revenue and contract costs associated with the contract should be recognized as revenue and expenses by reference to the stage of completion of the contract at the end of the reporting period. However, when the outcome of the contract cannot be estimated reliably, recognition of the revenue must only be made to the extent of contract costs incurred that is probable to be recovered and the contract costs should be recognized as an expense in the period in which they are incurred.

SECTION 24, GOVERNMENT GRANTS

Under this section, all government grants should be accounted for using a single, simplified model.

Income is recognized when the performance conditions are met (or earlier if there are no performance conditions) and it is measured at the fair value of the asset received or receivable.

SECTION 25, BORROWING COSTS

Under this section, the borrowing costs should be expensed to the statement of comprehensive income as and when incurred. This is a major deviation from the requirements of IAS 23, *Borrowing Costs,* in which borrowing costs that are directly attributable to the construction, production, or acquisition of a qualifying asset are to be capitalized.

SECTION 26, SHARE-BASED PAYMENT

All the principles adopted in this section are similar to those in the full IFRS relating to IFRS 2, *Share Based Payment,* except that this section also introduces a three-tier hierarchy on fair value measurement for determining the fair value of equity instruments granted to employees.

The share-based payments that are granted to employees should be recognized over the period of service that must be completed before they have become unconditionally entitled to the award.

The equity-settled share-based payment transactions are generally measured by reference to the fair value of the goods and services received. When the fair value cannot be estimated reliably or it is impracticable to determine, management must use their judgment to apply the most appropriate valuation method to obtain fair value. When these are transactions with employees, the value is measured with reference to the fair value of the equity instruments granted. In the case of cash-settled share-based payments, they are measured at the fair value of the liability.

SECTION 27, IMPAIRMENT OF ASSETS

This section is extremely simplified as compared to the requirements of IAS 36, *Impairment of Assets.*

Unlike the annual testing approach that is adopted under the full IFRS, an indicator approach to testing for impairment for goodwill and other intangible assets is adopted under this section. The indications of impairment may be external or internal and may include a decline in an asset's market value, significant adverse changes in the economic or legal environment, evidence of obsolescence or damage of an asset, or evidence from internal reporting.

If goodwill cannot be allocated to cash-generating units on a nonarbitrary basis, an entity shall test the impairment of goodwill by determining the recoverable amount of the acquired entity in its entirety that has not been integrated. If integrated, the recoverable amount of the entire group of entities shall be determined.

The required disclosures for impairment have been reduced. The impairment losses and reversals, if any, in a subsequent period must be disclosed.

SECTION 28, EMPLOYEE BENEFITS

Under the requirements of this section, actuarial gains on liabilities are recognized in full in the profit or loss or in other comprehensive income (without recycling) in the period in which they occur.

The costs relating to past service are recognized in full in profit or loss in the period in which they occur.

SECTION 29, INCOME TAXES

Although the fundamental principles of IAS 12, *Income Taxes,* have been retained, the changes proposed in the Exposure Draft of March 2009 have been incorporated, including the concept of a valuation allowance for deferred tax assets.

The tax basis of assets and liabilities is determined by the consequences of the sale of the assets or settlement of liabilities for their present carrying amounts. In IAS 12, *Income Taxes*, it is stated as "recovery through use" and not "sale."

SECTION 30, FOREIGN EXCHANGE TRANSLATION

The principles adopted in this section are similar to those in IAS 21, *The Effects of Changes in Foreign Exchange Rates*, except that in consolidated financial statements, SMEs must recognize in other comprehensive income a foreign exchange difference arising on a monetary item that forms part of the reporting entity's net investment in a foreign operation. They shall not again be recognized in profit or loss on disposal of the net investment.

In IAS 21, it is required that on disposal of the investment, the foreign exchange difference should be transferred to profit or loss.

SECTION 31, HYPERINFLATIONARY ECONOMY

All the principles adopted in this section are similar to those in IAS 29, *Financial Reporting in Hyperinflationary Economies.*

SECTION 32, EVENTS AFTER THE END OF THE REPORTING PERIOD

The principles adopted in this section are again similar to those in IAS 10, *Events After the Reporting Date.*

SECTION 33, RELATED PARTIES

The definition of *related party* has been split between *entity* and *person*. The main categories of related parties are subsidiaries, associates, joint ventures, key management personnel of the entity and its parent and parties with control or joint control or significant influence over the entity. Related parties do not include finance providers and governments who deal with the entity in the normal course of their business.

The disclosures that related-party transactions were made on terms equivalent to those that prevail in arm's length transactions are made only if such terms can be substantiated.

Key management compensation should however be disclosed in total.

SECTION 34, SPECIALIZED ACTIVITIES

Agricultural Activity

Under this section, in the case of an entity involved in agricultural activity, the biological assets are measured at fair value less estimated point-of-sale costs, where such fair value is readily determinable without undue cost or effort. When fair value is not readily determinable without undue cost or effort, such assets are measured at cost less any accumulated depreciation and any accumulated impairment losses. The agricultural produce harvested from biological assets is measured at fair value less estimated costs to sell at the point of harvest.

Extractive Industries

Under this section, an entity engaged in an extractive industry should recognize exploration expenditure as an expense in the period in which it is incurred. Entities accounting for expenditure on the acquisition or development of tangible and intangible fixed assets for use in extractive activities should follow the guidance in Section 17 (property, plant, and equipment) and Section 18 (intangible assets other than goodwill) of the IFRS for SMEs. However, when the entity has an obligation to dismantle or remove an item or restore a site, it should follow the guidance in Sections 17 (property, plant and equipment) and 21 (provisions and contingencies) of the IFRS for SMEs.

Service Concession Arrangements

A service concession is an arrangement in which a government or other public sector body (the grantor) contracts with a private operator to operate and maintain the grantor's infrastructure such as roads, bridges, tunnels, airports, energy distribution networks, prisons, and hospitals. Concession arrangements fall into two broad categories, which then determine the accounting that applies.

When, under the concession agreement, the operator has an unconditional contractual right to receive cash or another financial asset from or at the direction of the grantor, it should recognize a financial asset. The asset is measured at fair value and, for accounting purposes, management should follow the principles in Sections 11 and 12 (financial instruments) of the IFRS for SMEs.

When, under the concession agreement, the operator receives a right to charge the users of the public service, it should recognize an intangible asset. This intangible asset is measured at fair value and, for accounting purposes, management should follow the principles laid down in Section 18 (intangible assets) of the IFRS for SMEs.

SECTION 35, TRANSITION TO IFRS FOR SMES

A first-time adopter of the IFRS for SMEs will be an entity that presents its financial statements in accordance with the IFRS for SMEs for the first time, regardless of whether the previous financial statements were prepared under full IFRS or another set of generally accepted accounting principles.

A first-time adopter of the IFRS for SMEs shall apply this section in its first financial statements that conform to the IFRS for SMEs. The following are the salient provisions of this section:

- Since comparative information is required to be presented, the date of transition is the beginning of the earliest prior period presented for which the entity presents full comparative information.
- The adjustments that were required to be recorded before the date of transition shall be adjusted through equity.
- No retrospective restatement is required for assets or liabilities that are already derecognized or which otherwise would have been derecognized under this IFRS.
- An exemption is also available for not restating business combinations before the date of transition.
- The revaluation/fair value can be taken as the deemed cost for property, plant and equipment, investment property, and intangible assets.
- Any impracticability to restate amounts should be explained.
- An explanation as to how the transition has affected the financial position and performance of the entity in the first financial statements should be provided.
- Any change in accounting policy should be explained.
- A reconciliation of profit or loss and equity as per previous financial reporting compared to this IFRS should be provided.

INDEX

CPSIA information can be obtained
at www.ICGtesting.com
Printed in the USA
JSHW032224090822
29091JS00005B/161

9 780470 3991